Dogs on Cape Cod

Dogs do speak, but only to those who know how to listen.

— Orhan Pamuk, *My Name Is Red*

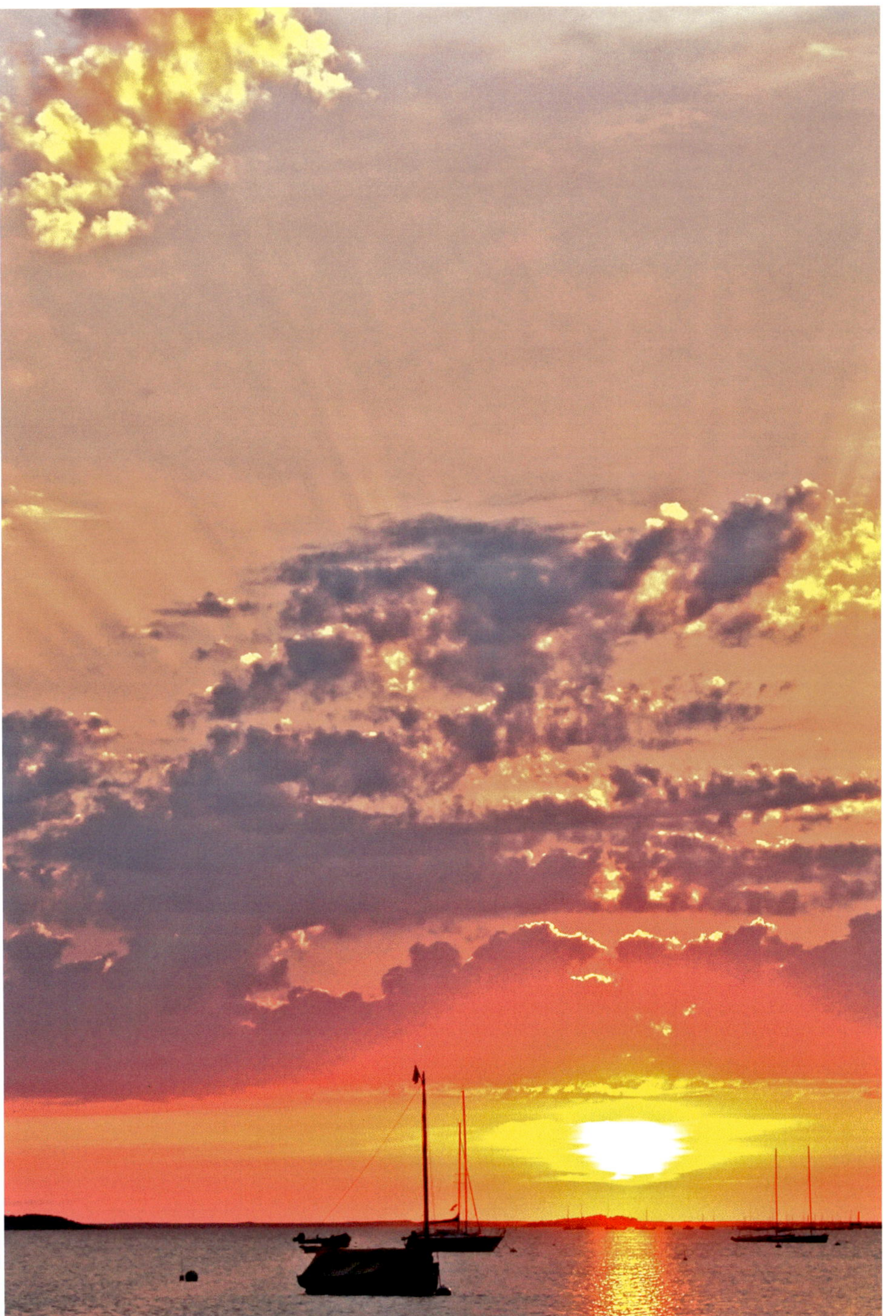

Pleasant Bay

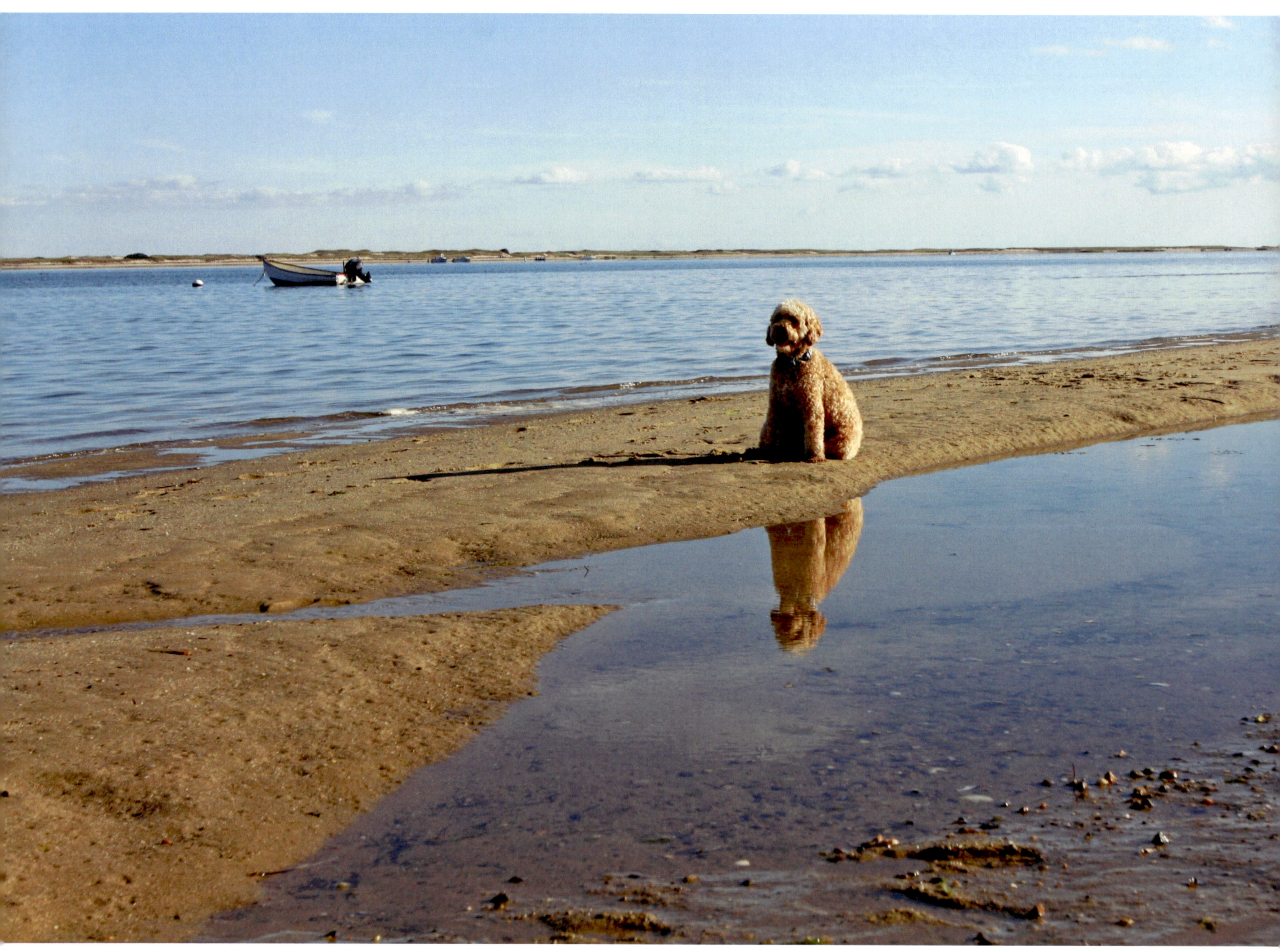

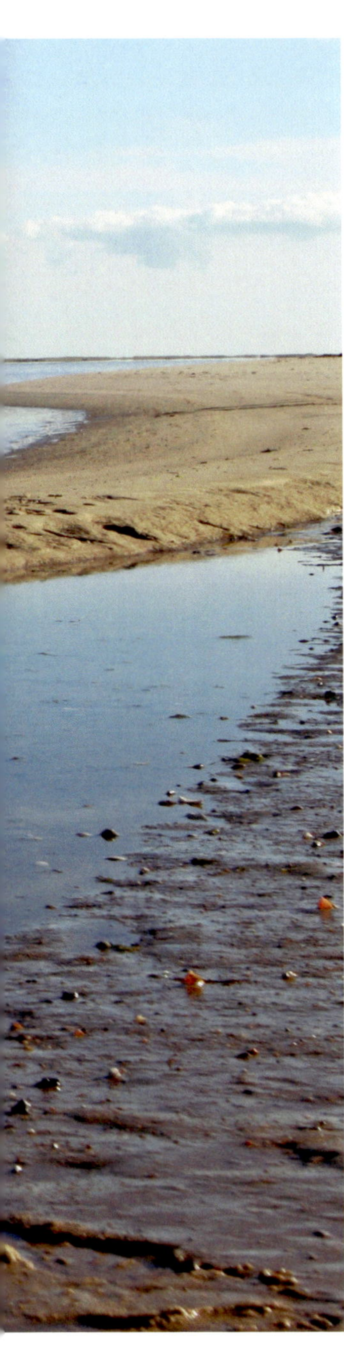

Dogs on Cape Cod

Kim Roderiques

Foreword by Brian Davies

Introduction by Sally Rosenthal

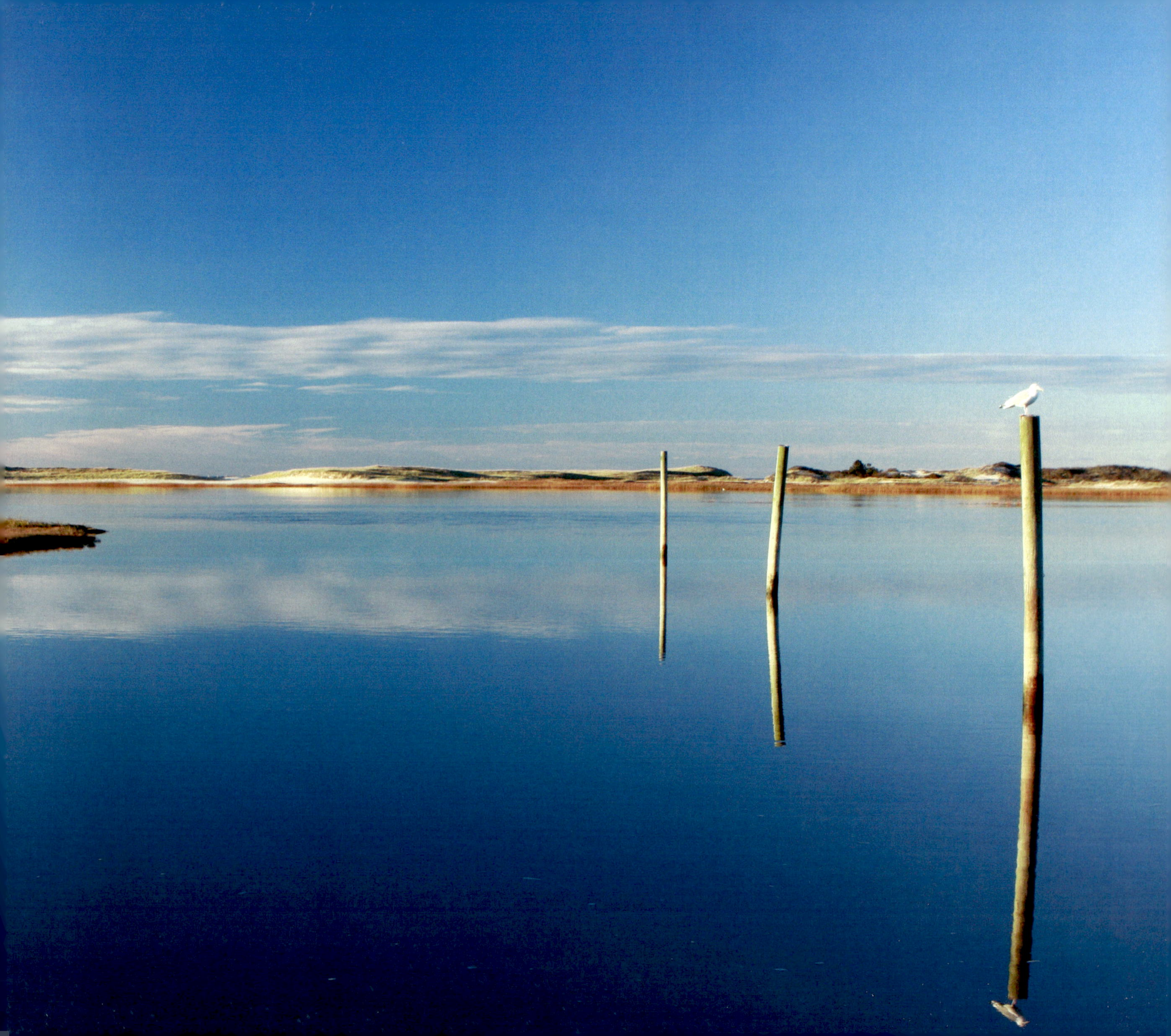

To the memory of my father, John Roderiques, who was
my mentor and protector and encouraged me to follow my passion.
My love for him is beyond words.

Gray's Beach (opposite)

Gioia (previous spread), Australian labradoodle, Monomoy Wildlife Refuge

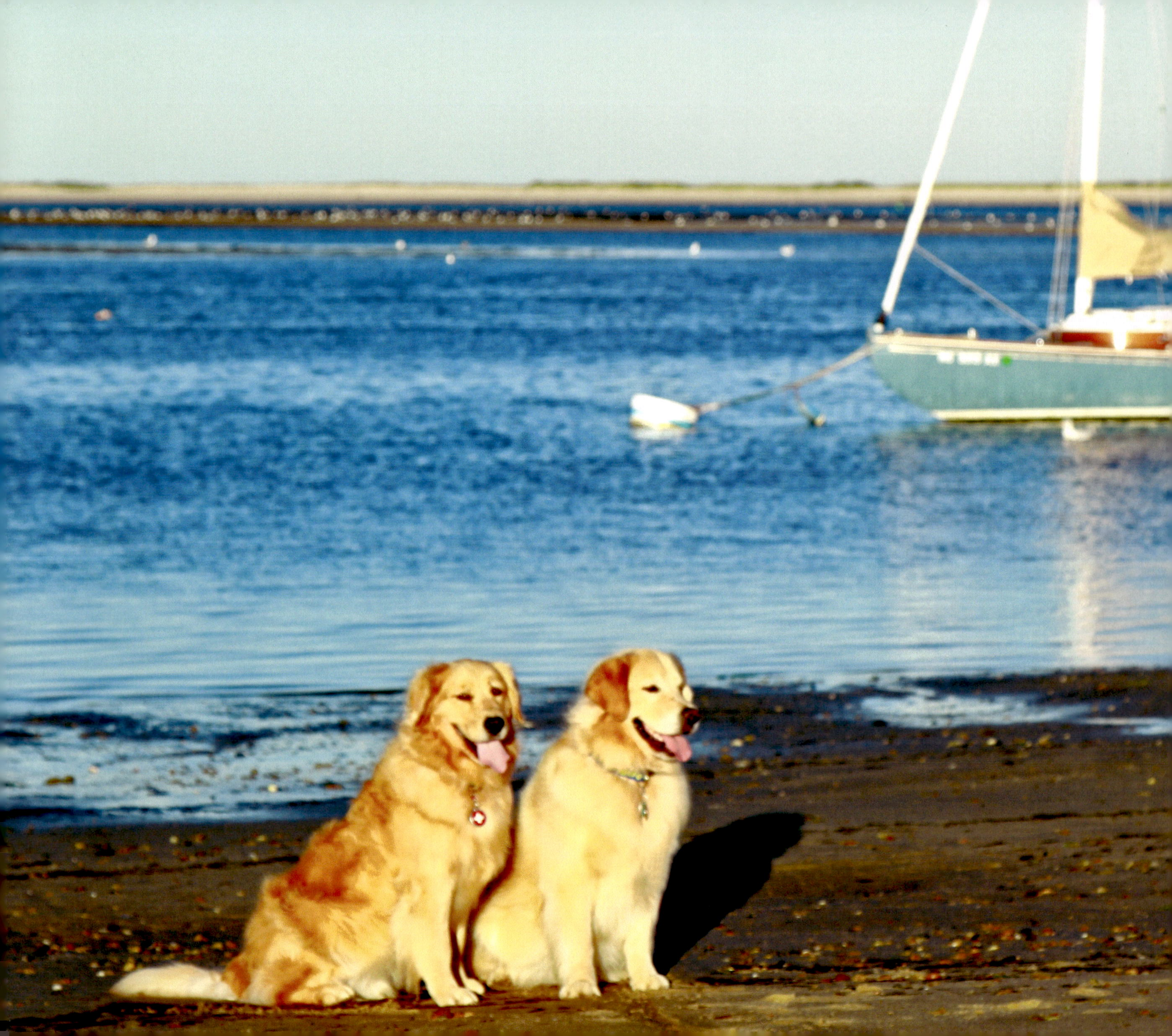

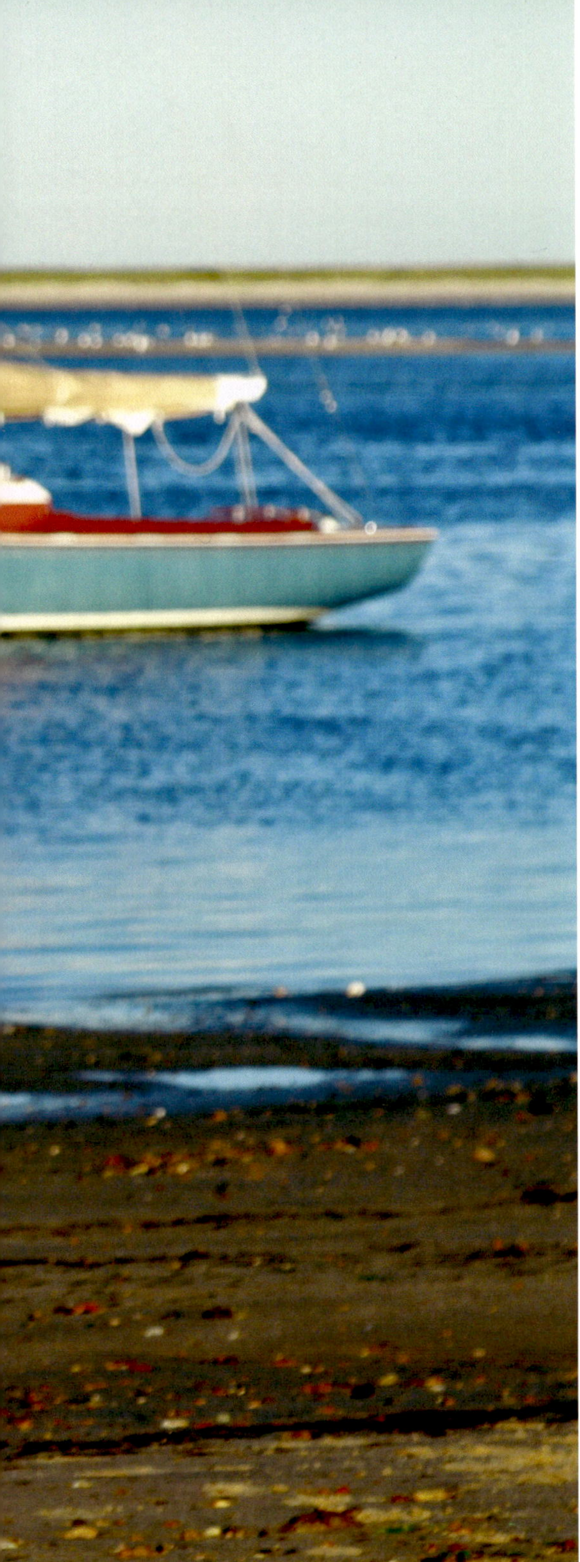

Logan and **Devon**,
golden retrievers,
Chatham Harbor

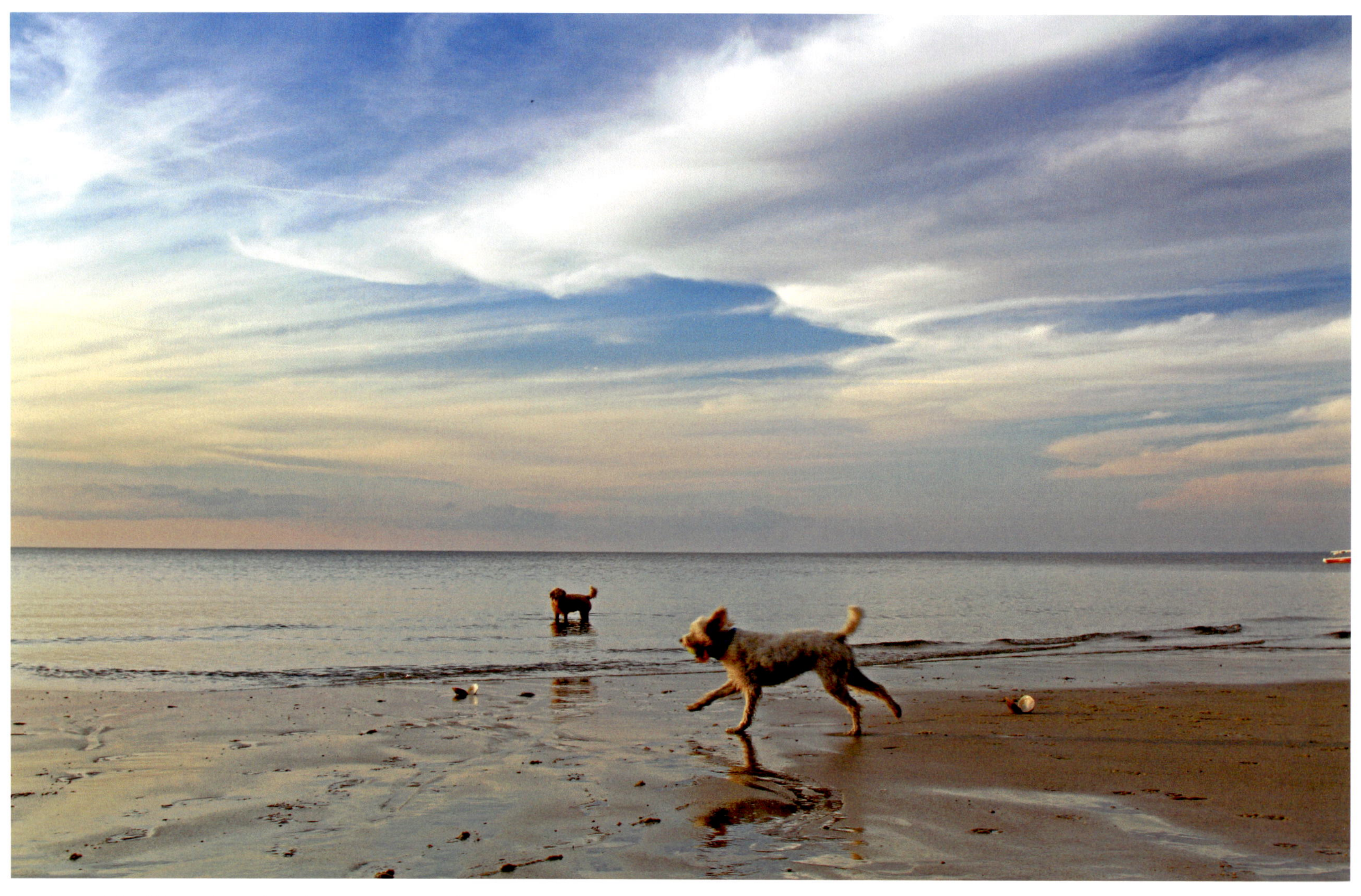

Lucie and **Nellie**, goldendoodles, Saints Landing Beach

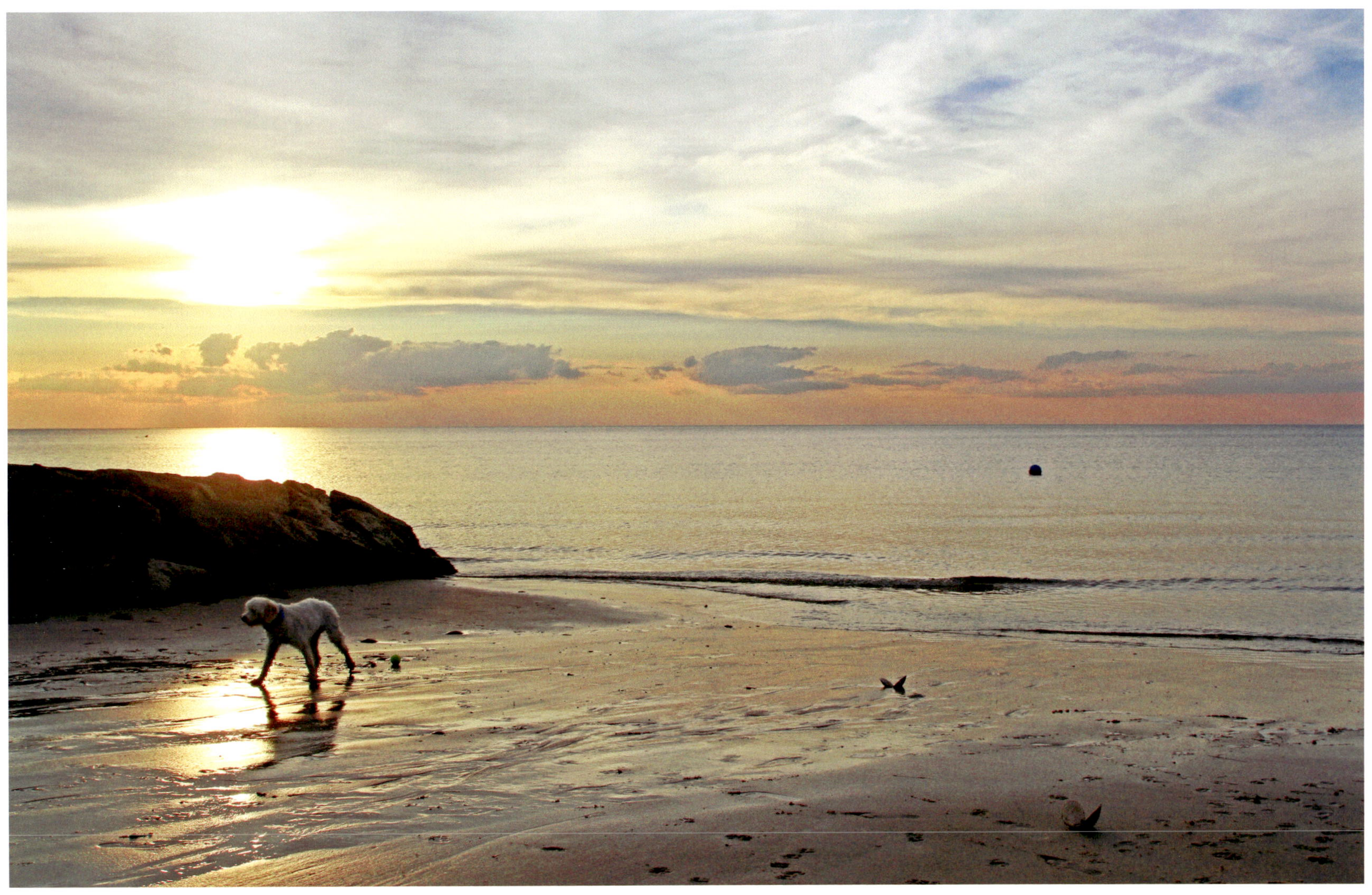

Lucie

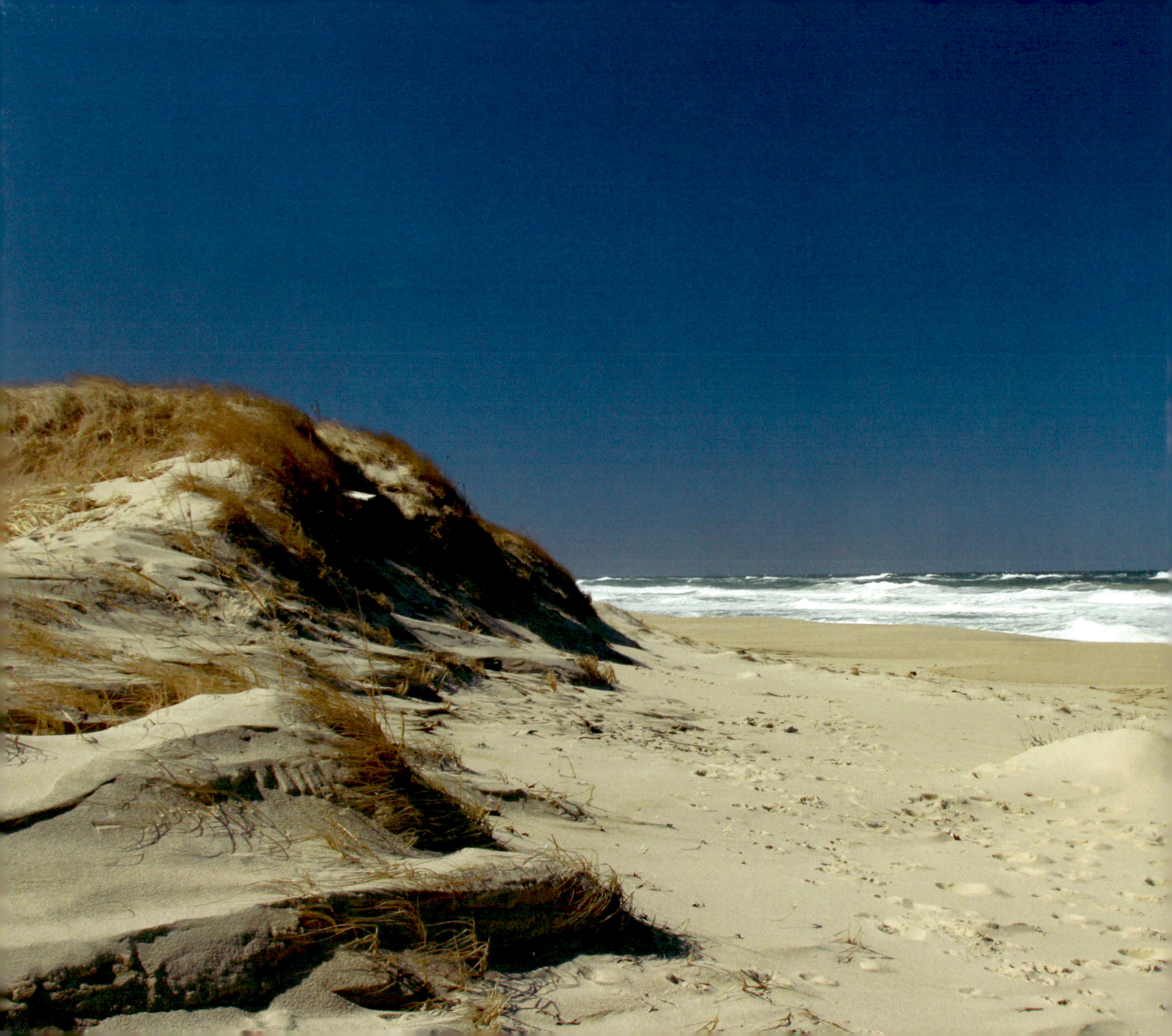

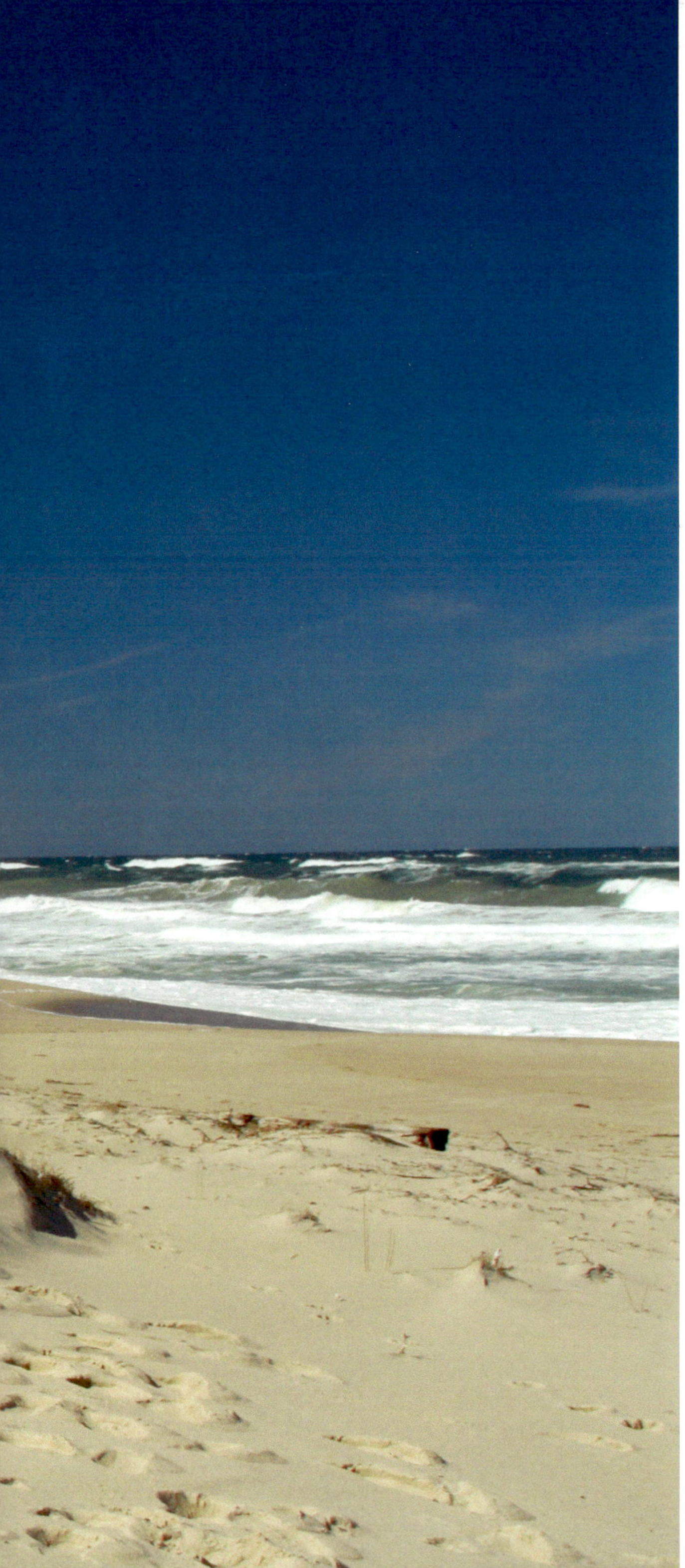

Foreword

When you truly love a dog with all your heart, you have been given a precious gift. When a dog loves you in return, you are doubly blessed. Dog lovers are so lucky.

A lifelong passion for dogs inspired photographer Kim Roderiques to create the pictures in this captivating book. *Dogs on Cape Cod* presents images of just about every kind of dog, each with its own unique personality and mood, captured against a stunning backdrop of Cape Cod scenes—ocean views, beachscapes, sand dunes, grasses, woodlands, and gardens.

Many of the dogs on these pages are rescues, which is an issue of particular concern to Kim and me. As founder (now retired) of the International Fund for Animal Welfare, based on Cape Cod, I spent a lifetime dealing with cruelty to animals. My wife Gloria and I found our dogs Taffy and Amber abandoned on the side of the road on an Italian island in the Mediterranean. Four months old, they were starving, smothered with ticks, near death, the little girl in agony from a barbed grass seed in her eye. Now, fifteen years on, these vibrant, healthy, happy dogs are the light of our lives.

Dogs on Cape Cod is a celebration of the delight that these amazing creatures give to the world, and to those who share their lives.

—Brian Davies

Head of the Meadow Beach

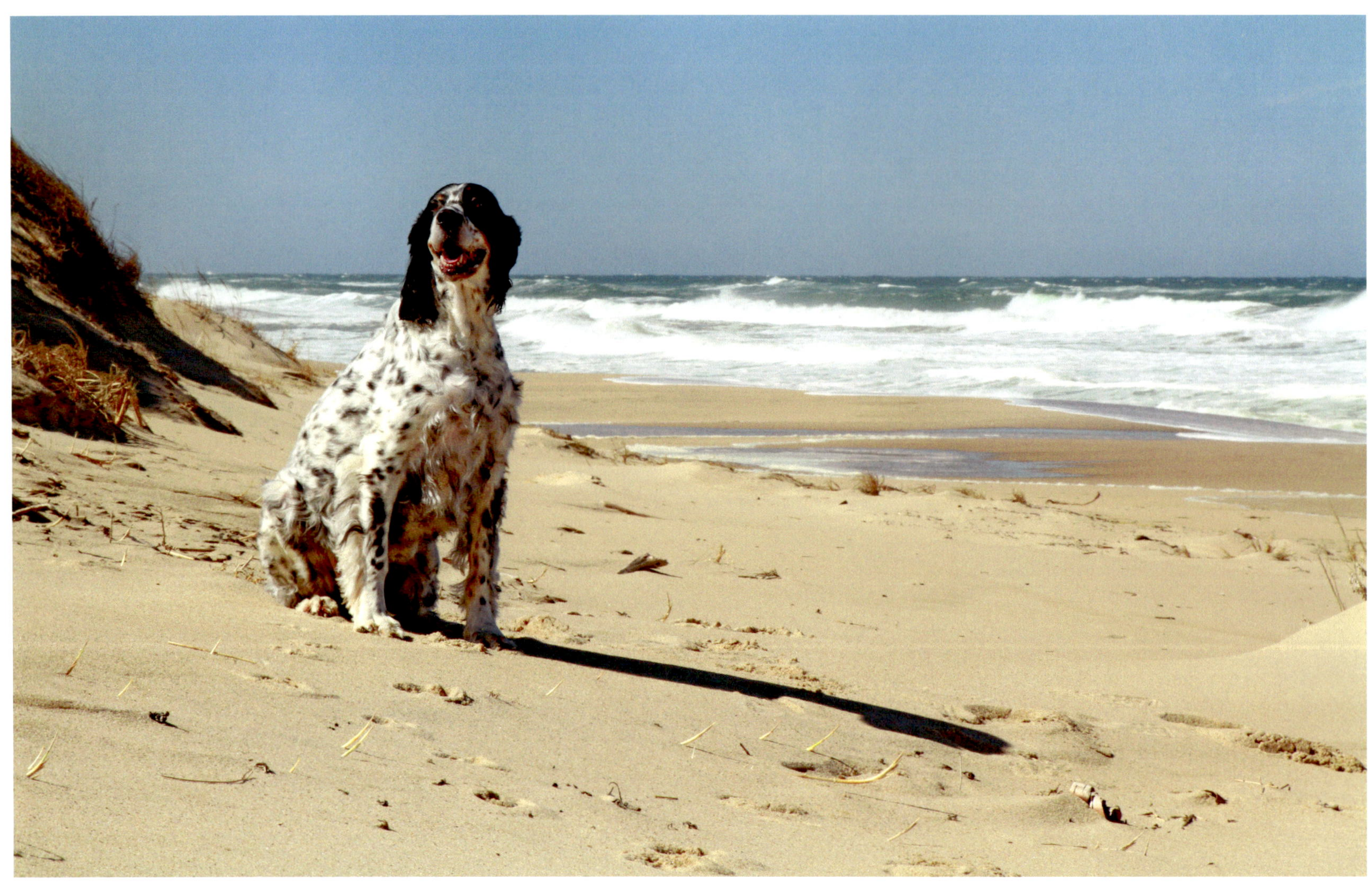

Monty, Llewellyn setter, Head of the Meadow Beach

Cape Reflections

I don't know many people who have been to Cape Cod just once. Either you've never been, or you return again and again. People here don't lament the lost beauty of a seaside that's been overdeveloped and robbed of its character. A unique, close-knit community protects the Cape's beauty fiercely, tightly restricting development and cherishing the old ways.

I first visited Cape Cod as a toddler in the mid-1970s. A friend of my father's from the Army Reserves had summered in Truro as a kid, and he suggested that our families rent a house together. We loved the Watson house, in the woods near Brush Hollow, and returned year after year. We spent our days at the ponds or at Ballston Beach, the adults relaxing on blankets, us kids digging in the sand until we hit water and burying each other up to our necks. We gathered around the picnic tables at PJ's to eat fried clams and onion rings, and shucked oysters on the beach where we found them, a few grains of sand always finding their way into the liquid inside the shell. In the evenings we went to the drive-in movie theater in Wellfleet, or to Ciro and Sal's in Provincetown for a slice of key lime pie. We rode bicycles along winding paths and climbed the spiral stairs of the Cape Cod Light. On rainy days we did jigsaw puzzles and painted small rocks.

That was almost four decades ago. In the early 1990s my parents built a house near Ryder Beach in Truro. Today we spend our days at the beach by our house, or on the ocean side at Longnook. We still eat fried clams at PJ's. We still go to the drive-in. We still bury each other in sand. We still paint rocks on rainy days.

The constancy of the Cape means that it always feels like home. It always looks just as you left it on your last visit. Wood is weathered. Signs are faded. New establishments crop up from time to time, but only in old buildings. Most restaurants know that your vacation would be incomplete without them; they don't reinvent themselves, and rarely change their menus or decor.

There is, of course, a large permanent community on Cape Cod. Although I visit year-round, I'm there most often in summer, and I associate my visits with long days, warm weather, and the beach. A full-time resident might think more about the quiet, the stark beauty, the community that draws together when the summer people go home. For me, the community is always waiting when I arrive. I feel it when the pilot on Cape Air turns around in his seat and chats with the passengers before takeoff, when the high school kids sitting on beach chairs at the entrance to Longnook check my beach sticker, when Cindy leads my family to our favorite booth at Front Street. Community is strong at the Wellfleet galleries featuring local artists, and at packed readings at the Fine Arts Work Center.

Growing up in the Boston suburbs, we would pile into the car on Friday after school or summer camp to try to make it to Truro by dinnertime. Now that I live in New York and don't have a car, I usually fly. The twenty-minute Cape Air flight from Boston to Provincetown is not for the skittish. Seats on the ten-seater plane are assigned by size, and as, at five foot two, I am usually the smallest traveler, I'm often assigned to ride shotgun next to the pilot. The plane flies so low over the Atlantic that you can sometimes see whales breaching. On one flight, there were so many whales breaking the water's surface that the pilot circled back for an impromptu aerial whale-watch. It is a testament to the power of that sight that the passengers agreed to this; the ten-seaters are small, and jiggle with every air pocket, and no one would normally spend a second more than necessary in one of them. But just as you're promising yourself that next time you'll take the ferry, Provincetown's national seashore comes into view, all pristine beaches and grassy dunes, and there's nowhere you'd rather be than that little flying oven. The plane crosses the rail trails and the Cape Cod lifesaving station, before finally descending toward the runway of the Provincetown Municipal Airport. Once a one-room shack, the airport was renovated about fifteen years ago and now boasts high, beamed ceilings, sweet old-fashioned benches, and an arrow pointing to the one spot in the building where cell phones work. My family greets me, and we head home, my mother invariably telling me on the walk to the car about all the food that awaits us back at the house.

One of my favorite Cape traditions is our family's lobster lunch. It started as a Fourth of July treat, but now we use every houseguest as an excuse to sit down together for a long, leisurely meal. With my parents at either end of the table, and my brother, his family, my friends, my niece's friends, my parents' friends, and me in between, we begin with a Caprese salad with tomatoes from the produce stand on Route 6 and herbs from my dad's garden. Then the lobsters come out, from Hatch's in Wellfleet: perfectly steamed and cut down the center. The large ceramic bowls along the table begin to fill up with discarded shells. When everyone's plate is a mess of gnawed corncob and excess butter, my mother politely forces us all to make room for a slice of watermelon. Afterward, many hands make short work of the dishes. Then we grab our towels and drag our overstuffed bellies to the beach.

In the summer on the Cape, plans for the day often follow the tide clock. The best time to be at Longnook, my favorite ocean beach, is halfway between high and low tide, when the water is heading out and the waves are breaking. Every summer the ocean floor is different, depending on how storms have pummeled it over the winter. A nor'easter that hits at high tide on a full moon in December will change the break points for the waves the next summer. One recent summer there were hardly any waves at all. But typically, at that halfway point between tides, a wave caught on a bodyboard can propel its rider all the way up onto the sand. A long, uninterrupted ride is pure bliss. When I was a kid, my only concern was that a parent would eventually notice my blue lips, check my pruny fingers, and order me out of the water. Since that time, though, hordes of surfers have arrived, many of them novices with little control. Plenty of people still ride bodyboards, myself included, but with a caution that wasn't necessary before the surfers came.

Low tide on the ocean side is young-family time. As the water recedes, shallow tide pools and sandbars appear over the same stretches where the best waves were two hours earlier. Toddlers splash in the pools, and older kids slide around on bodyboards. Some people carry their chairs out to the sandbars and let the water roll over their feet as they sit in the ocean shallows.

On the bay side, when the tide comes in, the stony bottom retreats to the depths, and the water reaches up the beach. Wading in becomes much more comfortable, as sand replaces rock underfoot. A tiny crab might bump against your ankles, but he's not there to nibble. The water stays calm. The big rocks in front of our house where the seals congregate at low tide disappear. Sometimes the bay is still, as it was the day I learned to swim. My father stood with his arms outstretched before him as I floated just above them, discovering the concept of buoyancy as my body rose and fell to meet his arms with each subtle hint of a wave. High tide at the bay is soft and easy.

High tide on the ocean side is different. The water at Longnook becomes a pool with no shallow end, and pulls you back in when you try to get out. I learned this when I was seven years old. A friend and I had found a bottle in the sand, and we decided to put messages in it and send it floating to China. We scribbled notes and flung the bottle into the ocean, but as soon as we'd released it, I decided I didn't like what I had written and stepped into the water to retrieve the bottle. Within seconds I was in over my head, lost in dark water, the strong undertow pulling me away. My mother saw me go under and dove in to pull me to safety. I didn't get the bottle, and I didn't go into the ocean at high tide again until I was much taller.

Longnook is not like other ocean beaches. Walking through the parking lot, all that is visible is the dunes, with a dip in the middle and sky ahead. Where the pavement hits the sand, lies a jumble of flip-flops and sandals, temporarily abandoned by beachgoers. As you keep walking, the parking lot drops away and the water suddenly comes into view; far below, the beach seems to stretch infinitely in either direction, umbrellas dotting the sand, the ocean a distant roar. A steep path cuts down through the dunes to the beach, an orange sediment in the sand staining your feet. Longnook's dunes loom over sixty feet above the beach, casting shade in late afternoon, still as stone save for the occasional pebble rolling down from the top and coming to rest beside your towel. They seem immutable, fixed in place, yet a glance up confirms their fragility; they are broken off at their peaks like the upper reaches of the Alps, and just as capable of collapsing in an avalanche when disturbed. These dunes are meant for admiring, not frolicking.

Which isn't to say that all dunes in the Cape are hands-off. Some, like those in Provincetown, are meant to be experienced in a dune buggy. On a packed sand road, our buggies' tires filled only halfway so they don't pop on the beach, we wind through the dunes, avoiding the areas where the piping plovers nest, until the Atlantic stretches before us. Turning right, we bounce past the campground and the surfcasters, lurching with every bump, hidden by beach grass, in the terrain. Tucked into the sandy hills where Provincetown starts its curve are the dune shacks: tumbledown structures from the earliest days of the artists' colony, passed down from parent to child for a hundred years, with wide plank boards, one room, outhouses, no electricity, and uncompromisingly beautiful views of the water.

It's stunning there at sunset—but there's nothing like sunset at home. At our house in Truro, no matter what we're doing at day's end, we drop it and go out to the deck to "watch the red ball." When the sun goes down, the sky lights up with brilliant pink and blue and yellow, and the fireball seems to pour itself into the horizon. We'll stay a few minutes after that last line of gold-red has disappeared, enjoying the wild colors of the sky. When darkness sets in, the curve of the Cape tip glitters with the lights of Provincetown, the monument clearly visible. The music of the Cape at night is crickets and waves.

I can't count the number of times I've looked up on a lazy afternoon of beach lounging and book reading at Longnook to realize the sun is starting to duck behind the dunes, and it's time to head home for dinner. I suppose more energetic types schedule activities. Many people on the Cape sail, but our family's vessel of choice is the kayak. Paddling along the winding narrows of the Pamet River, you don't long for company: egrets hop along the banks, bullfrogs croak, fish whiz by your oar, turtles sit, contentedly still, underwater. One time, with almost a dozen guests, we put in at a spot in Wellfleet and kayaked down the Herring River estuary. At low tide, we reached the bridge that goes over the dike on its way to Great Island and pulled our kayaks up on the narrow riverbank. A stash of oysters lay half-buried in the sand, as if waiting for us. I don't remember who had the foresight to bring the knife, but slurping the oysters down on the spot reminded me of that childhood Cape pleasure, which is now frowned upon.

One place you can still eat an oyster seconds after it's shucked is the agricultural fair Truro hosts every summer. At the Ag Fair, in addition to buying a dozen oysters from lightning-fast shuckers, you can vote for your favorite turkeys or alpacas in the Barnyard Beauty Contest, admire the Strangest Veggie and Best-Looking Dozen Eggs, and avert your eyes from the popular but revolting pie-eating contest.

Another of Truro's oddly beloved institutions is the town dump. Disposing of trash on the Outer Cape is an adventure and an exercise in sequencing precision: drive down the hill; stop; chuck garbage bags into the giant metal pit; drive to the cardboard station; stop; dispose of flattened boxes; drive to the paper station; stop; dispose of newspapers and magazines; drive to the deposit station; stop; dispose of bottles and cans (which the Council on Aging and the Boy Scouts turn in for the deposit); drive to the glass station; stop; dispose of glass bottles; drive to the metal waste station; stop; dispose of aluminum containers; drive to the swap shop; stop; browse the used paperbacks. To the right of the swap shop is the area where contractors leave items they've removed from torn-down houses; it's not uncommon to see a row of toilets, or a line of refrigerators standing at attention. At the rear of the dump, all the nearby restaurants dispose of their lobster bodies in a shellfish graveyard. In this landscape of hollowed-out claws, split tails, broken knuckles, and empty torsos, a million flies buzz in a loud, constant drone. The stench is staggering. The Cape is at once an oasis of calm and an onslaught on the senses.

In almost forty years of visits to the Cape, as much as I adore its beauty, its beaches, its food, its local amusements, I've come to cherish it most as a gathering place for the people I love, especially as the number of those people has grown. It holds us close. My parents furnished the house with all twin beds so that as we got older, my brother and I would bring our families, and everyone would have somewhere to sleep. I don't think my parents considered that we would bring our friends year after year, that our friends would become my parents' friends, that they would bring their families too, and how close it would keep us all. Everyone I know on the Cape feels like family. Everyone I bring says it feels like home. I've brought Australian friends who love Truro because it reminds them of Sydney. My Dutch friends identify with the live-and-let-live ethos of the Outer Cape (and the constant presence of bicycles!). My New York friends spend a weekend here and vow never to return to the Hamptons. My best friend from childhood recently bought a house in Osterville, and I see her sons discovering those same pleasures that enchanted my brother and me. I still see the family we came to the Watson house with that first summer; our lives keep changing, away from each other and back again, to school, careers, marriage, children, grandchildren. The constant in all our lives is the Cape. Anyone who has known the unique joys of Cape life finds it hard to leave, and conspires to return. It becomes part of them. It's the most beautiful, welcoming, quirky, energized, lazy, restorative, gluttonous, artistic, indulgent, lush, stark, warm, and wonderful place on earth.

—Sally Rosenthal

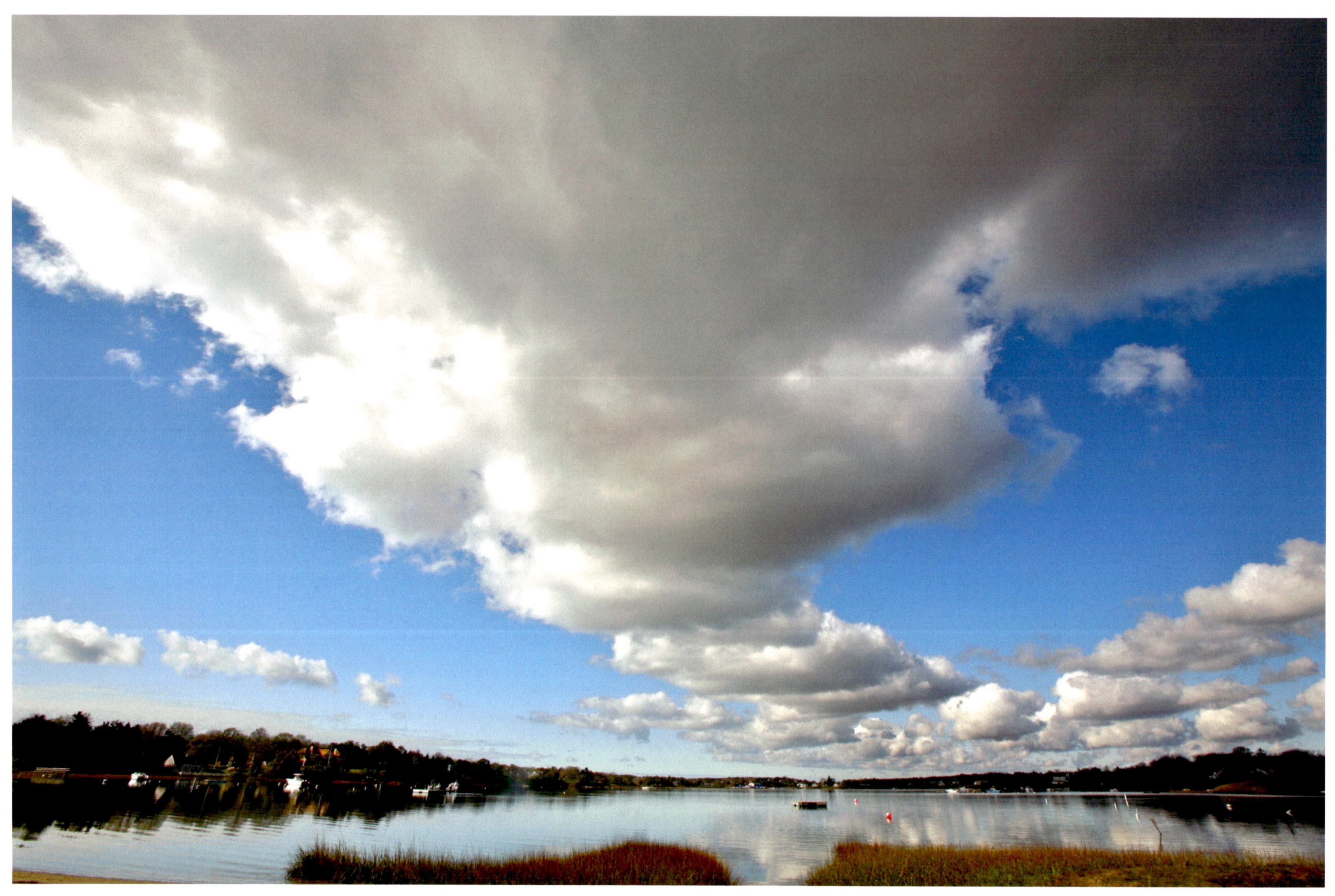

Oyster Pond

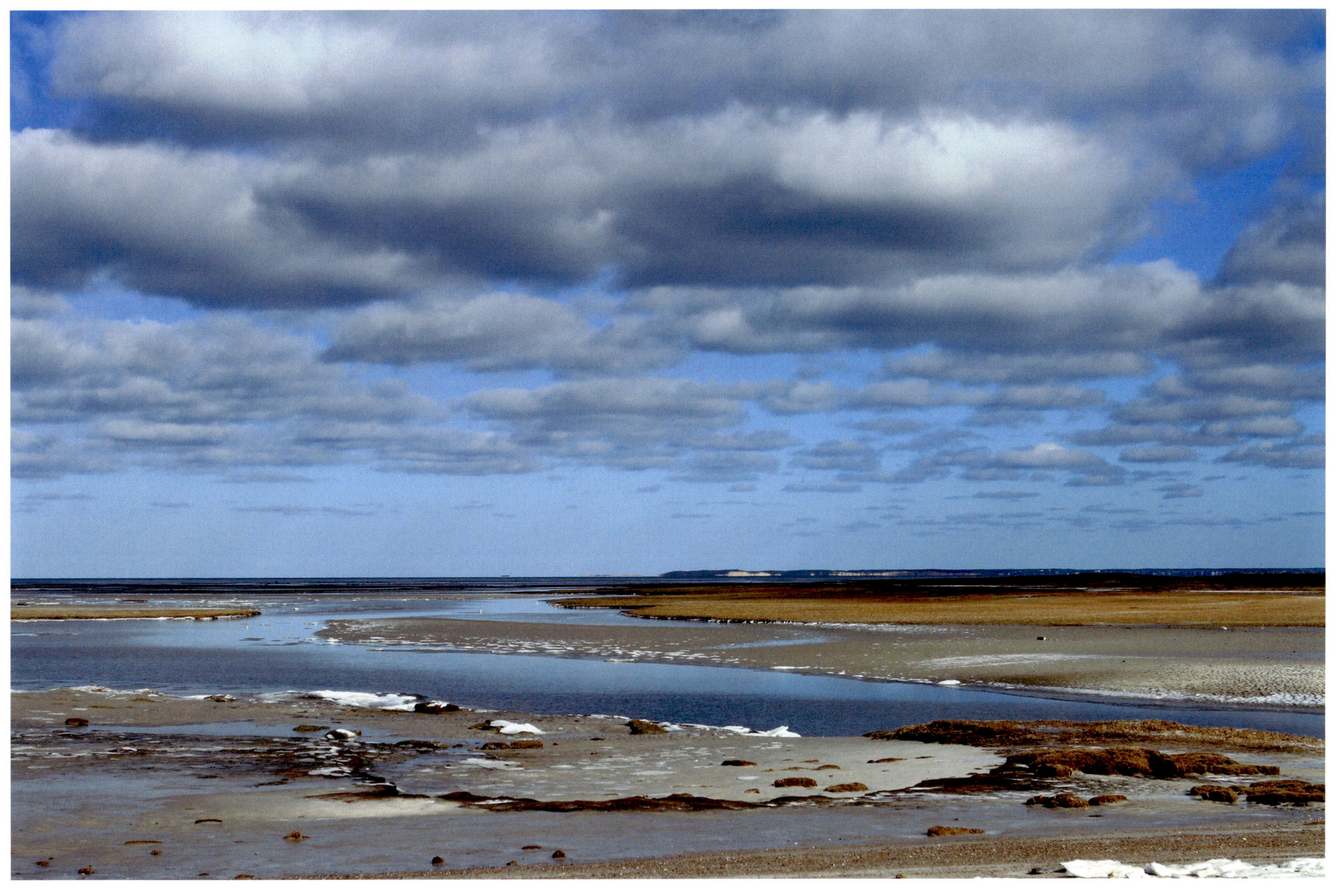

Boat Meadow Beach

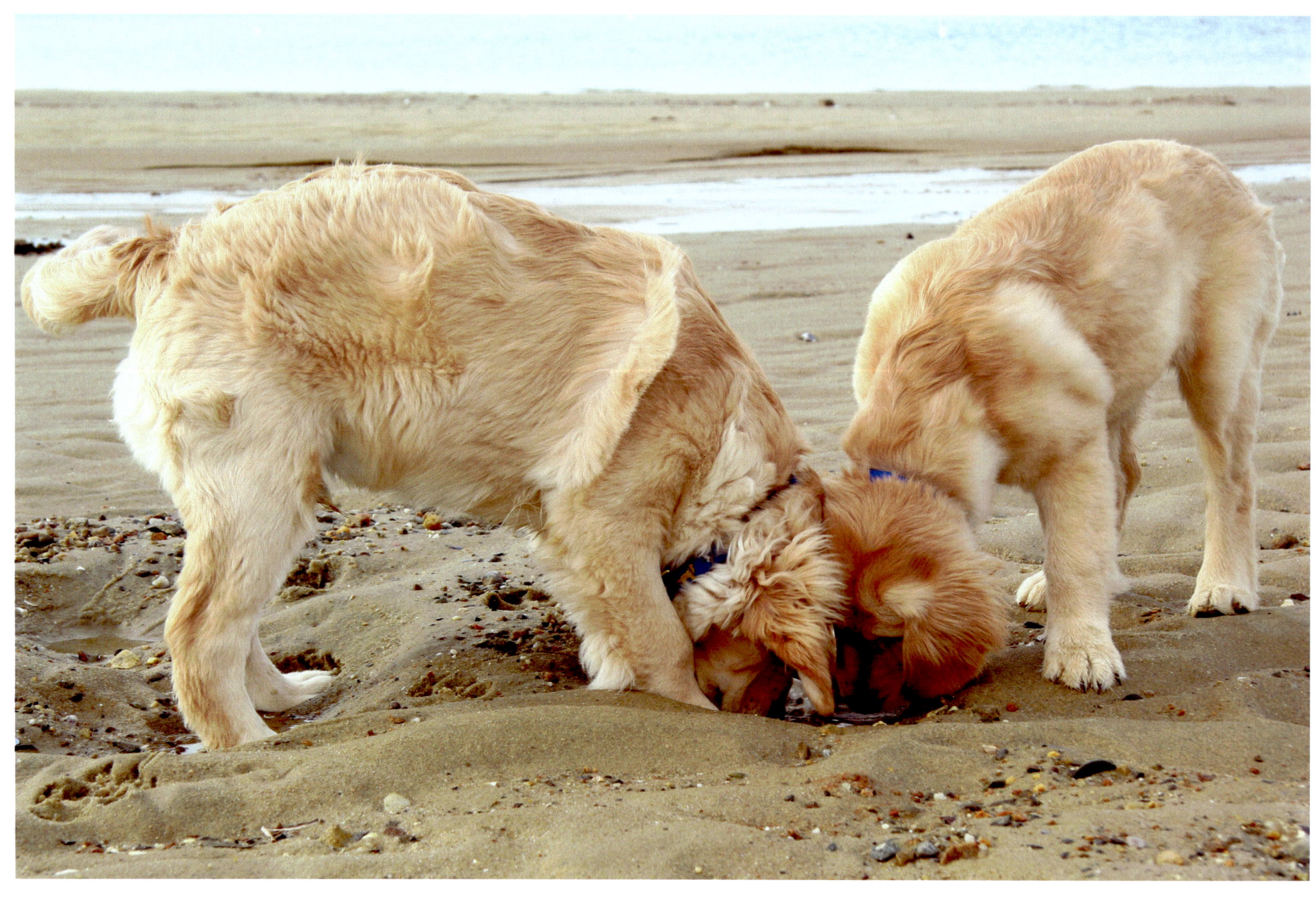

Graham and **Kelly**, golden retrievers, Scatteree Landing

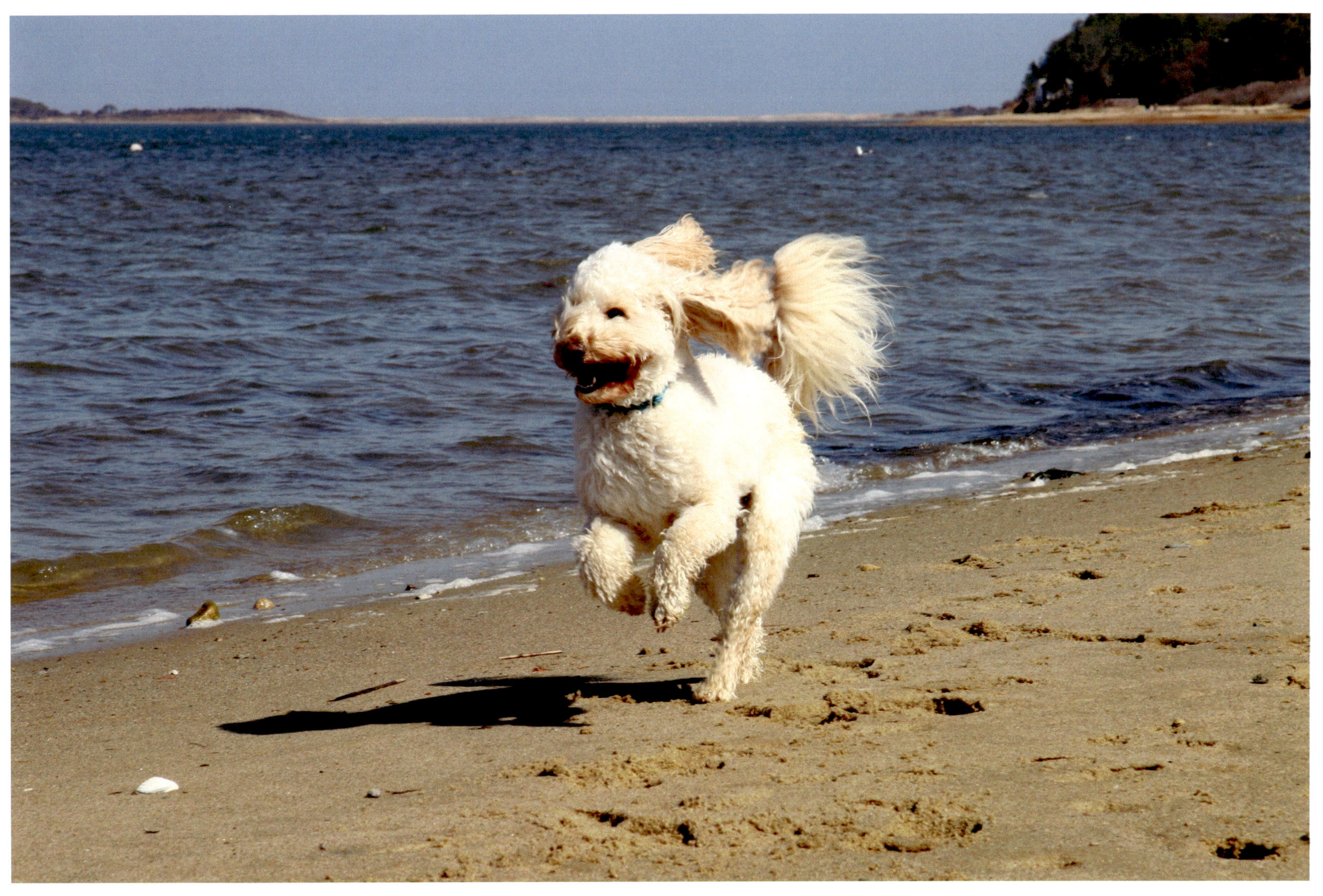

Georgey, Australian labradoodle, Pleasant Bay

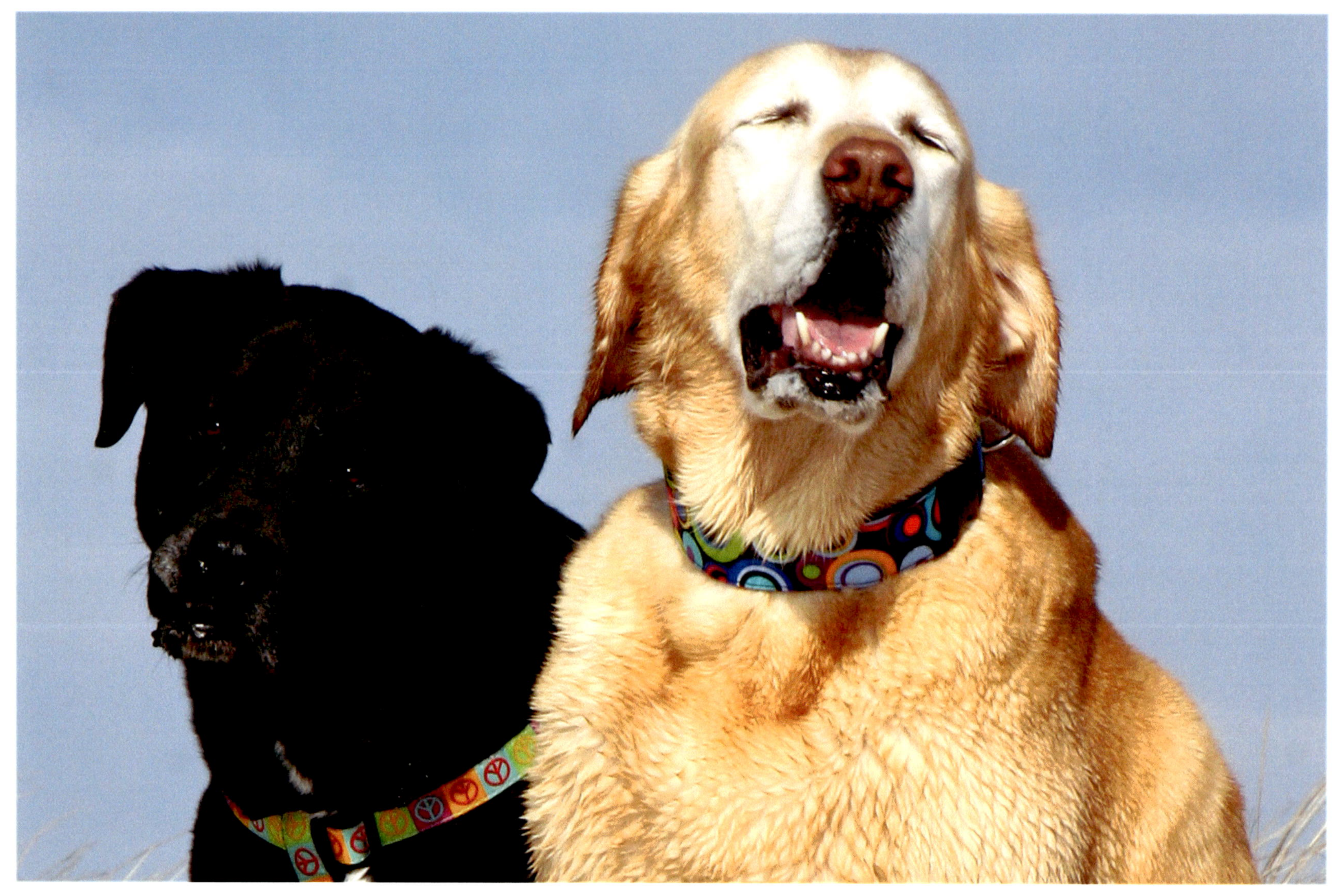

Rooney, labrador retriever mix, and **Jack**, golden retriever mix, Harding's Beach

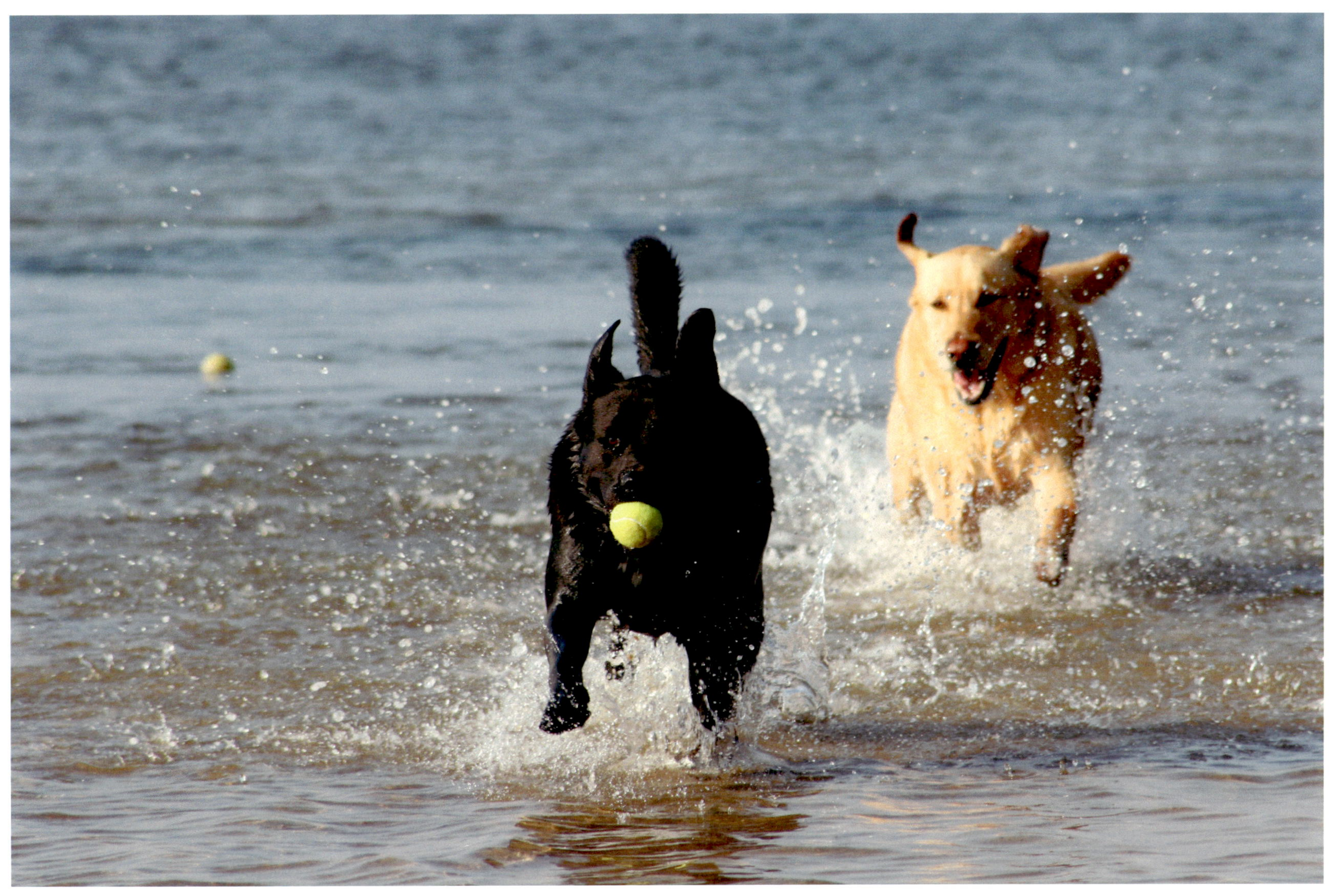

Rooney and **Jack**, Jackknife Beach

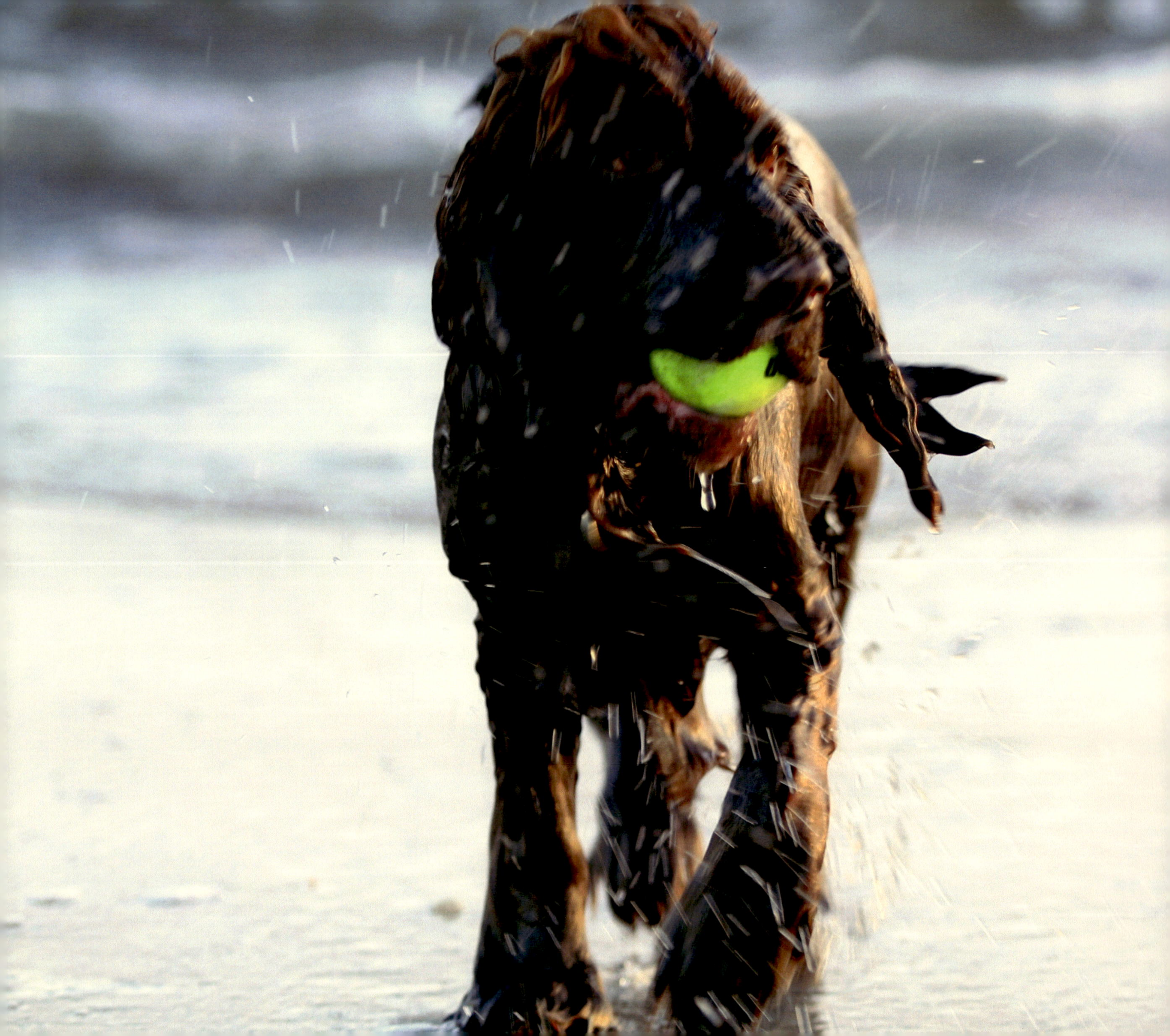

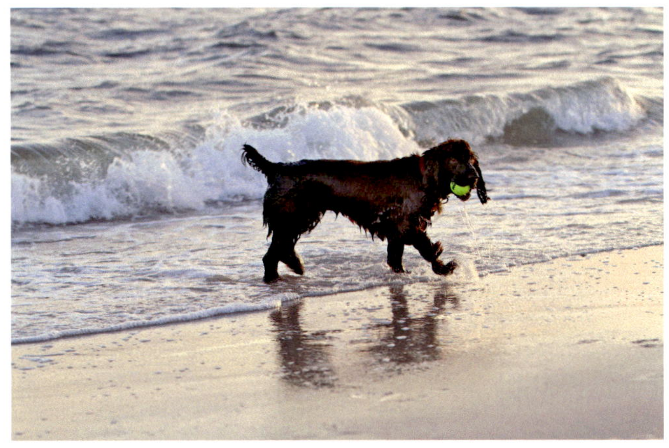

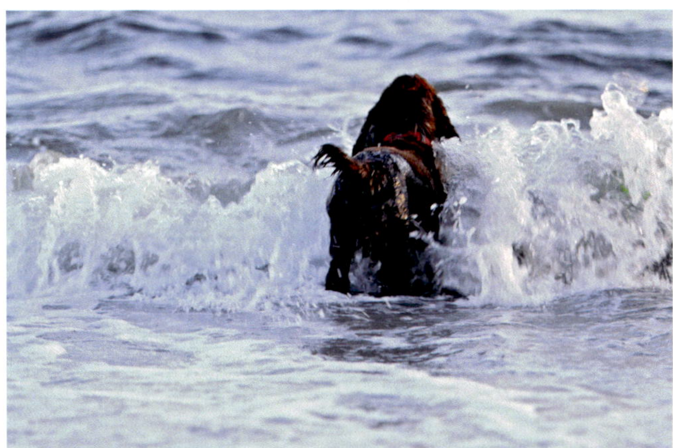

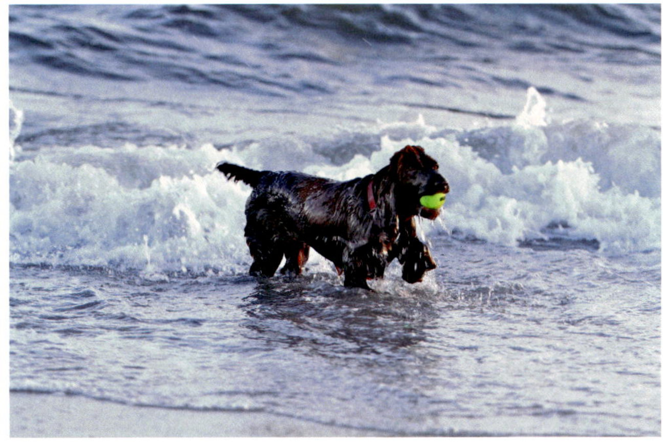

Lola, field spaniel, Red River Beach

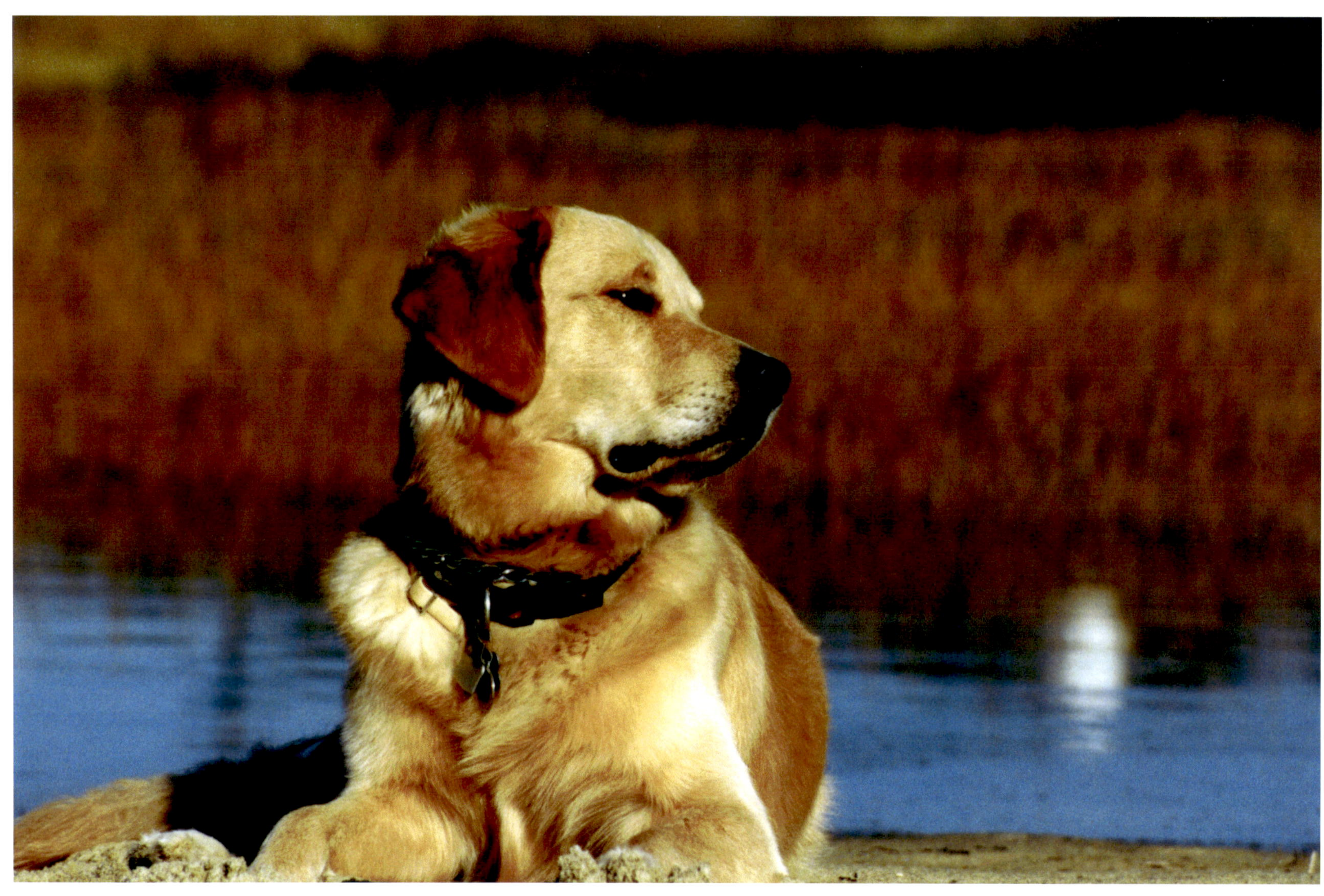

Max, golden retriever, Ridgevale Beach

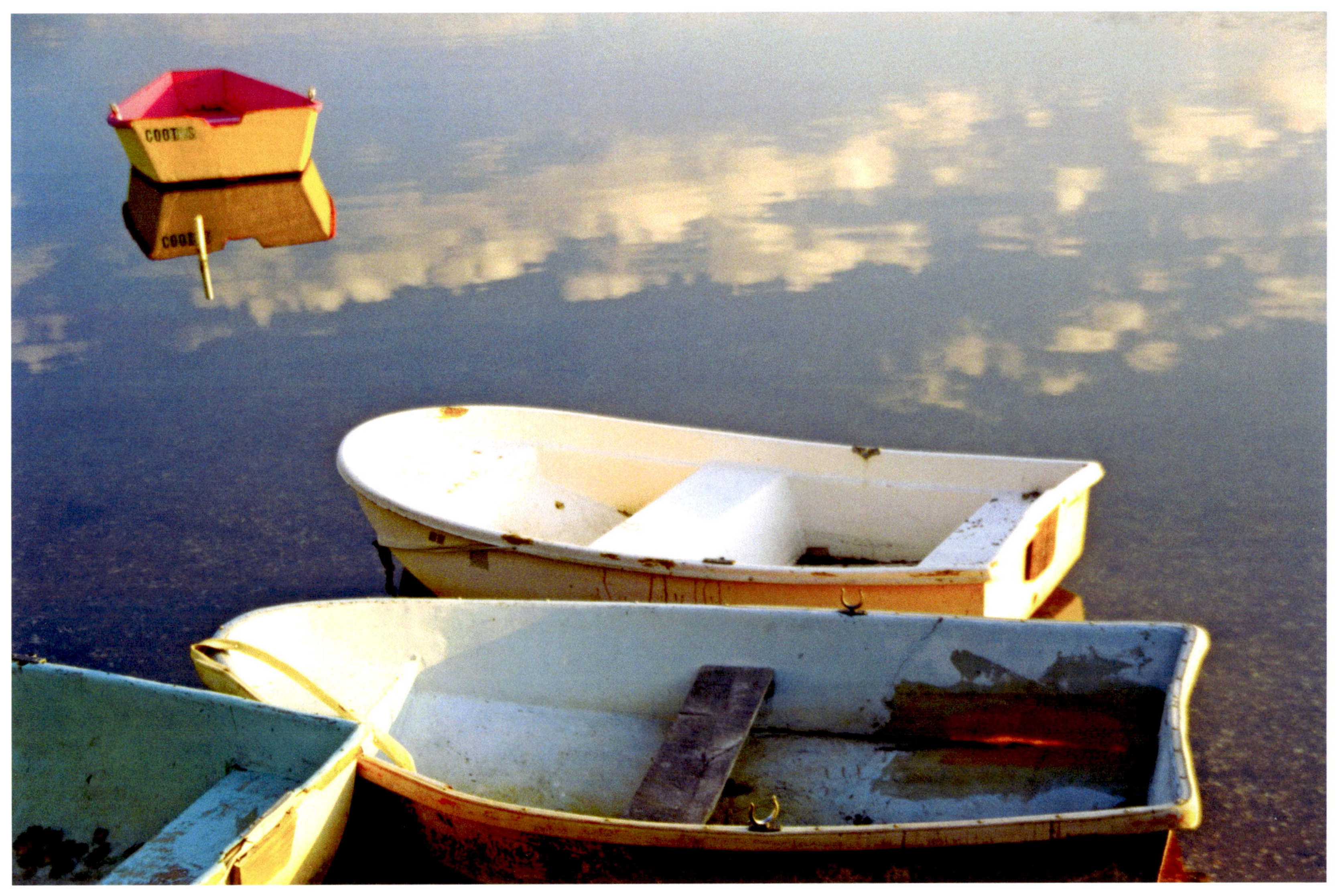

Oyster Pond

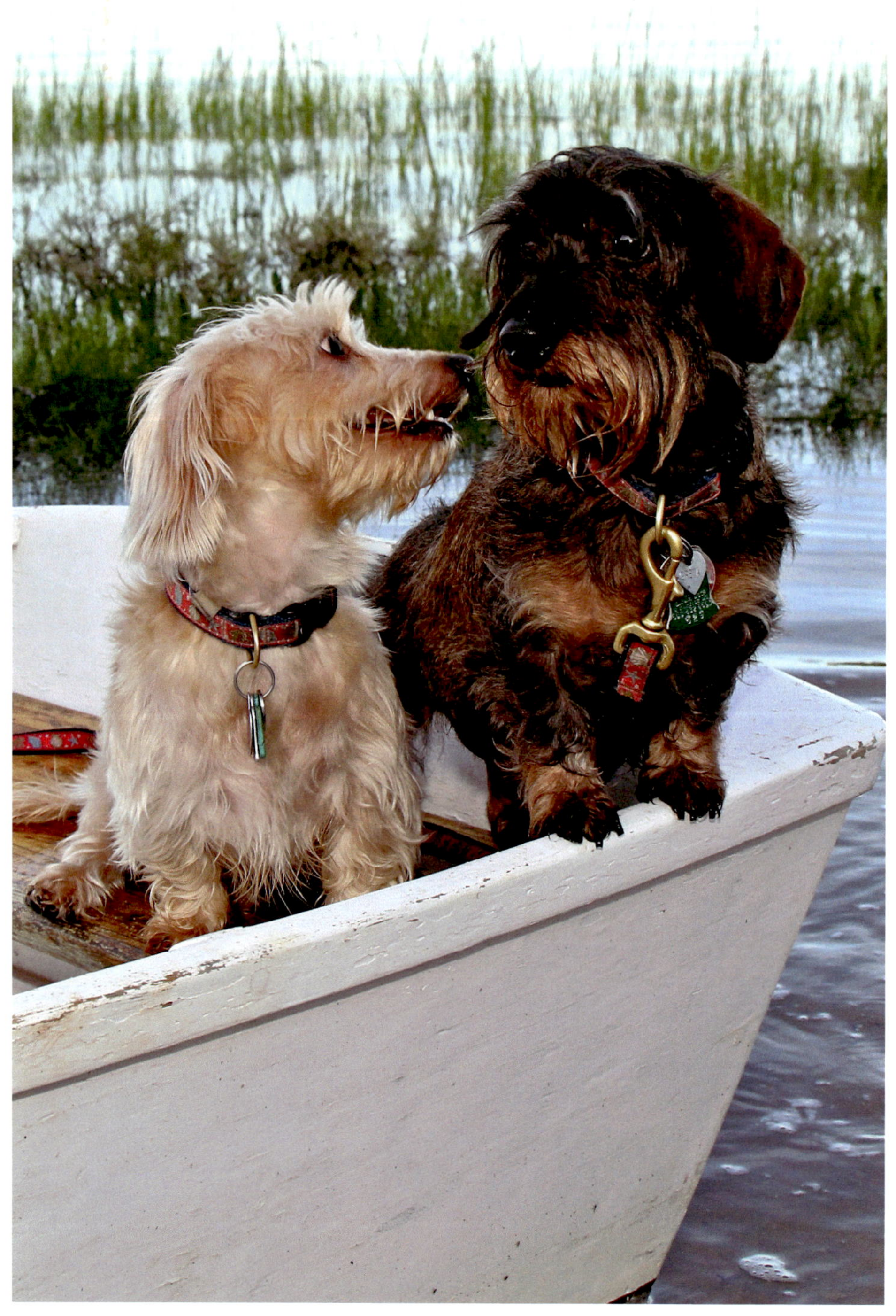

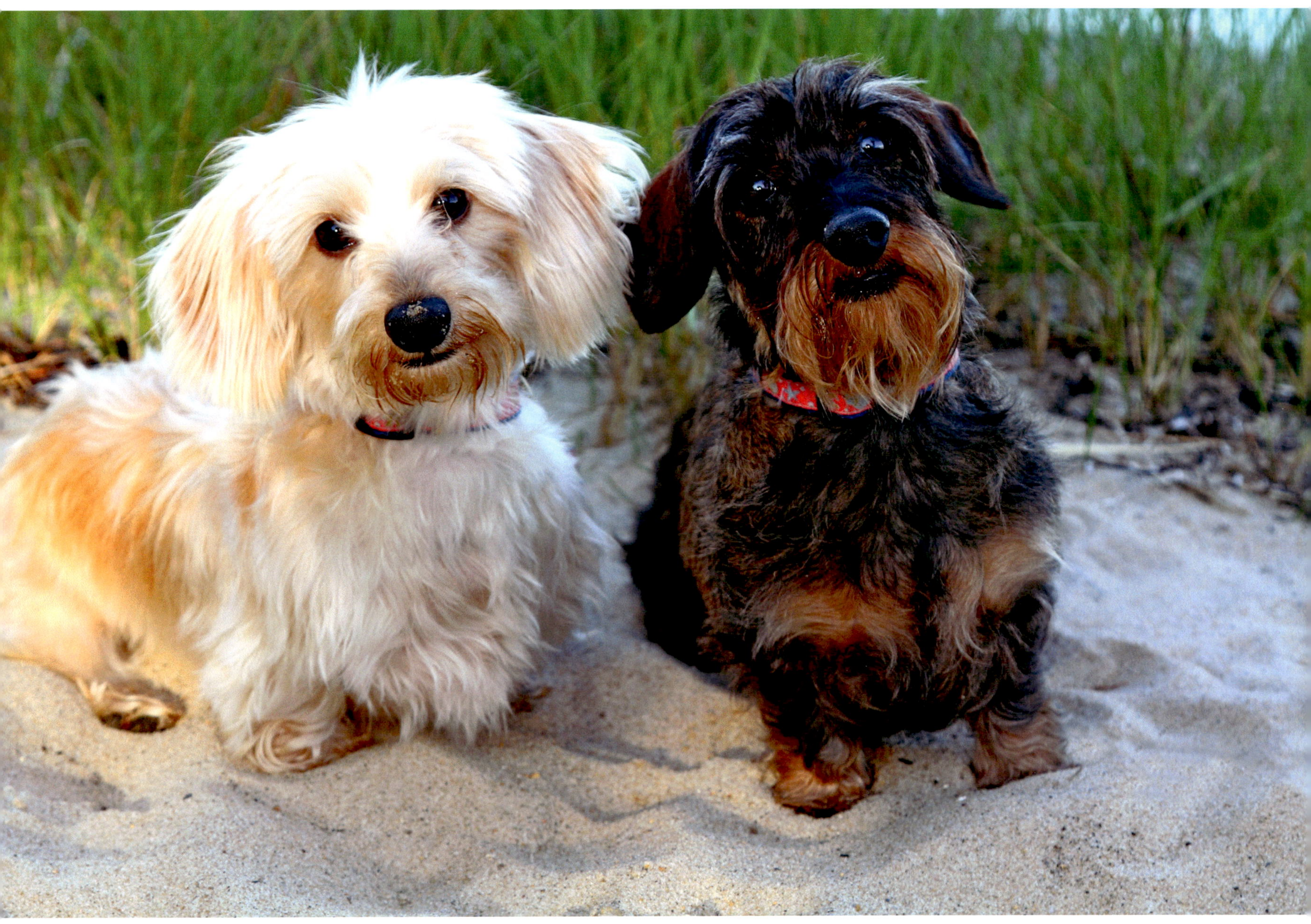

Elsa and **Greta**, wirehaired dachshunds, Chatham Harbor

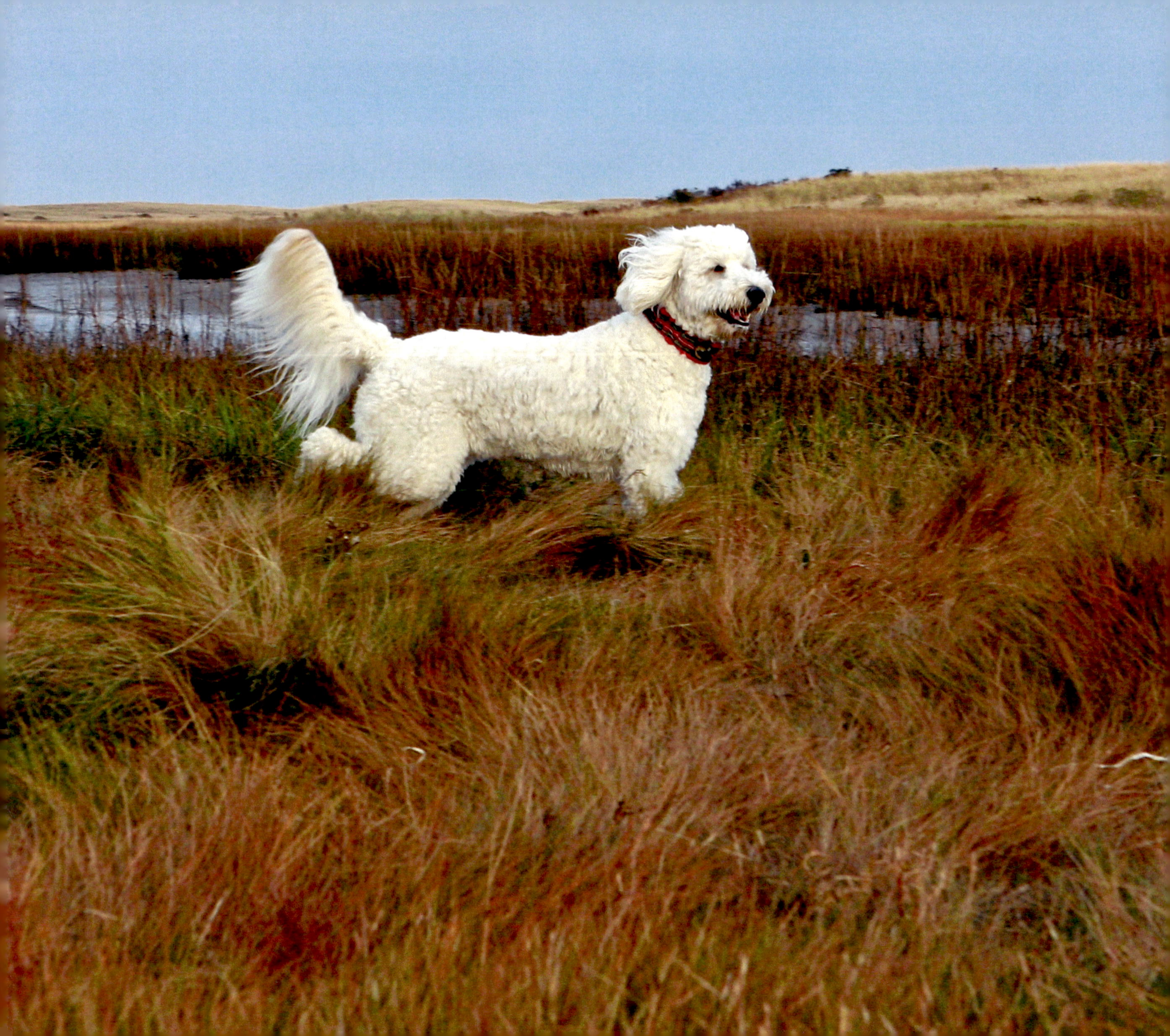

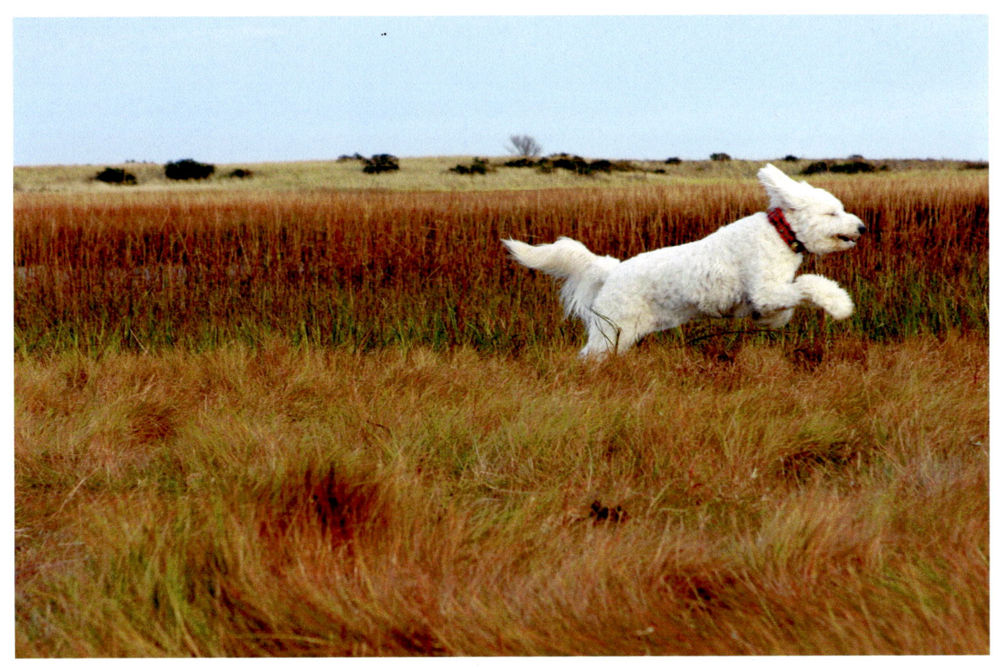

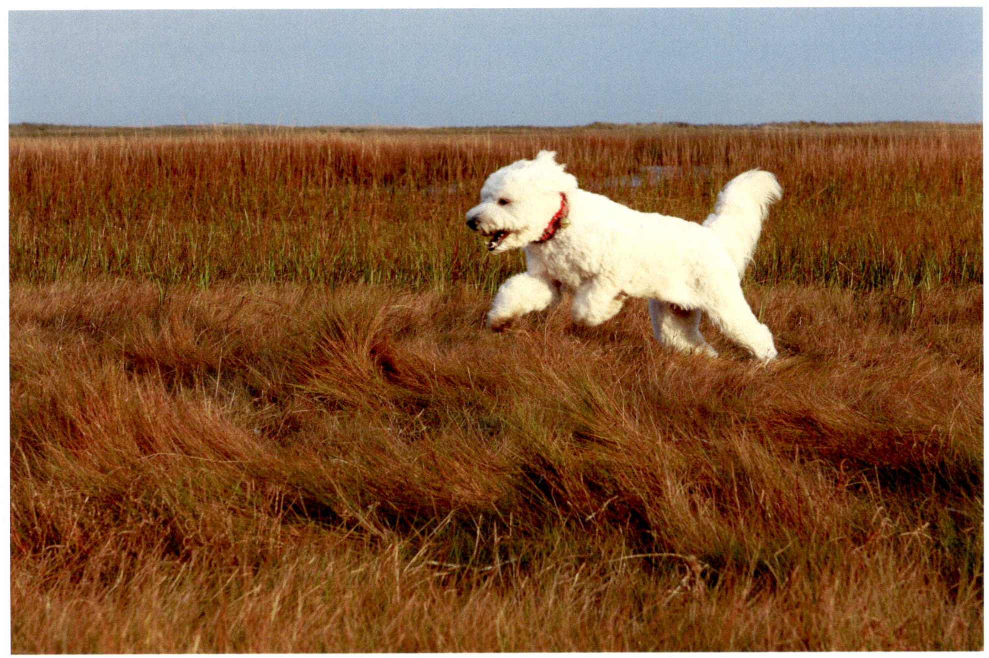

Bella, goldendoodle, Morris Island

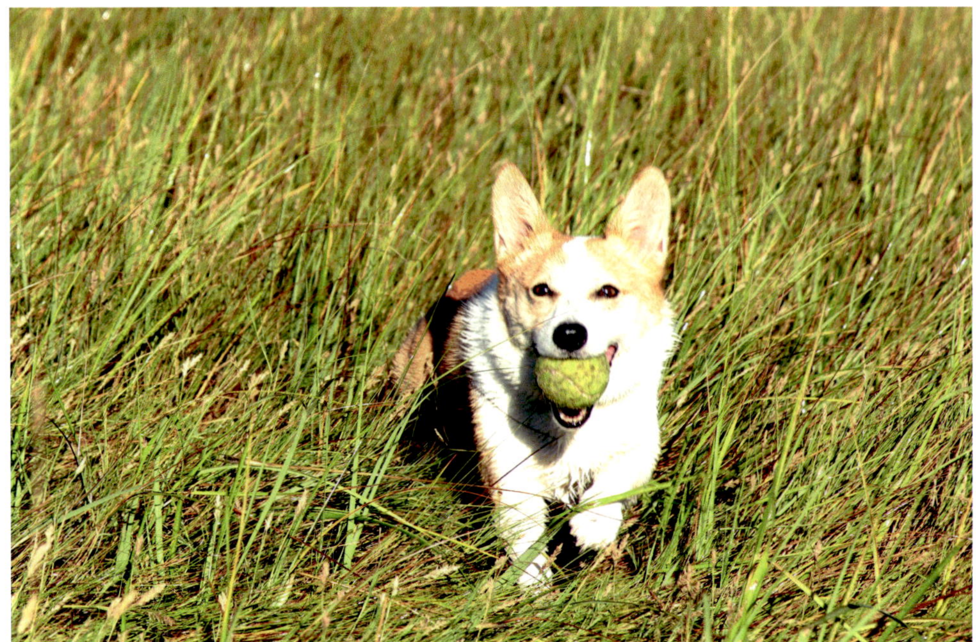

Cricket, Pembroke Welsh corgi, Ridgevale Beach

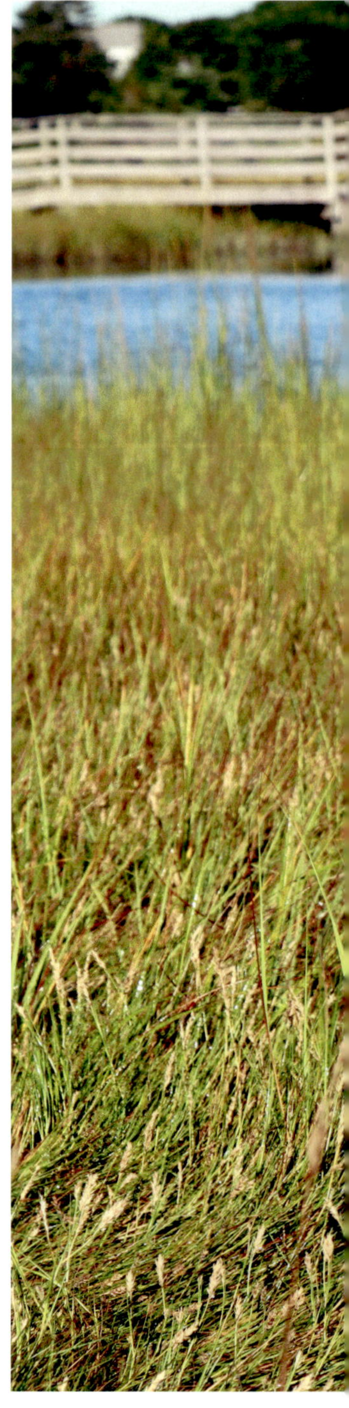

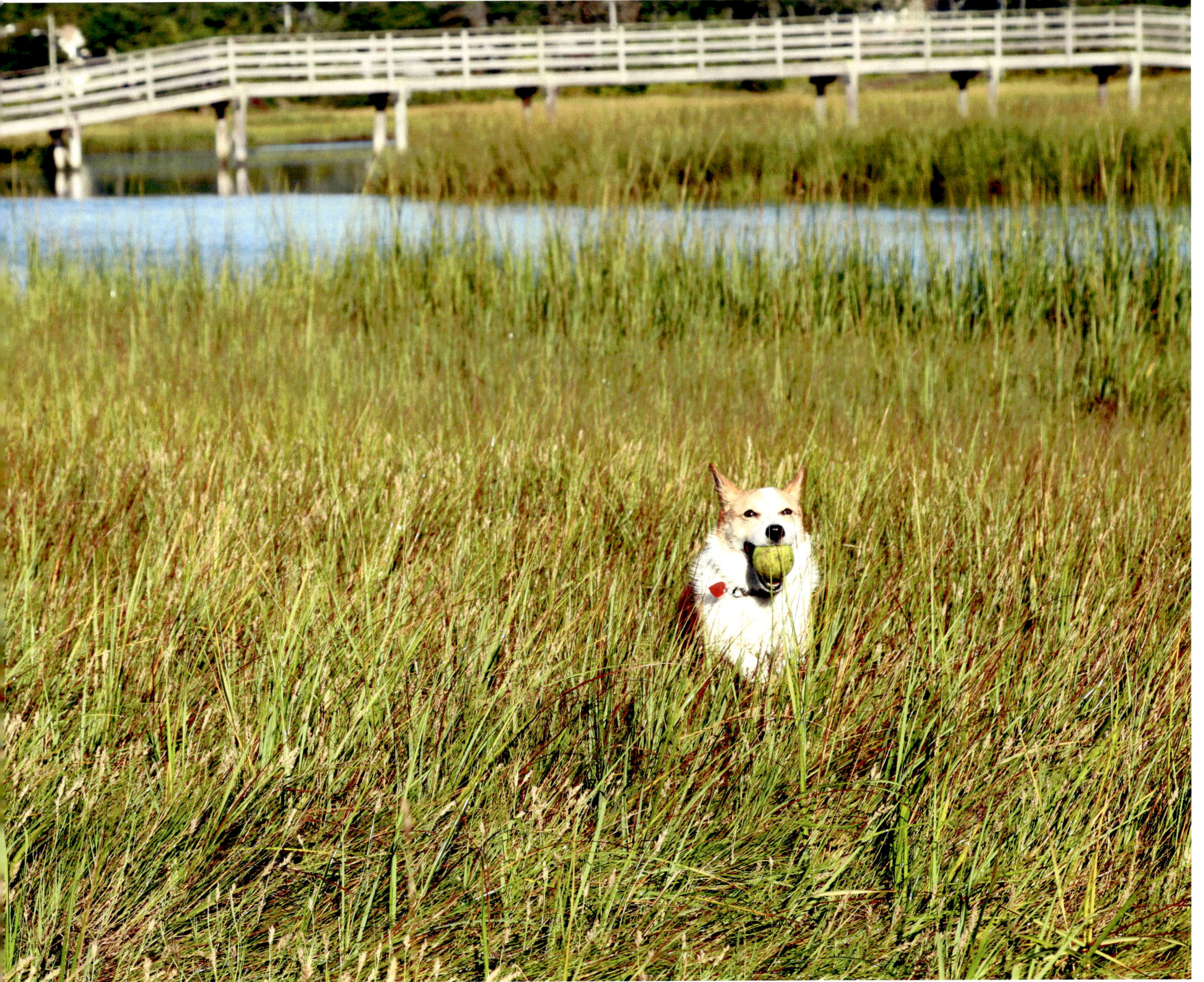

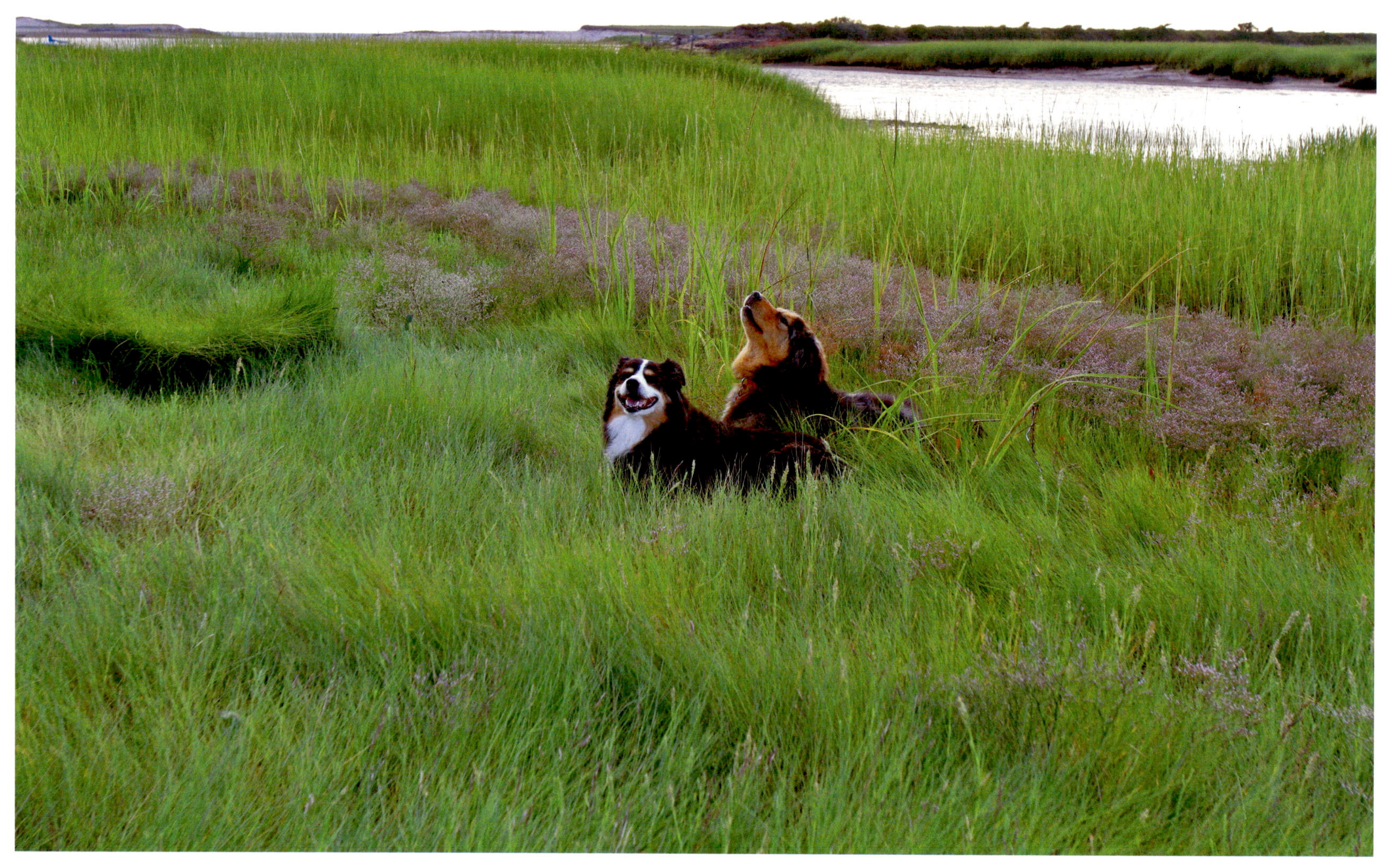

Heidi and **Kota Bear**, Australian shepherds, Pamet Harbor

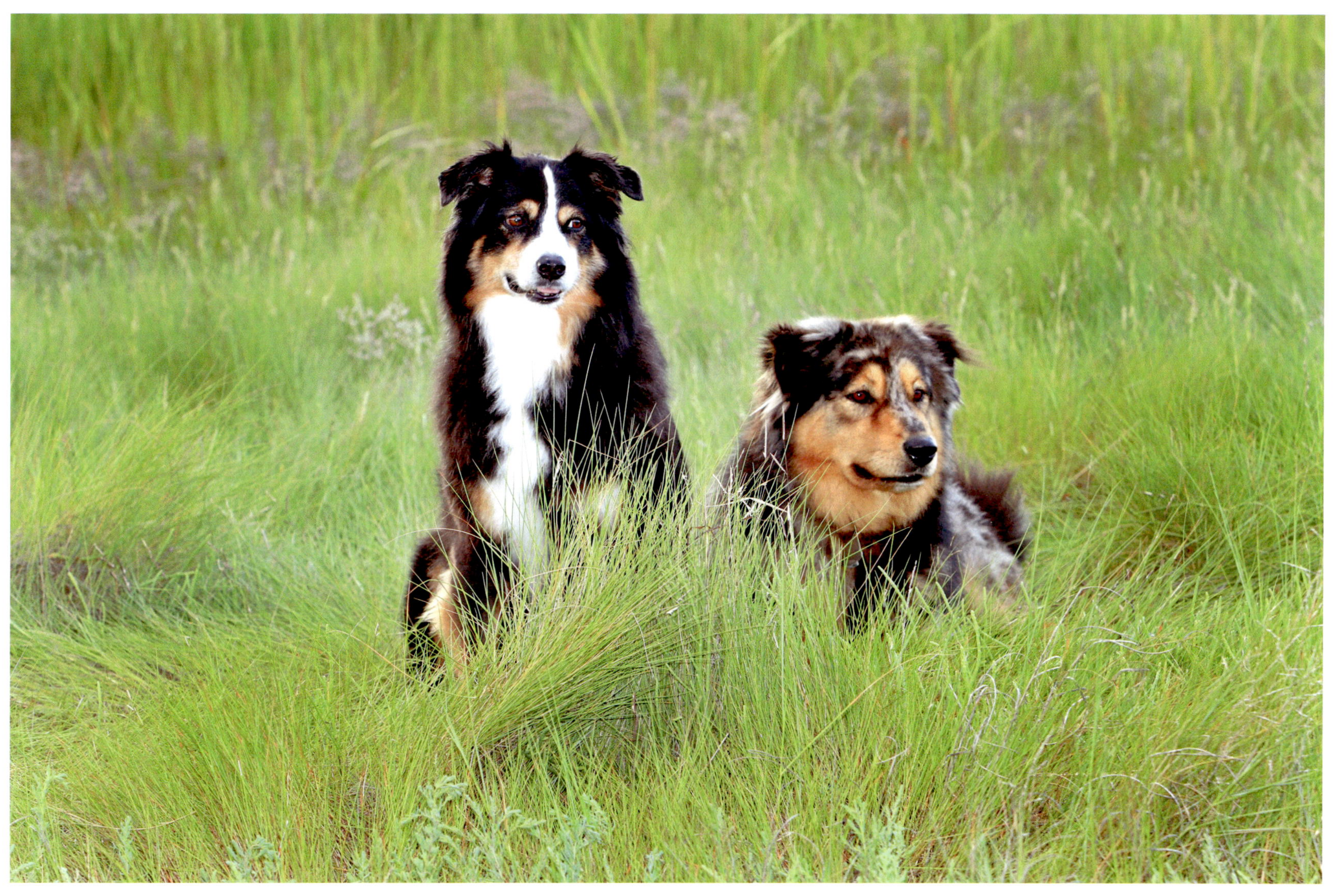

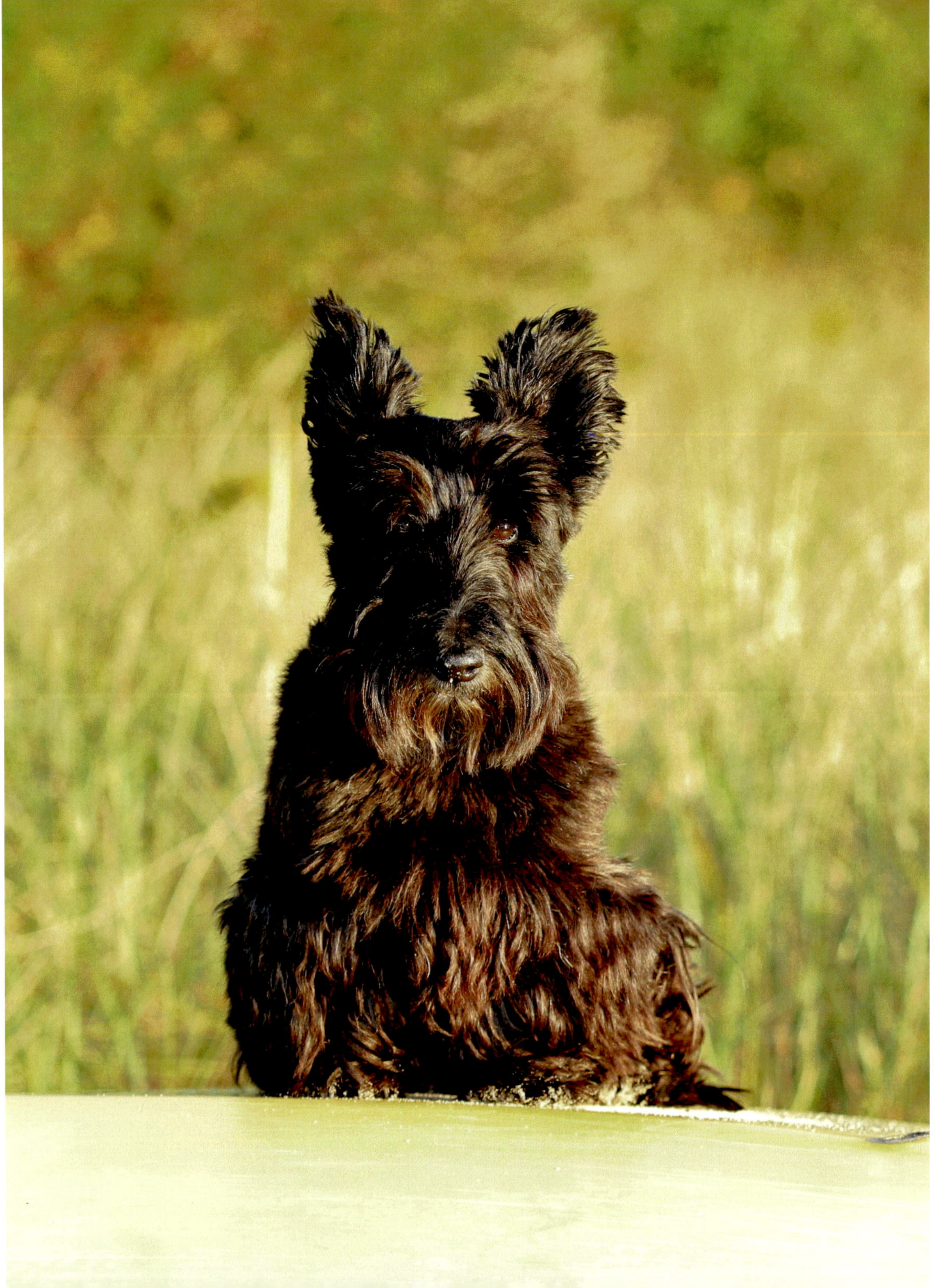

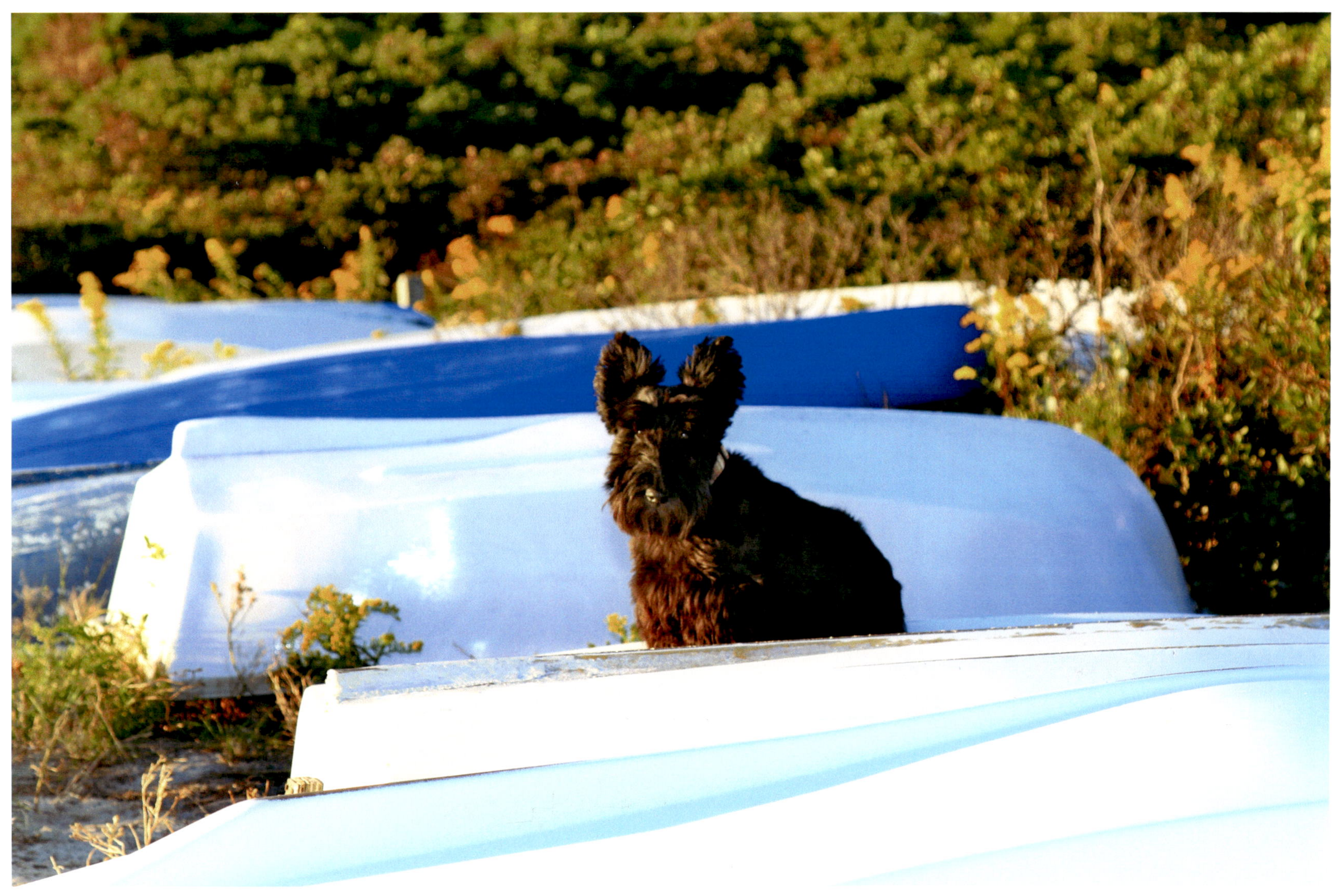

Griffin, Scottish terrier, Stage Harbor

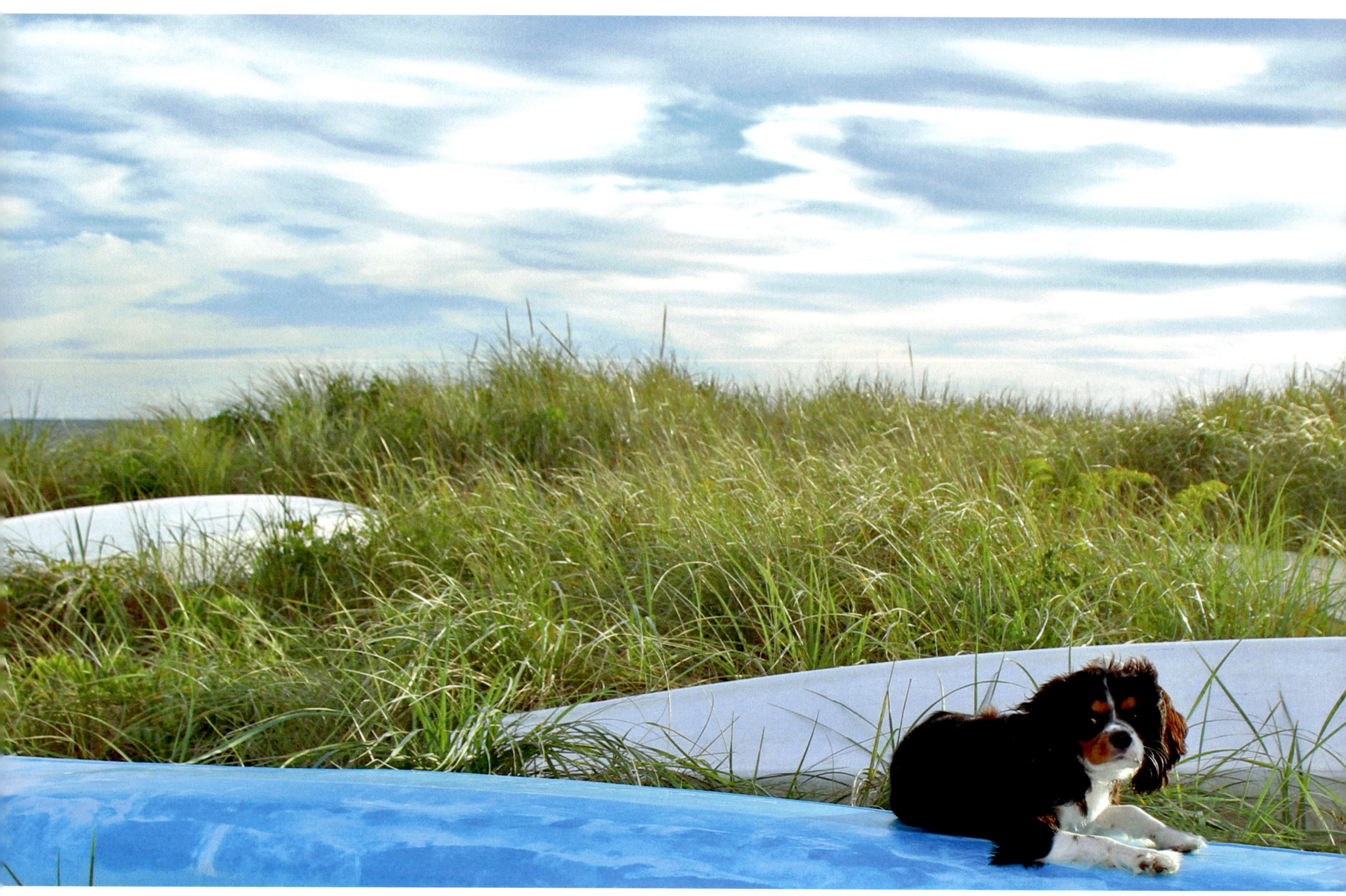

Murphy, Cavalier King Charles spaniel, Ridgevale Beach

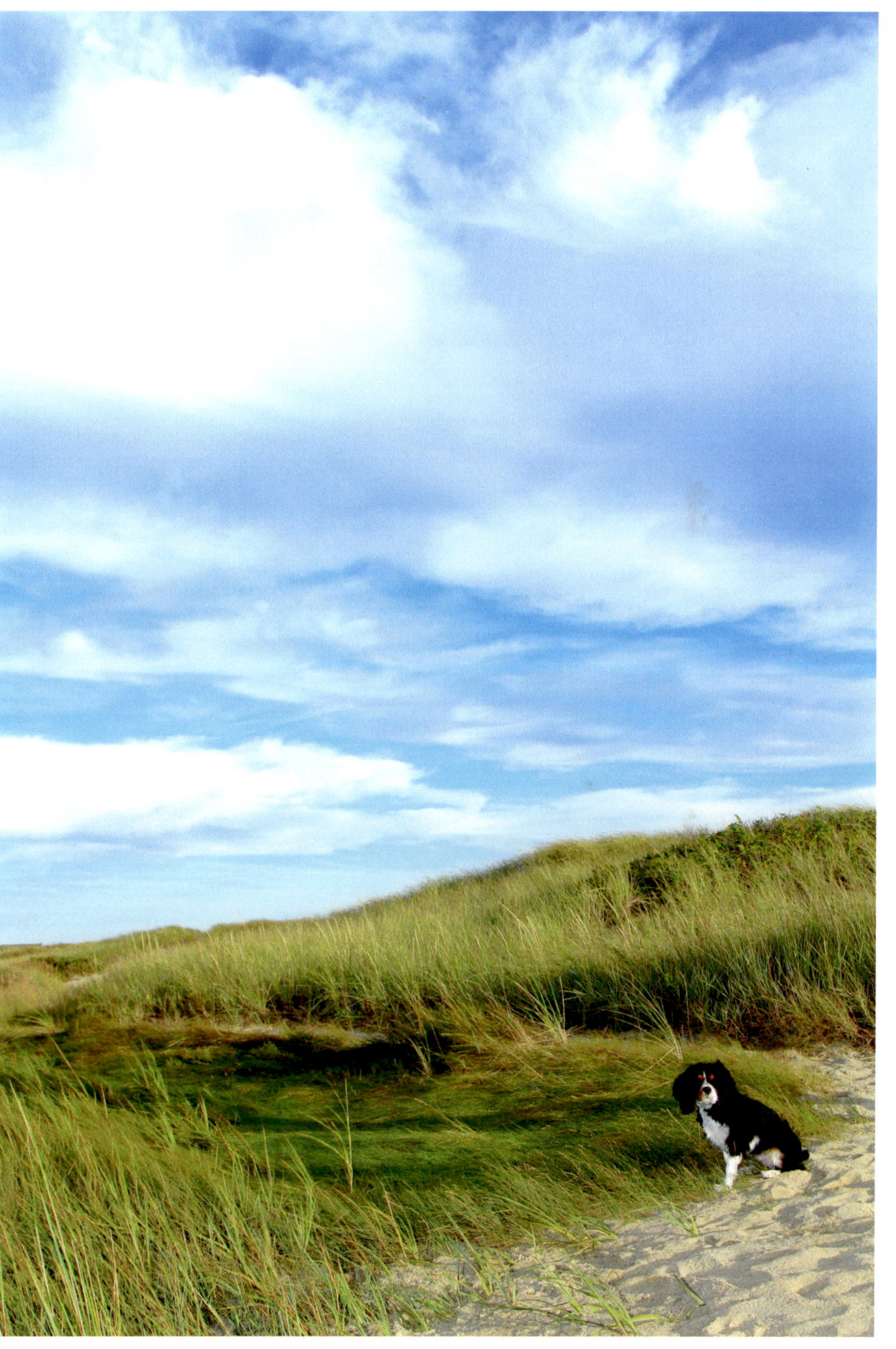

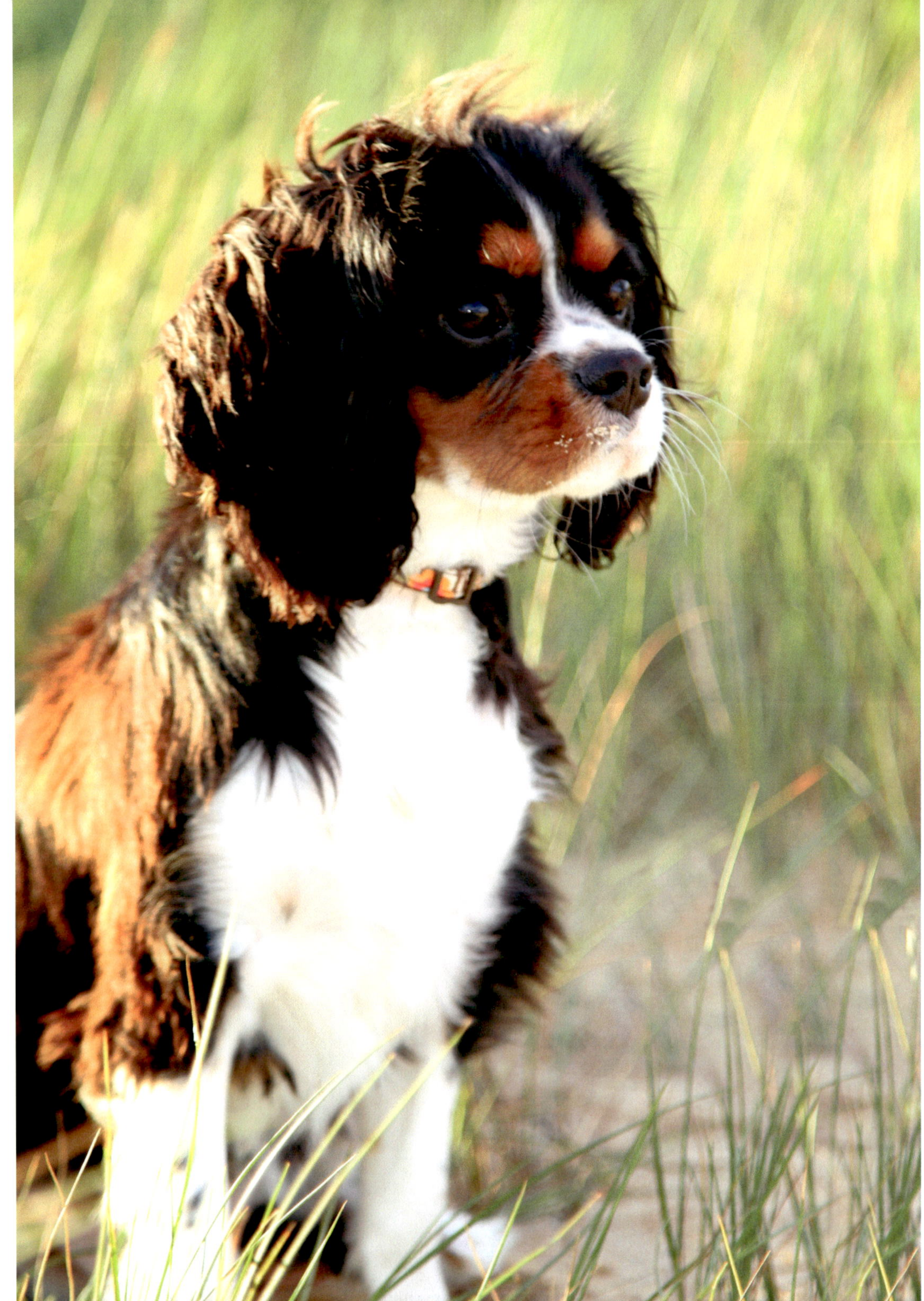

Murphy (opposite), Ridgevale Beach

Jameson, Cavalier King Charles spaniel, Ridgevale Beach

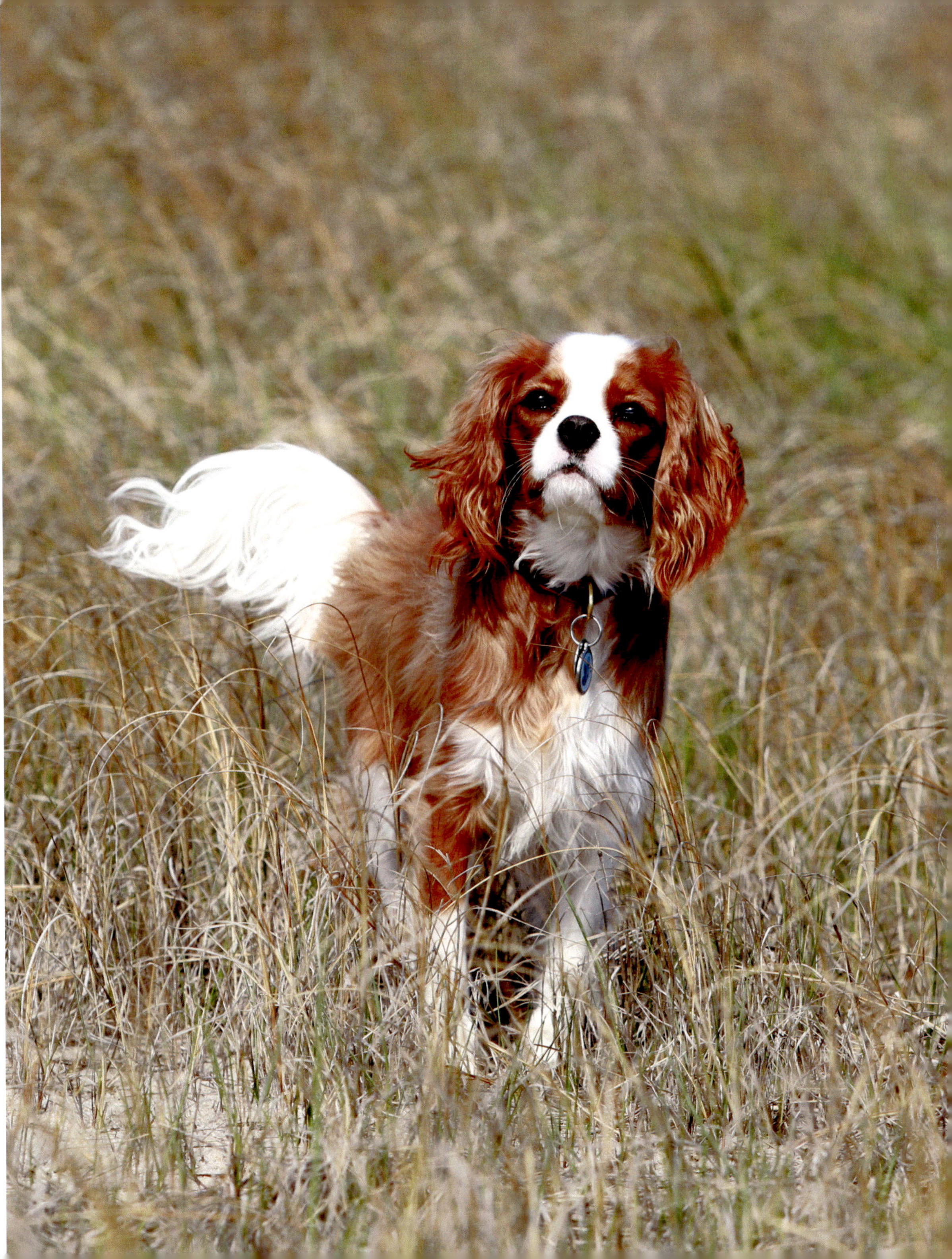

Teaka, Australian shepherd, and **Scout**, Australian cattle dog, Harding's Beach

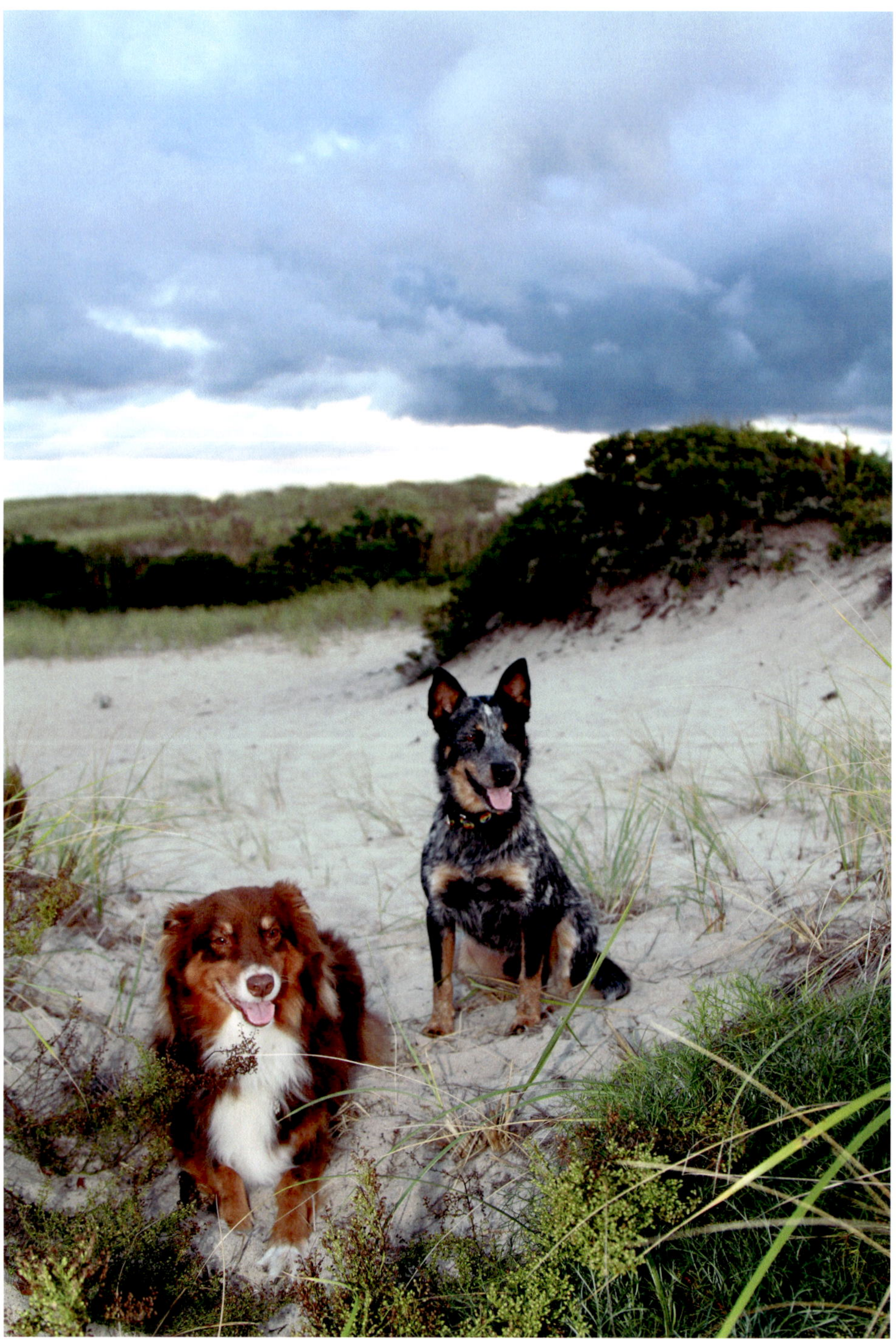

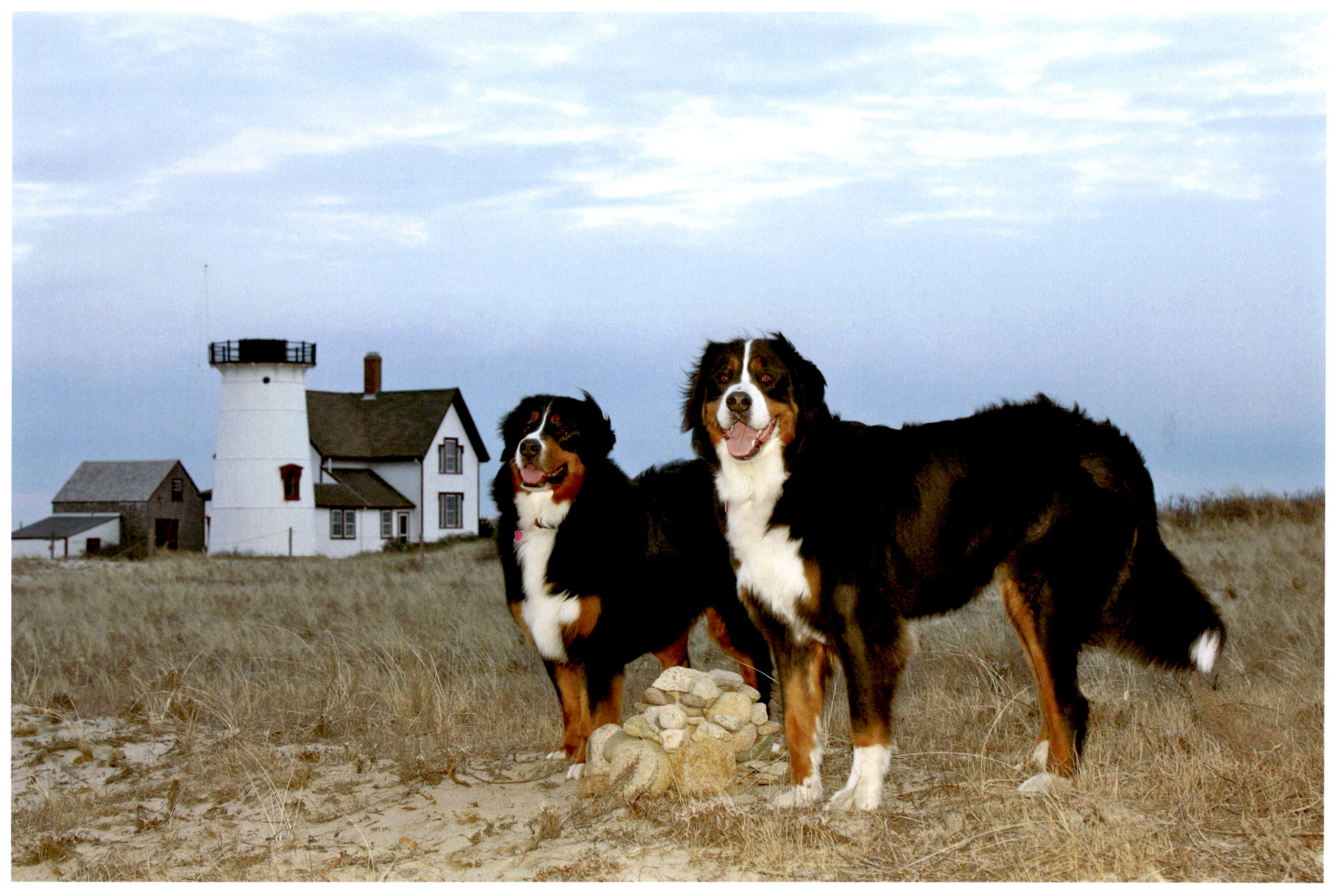

Sweetie and **Balto**, Bernese mountain dogs, Harding's Beach

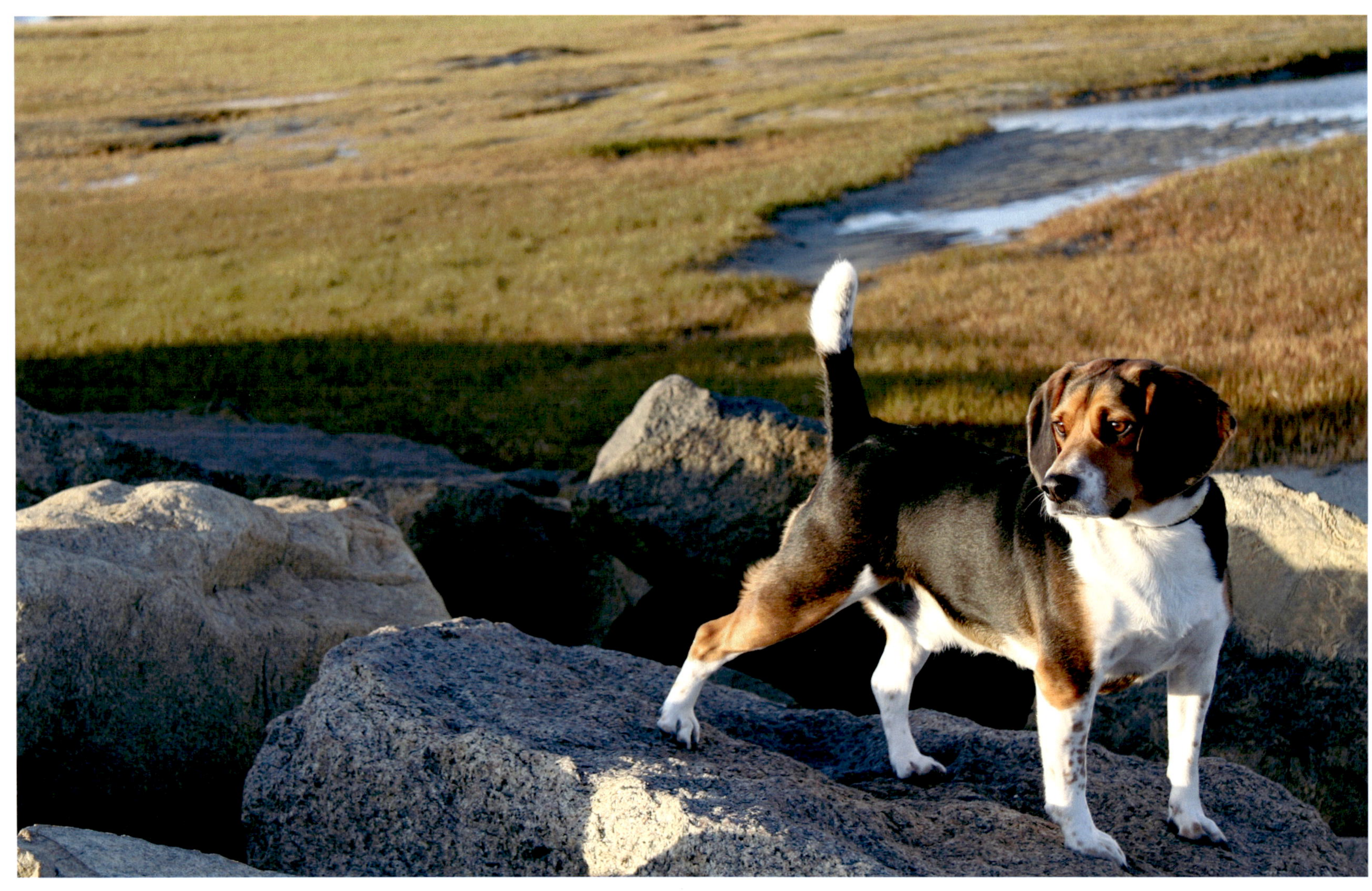

Napoleon, beagle, Paine's Creek

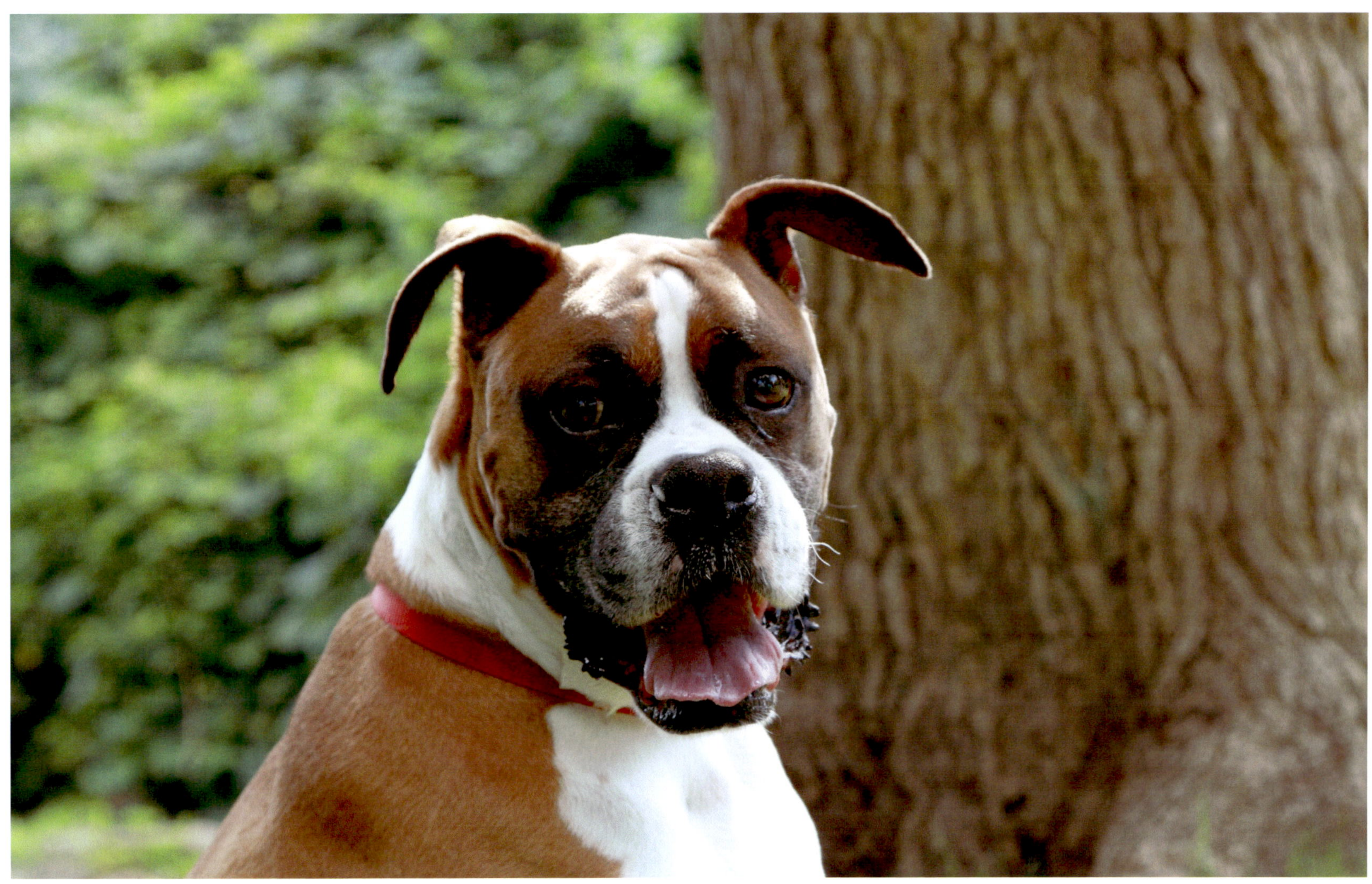

Porter, boxer, Grist Mill

Sailor, Welsh terrier,
Boat Meadow Beach

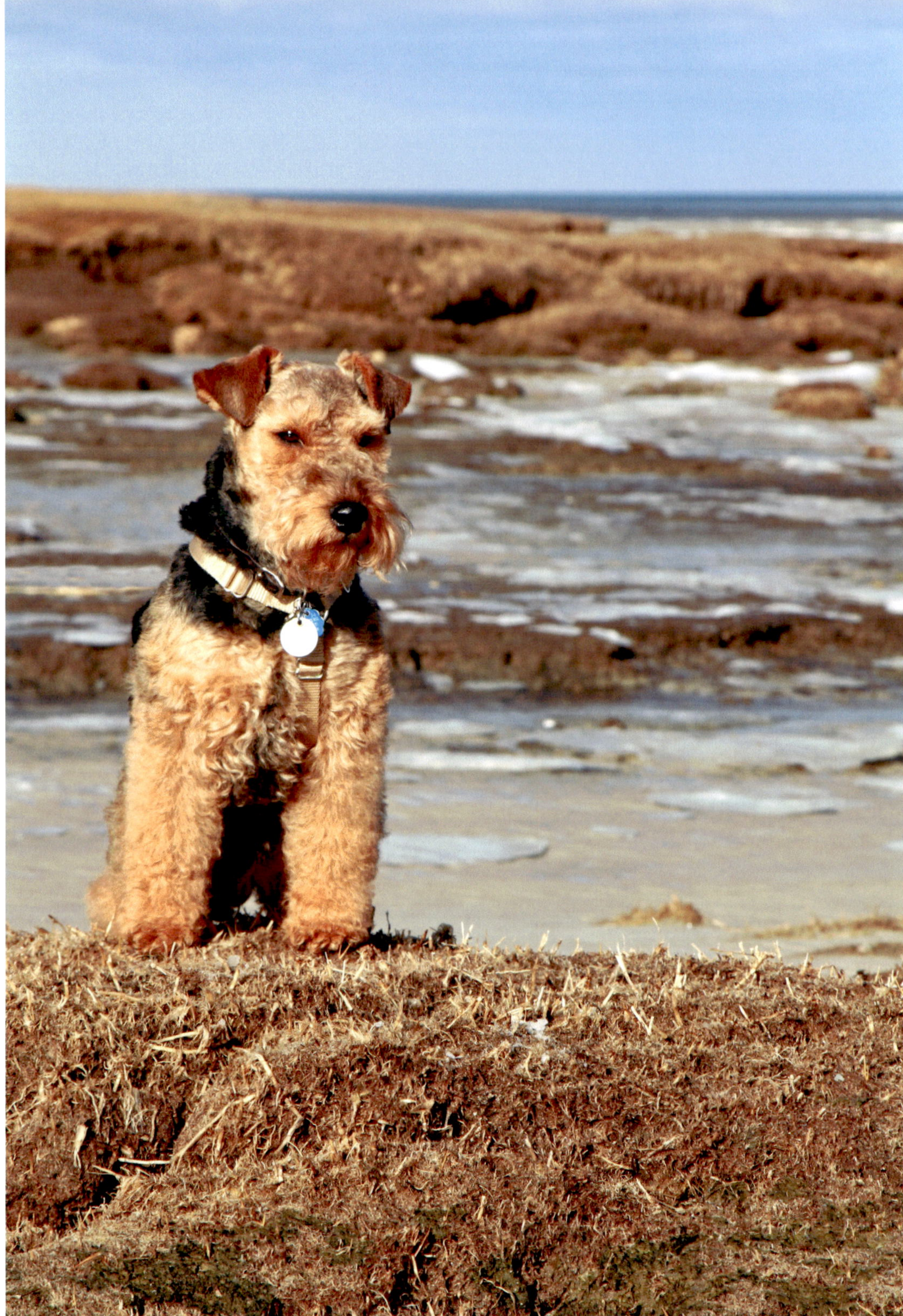

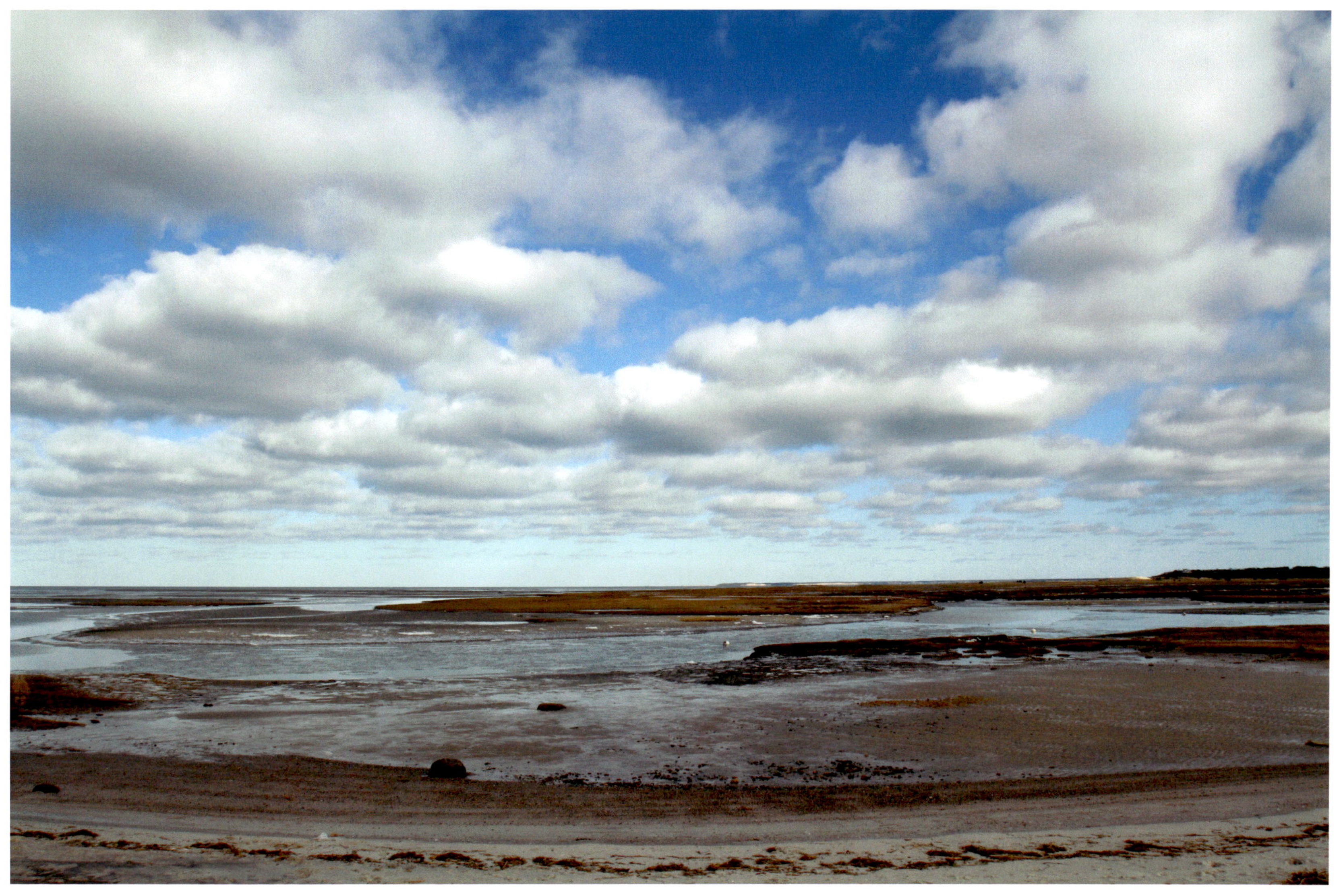

Boat Meadow Beach

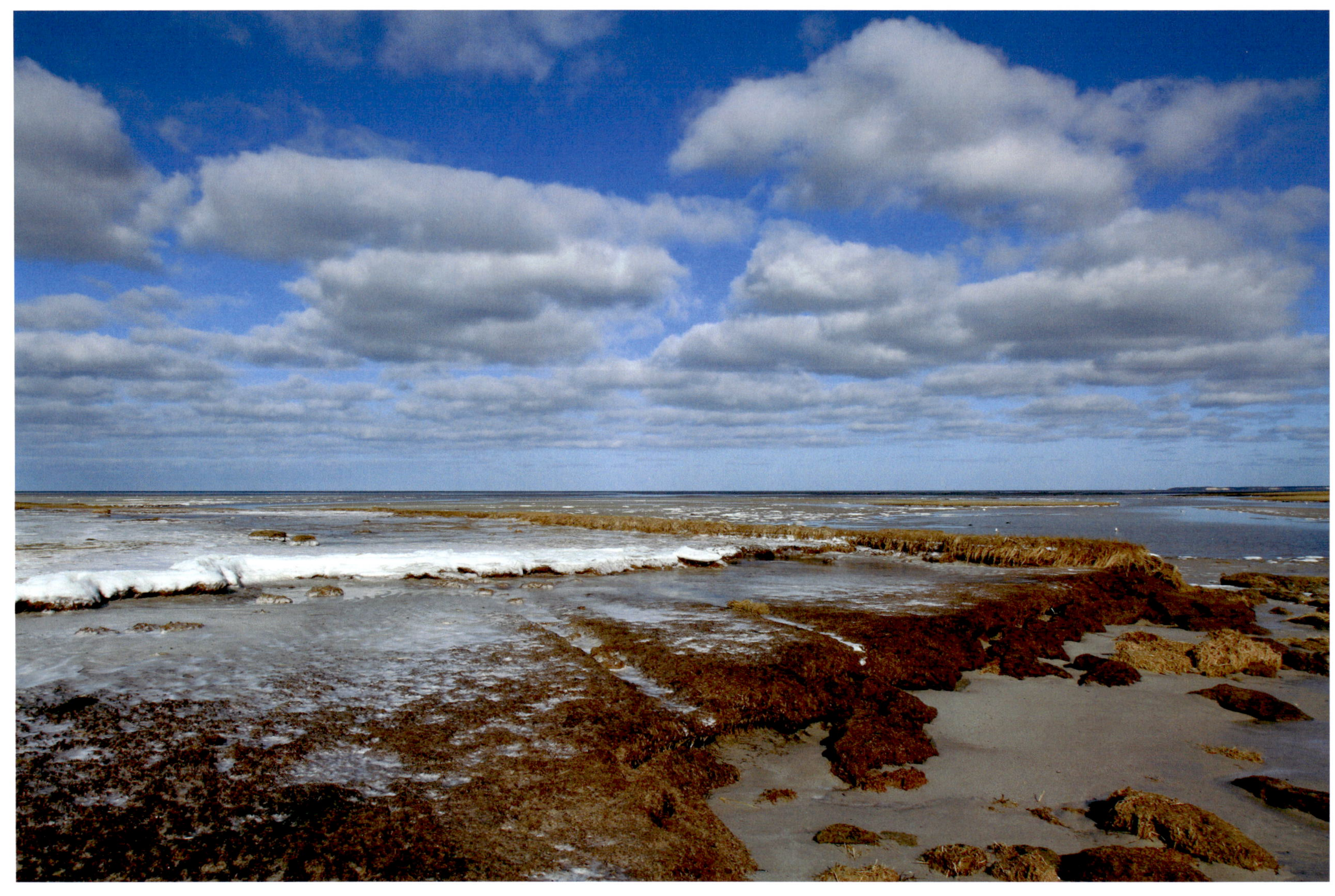

Boat Meadow Beach

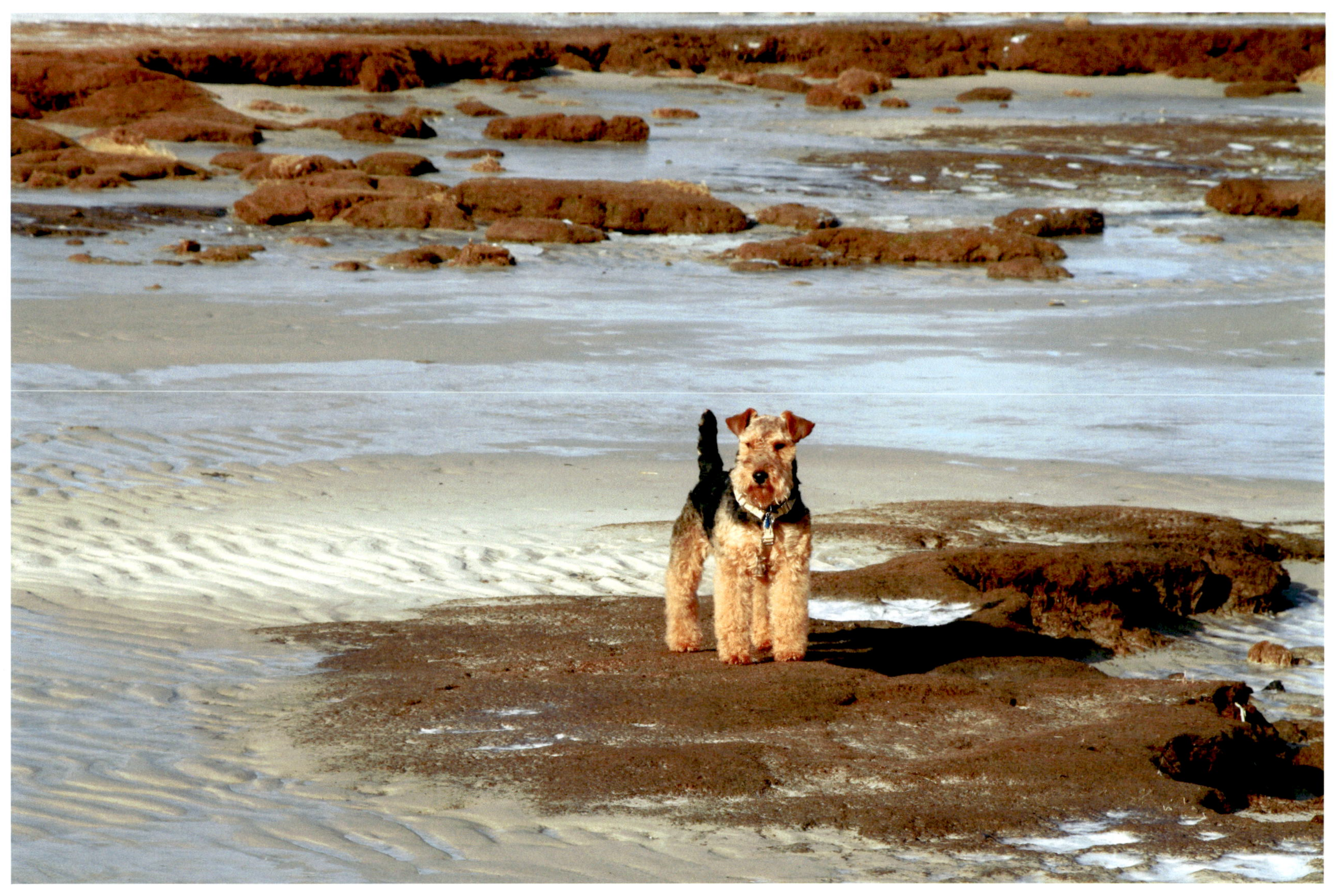

Sailor, Boat Meadow Beach

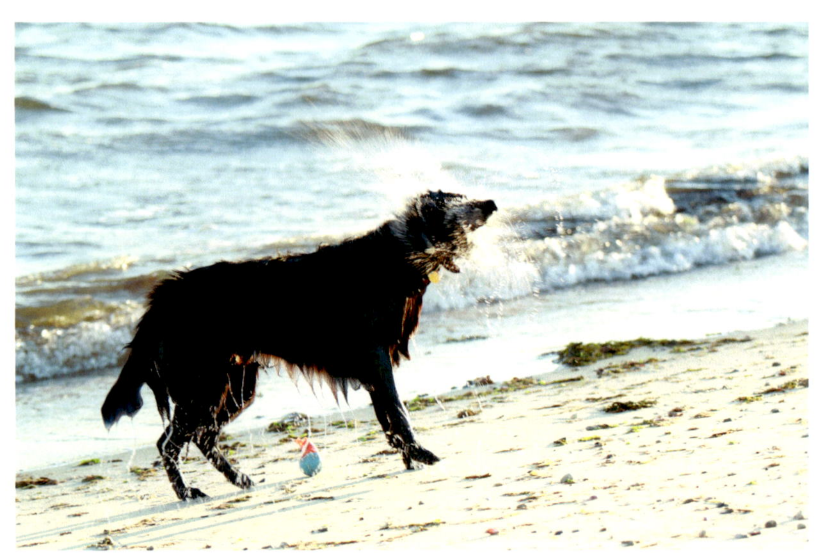

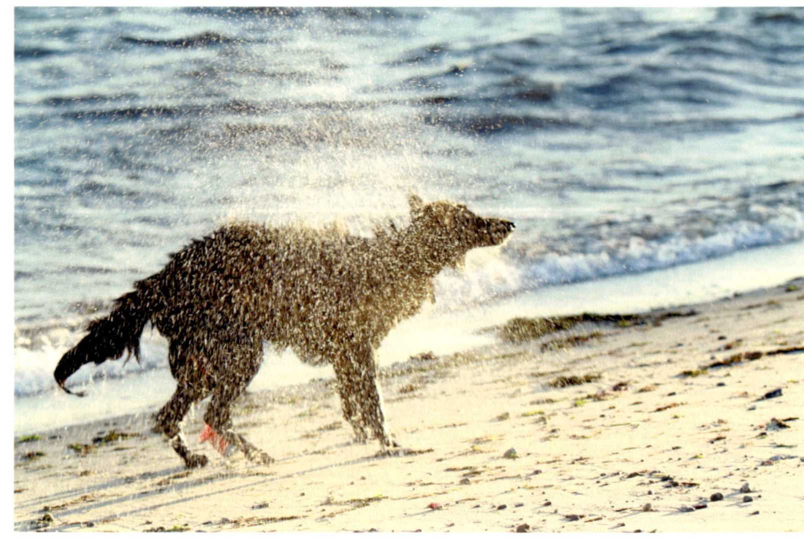

Cadence, Belgian shepherd, Forest Beach

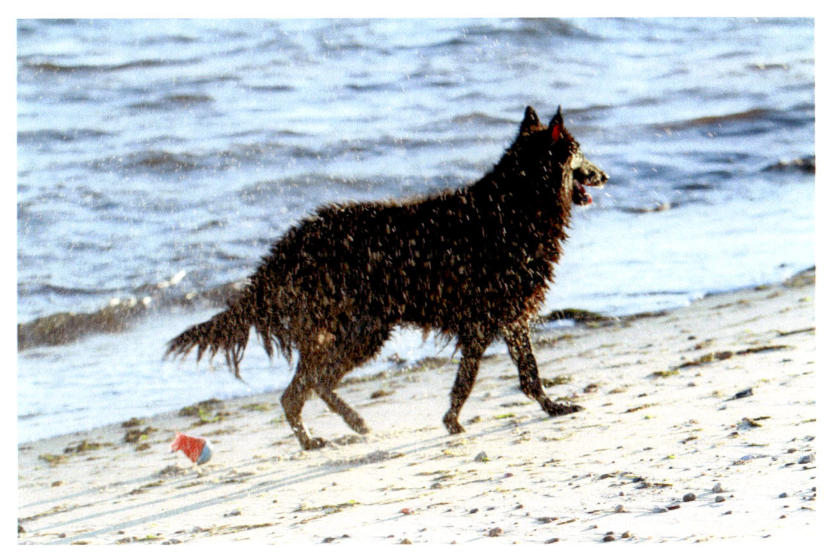

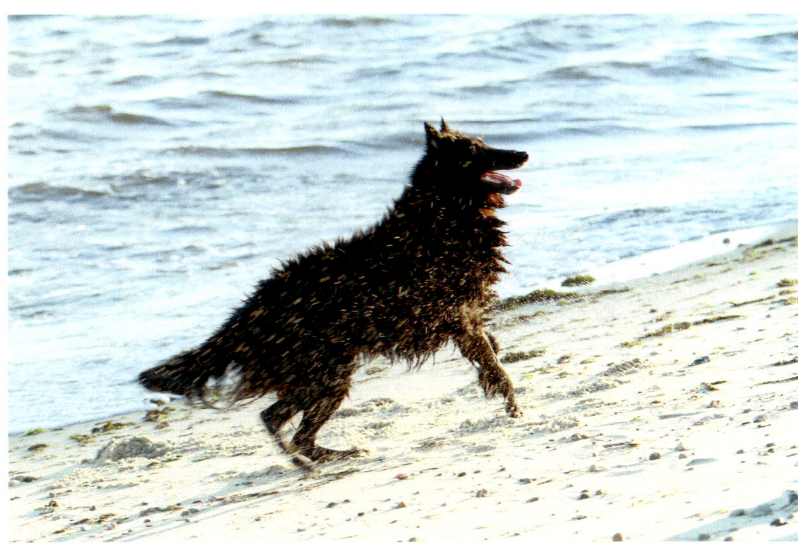

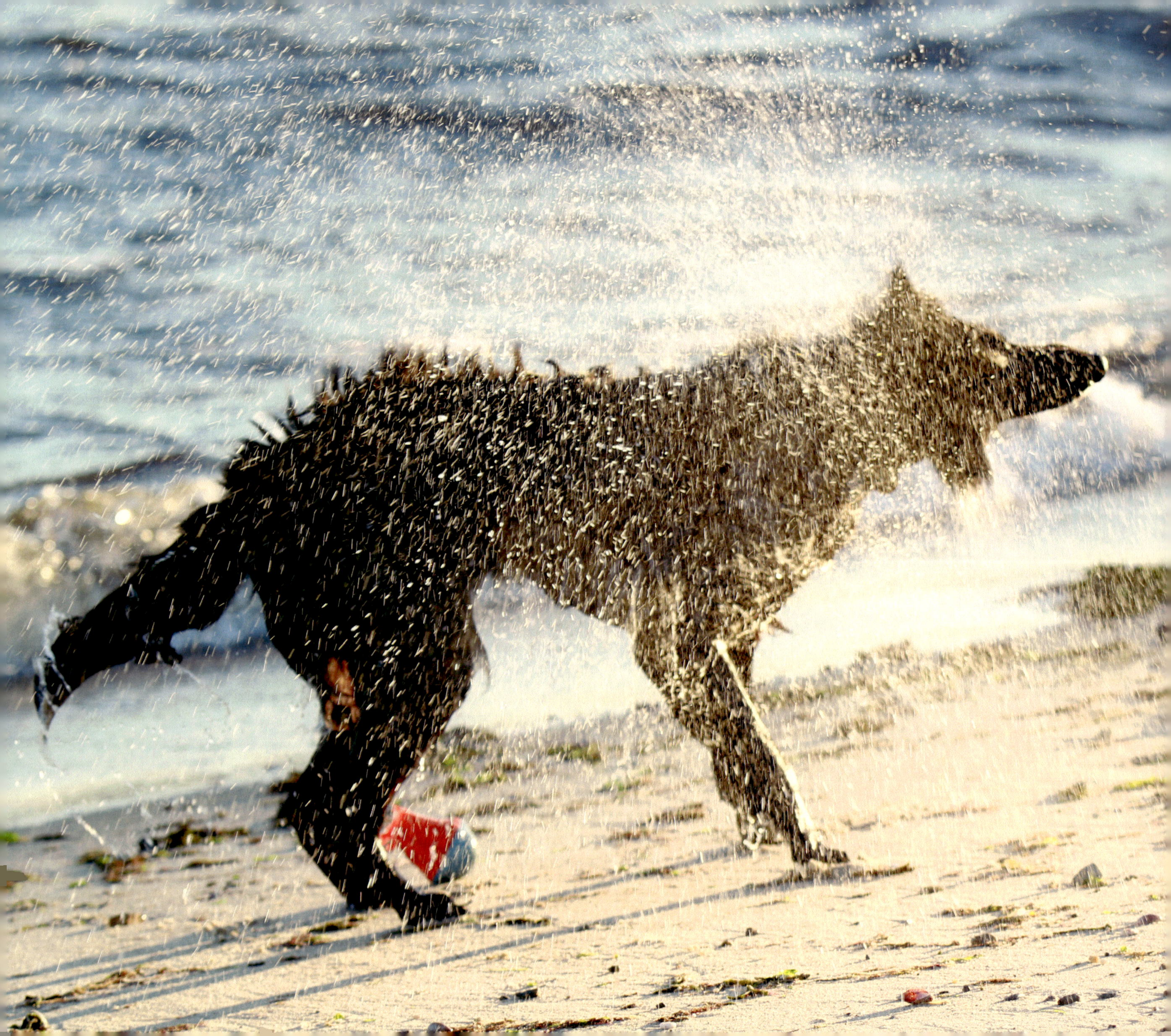

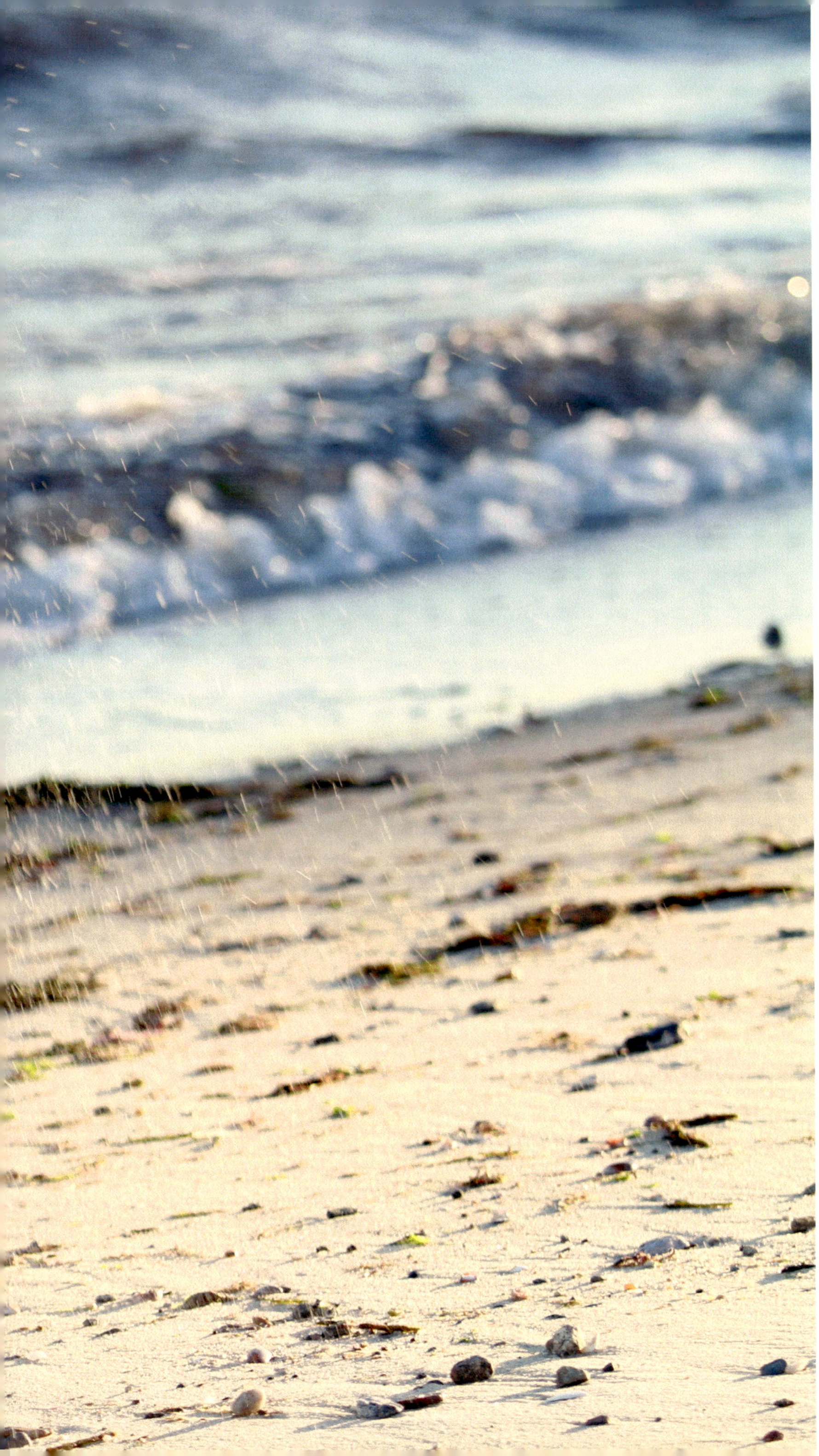

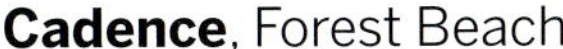

Cadence, Forest Beach

The truth I do not stretch or shove
When I state the dog is full of love.
I've also proved, by actual test,
A wet dog is the lovingest.

— Ogden Nash, "The Dog"

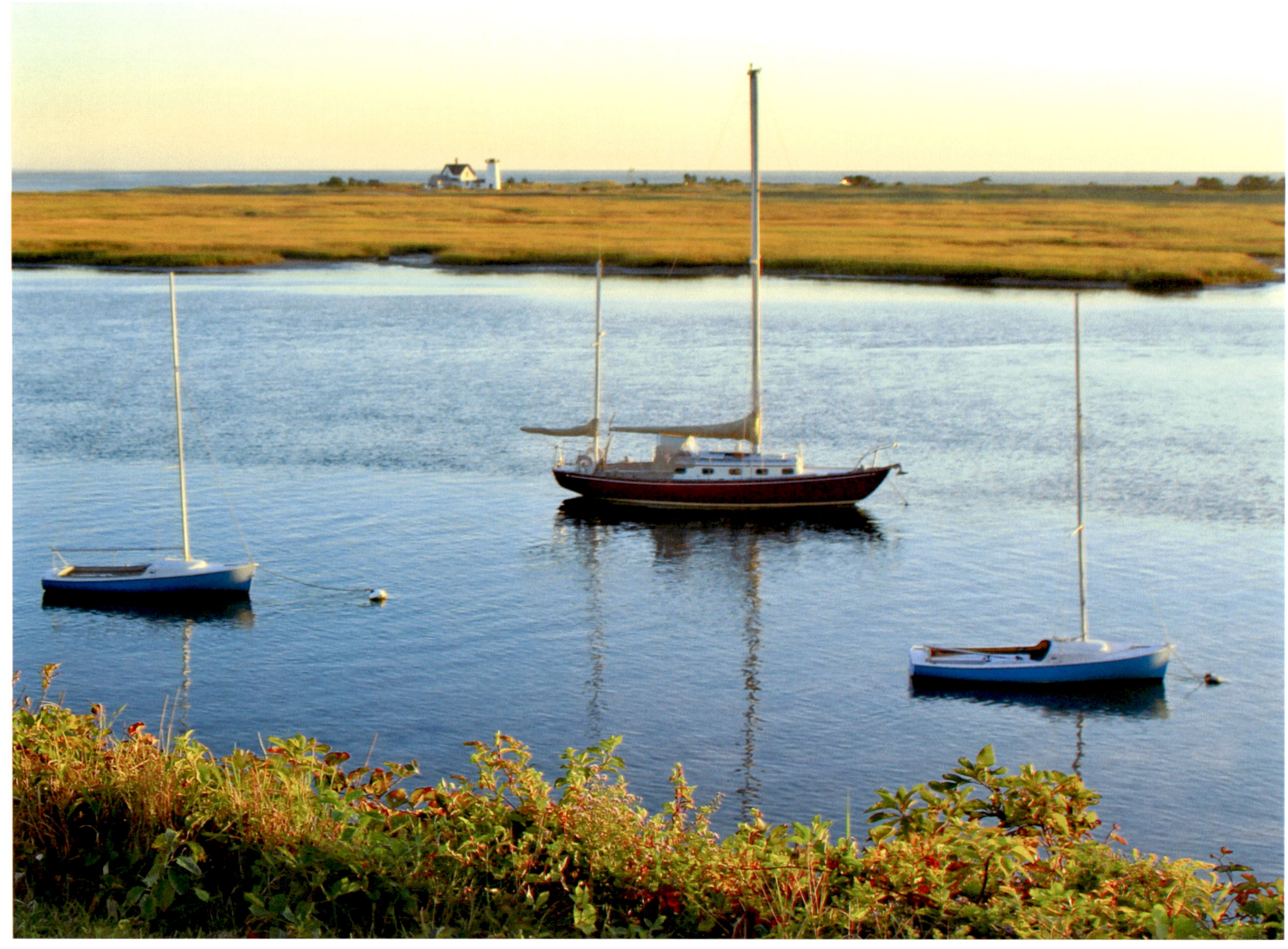

Oyster River

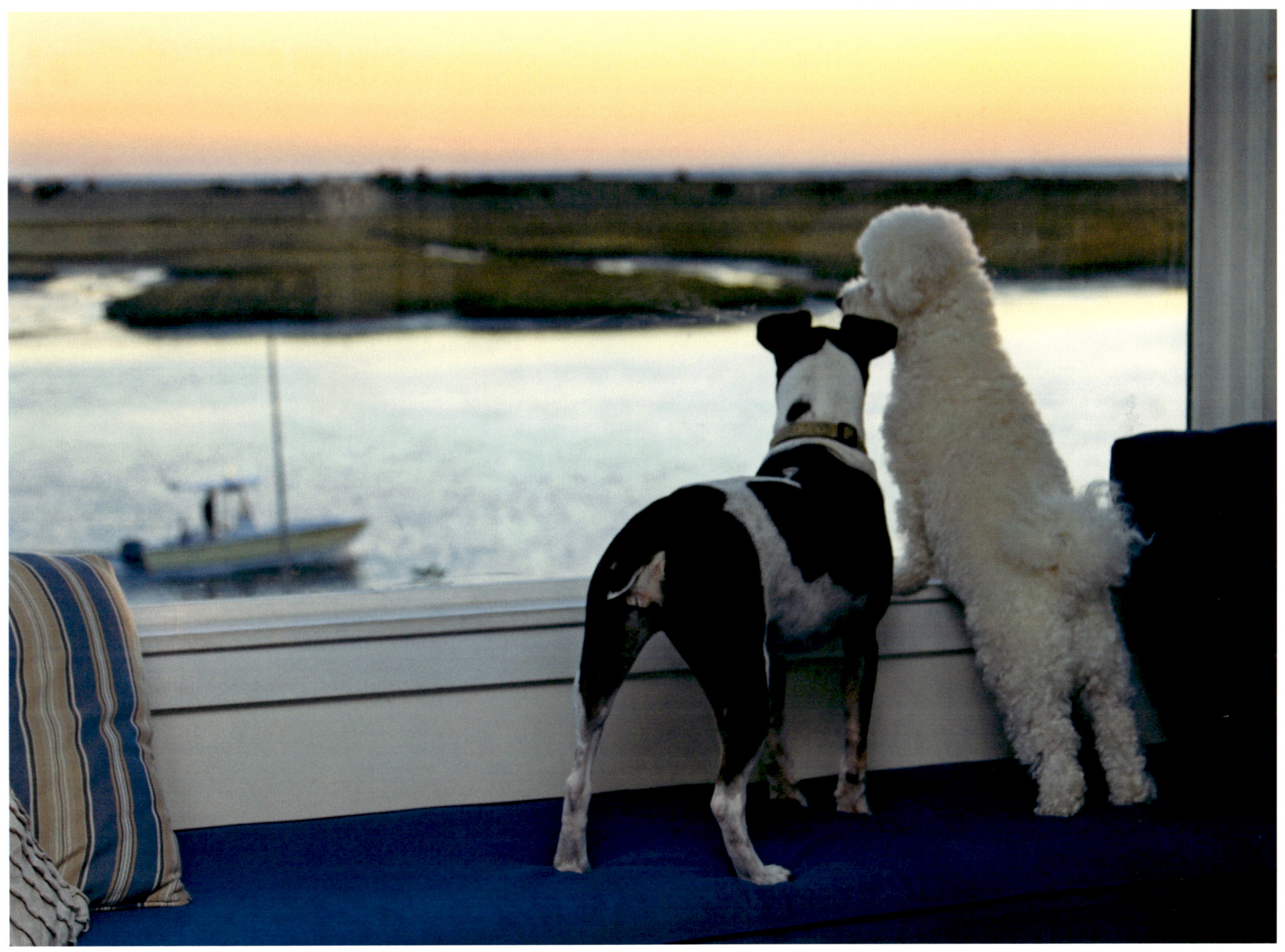

Polly, rat terrier, and **Ziva**, bichon frise, Oyster River

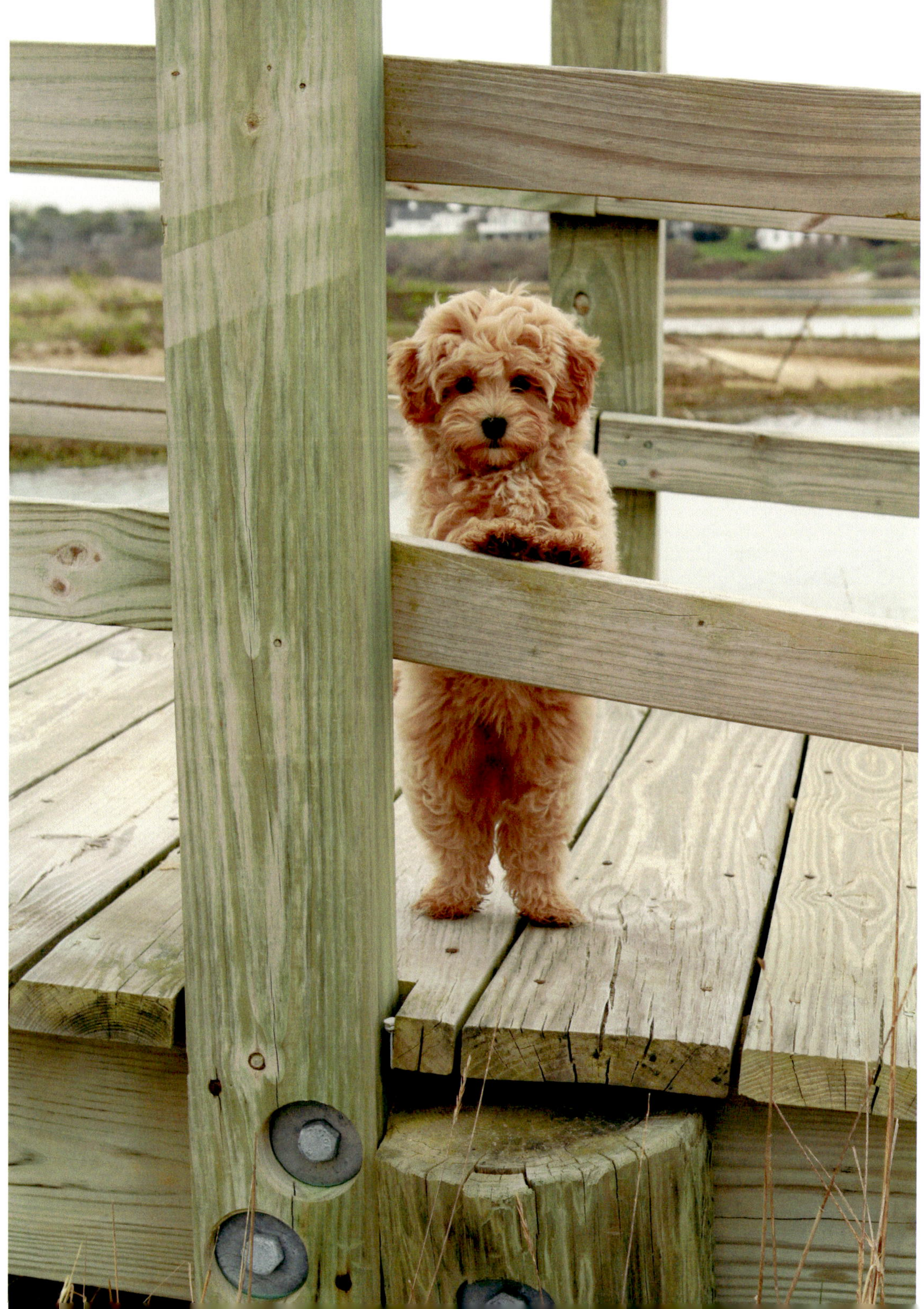

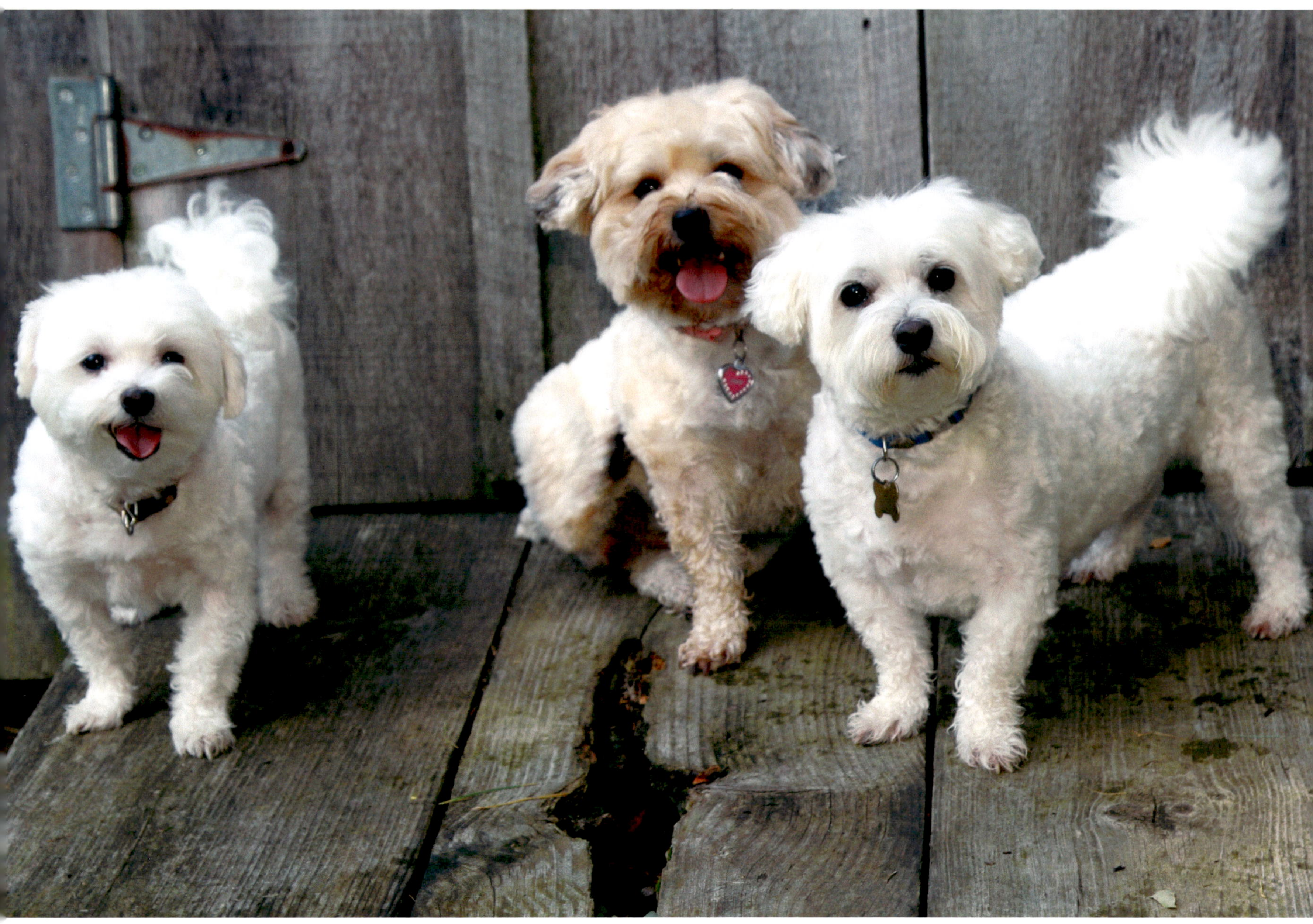

Chenin, Maltese, **Coco**, Morkie, and **Cotton**, Maltese (above)

Gadget (opposite), Maltipoo, Ridgevale Beach

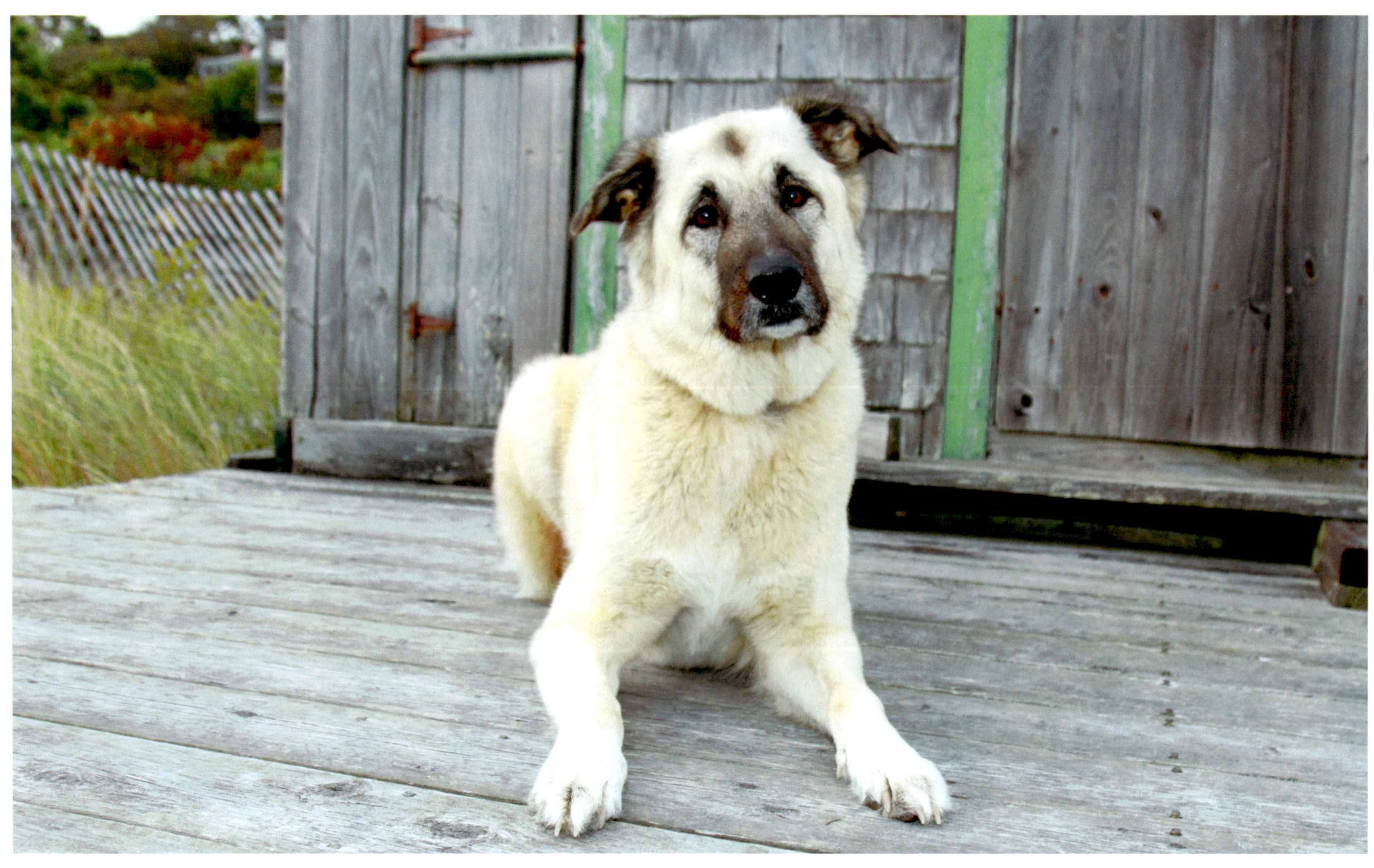

Oscar, Anatolian shepherd, Forest Beach

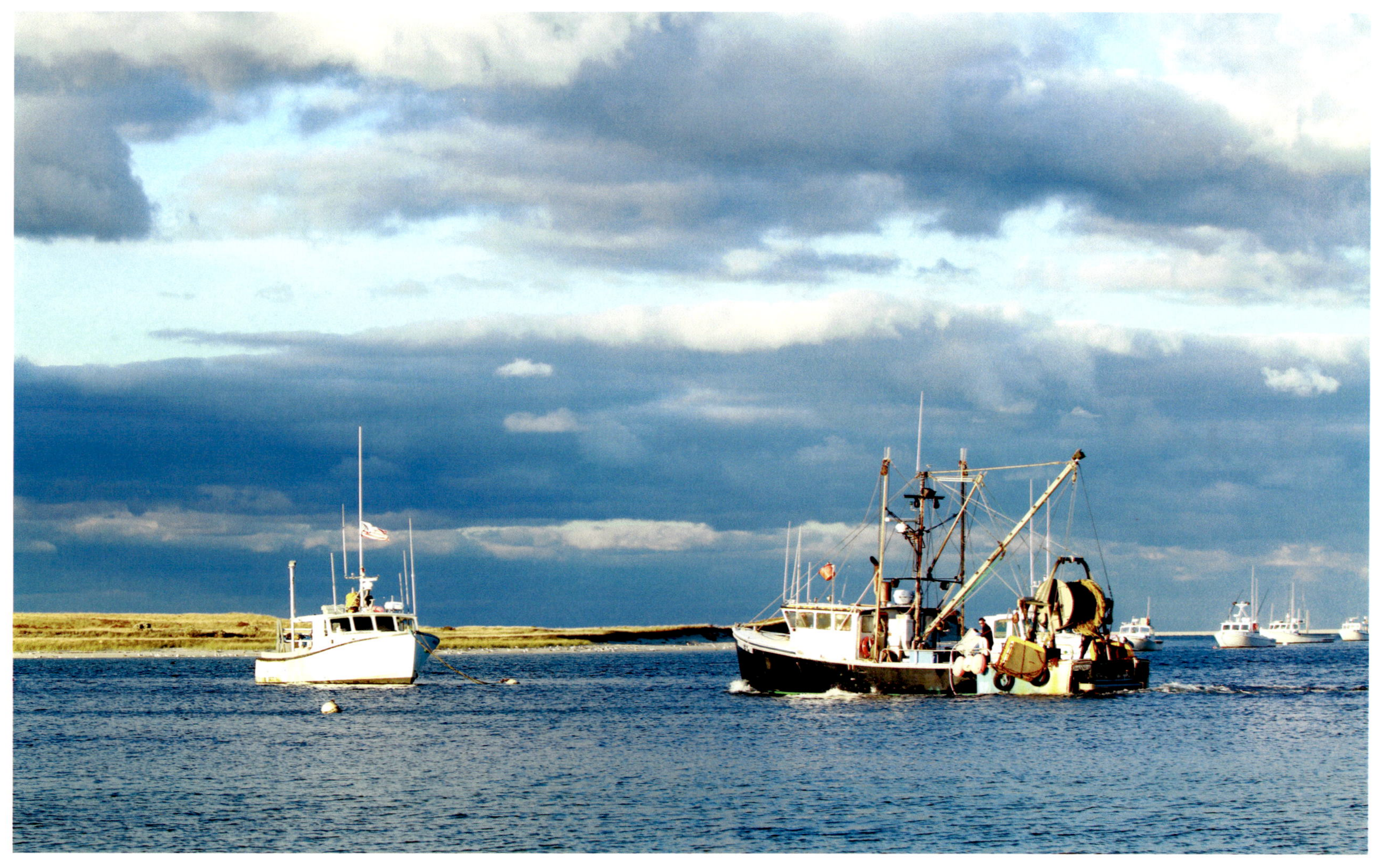

Chatham Harbor

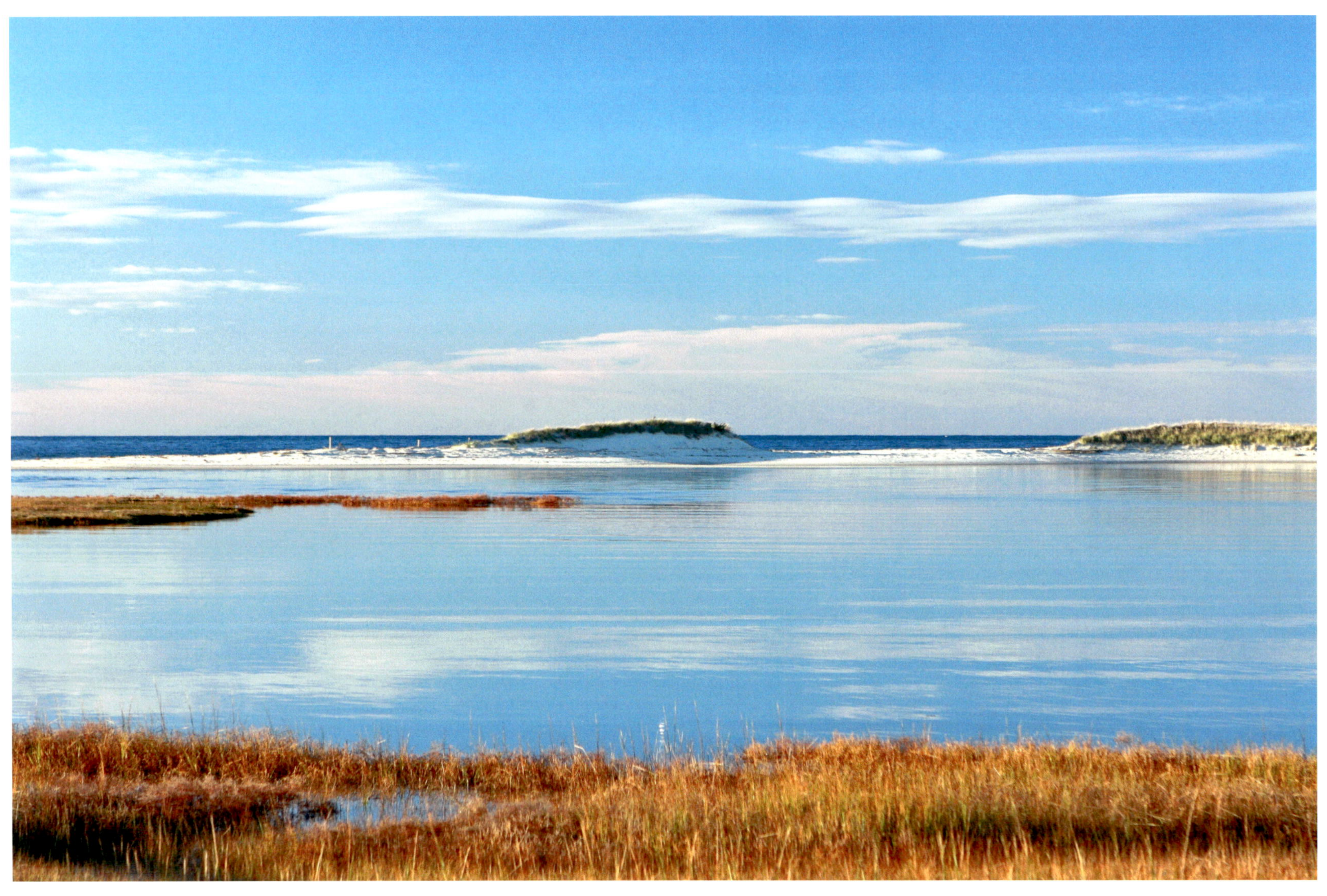

Gray's Beach

Eloise, Maltipoo, Neel Beach

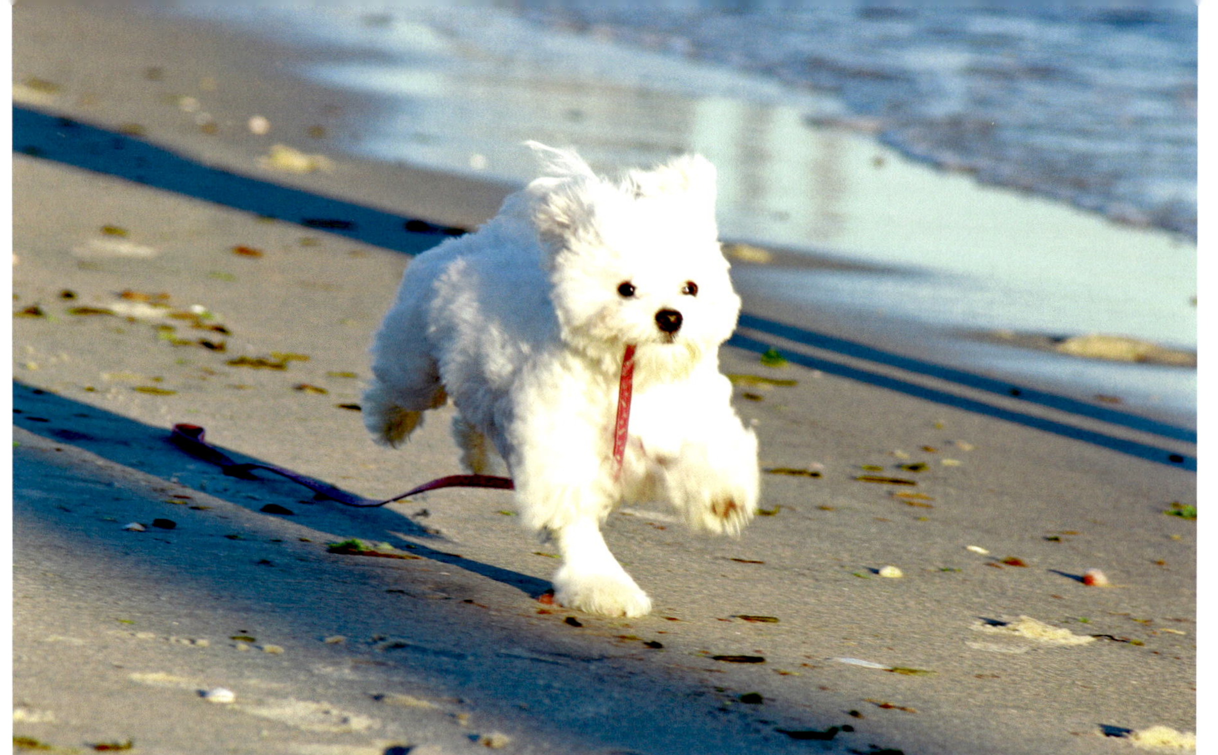

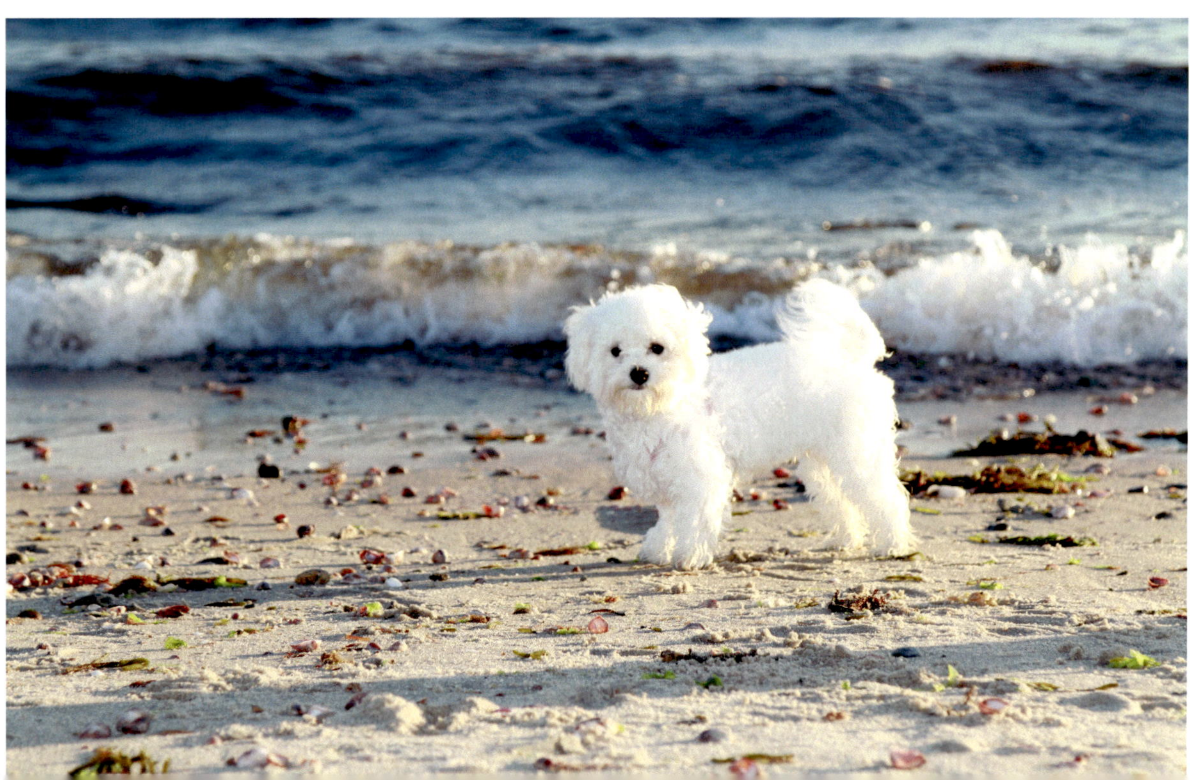

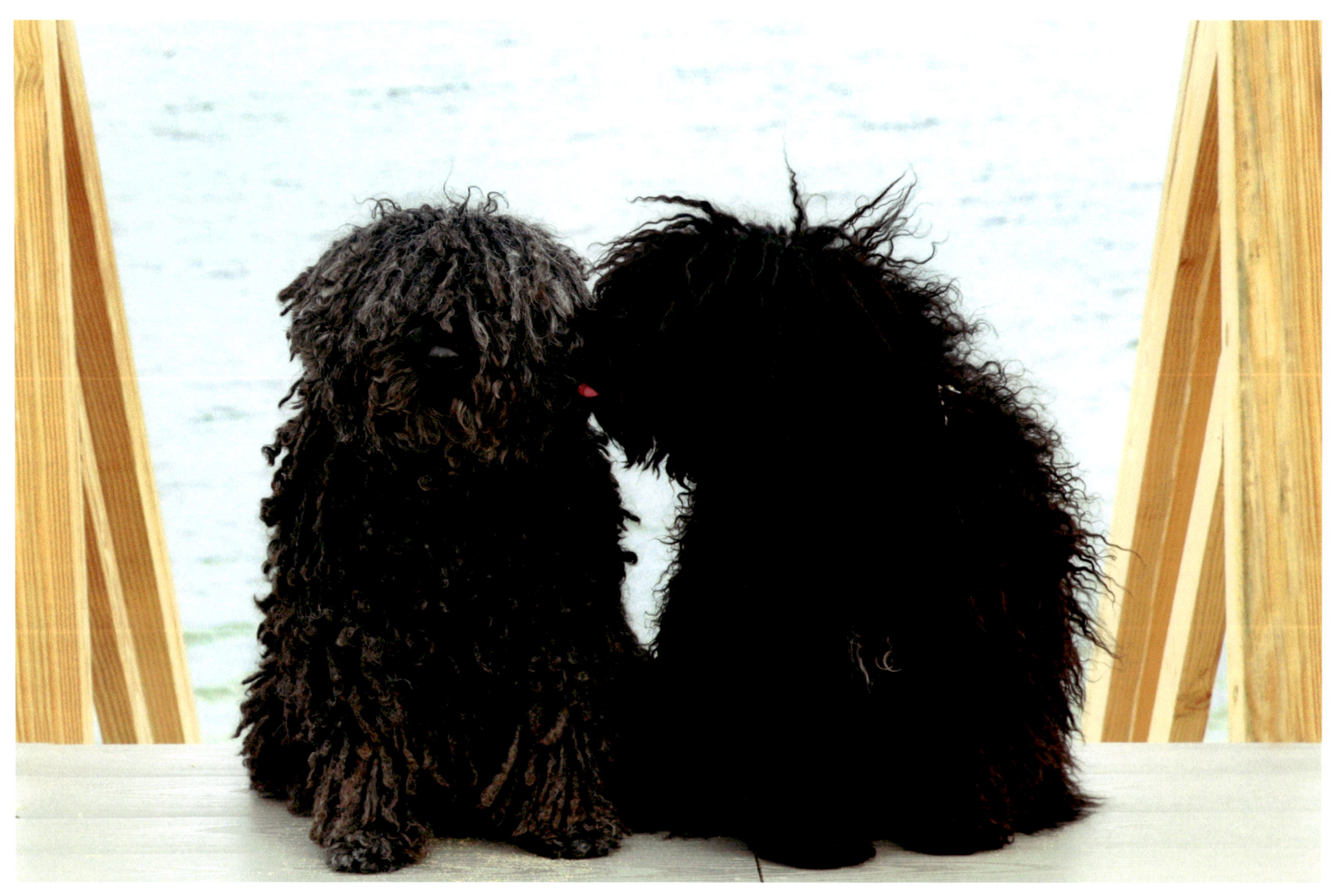

Polly and **Rory**, pulis, Provincetown Harbor

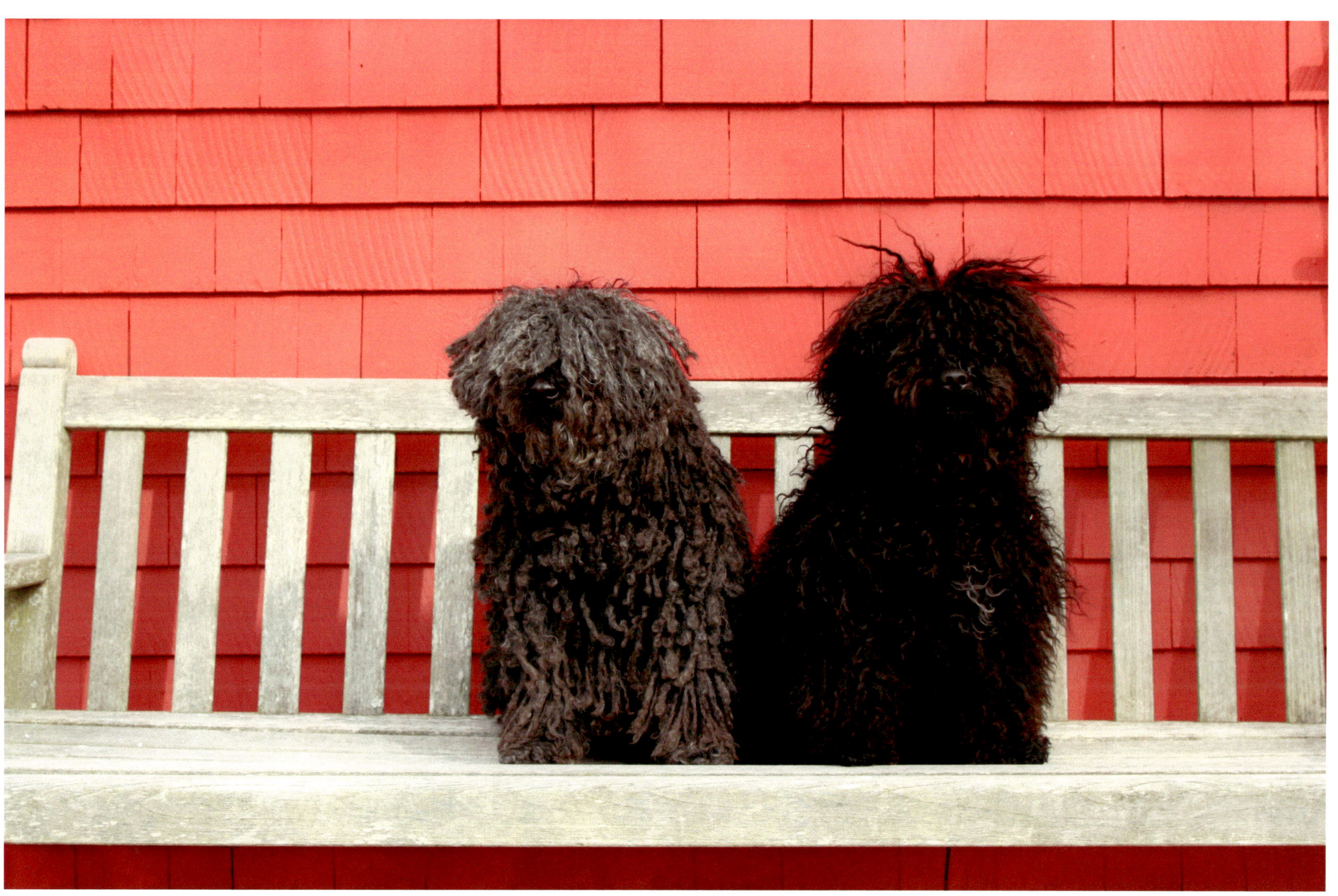

Bridey Mahoney, soft-coated wheaten terrier, Oyster River

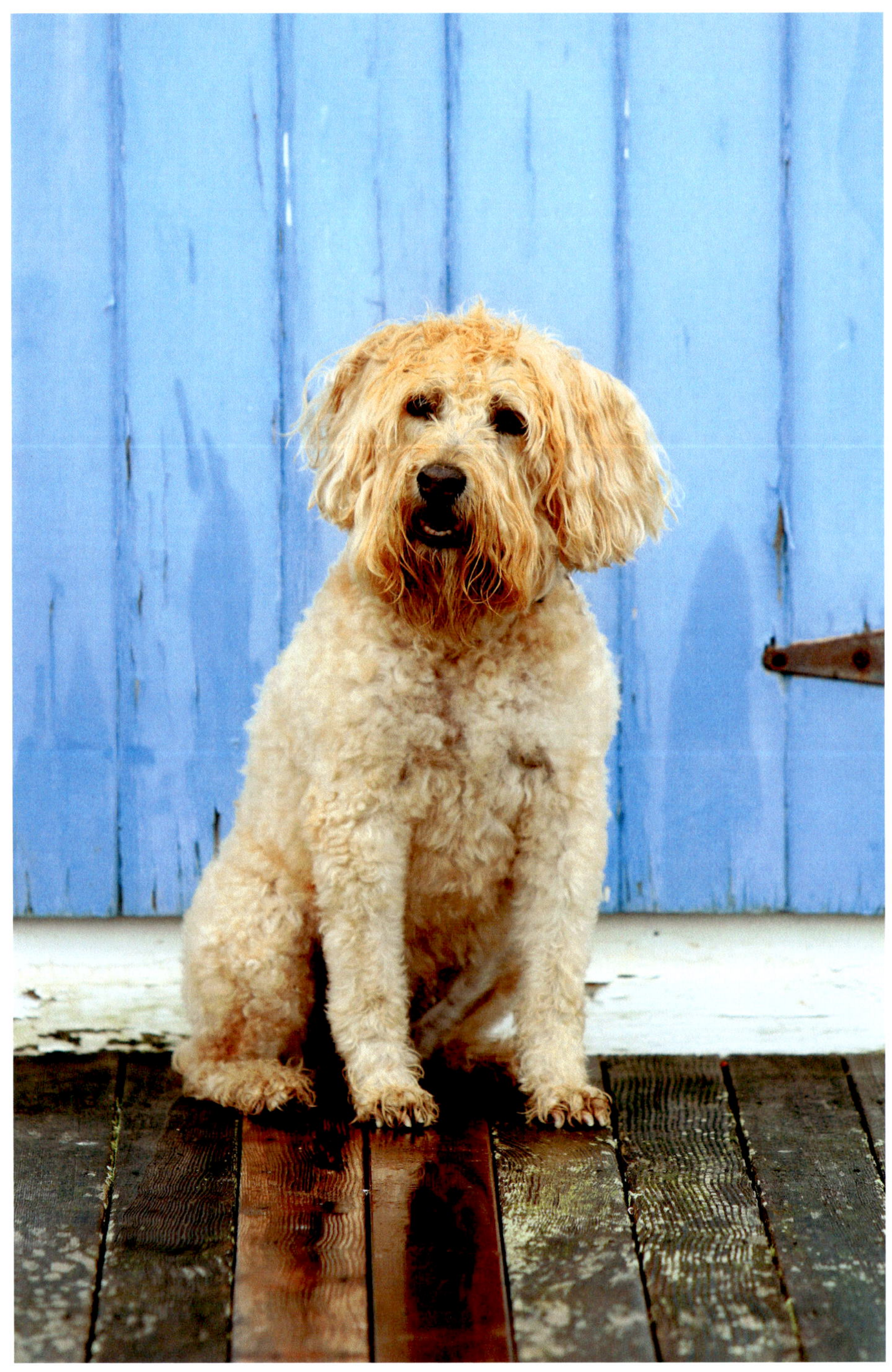

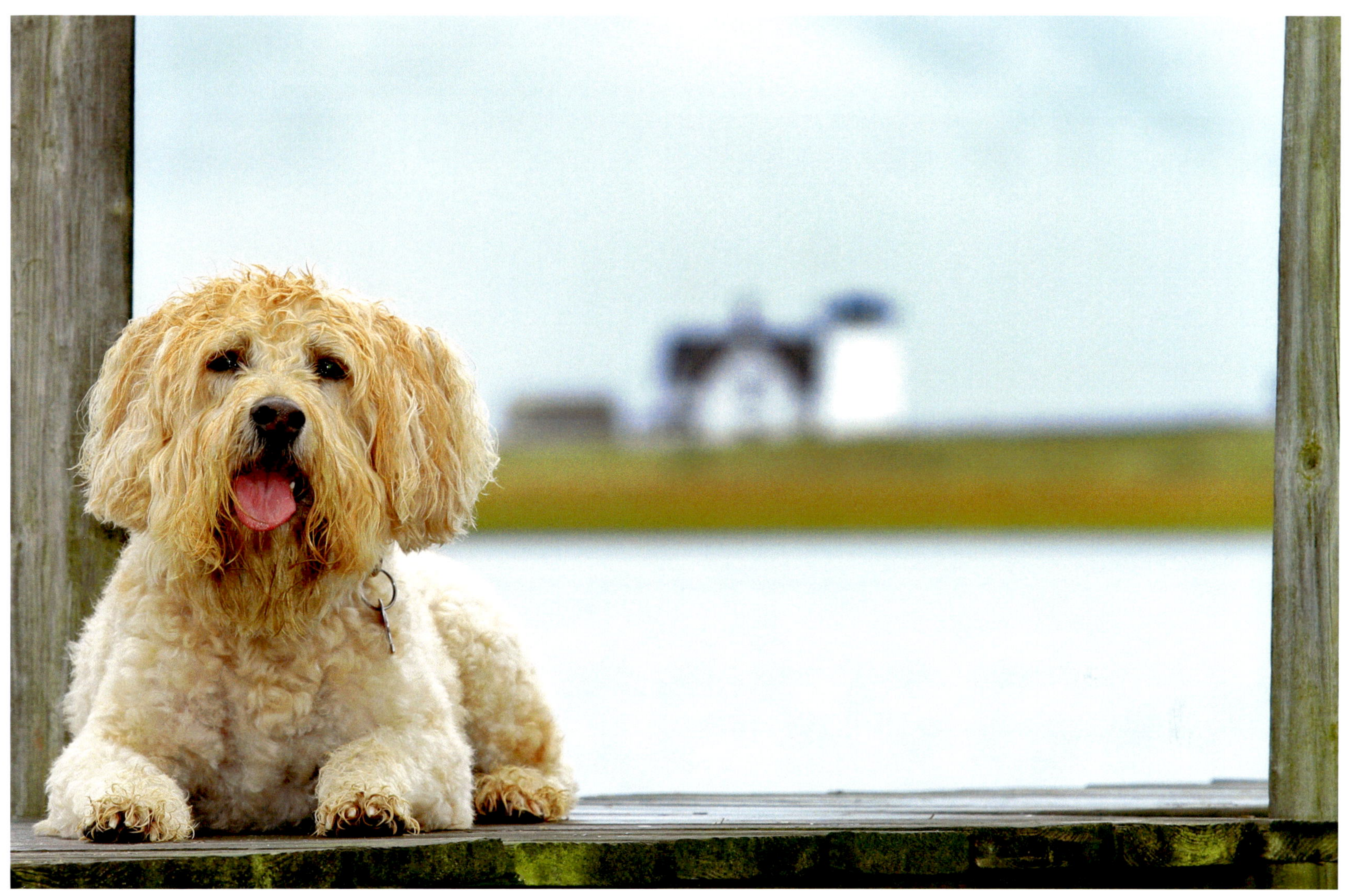

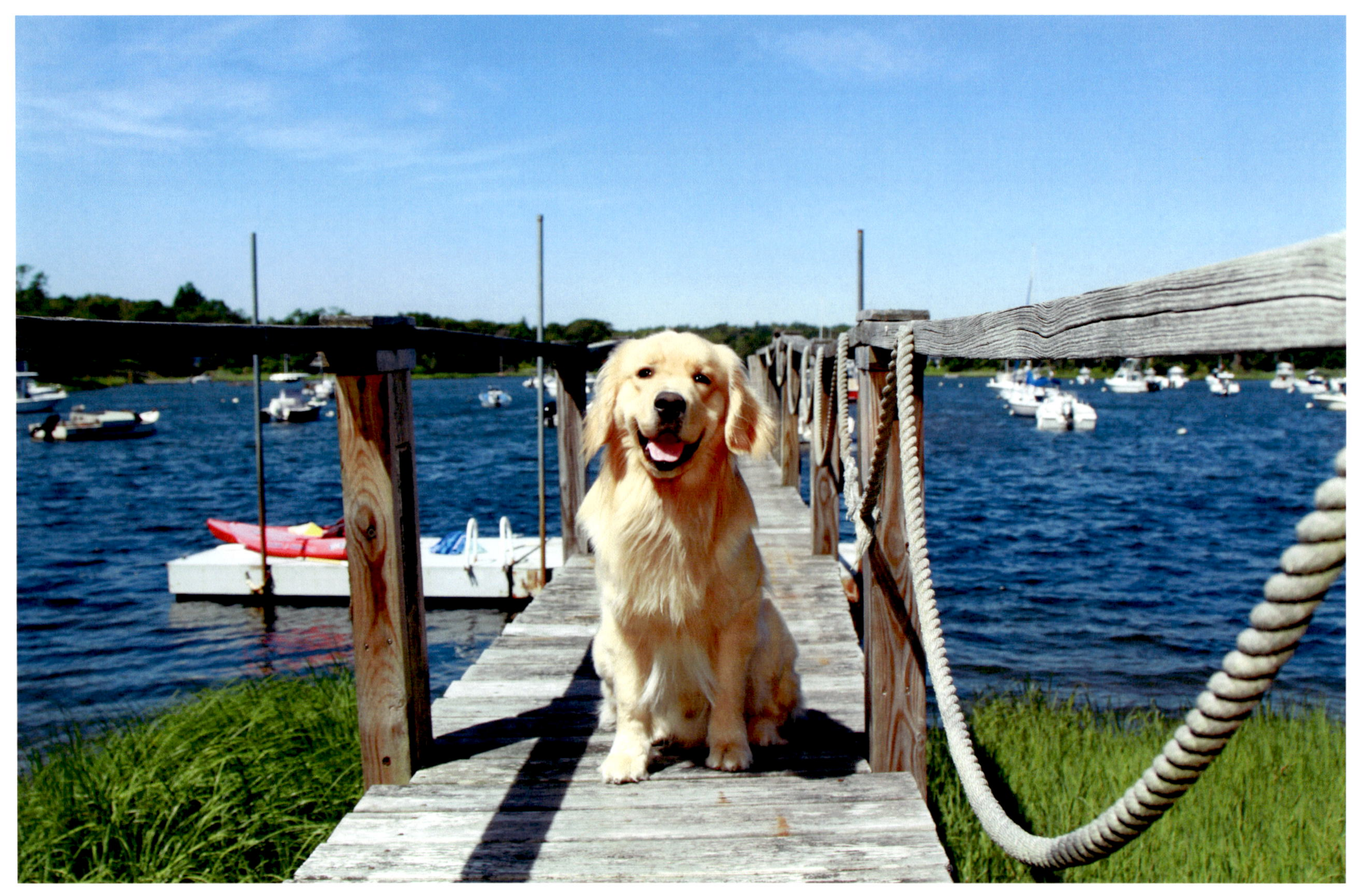

Charlie, golden retriever, Meetinghouse Pond

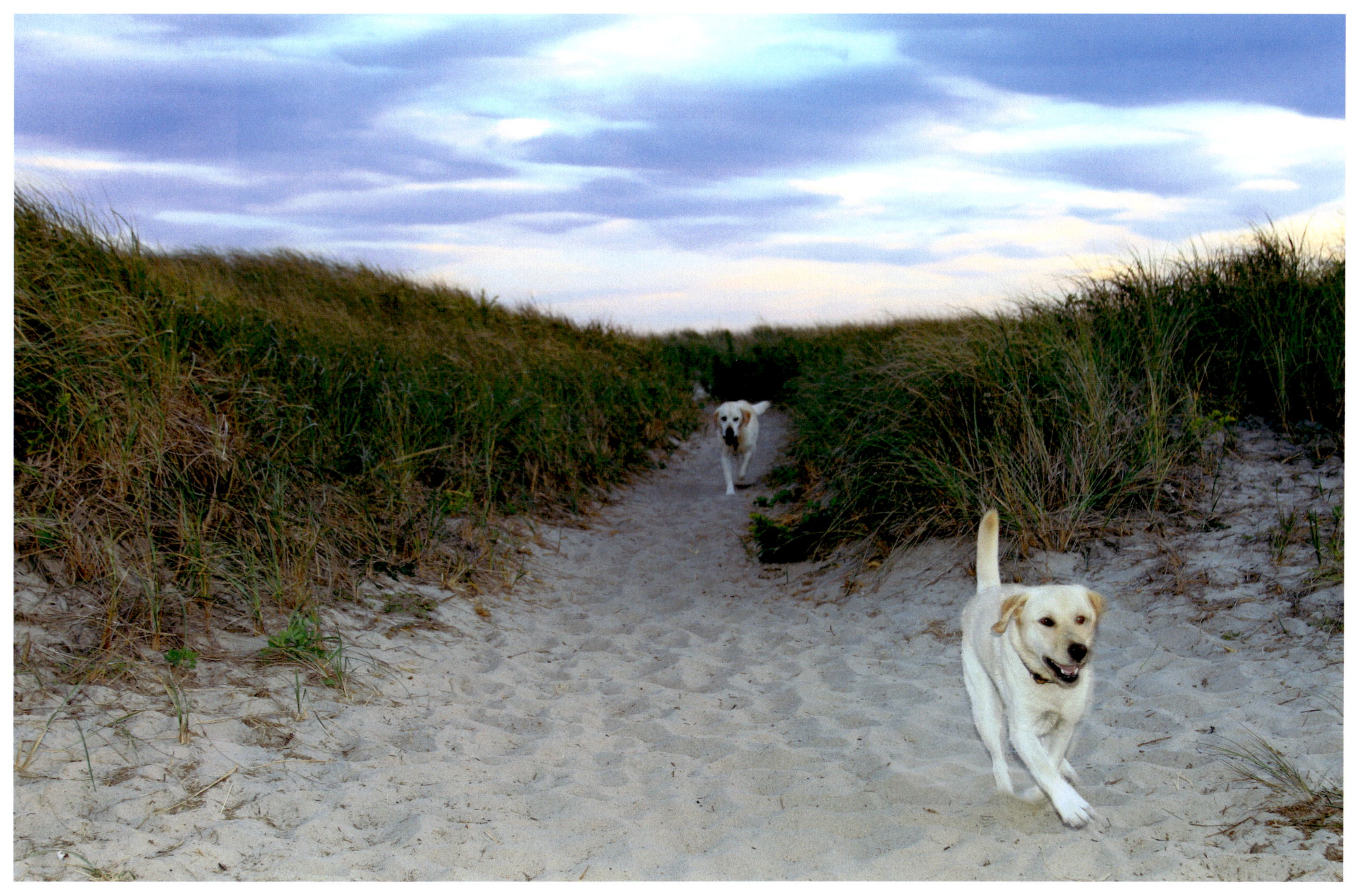

Gunnar and **Kaylee**, Labrador retrievers, Ridgevale Beach

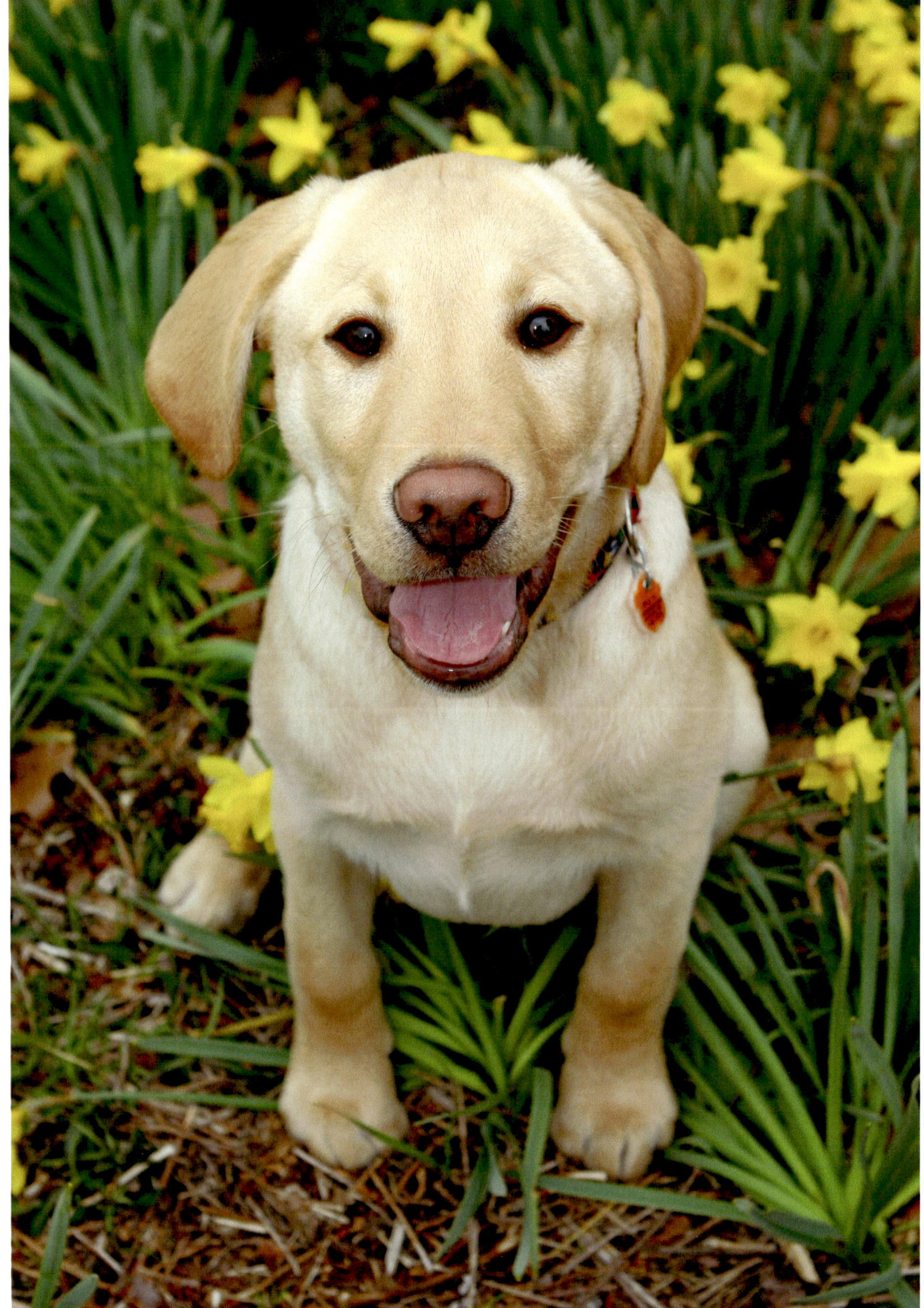

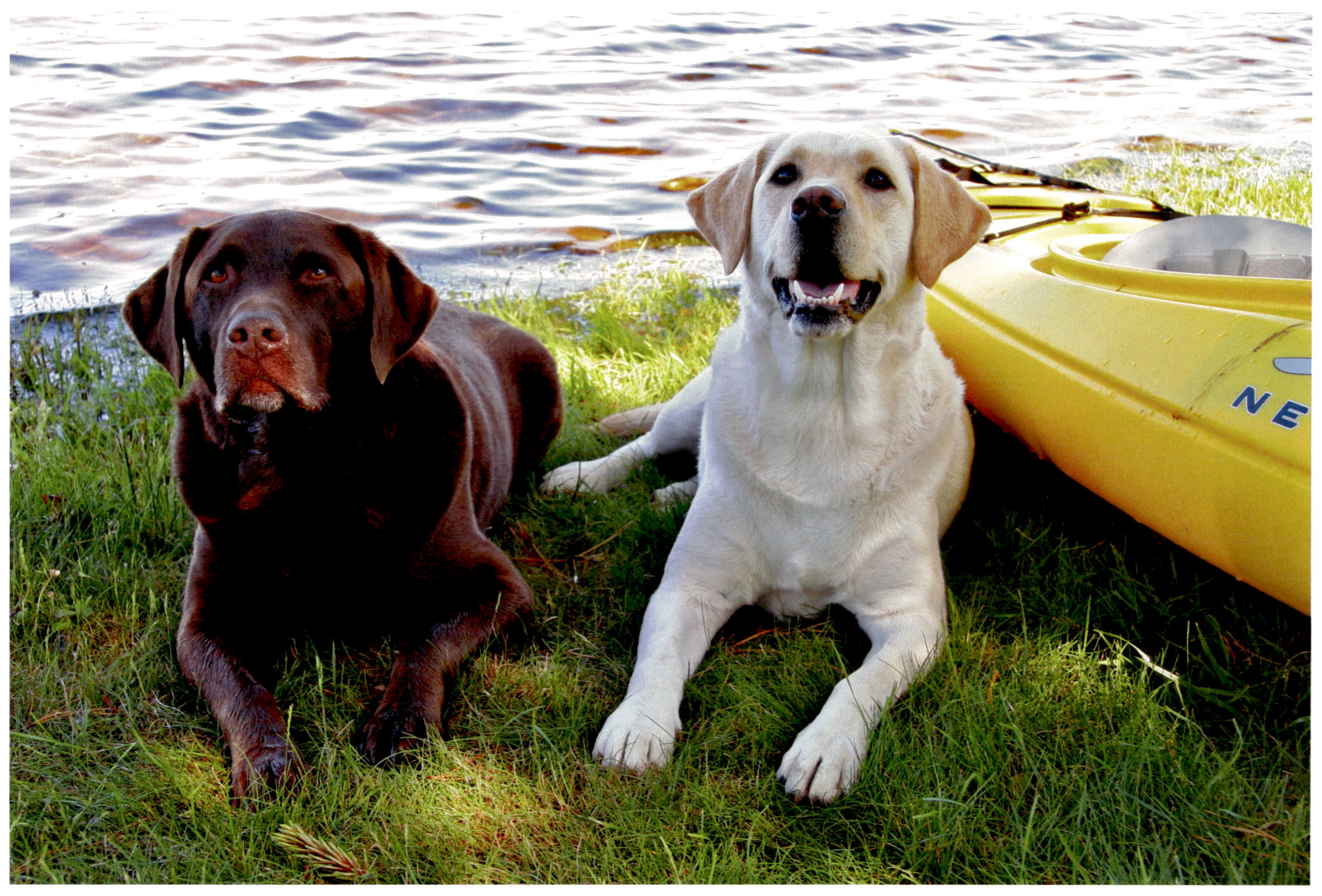

Quinn and **Cedar** (above), Labrador retrievers, Depot Pond

Henry (opposite), Labrador retriever

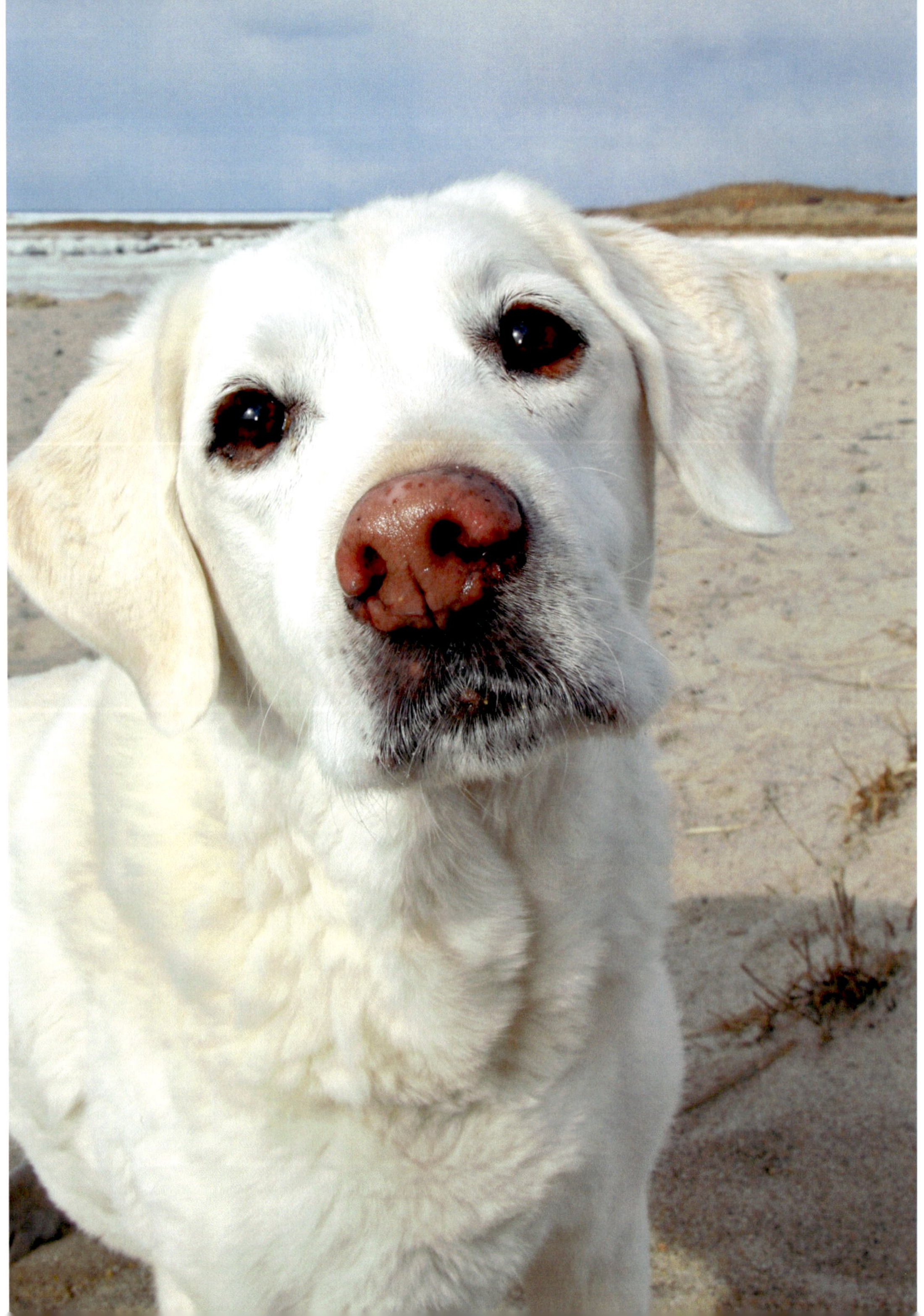

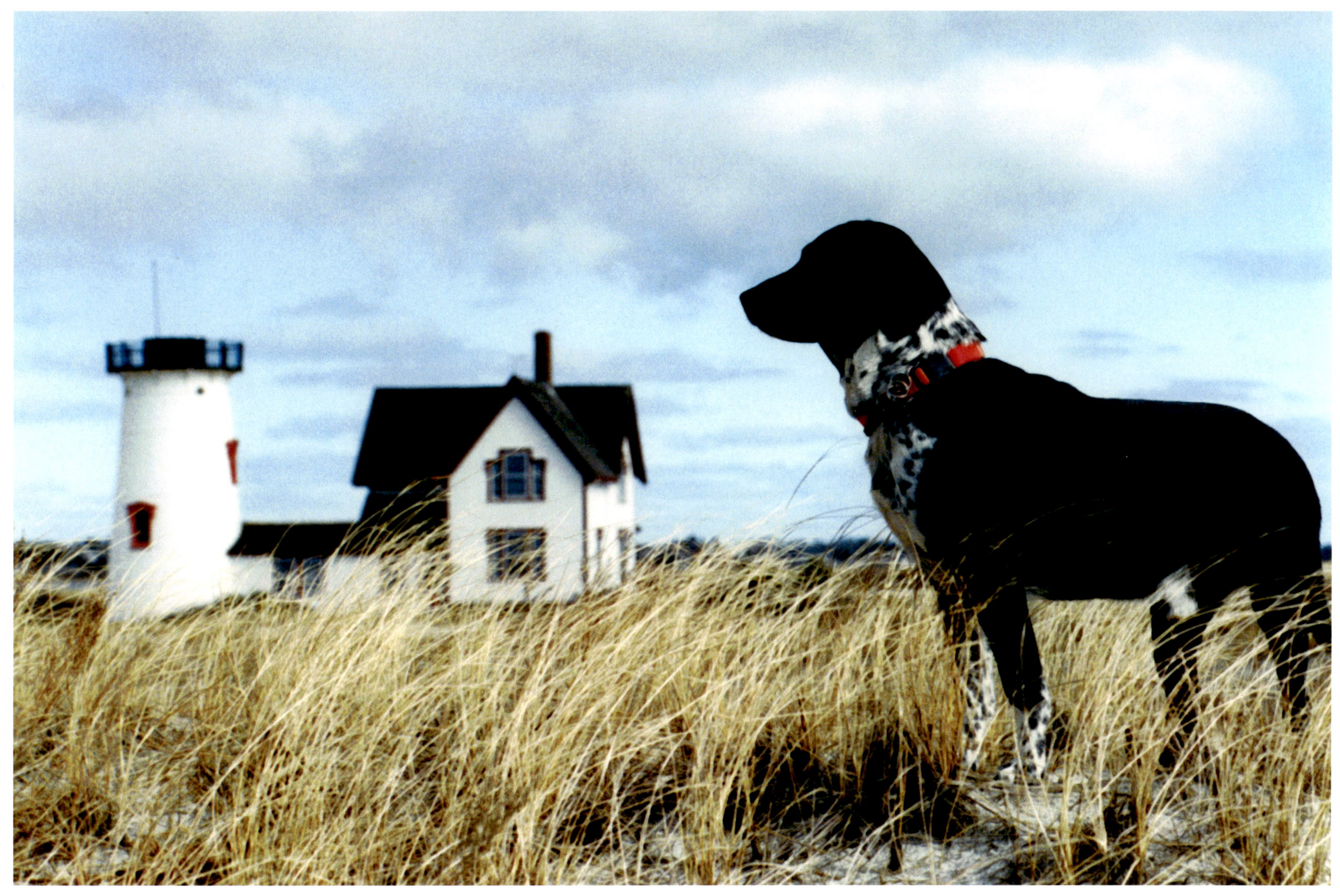

Ocean (above), Dalmatian mix, Harding's Beach

Belle (opposite), Labrador retriever, Skaket Landing

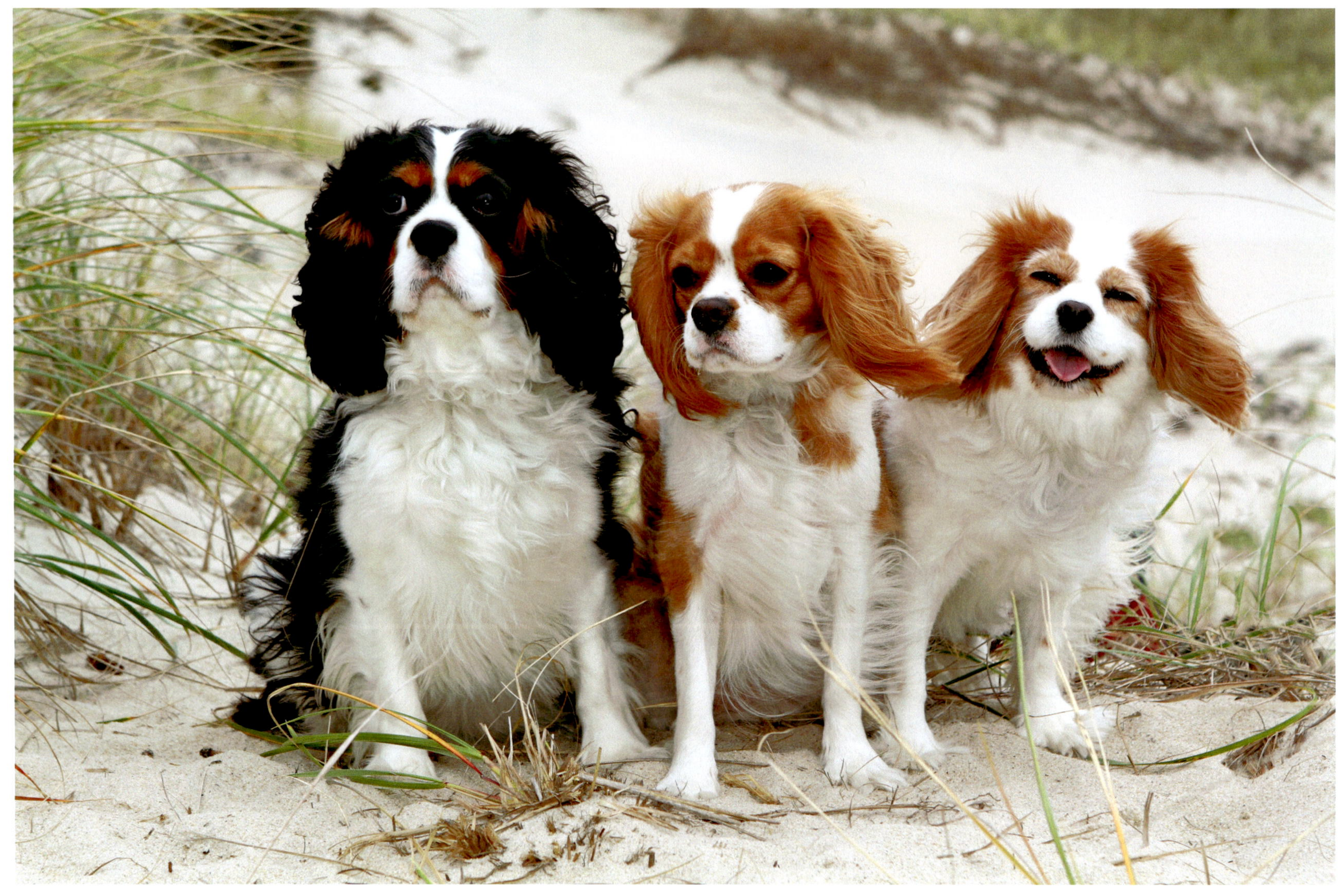

Bridget, **Lily**, and **Pippa**, Cavalier King Charles spaniels, Chapin Beach

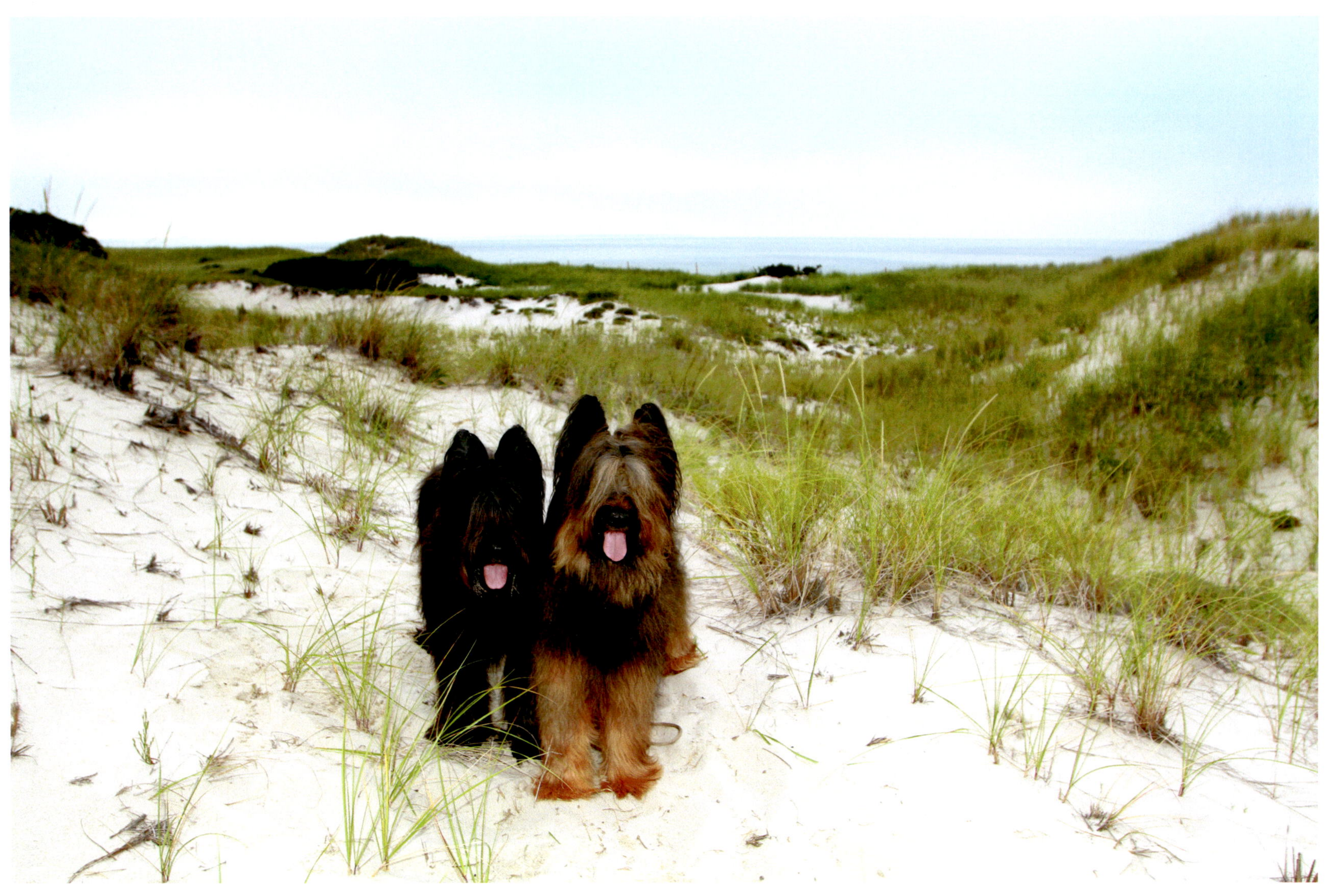

Coco and **Russet**, briards, Chapin Beach

Rosie (below), miniature sheepadoodle; **Coco** and **Russet** (bottom), briards

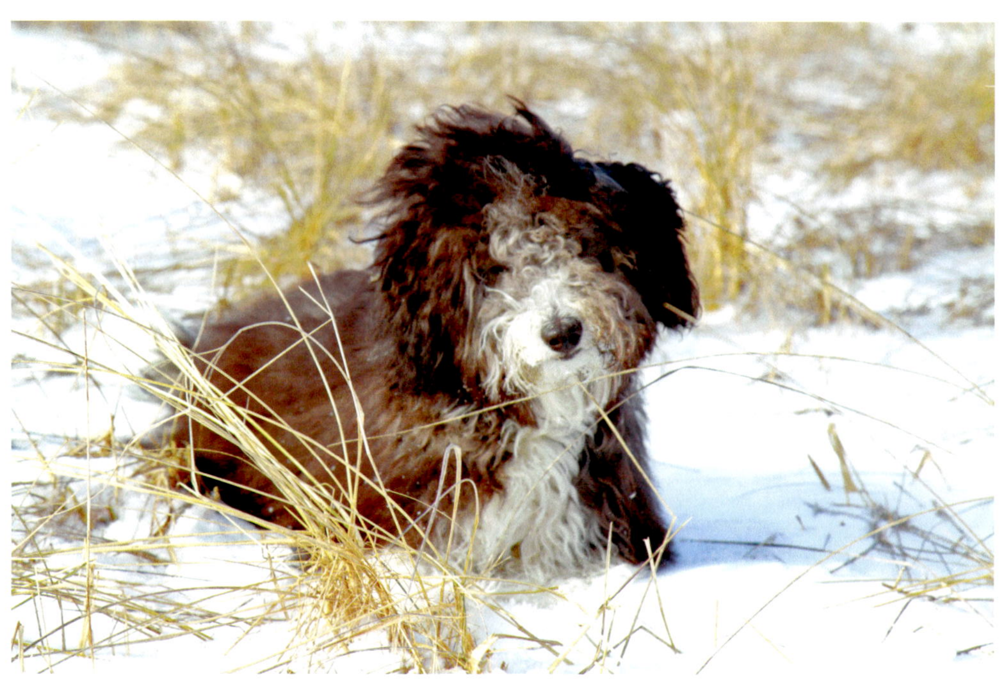

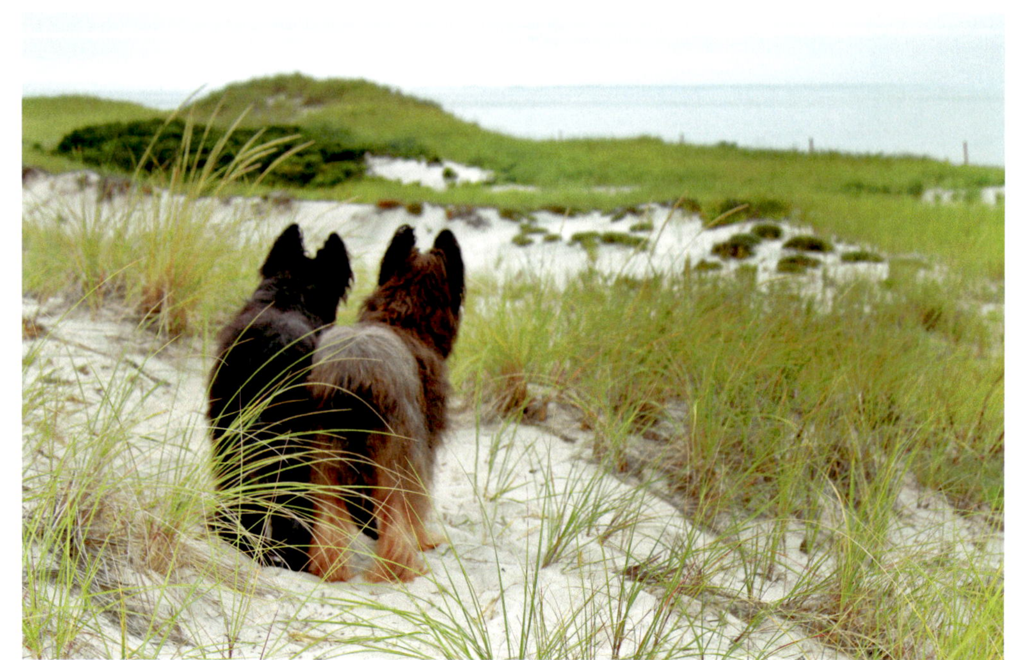

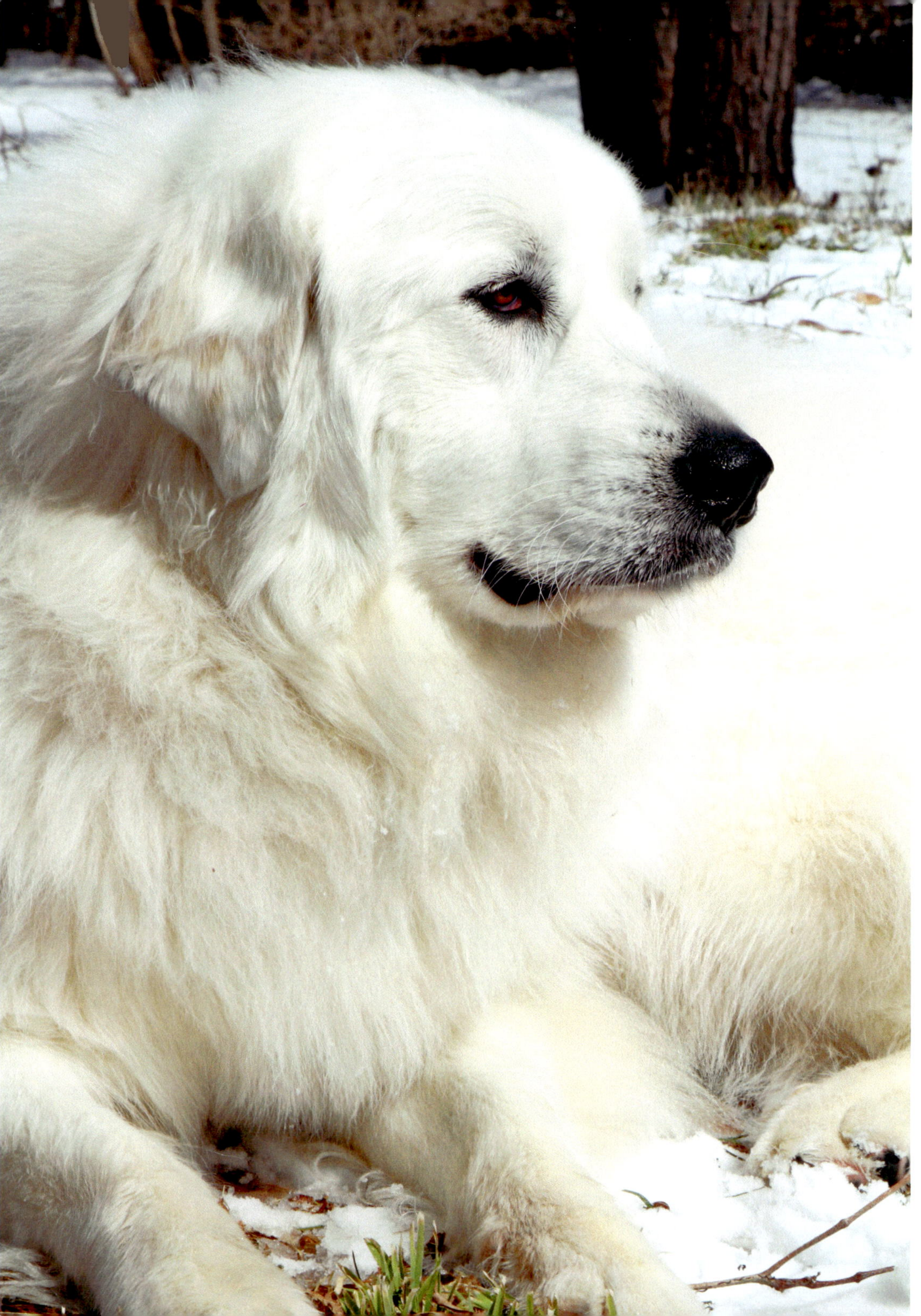

Sugar,
Great Pyrenees

Midget, vizsla

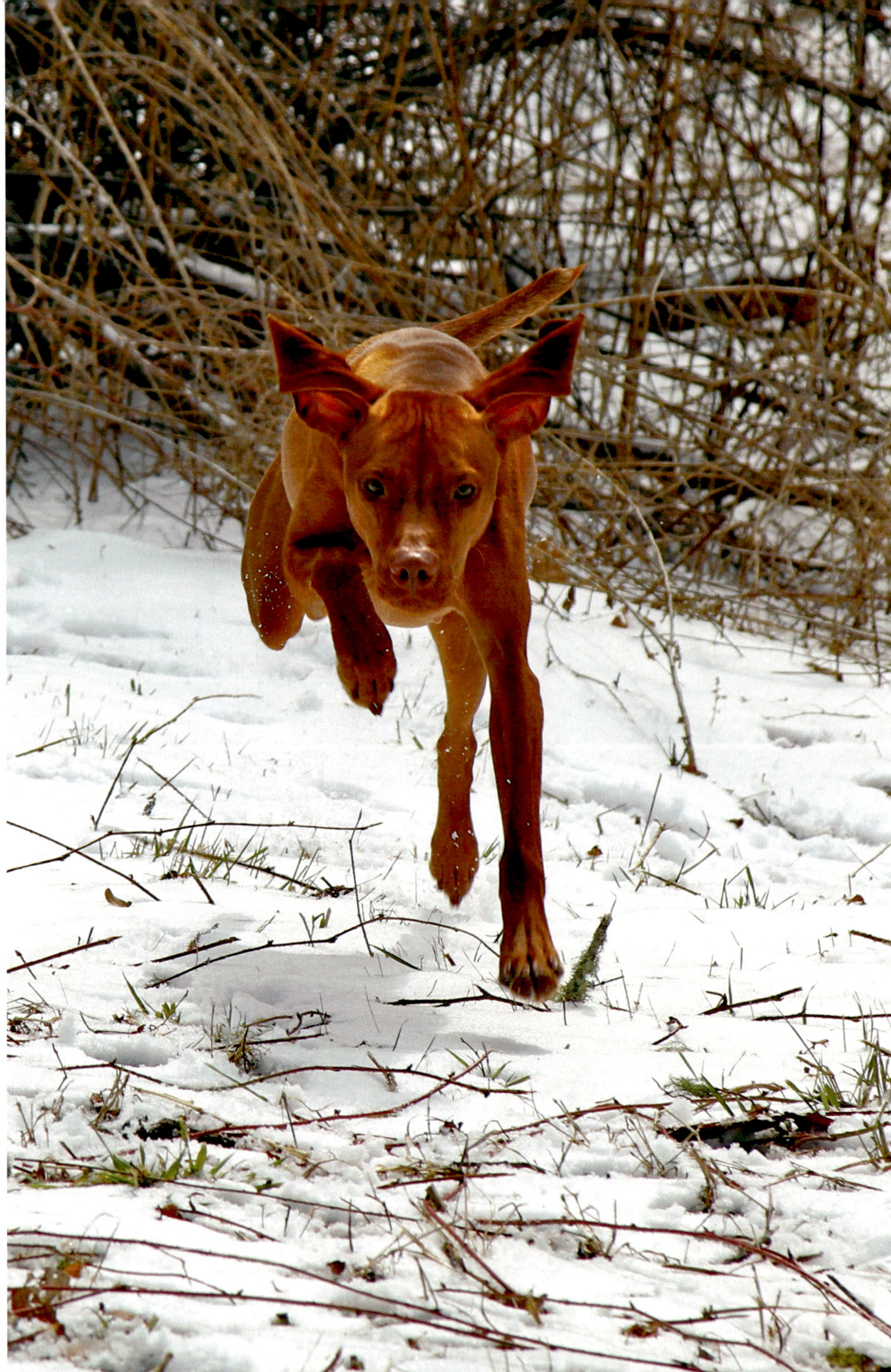

Midget (below) and **Mimosa** (bottom), vizslas

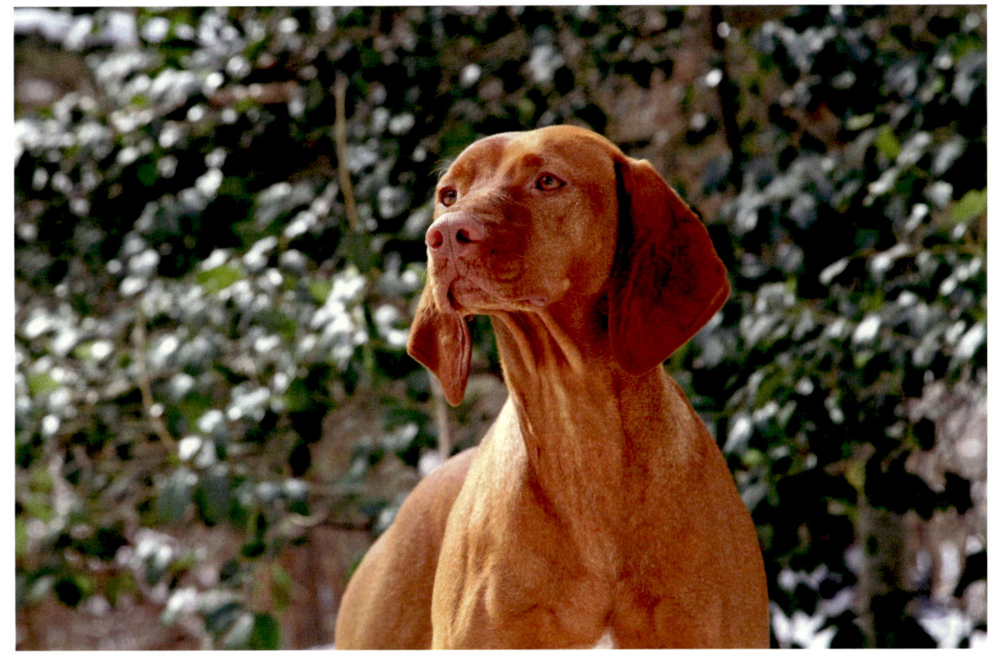

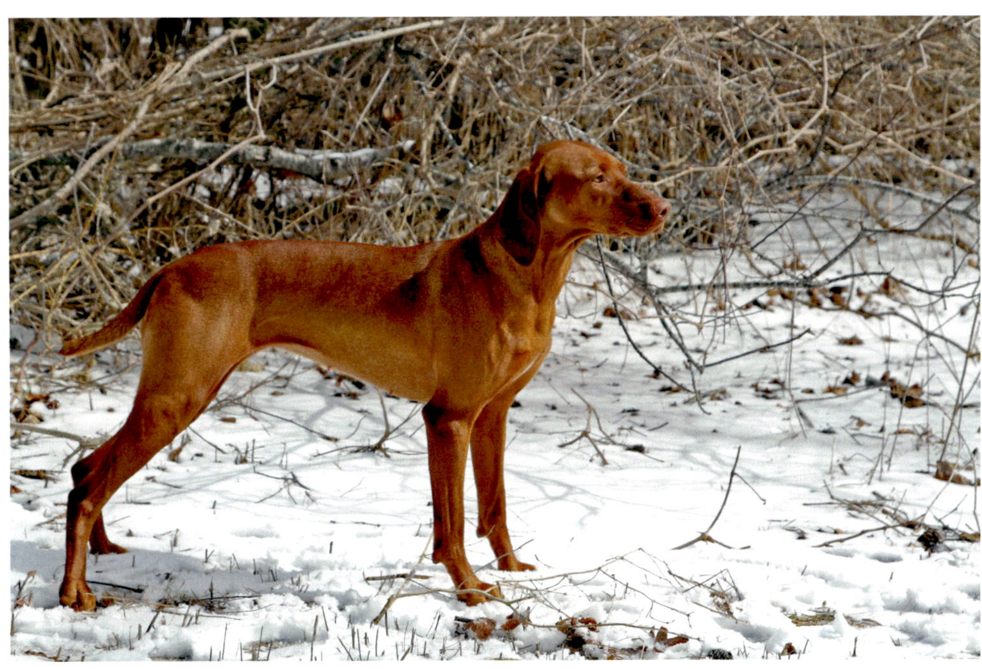

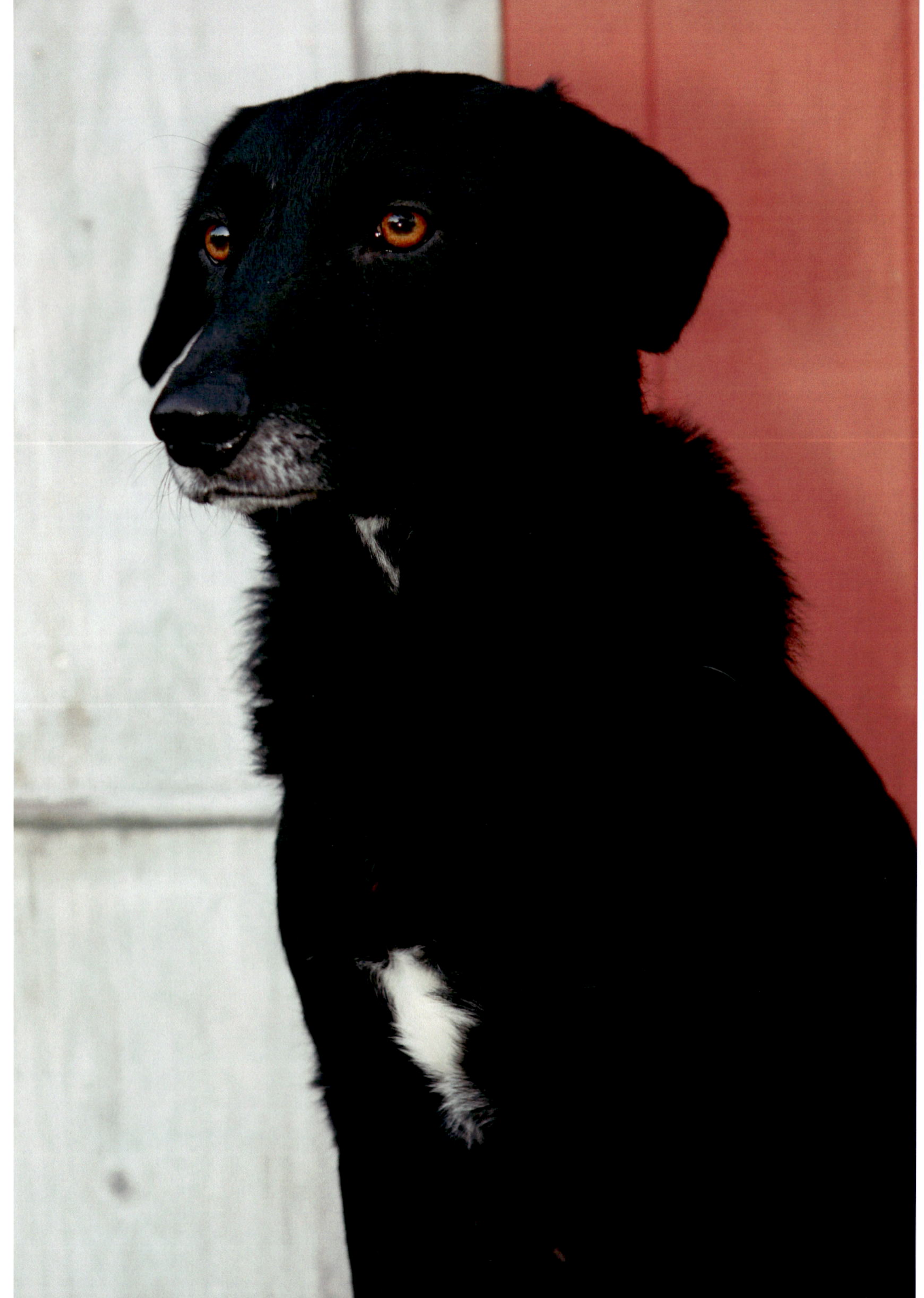

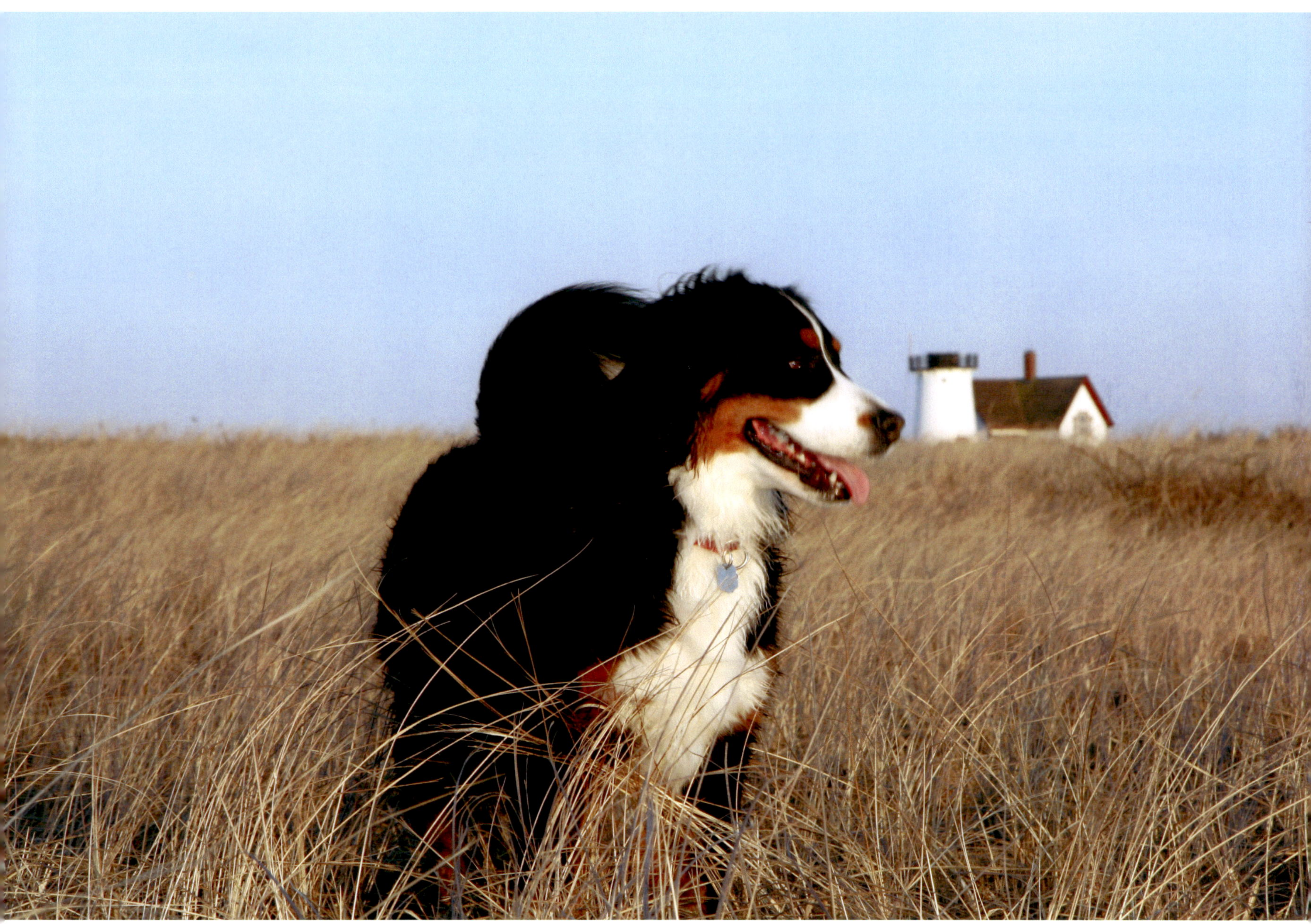

Nettie (above), Bernese mountain dog

Sam (opposite), Labrador retriever mix

Sonja, standard poodle, Bank Street Beach

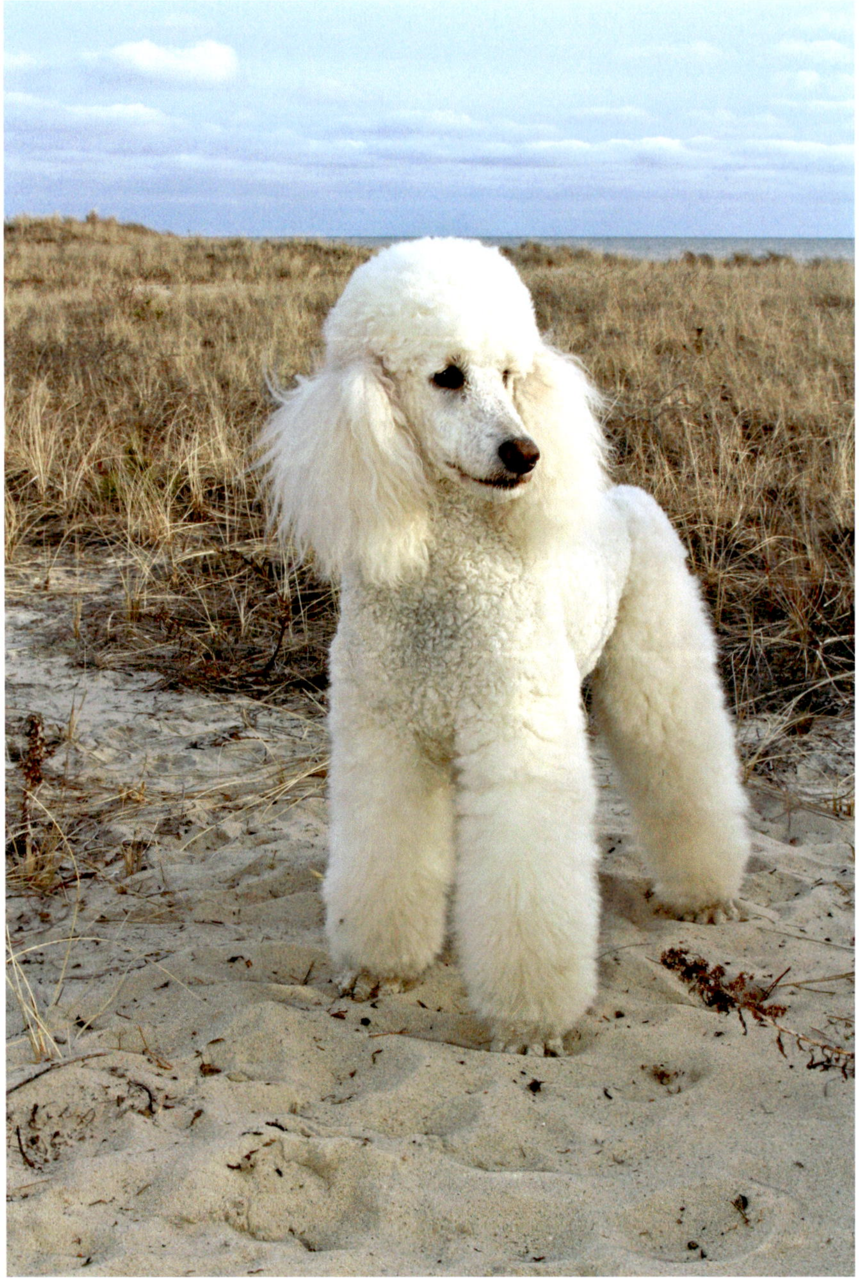

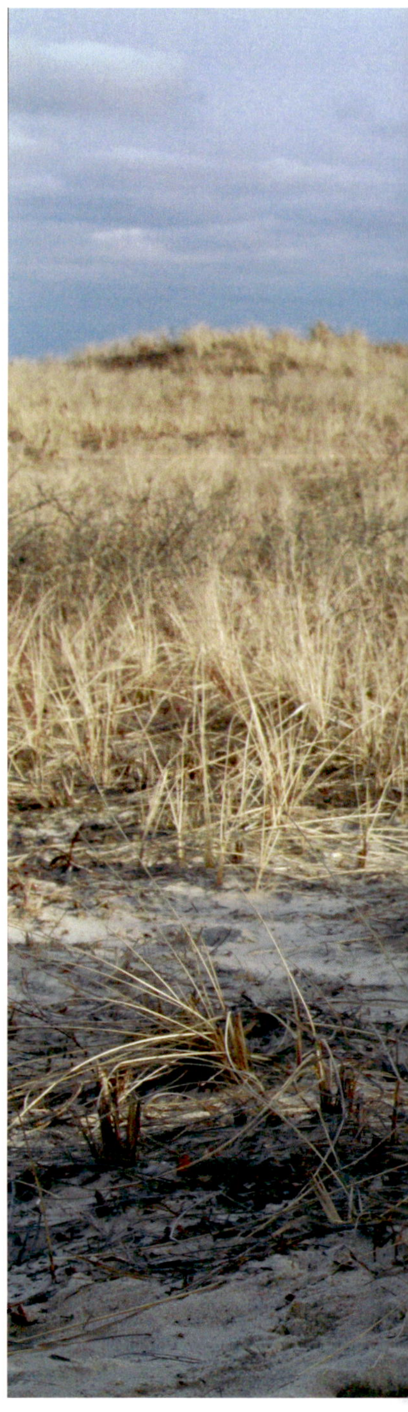

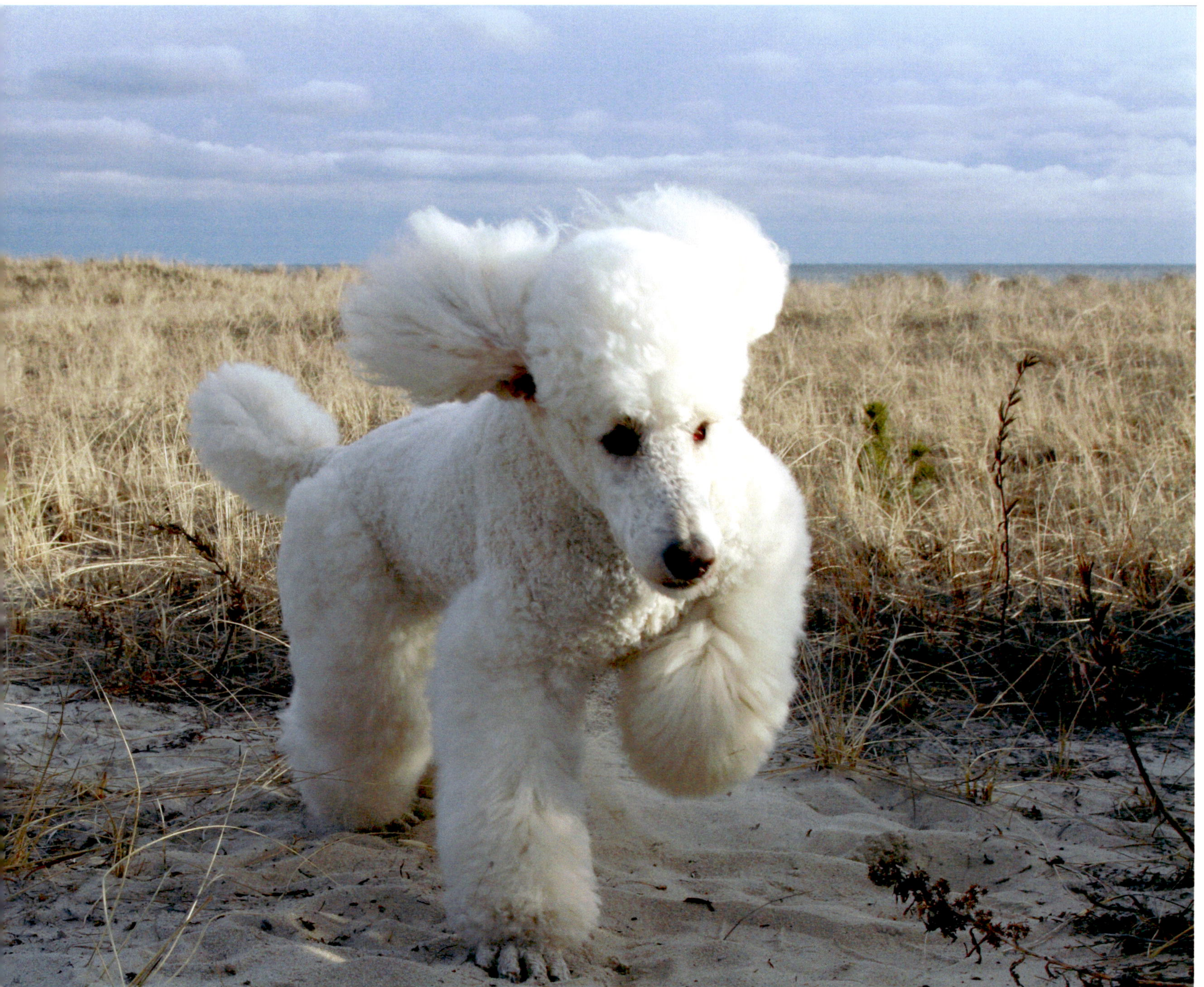

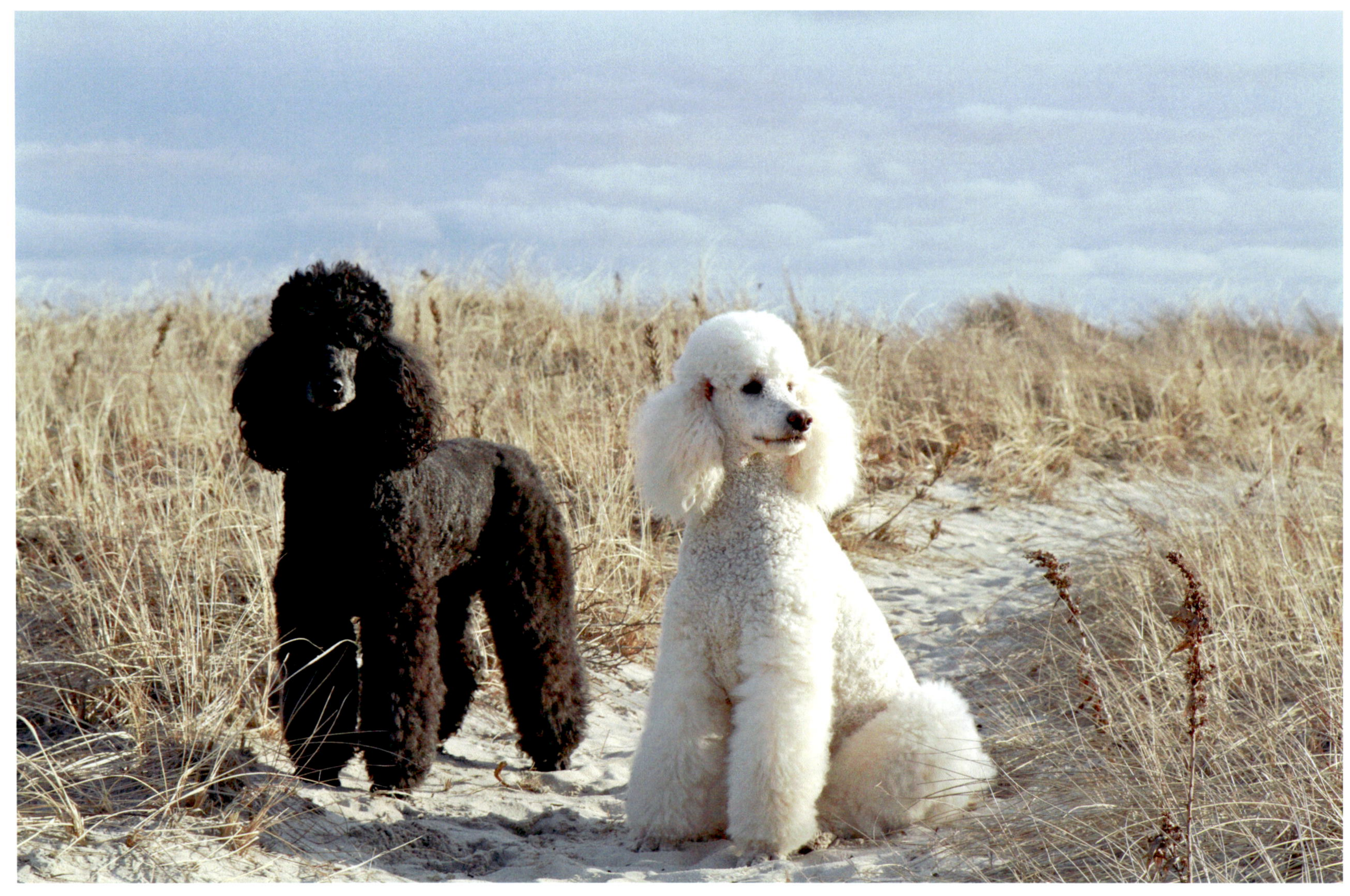

Martina and **Sonja**, standard poodles, Bank Street Beach

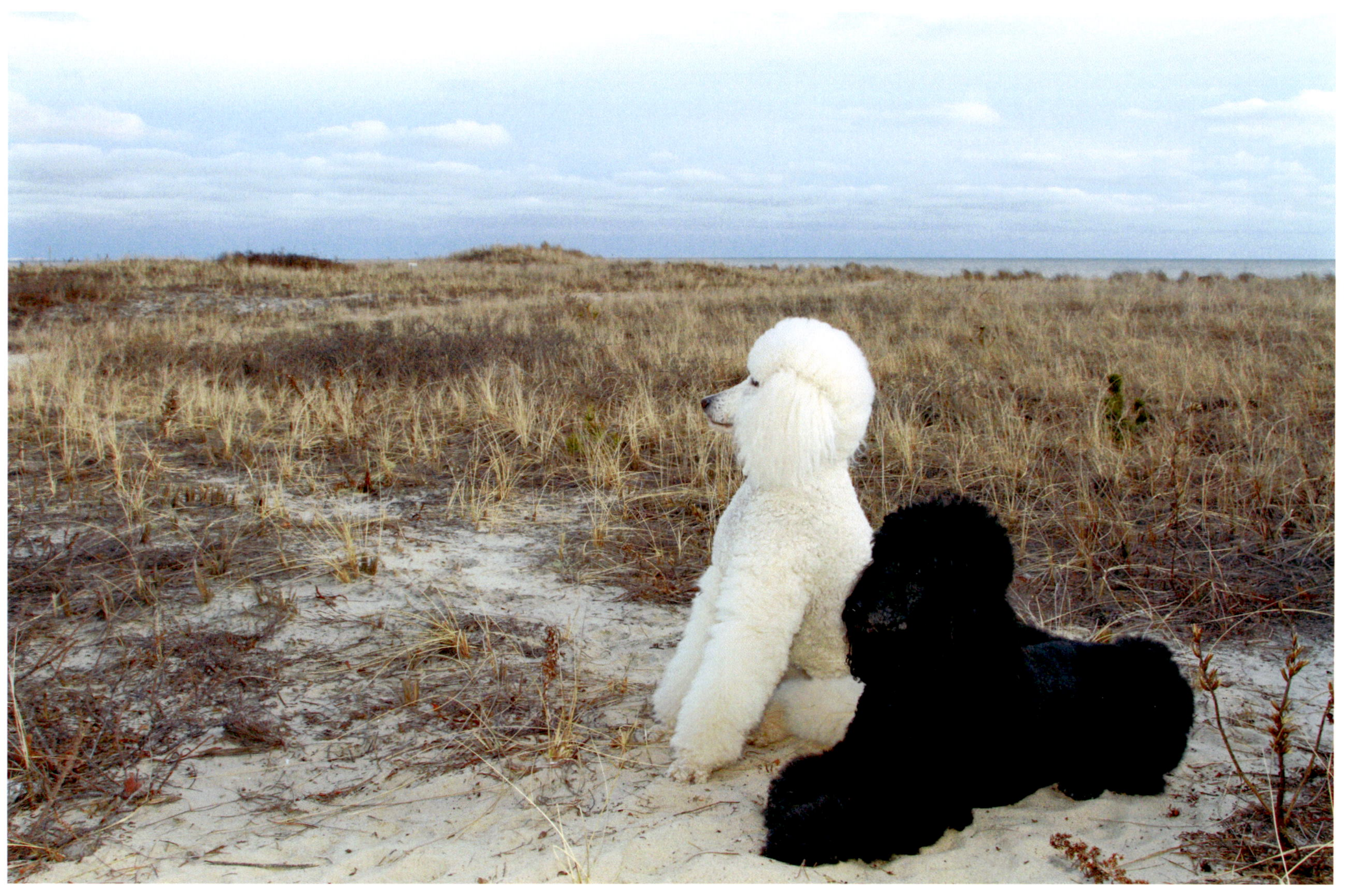

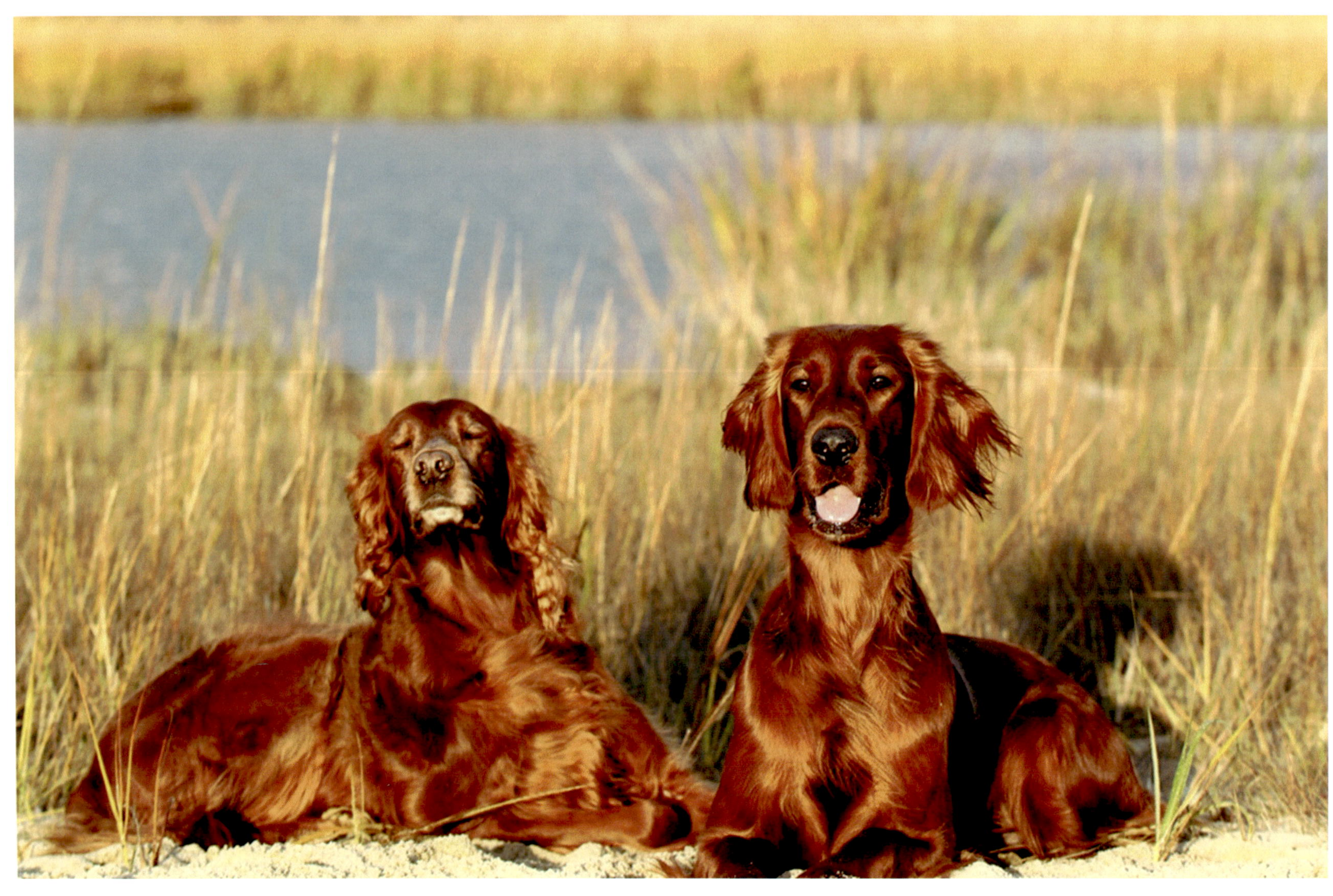

Ruby and **Georgia**, Irish setters, Ridgevale Beach

Georgia

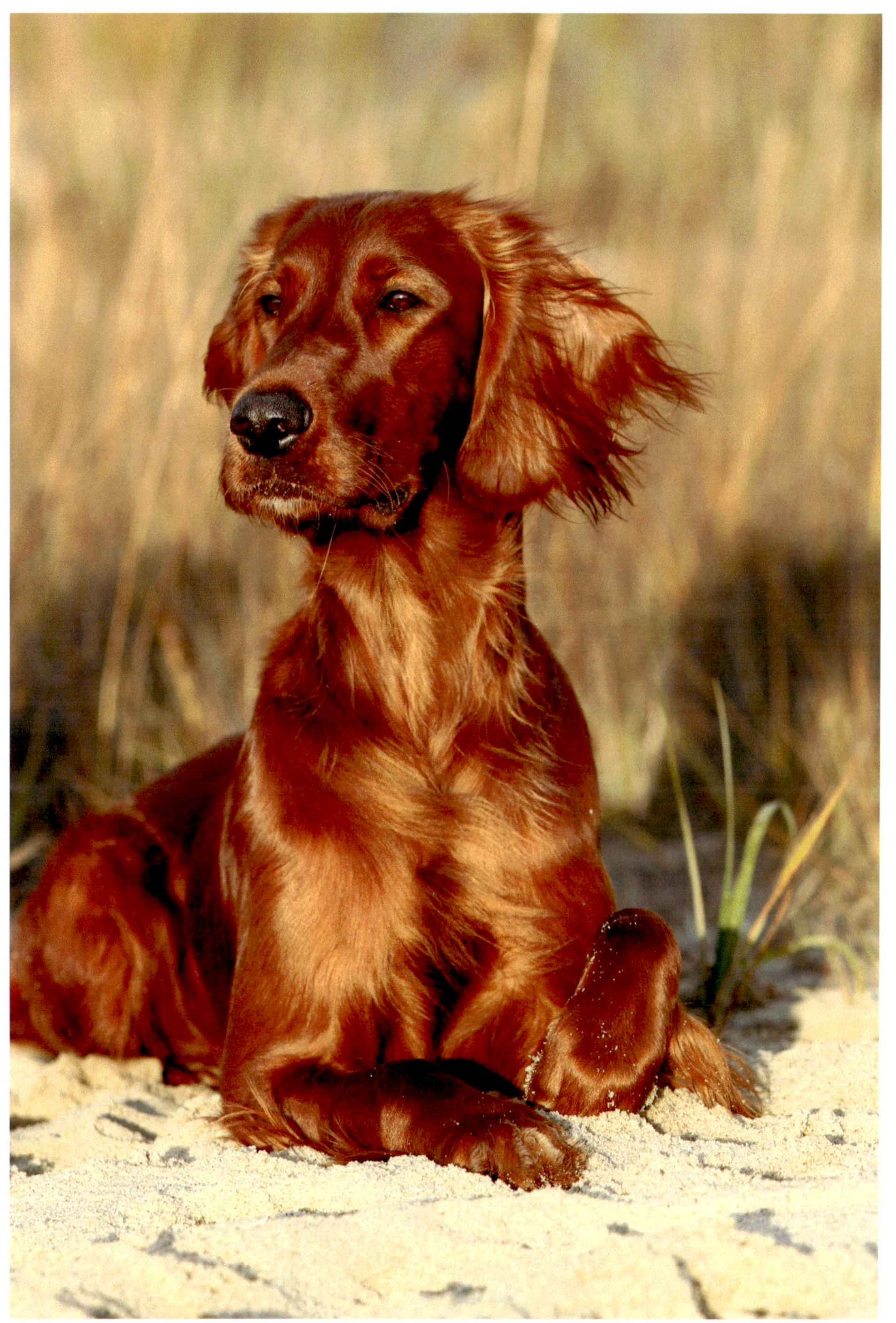

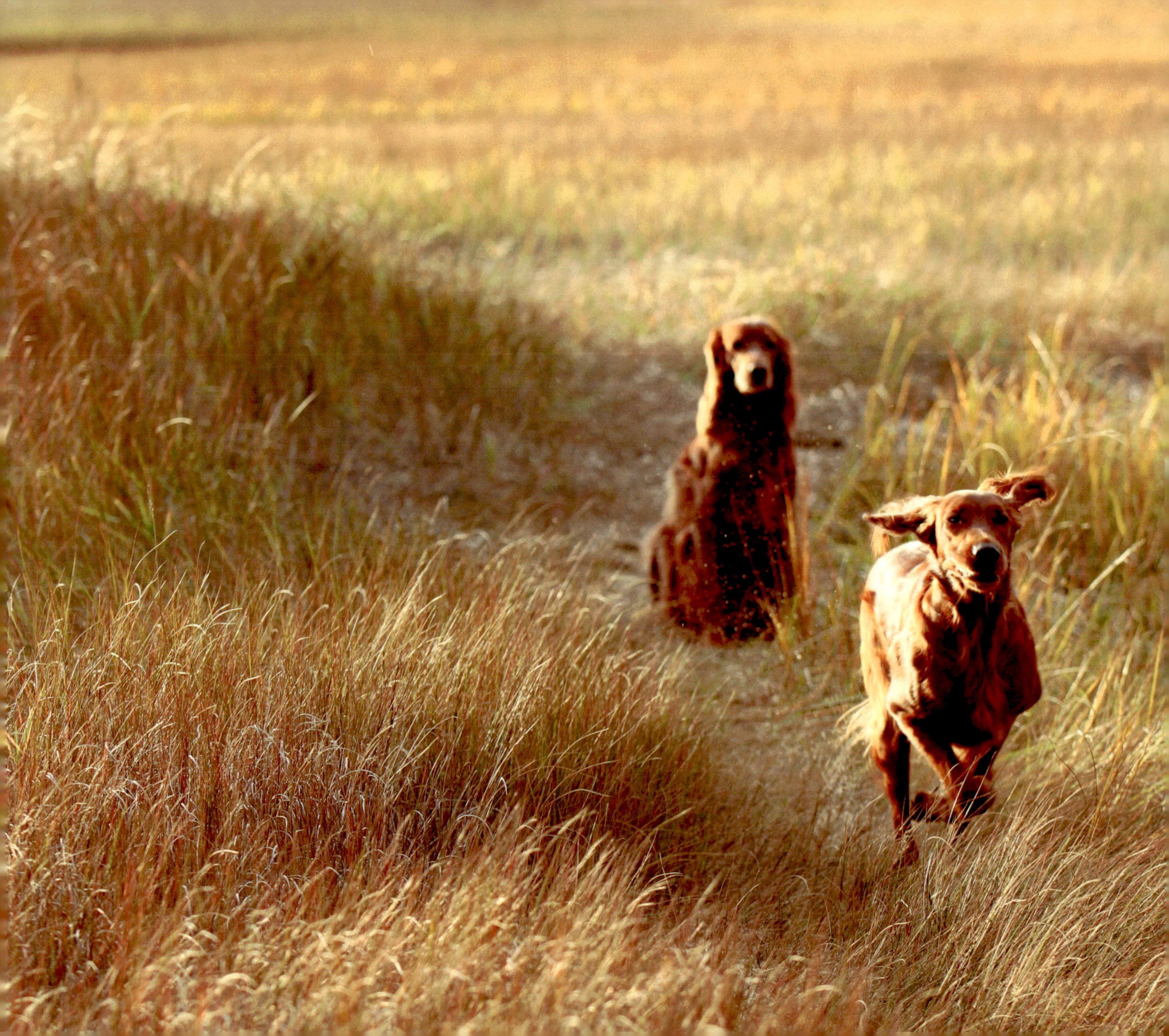

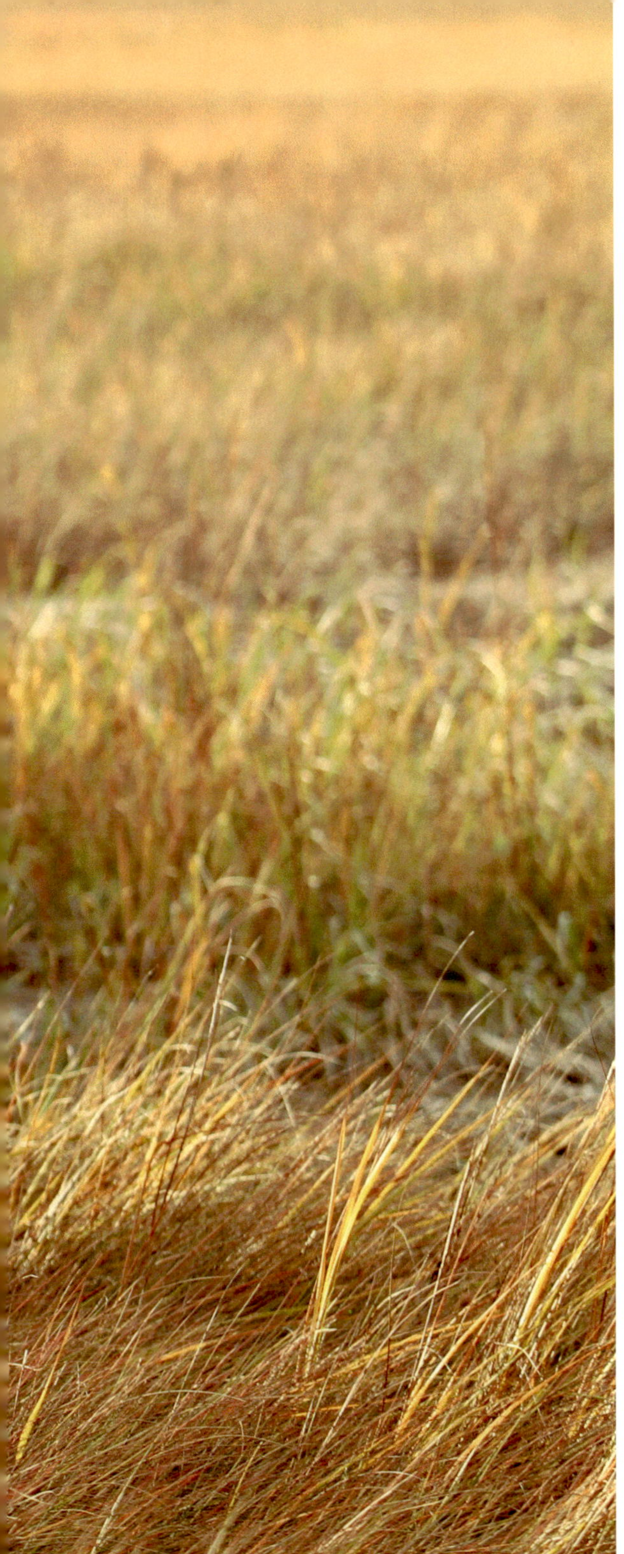

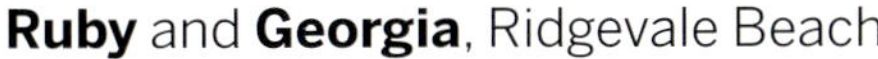

Ruby and **Georgia**, Ridgevale Beach

You may not agree, you may not care, but
If you are holding this book you should know
that of all the sights I love in this world—
and there are plenty—very near the top of
the list is this one: dogs without leashes.

— Mary Oliver, *Dog Songs*

Taffy, Nova Scotia duck tolling retriever, Paine's Creek

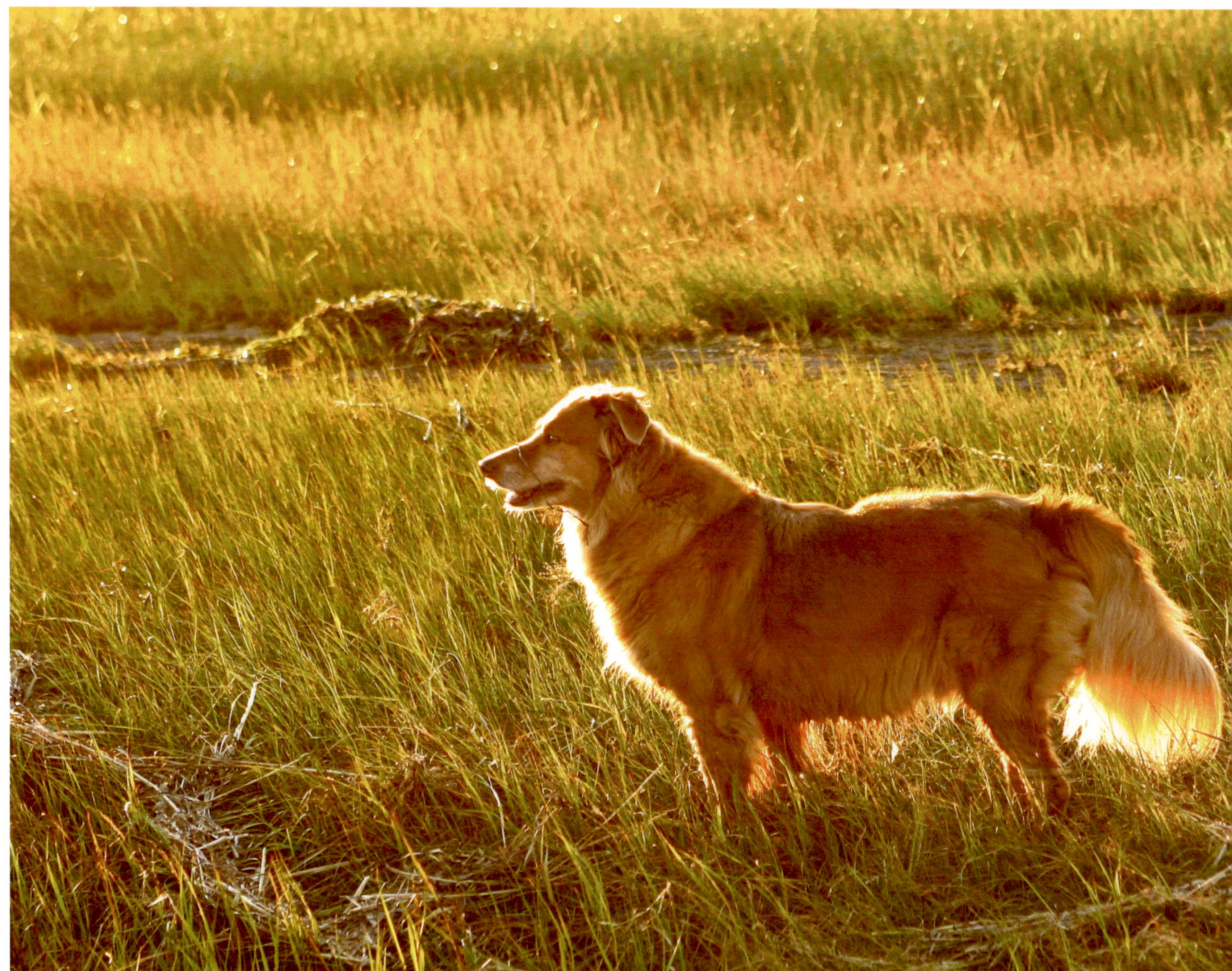

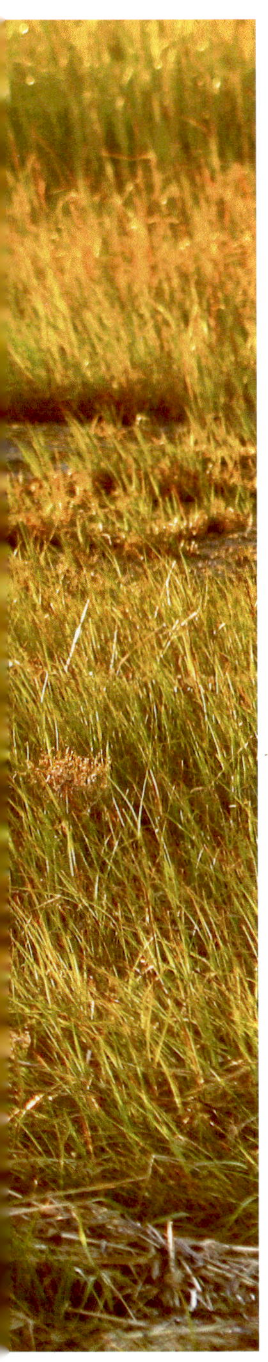

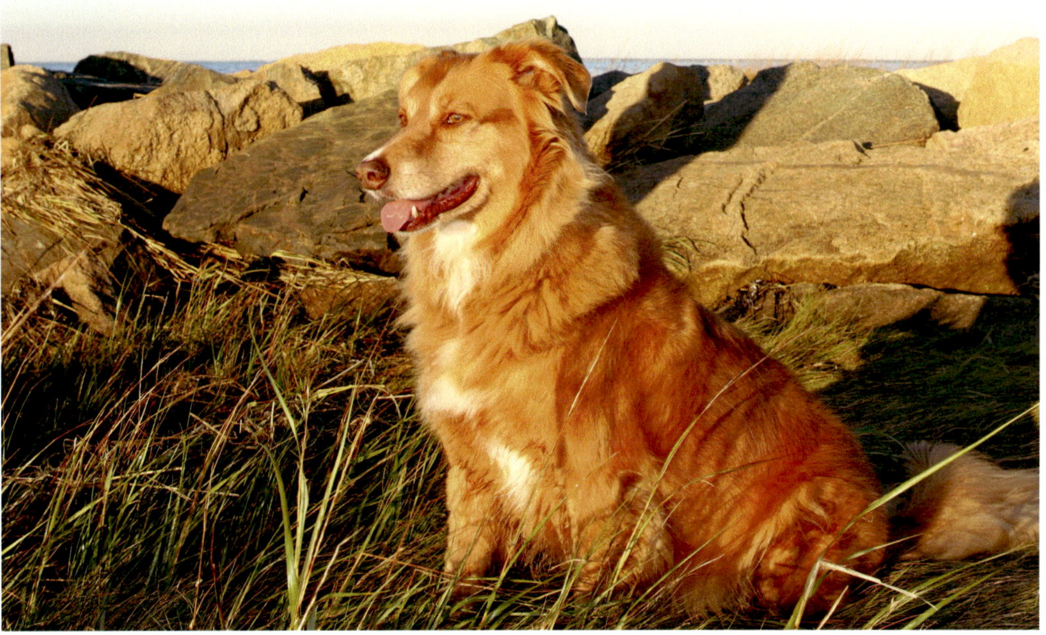

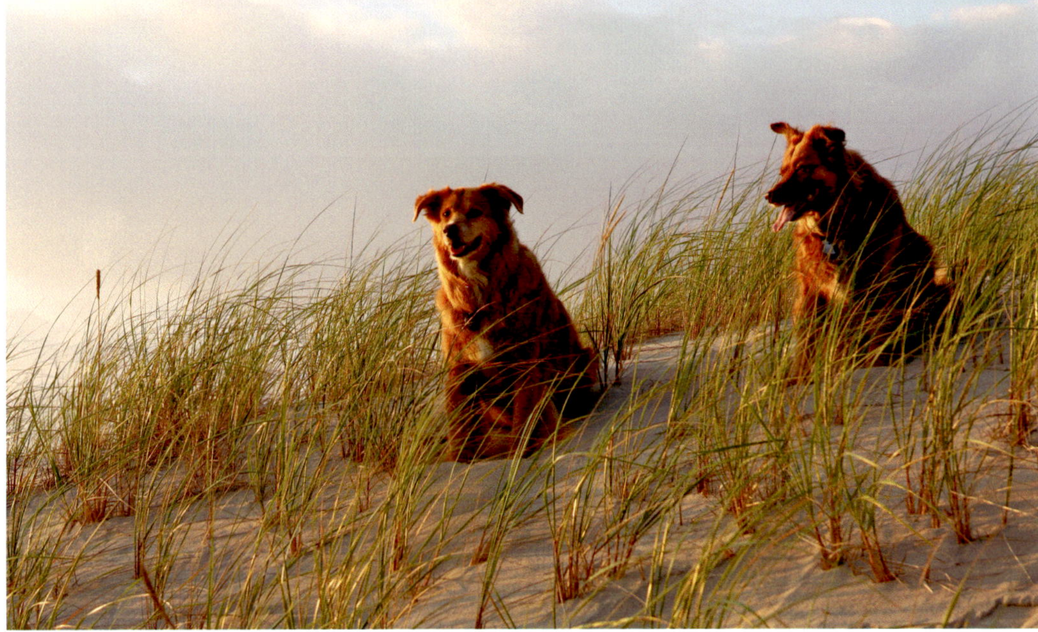

Taffy (top) and **Taffy** and **Amber** (above), Nova Scotia duck tolling retrievers, Chapin Beach

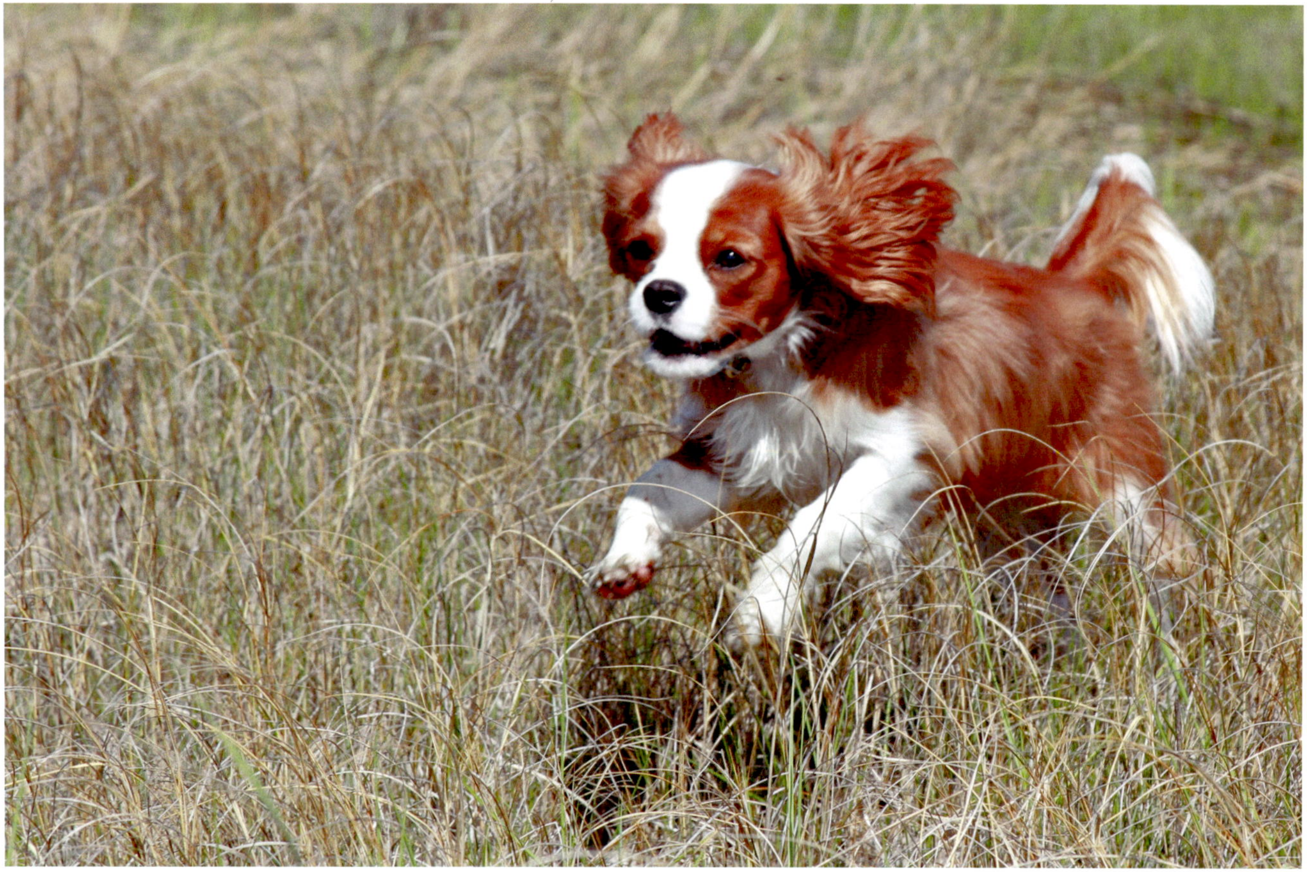

Jameson, Cavalier King Charles spaniel, Ridgevale Beach

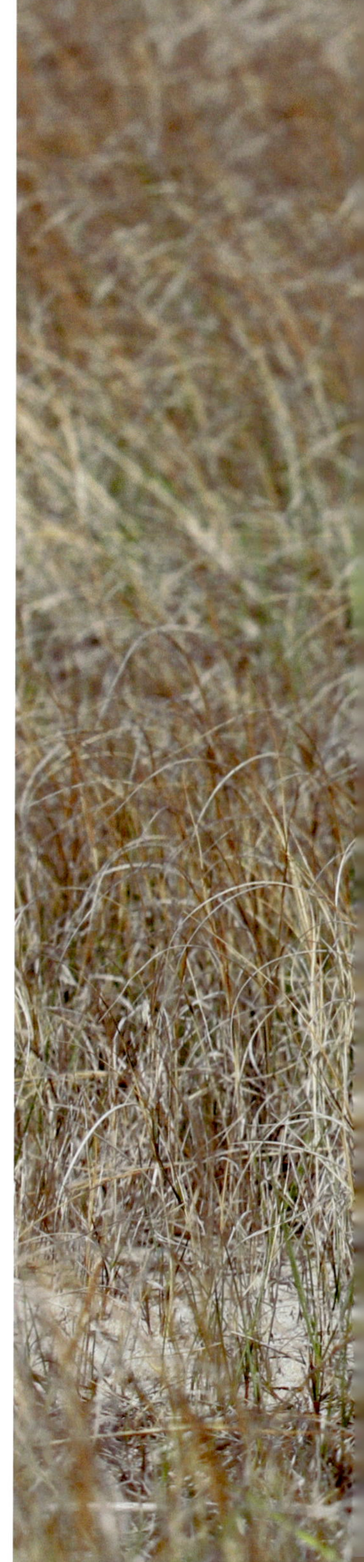

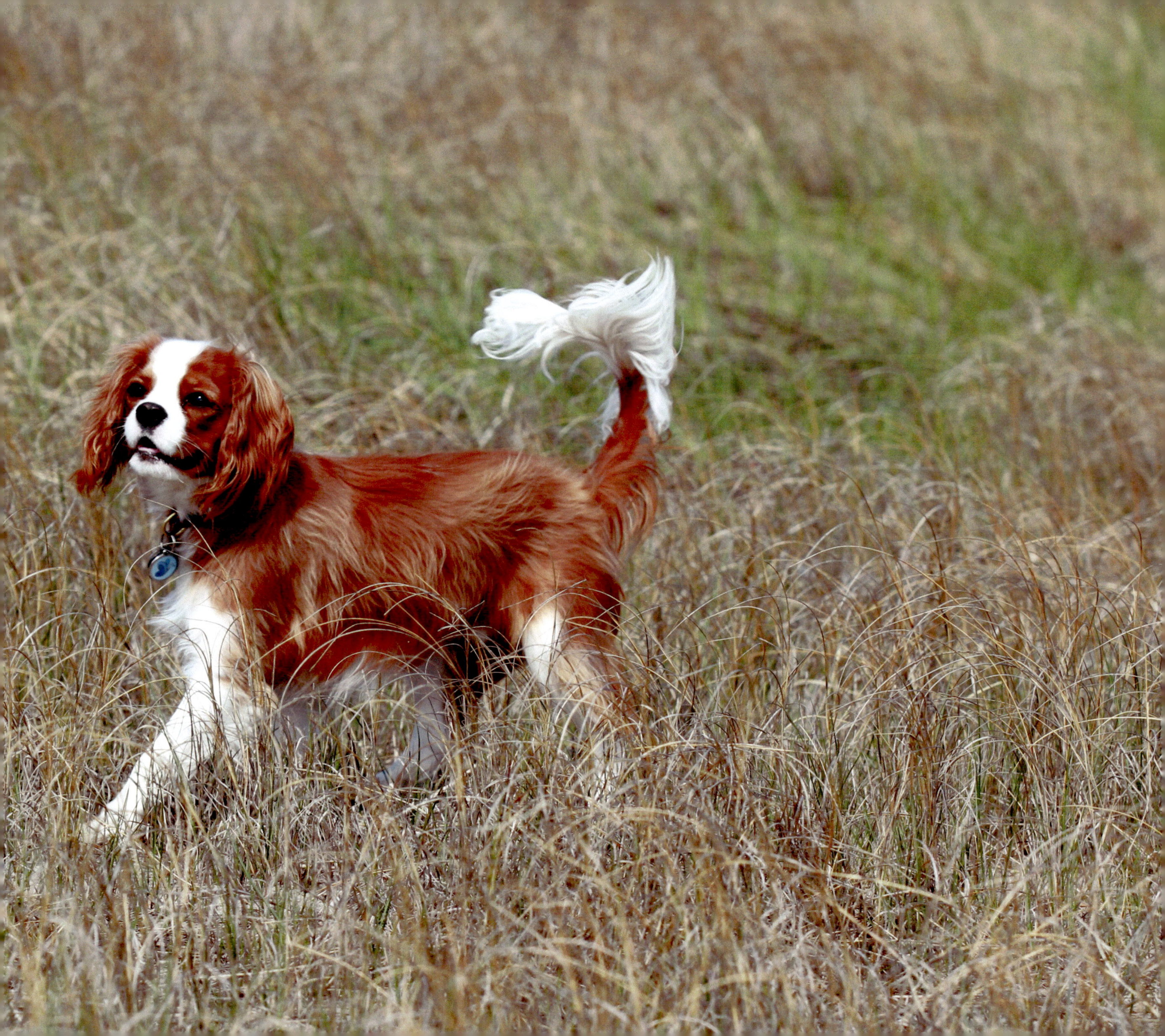

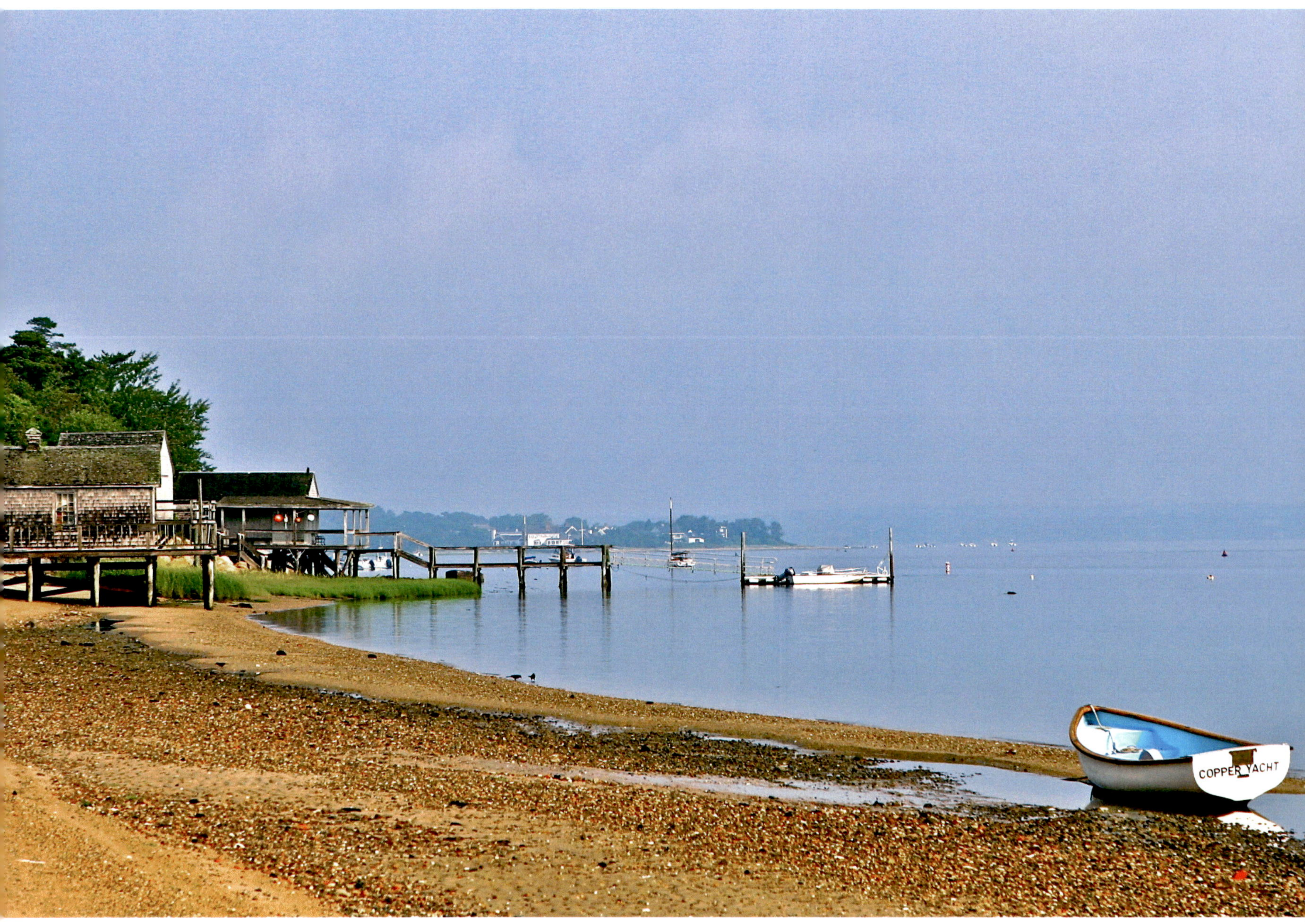

Scatteree Landing

Dogs are a link to paradise. They don't know evil or jealousy or discontent. To sit with a dog on a hillside on a glorious afternoon is to be back in Eden, where doing nothing was not boring—it was peace.

— Milan Kundera

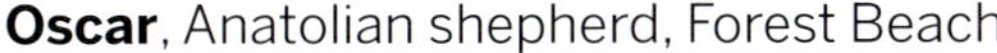

Oscar, Anatolian shepherd, Forest Beach

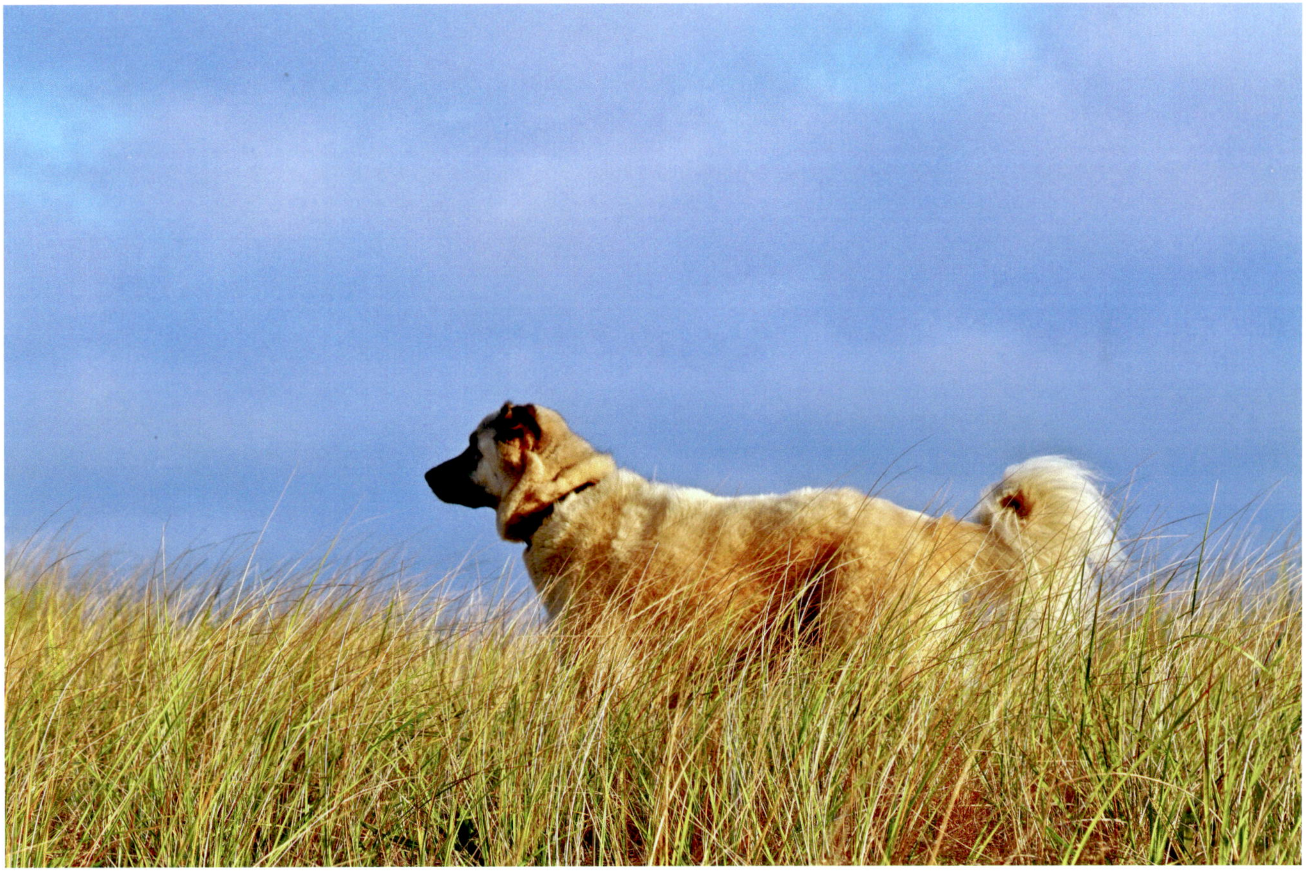

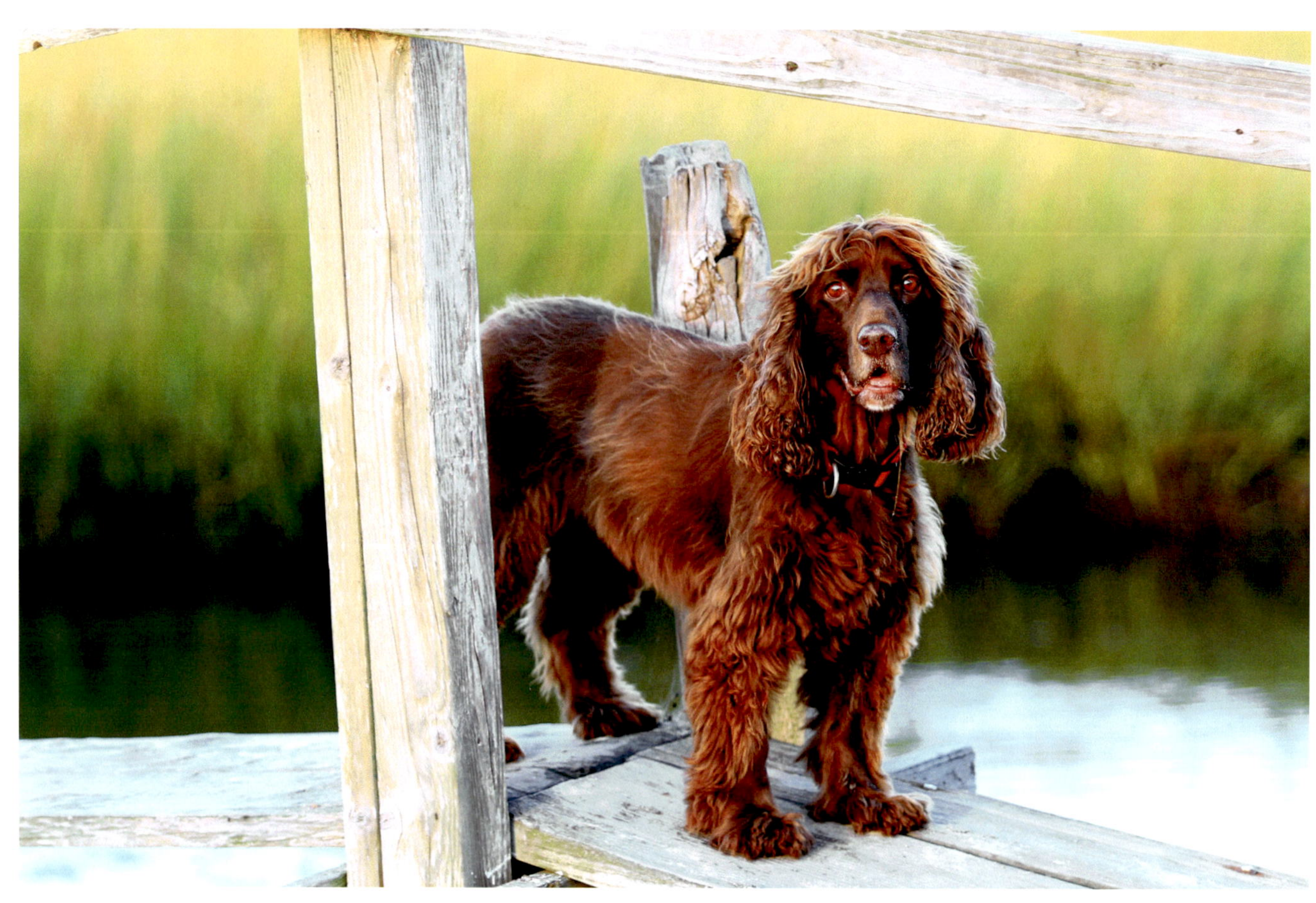

Lola, Field spaniel, Red River Beach

Knuckles, boxer

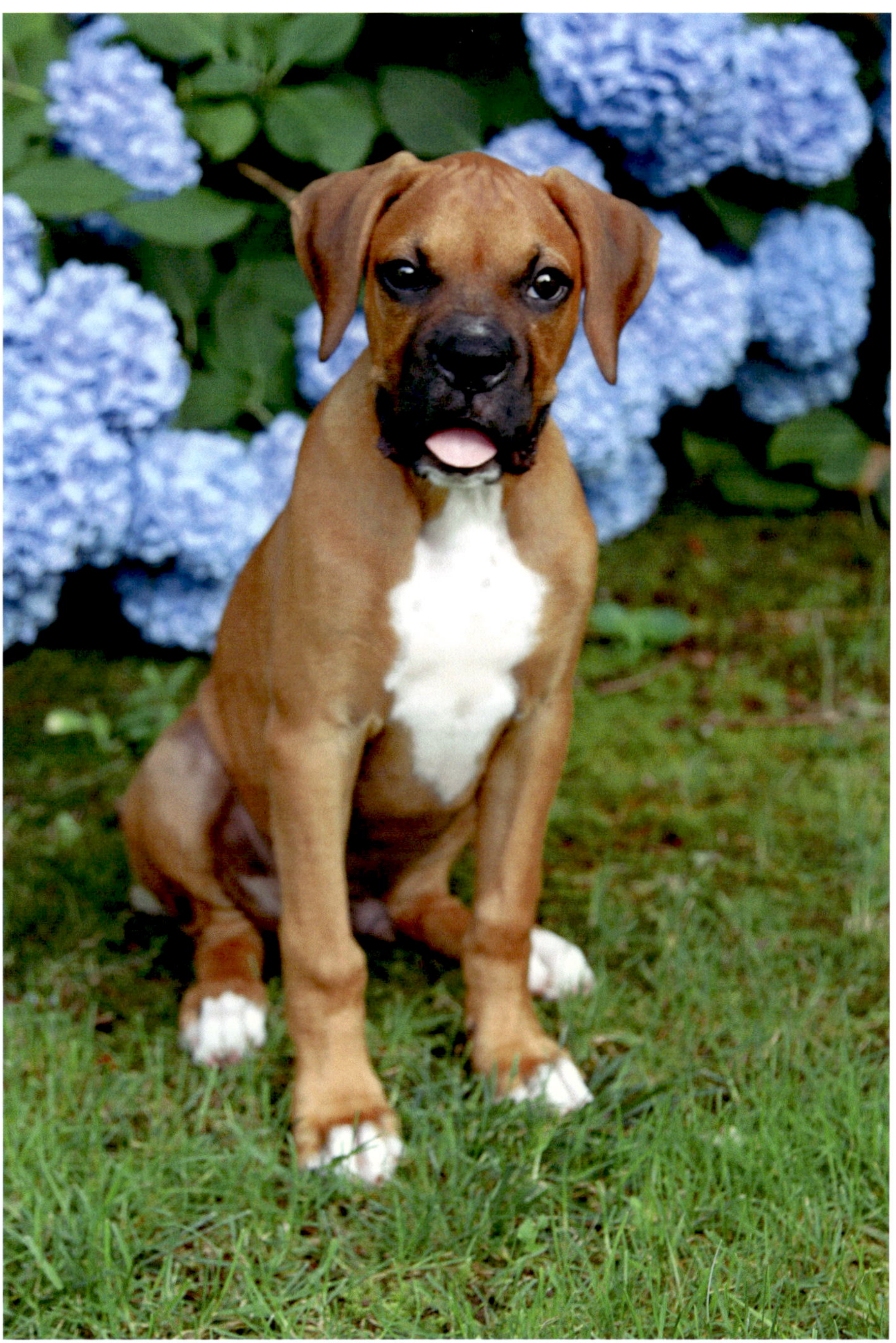

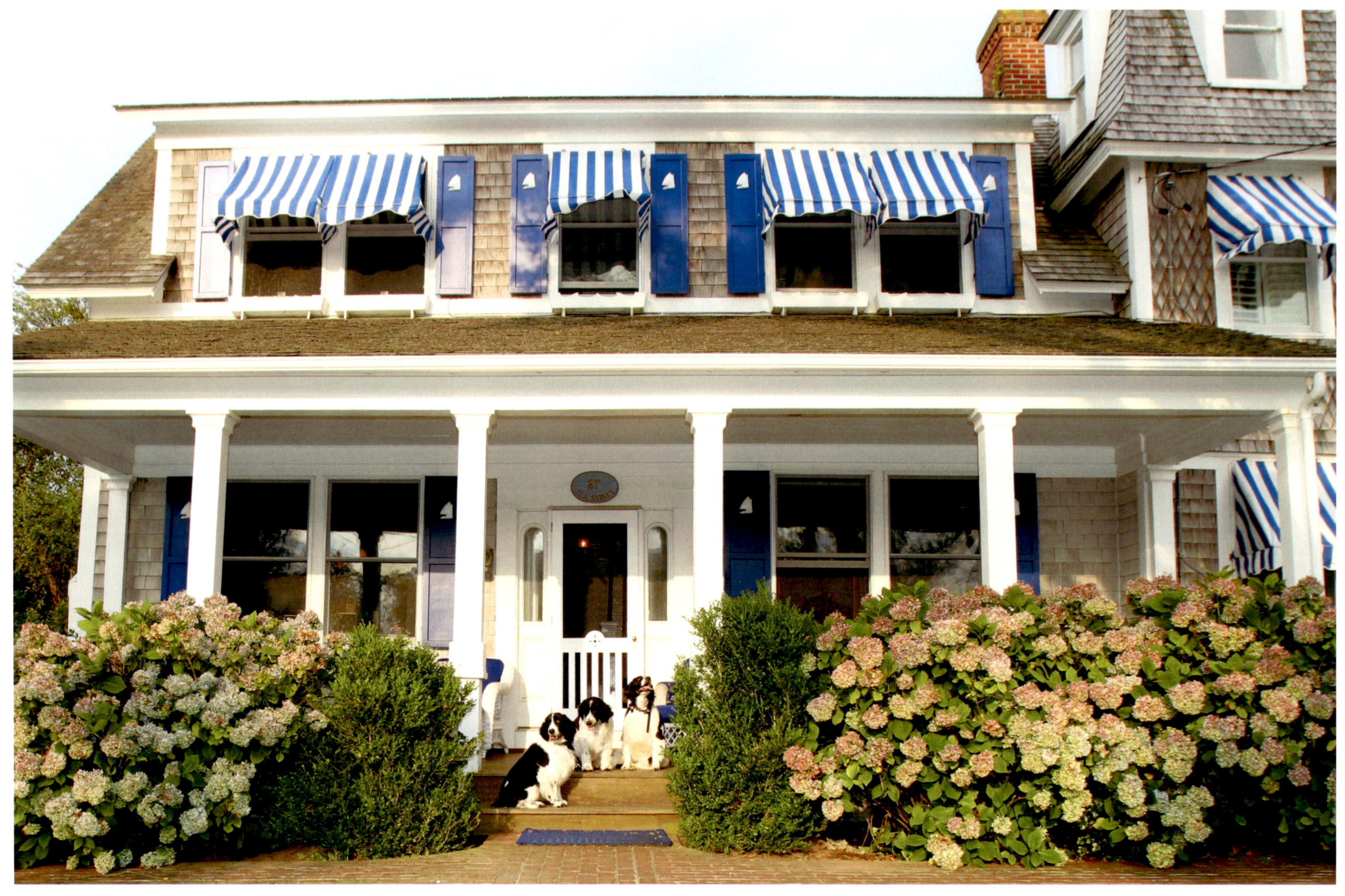

Bridget, **Leah**, and **Bella**, springer spaniels

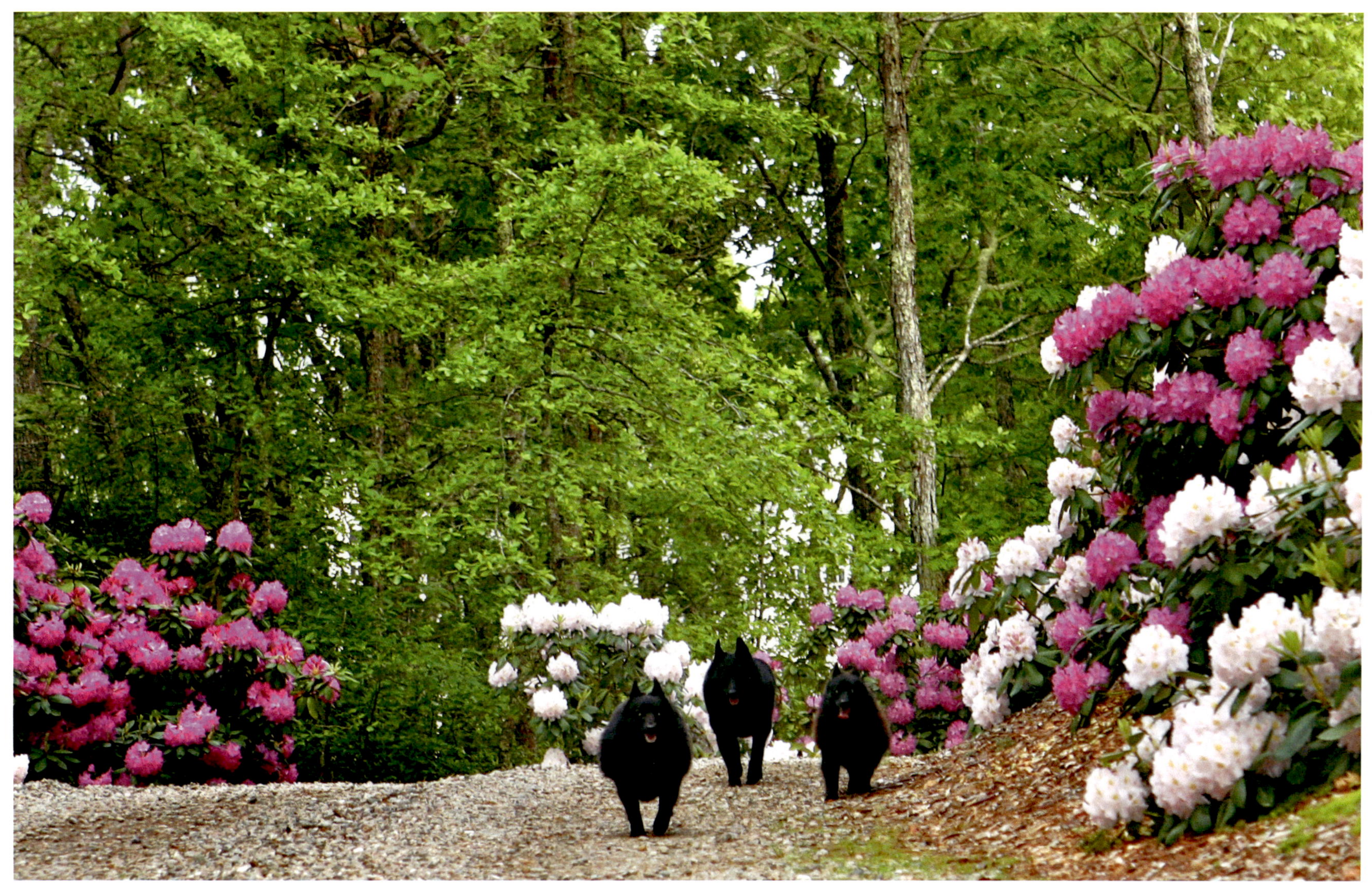

Billy, **Bobbi**, and **Freddi**, schipperkes

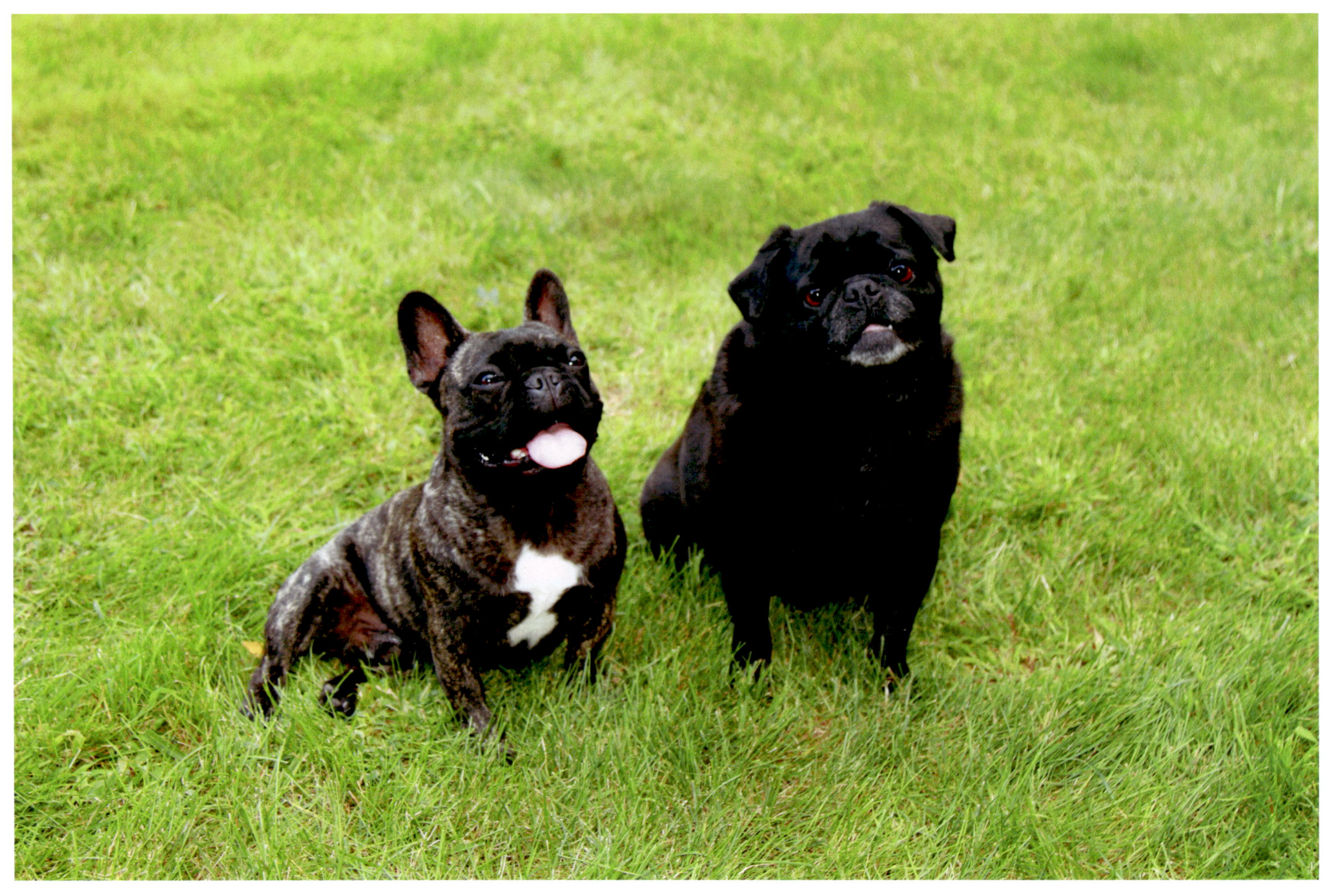

Bentley, French bulldog, and **Nelson**, pug

Dogs are great. Bad dogs, if you can really call them that, are perhaps the greatest of them all.

—John Grogan,
Marley and Me

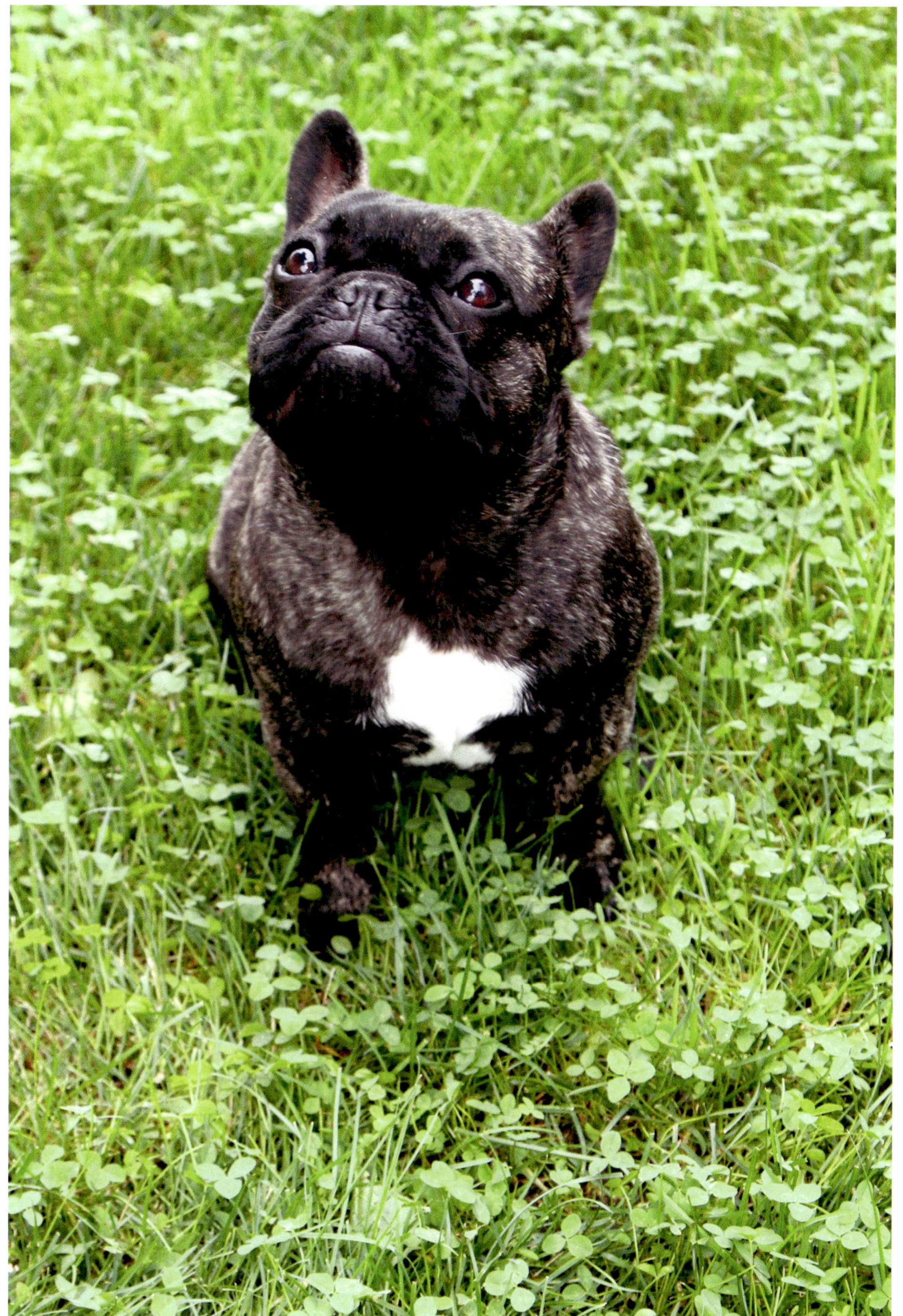

Bentley

Pandit, wirehaired Parson Russell terrier

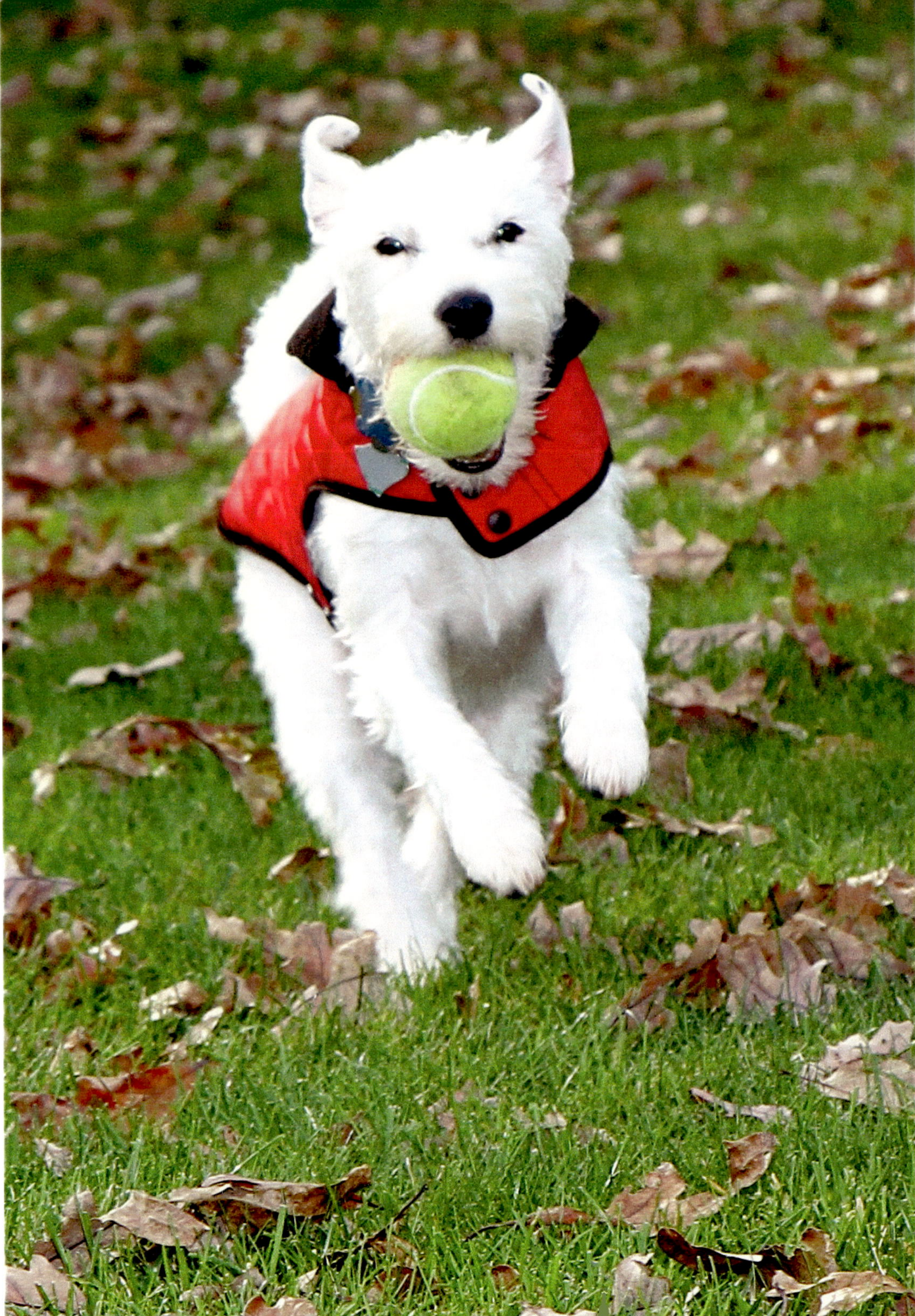

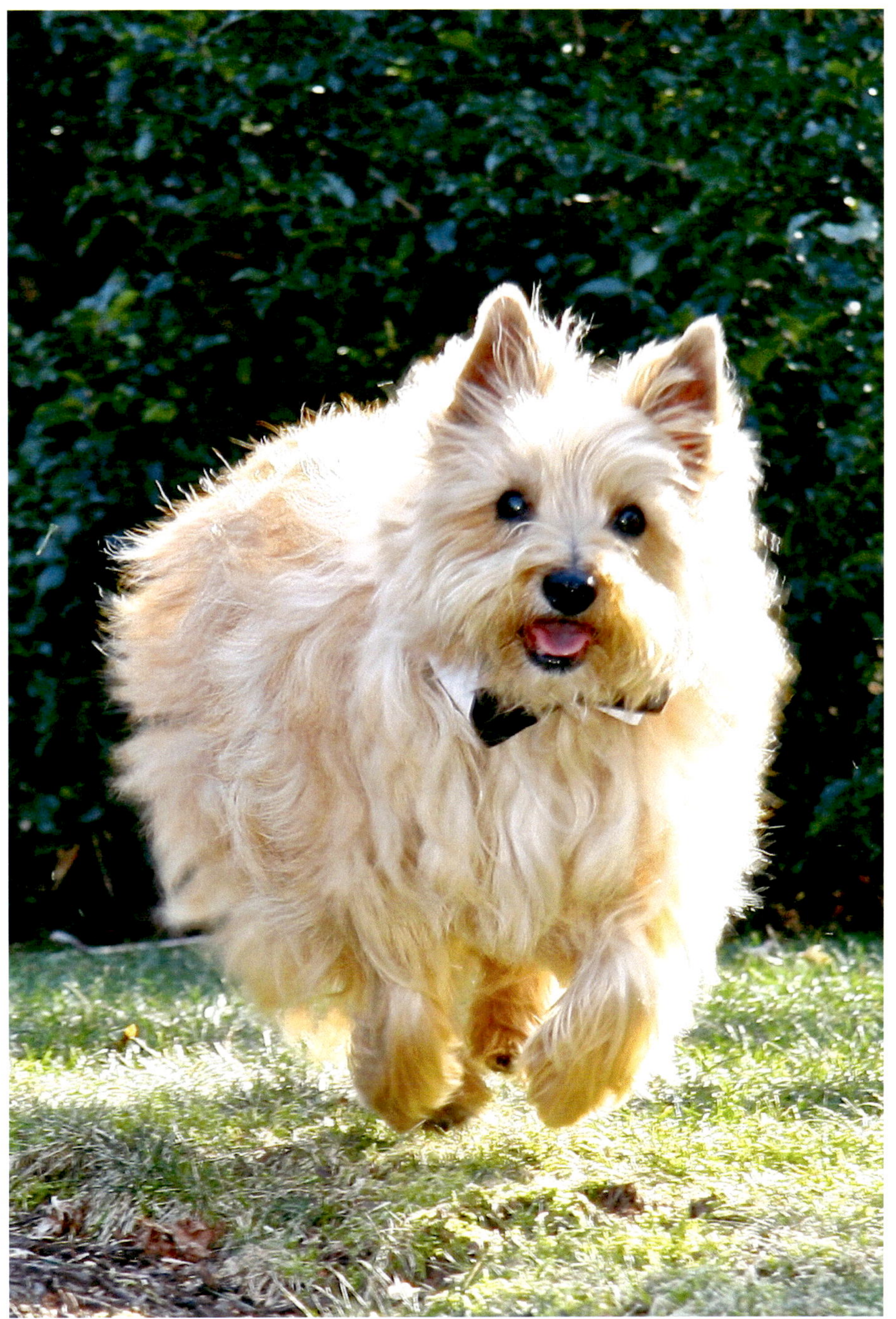

Patrick, Cairn terrier

Her white hair was long and silky, blinding in sunlight, the orange mask on both eyes matched by orange freckles that looked as if she had been dappled by curry. The eyes, shiny brown, seemed to know aforehand anything that came into my head. They looked back wherever I looked.

— Dave Smith, *How I Came to Live with Bird Dogs*

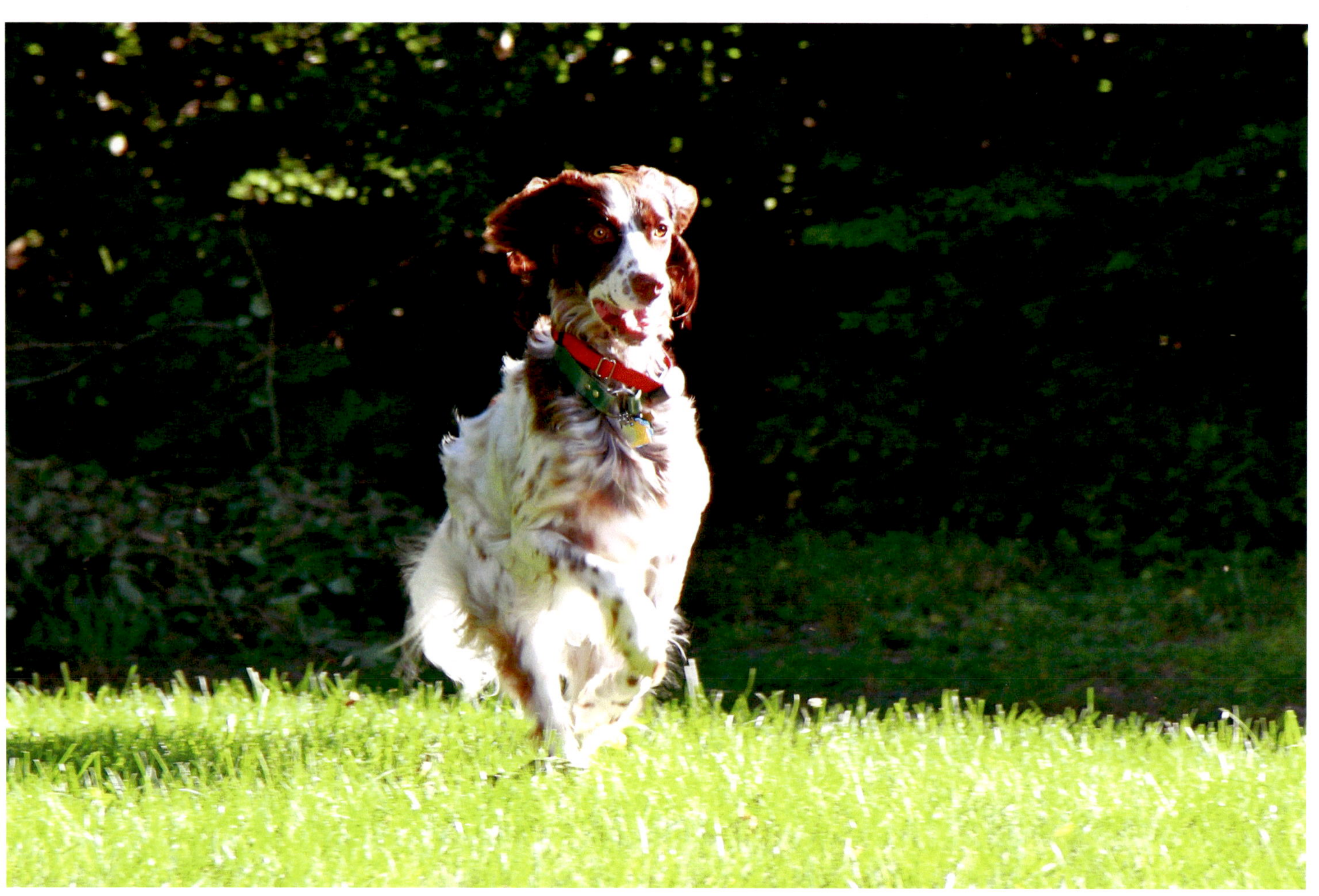

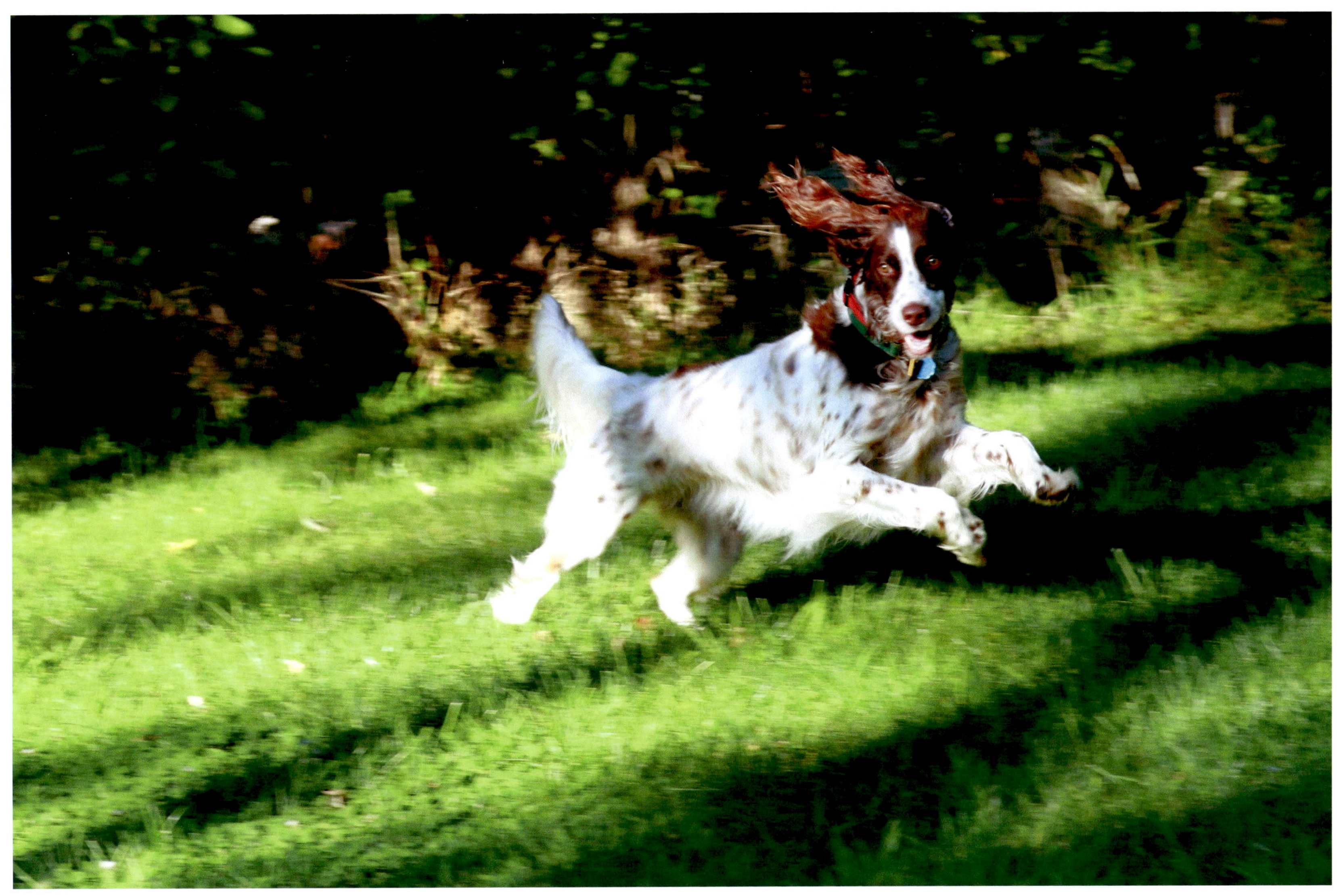

LuLu, Llewellin setter

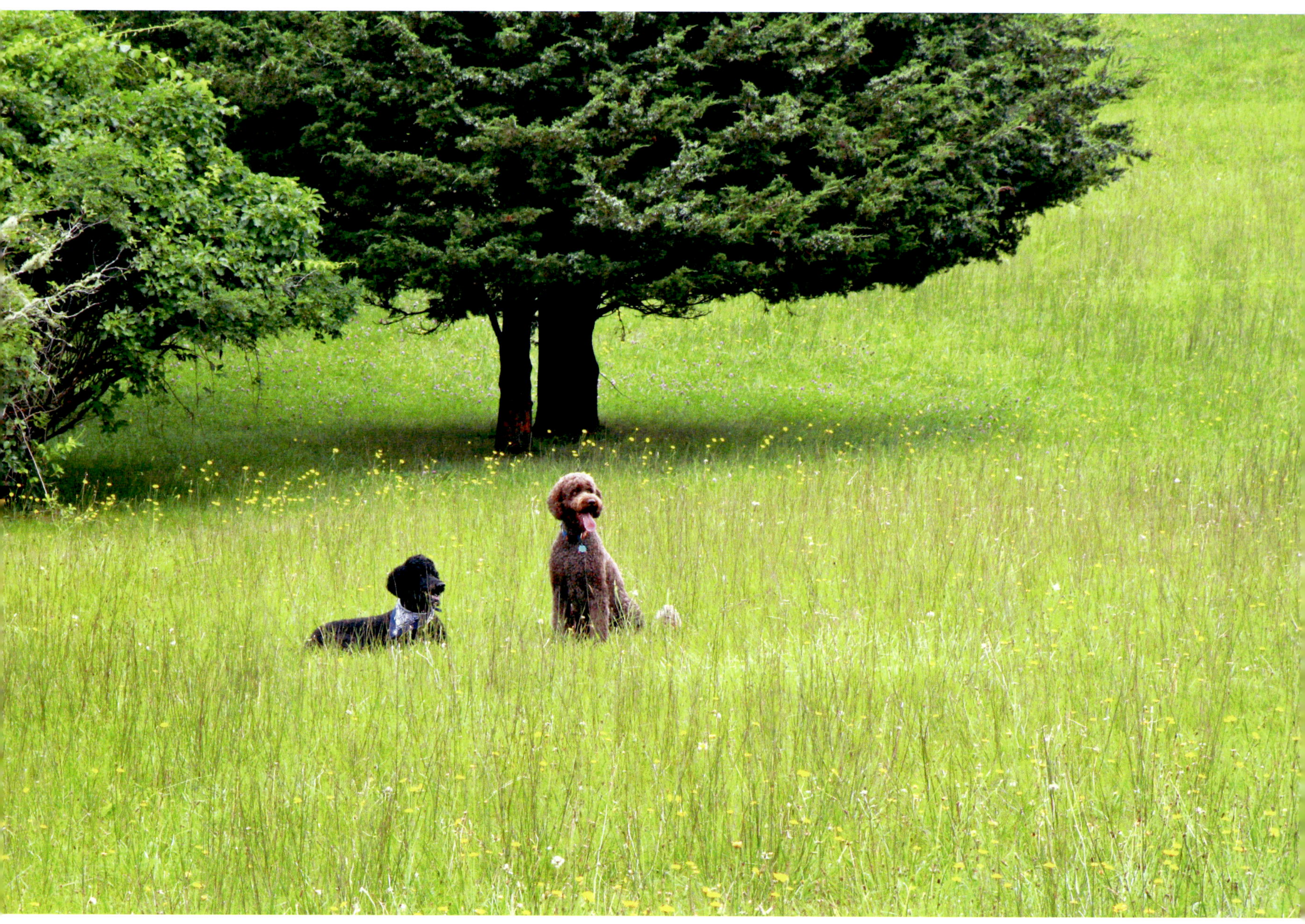

Bandit, standard poodle, and **Wilbur**, Australian labradoodle (opposite)

Wilbur (right)

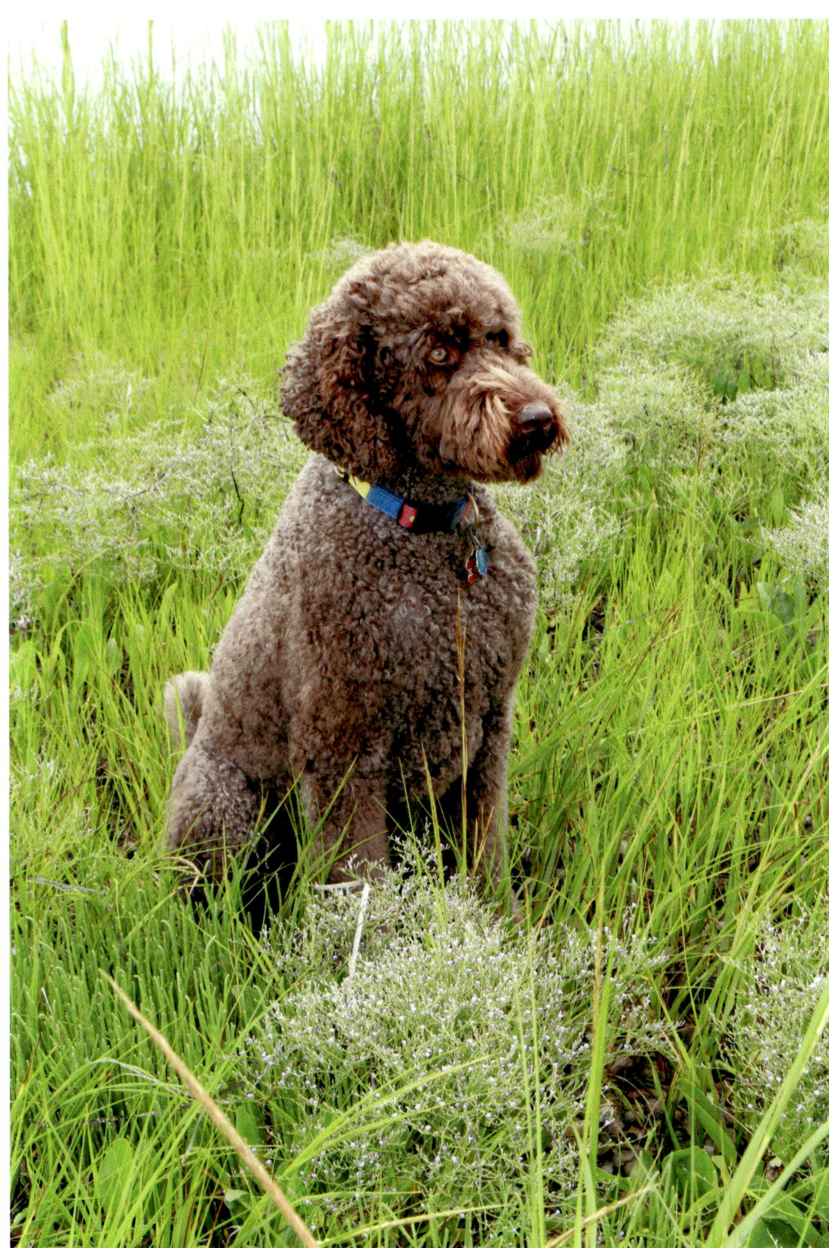

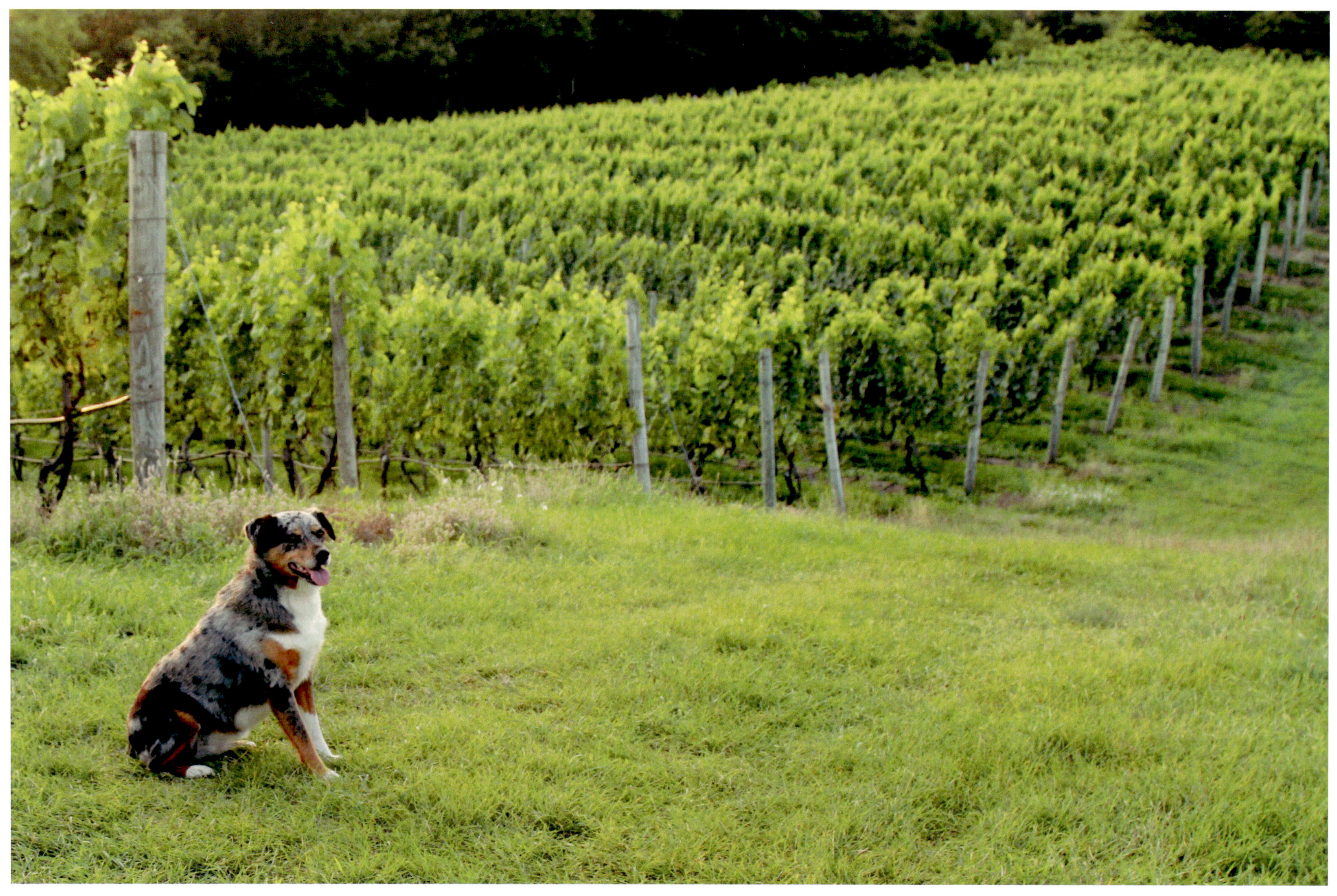

Shug, miniature Australian shepherd, Truro Vineyard

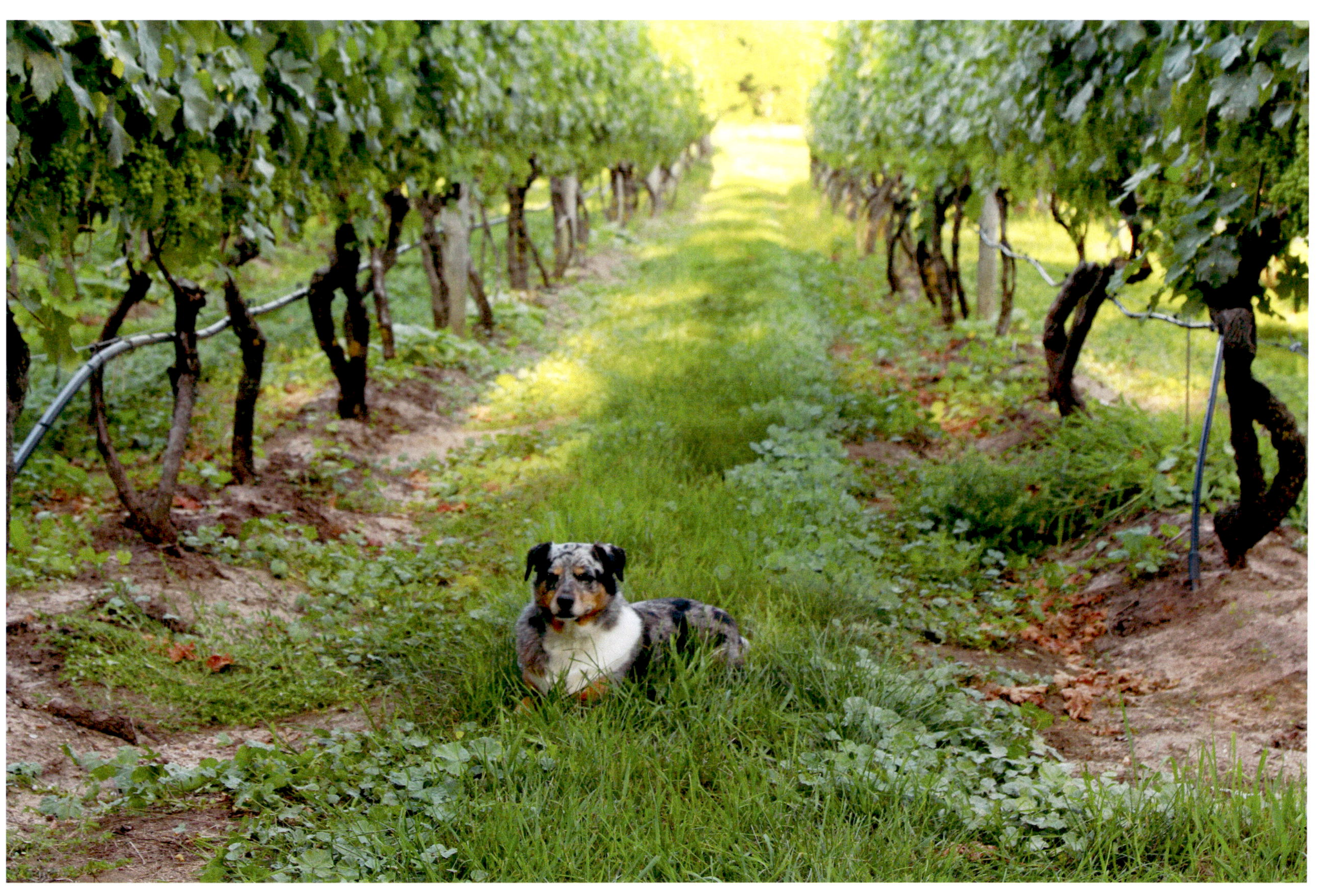

Obie (below); **Obie**, **Sumo**, and **Gingko** (bottom), Labrador retrievers, Cape Cod Lavender Farm

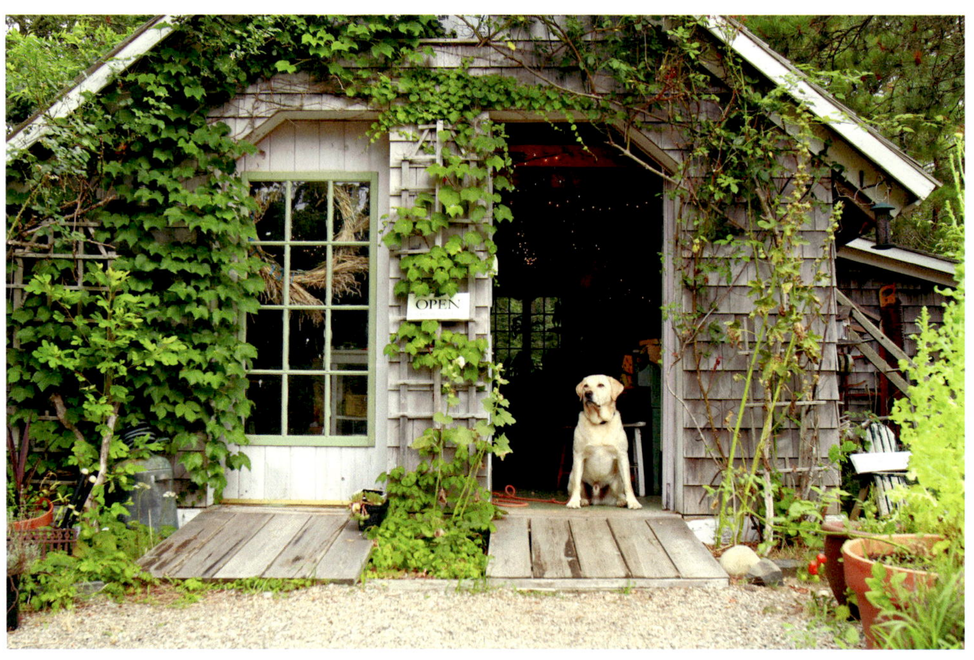

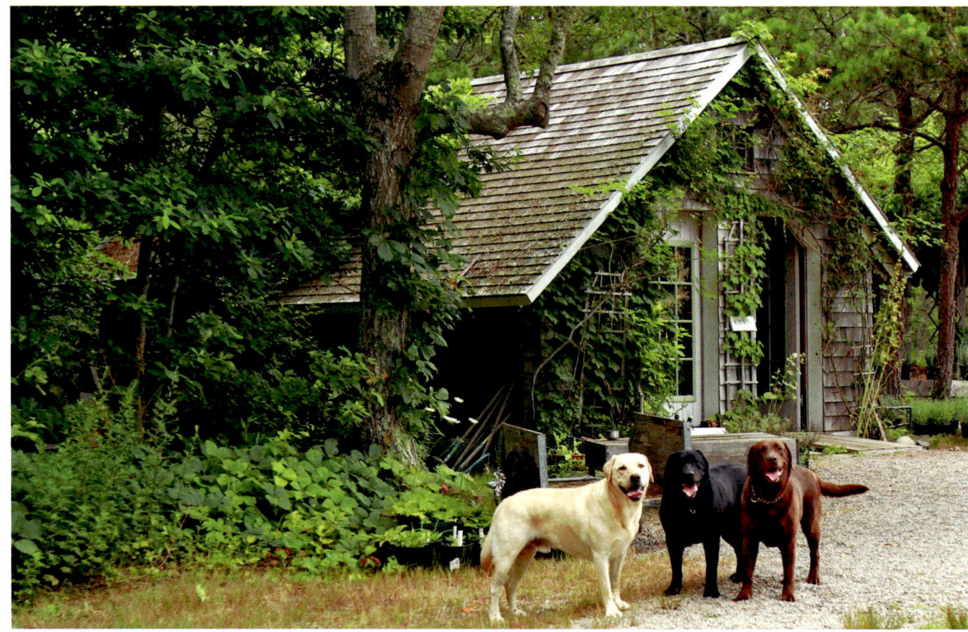

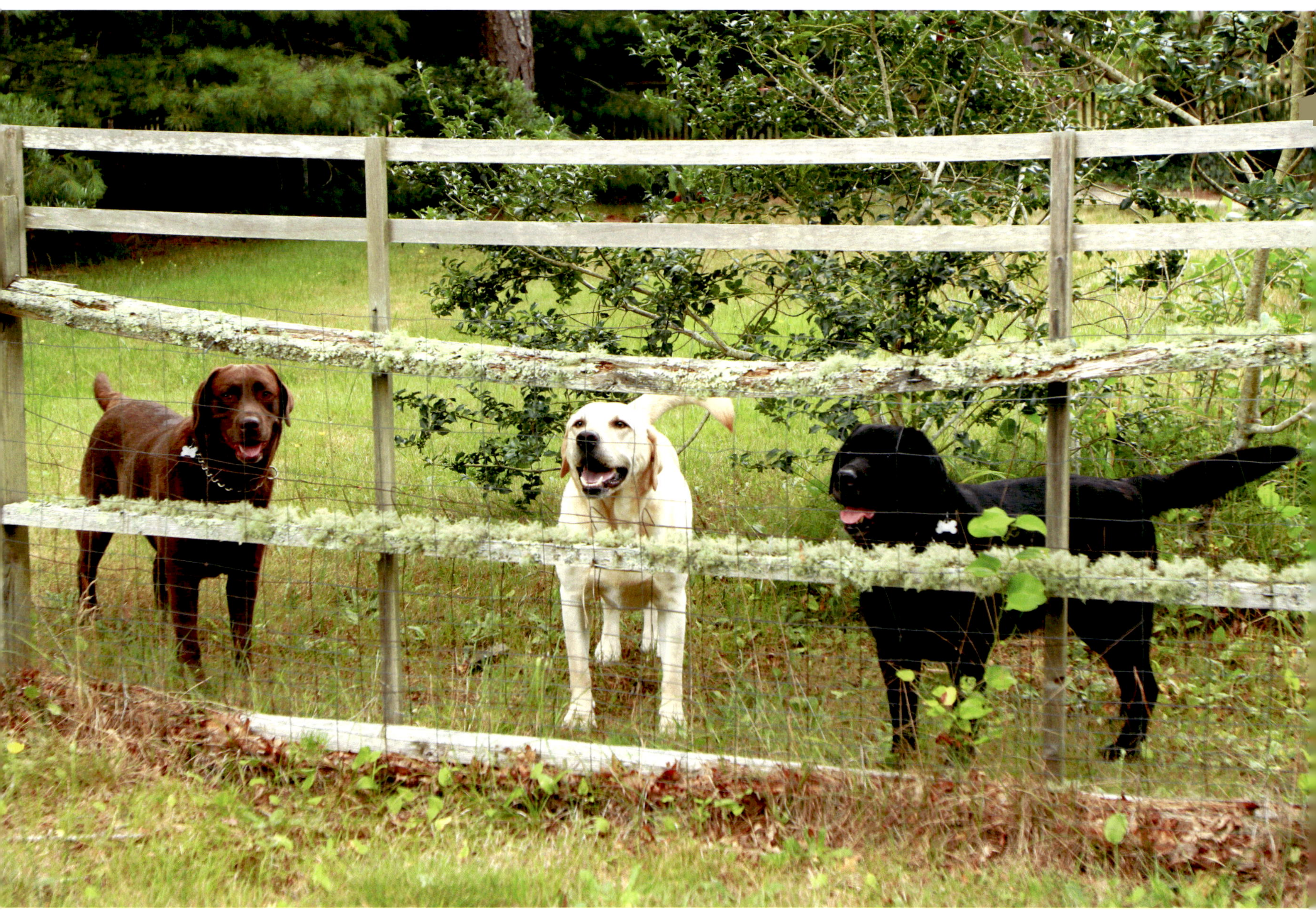

Gingko, **Obie**, and **Sumo**

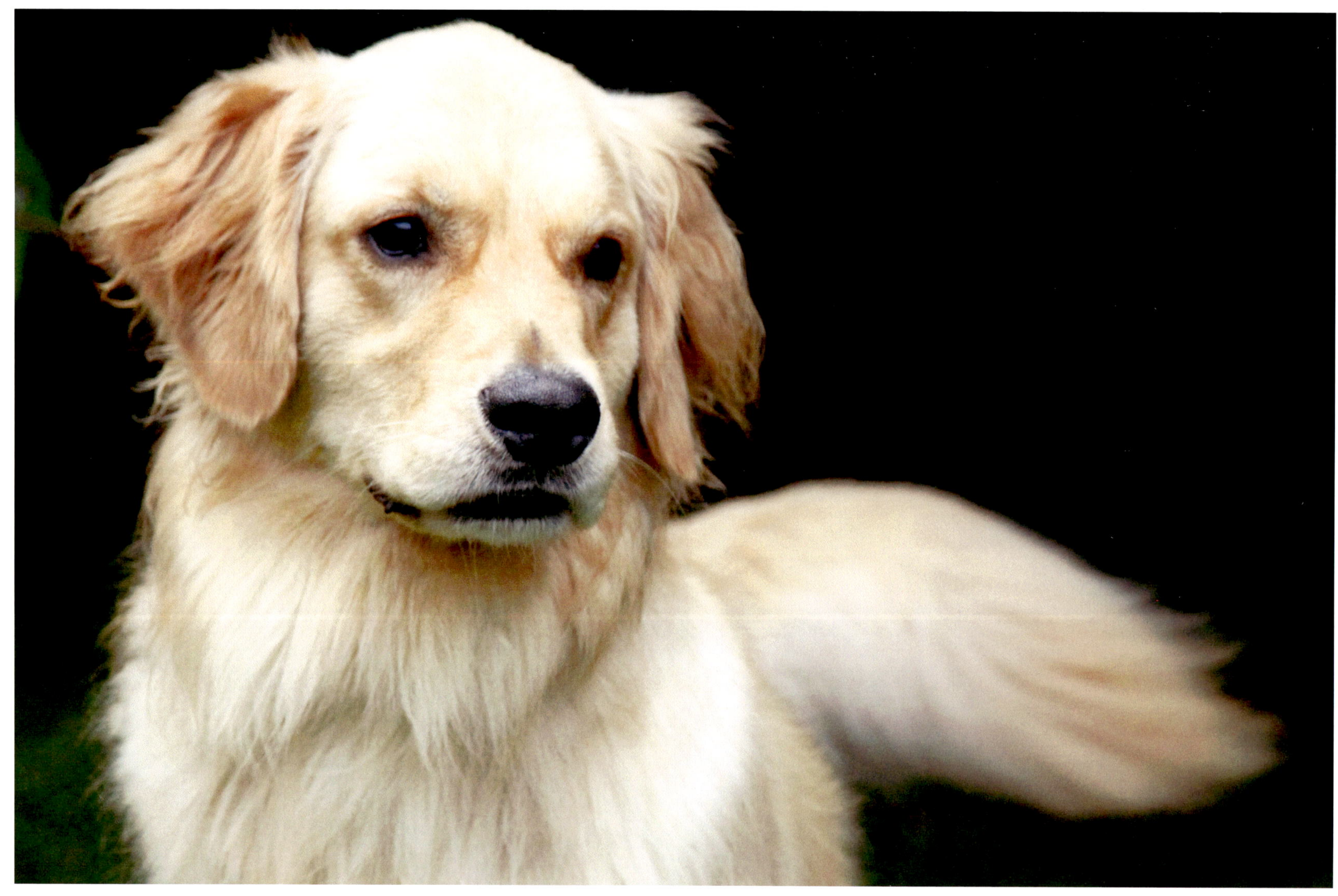

Louie, golden retriever

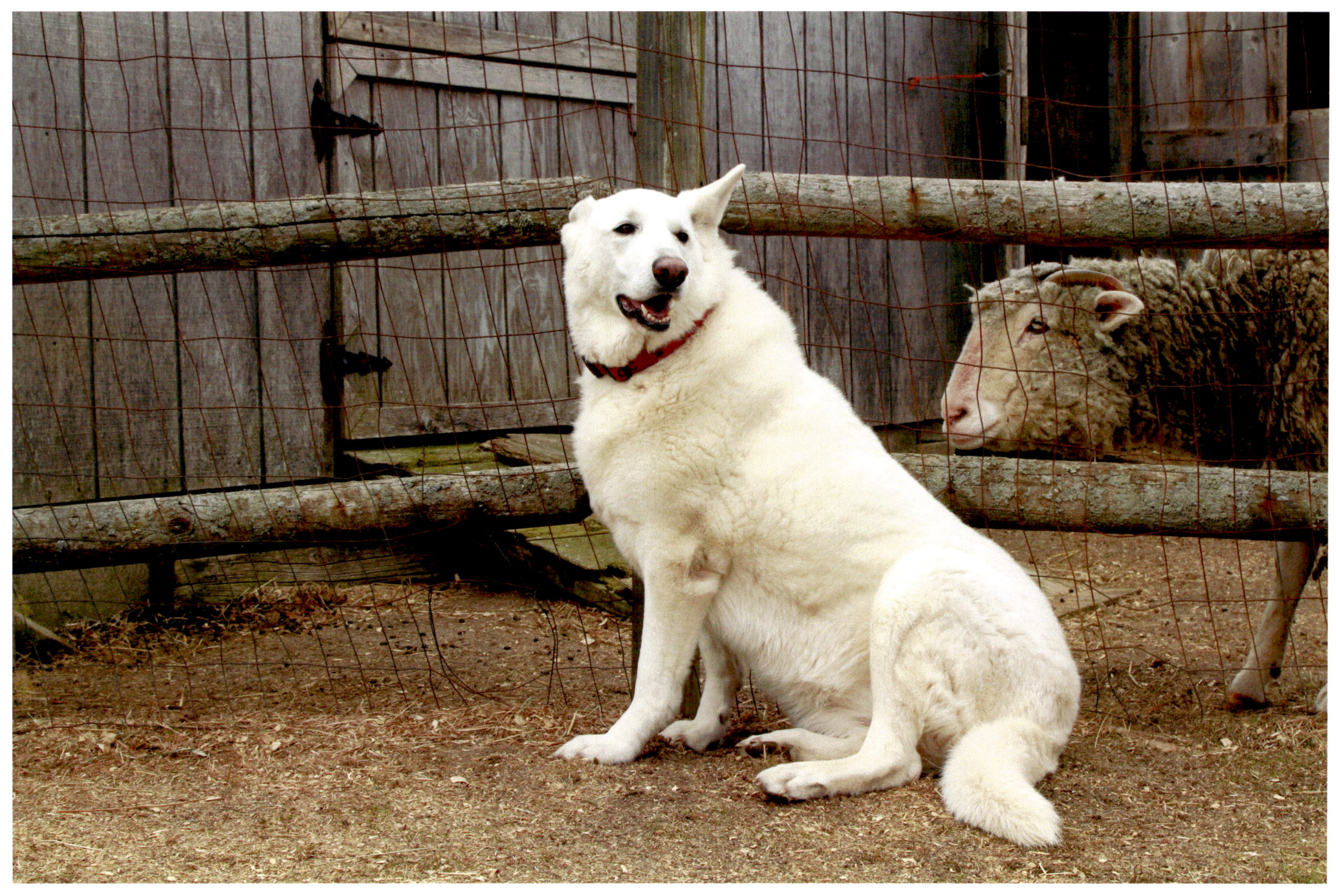

Crystal, white shepherd, South Chatham Farm

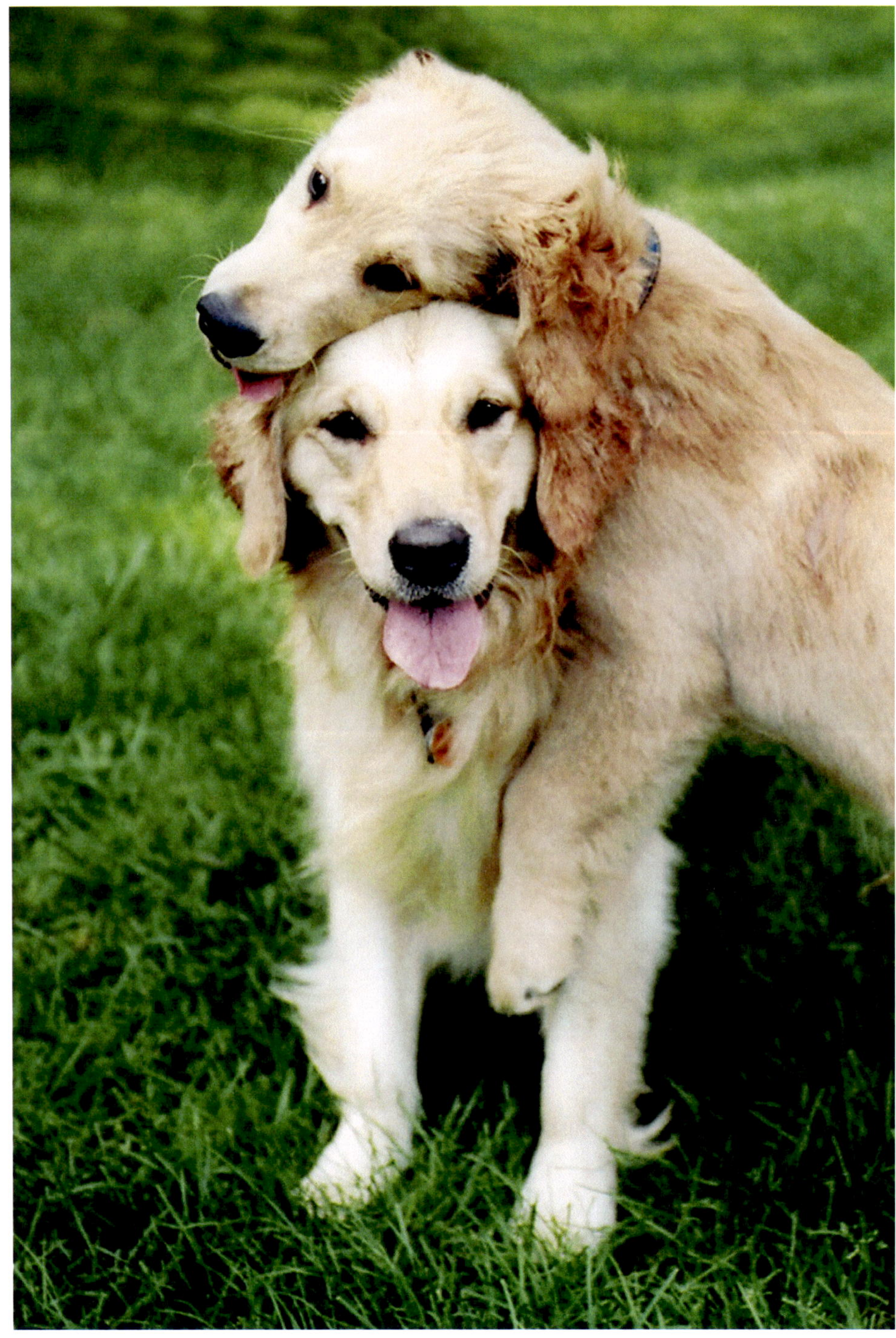

Otis and **Cassie**, golden retrievers

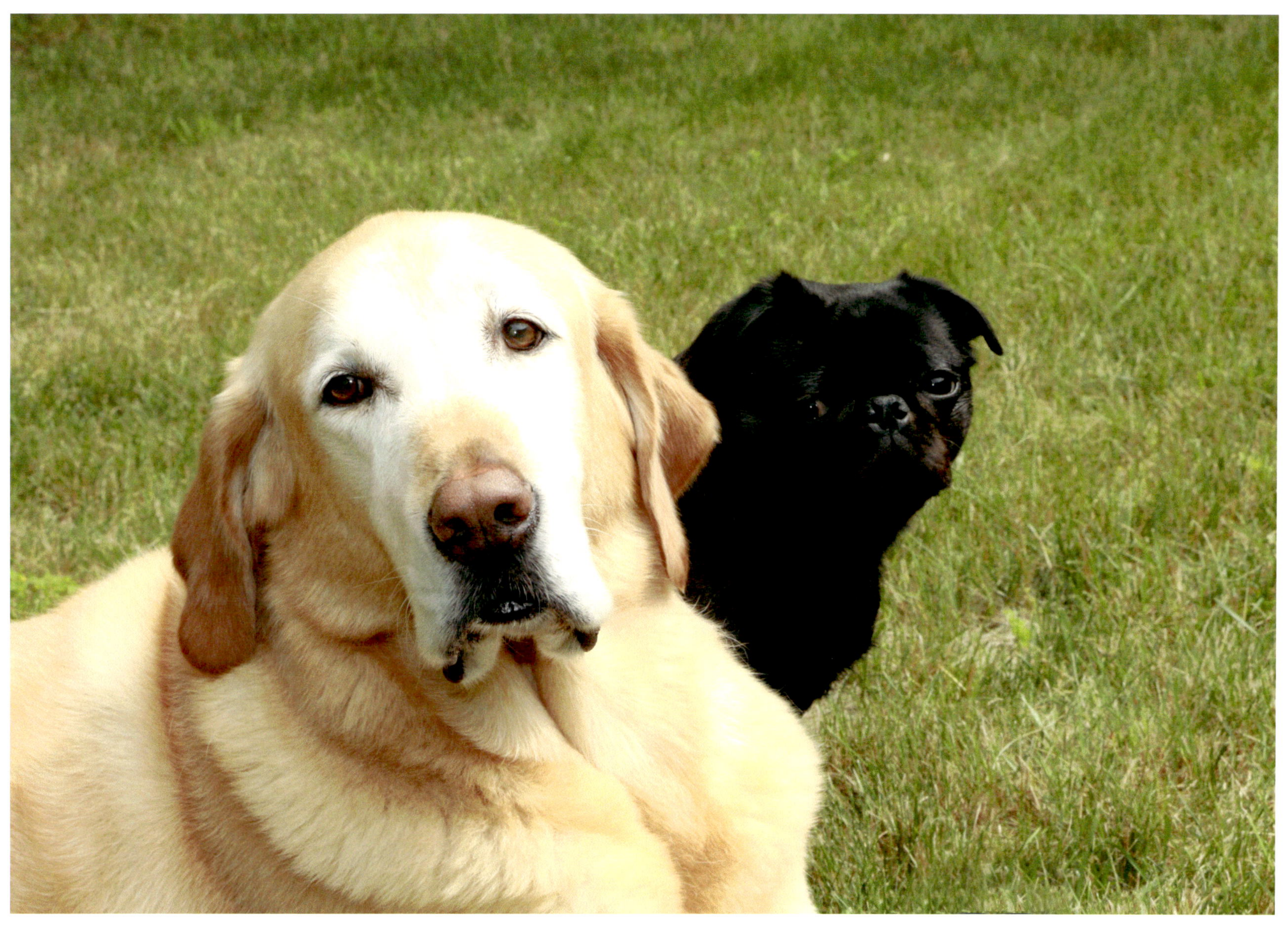

Jack, golden retriever mix, and **Olive**, pug

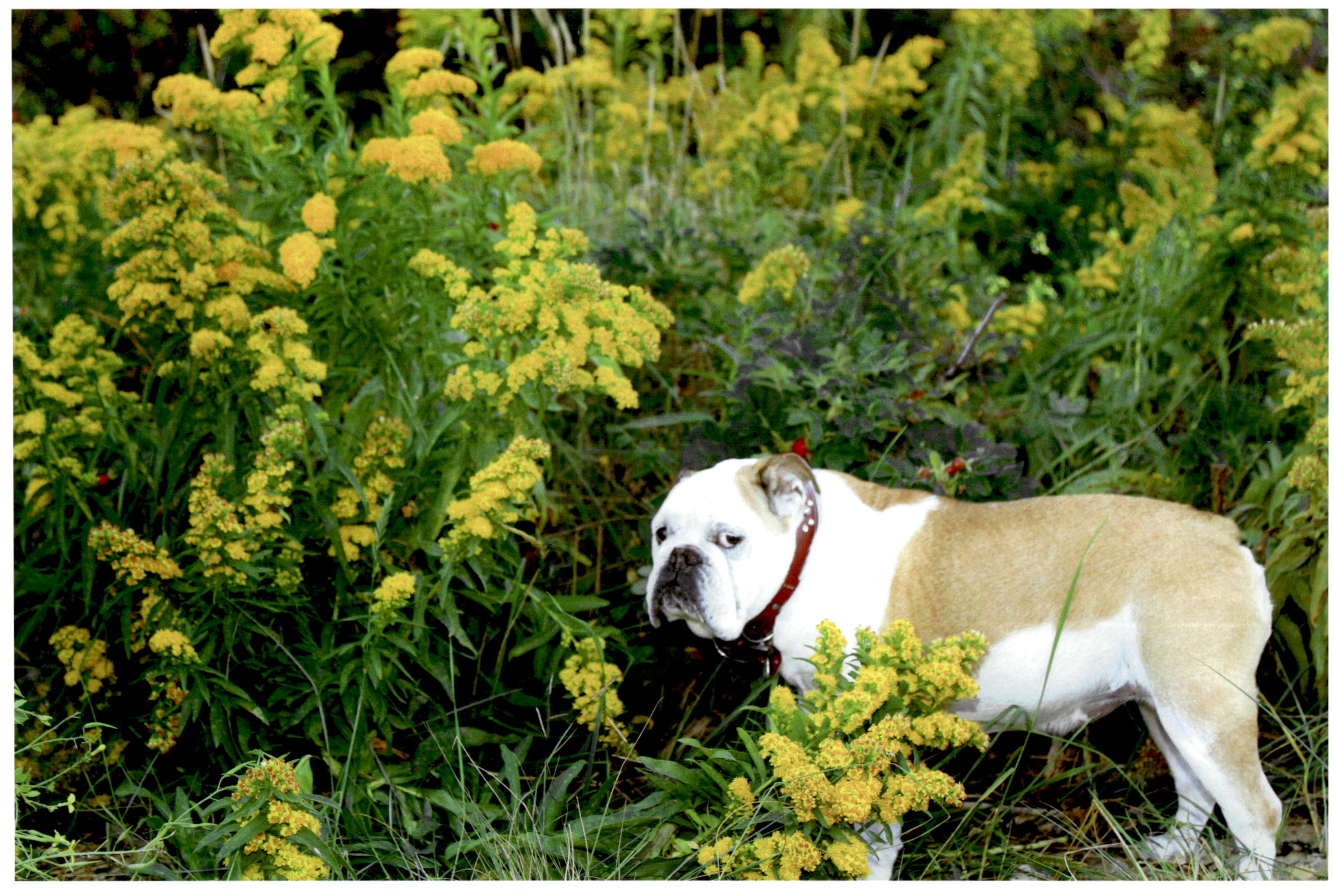

Bellarossa (above), bulldog

Olive (opposite), pug

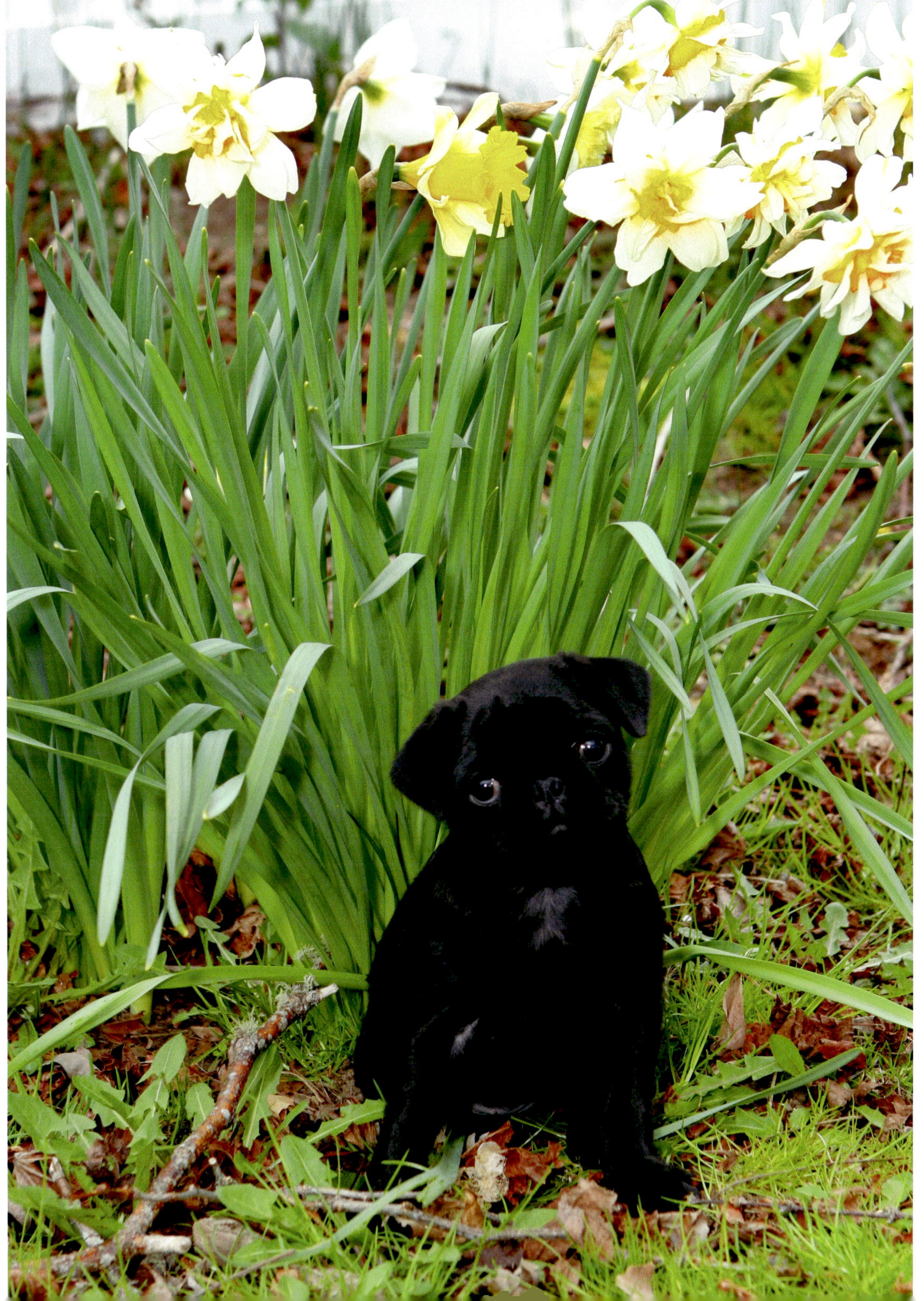

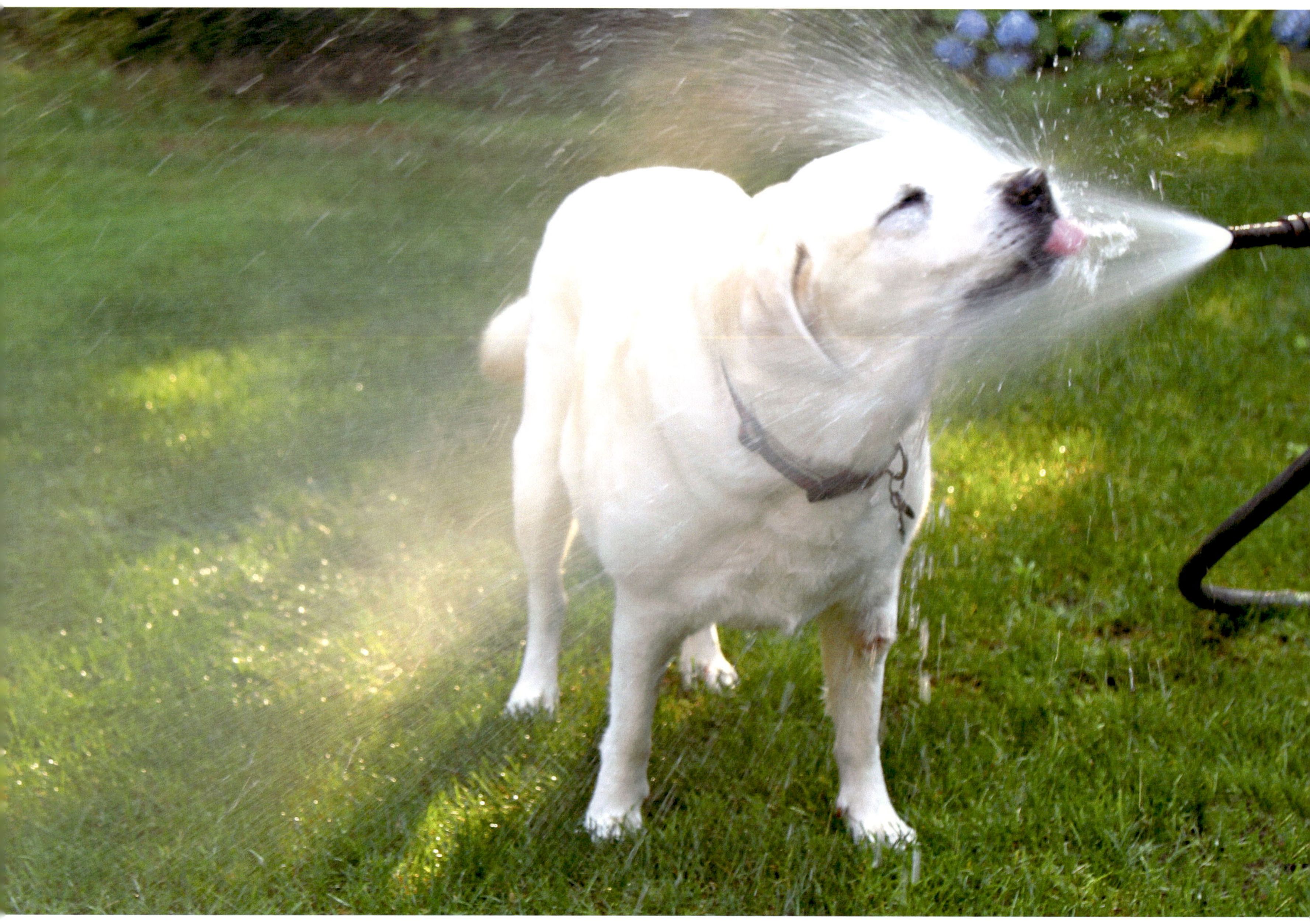

Seve, Labrador retriever

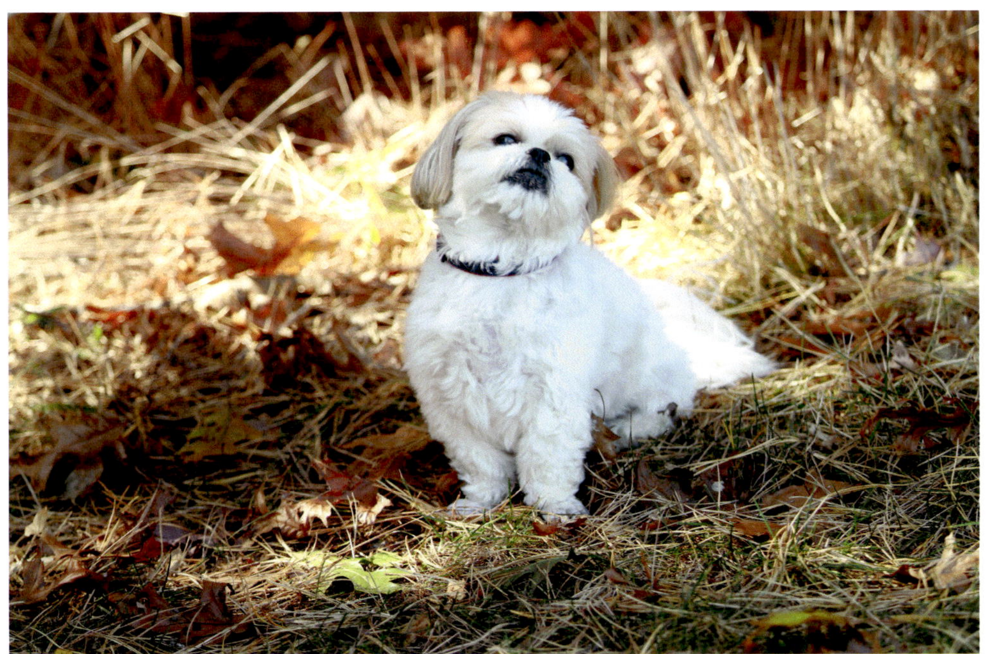

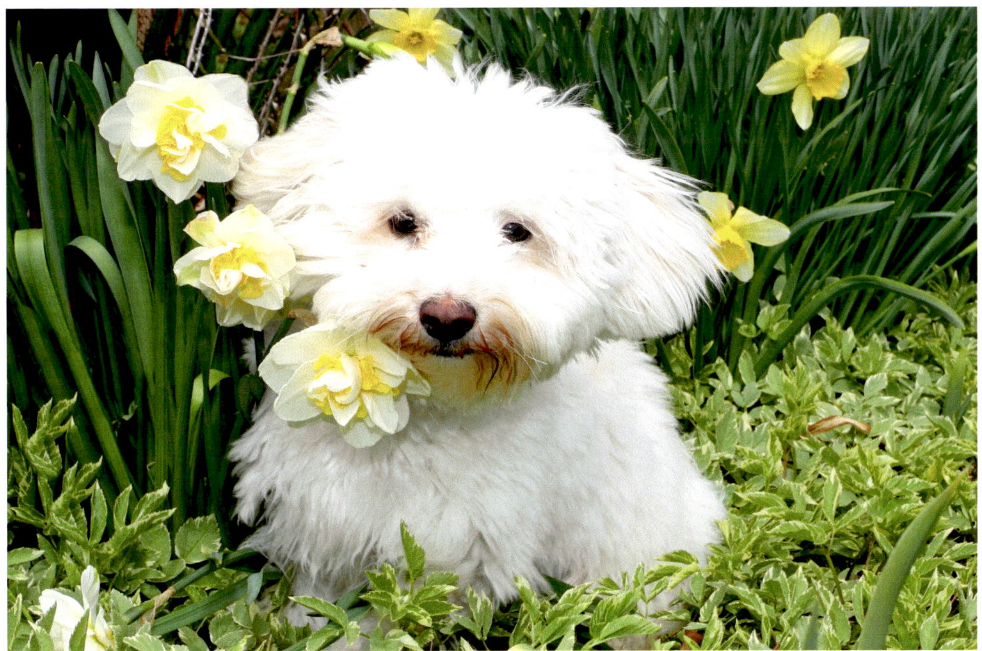

Zoe (top), shih tzu; **Tucker** (above), Havanese

Sabrina, Cavalier King Charles spaniel

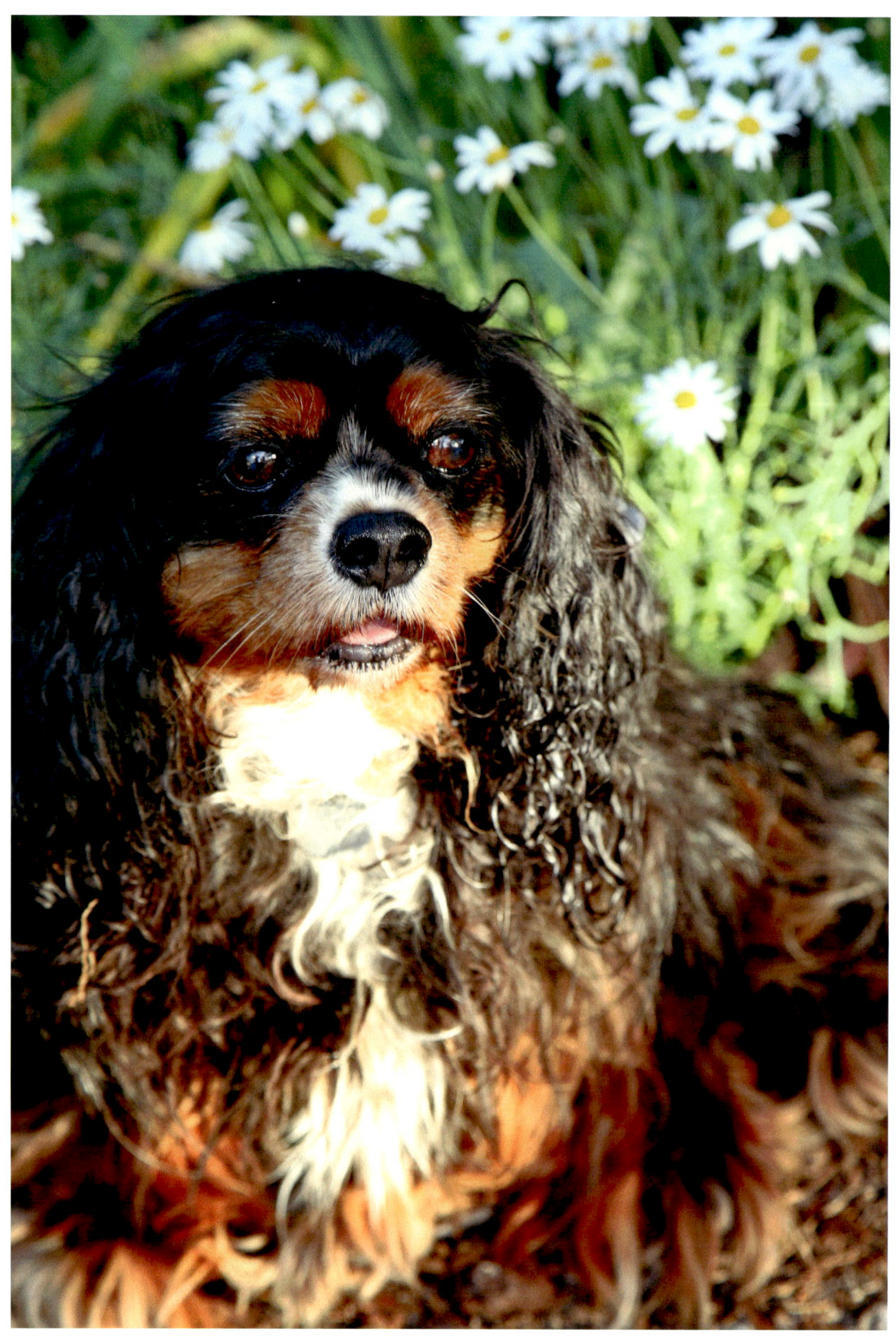

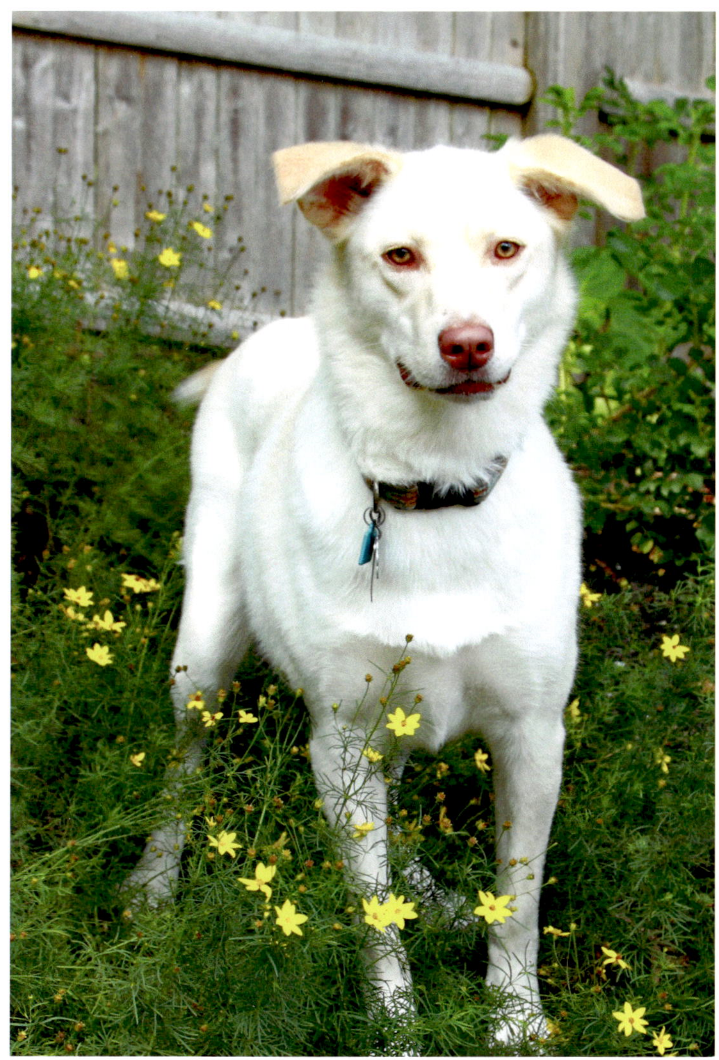

Derby, husky mix

Lacey, collie mix

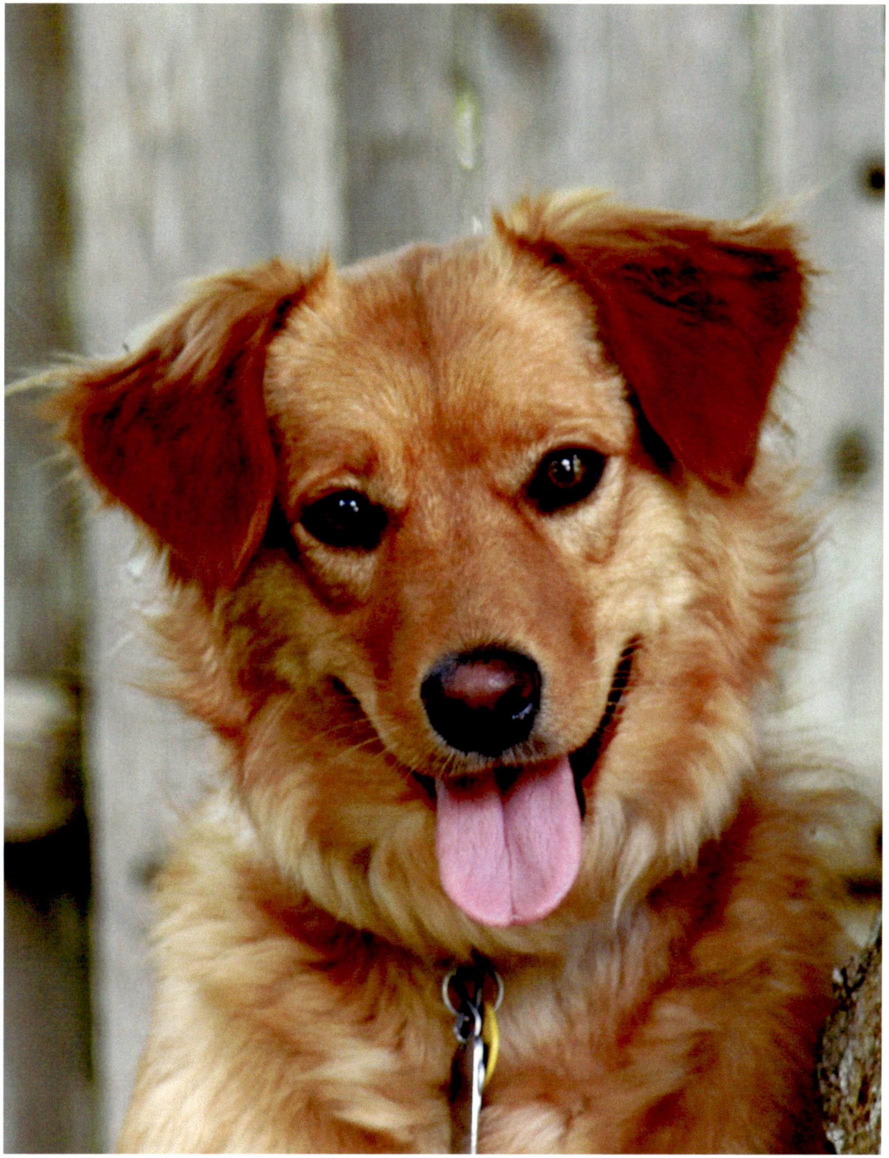

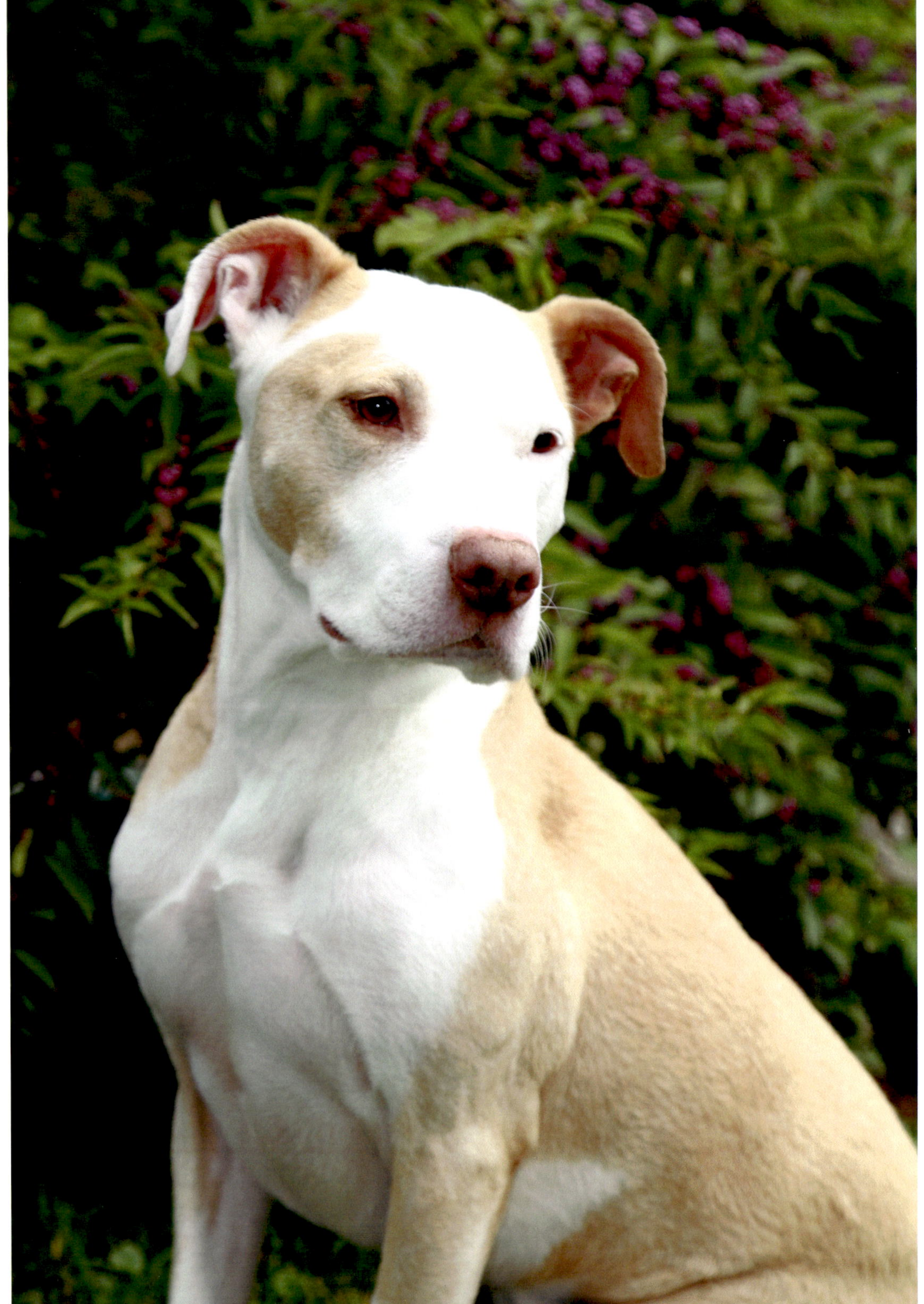

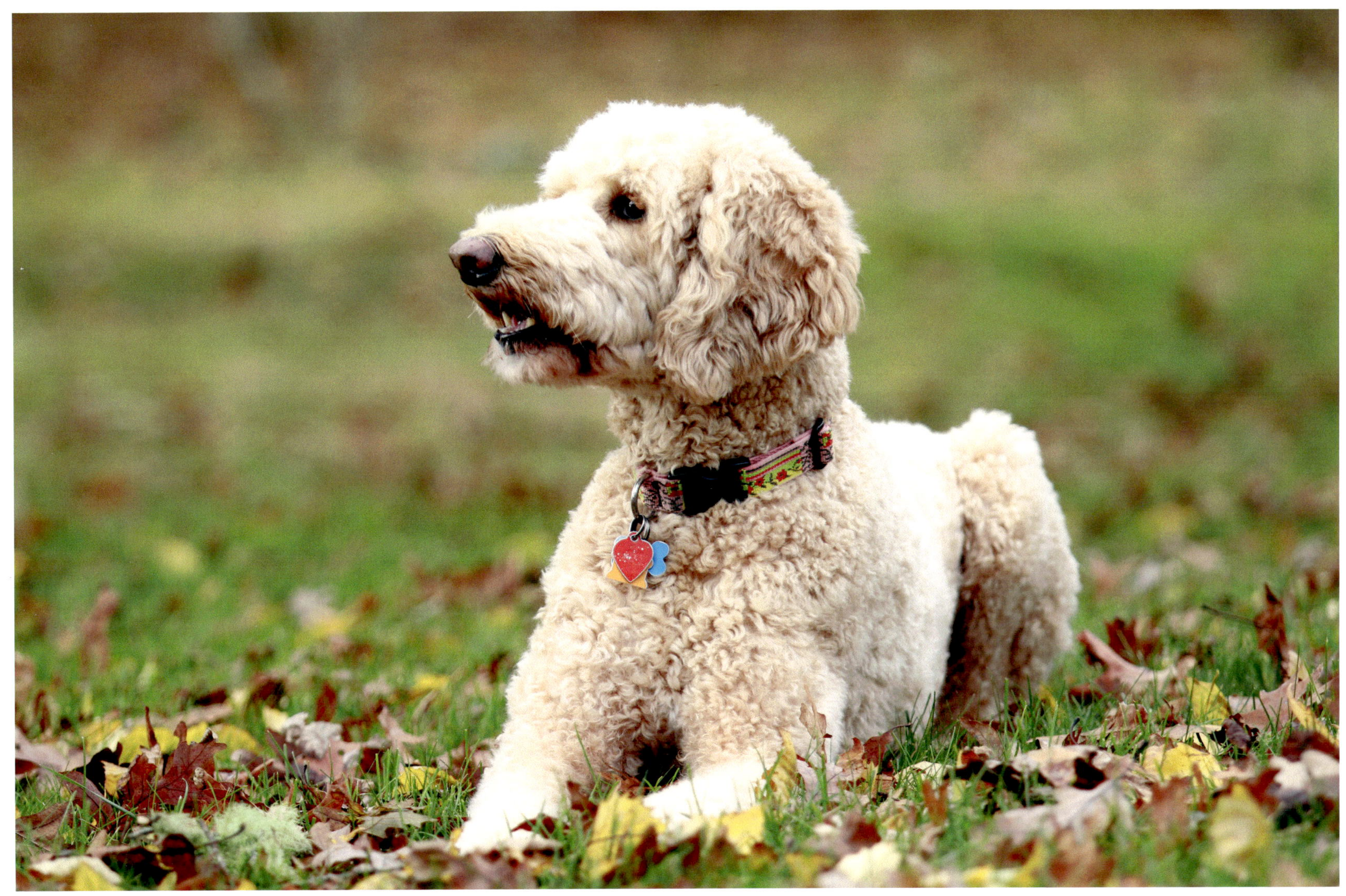

Cortland (above), standard poodle

Tucker (opposite), American Staffordshire terrier mix

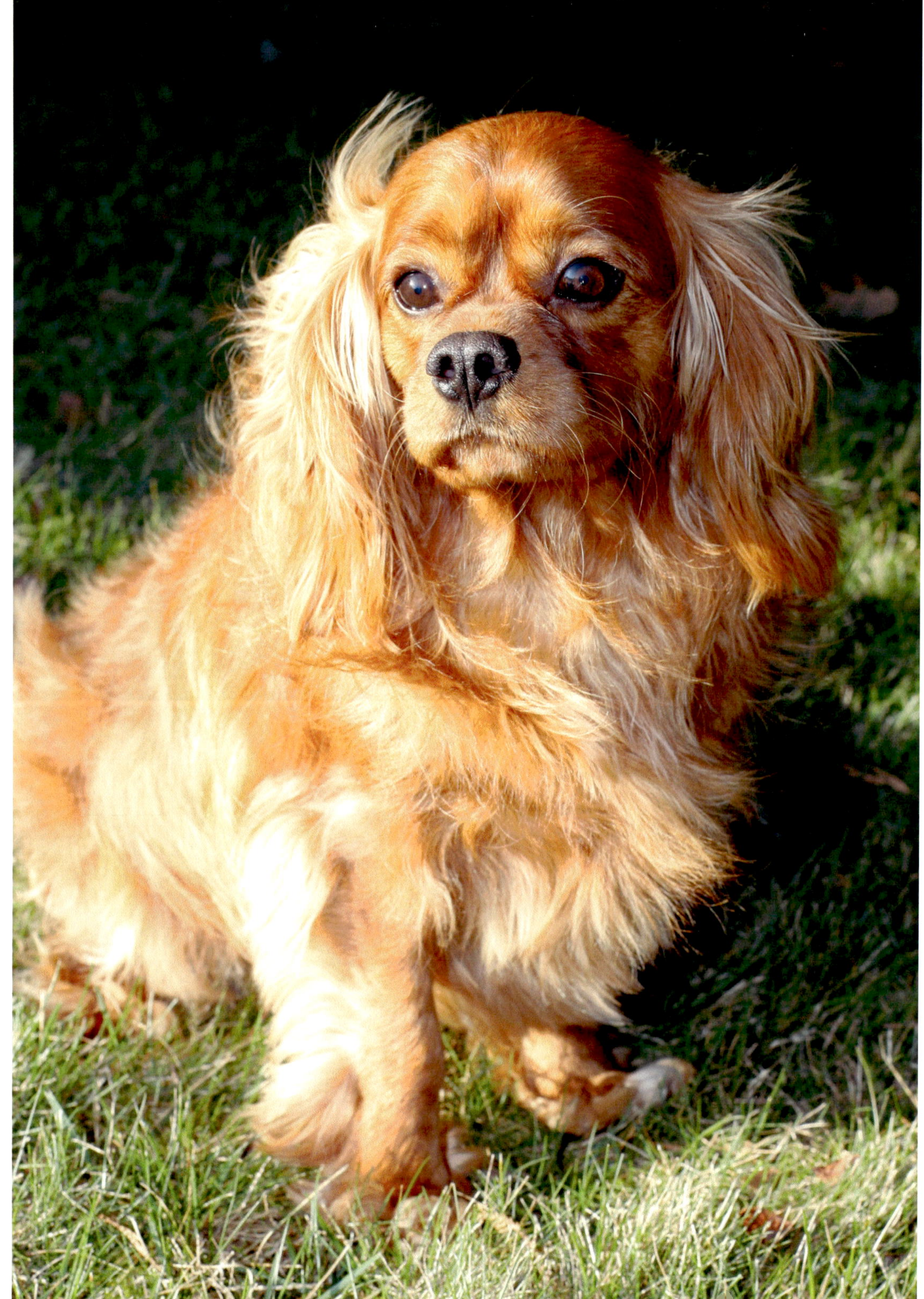

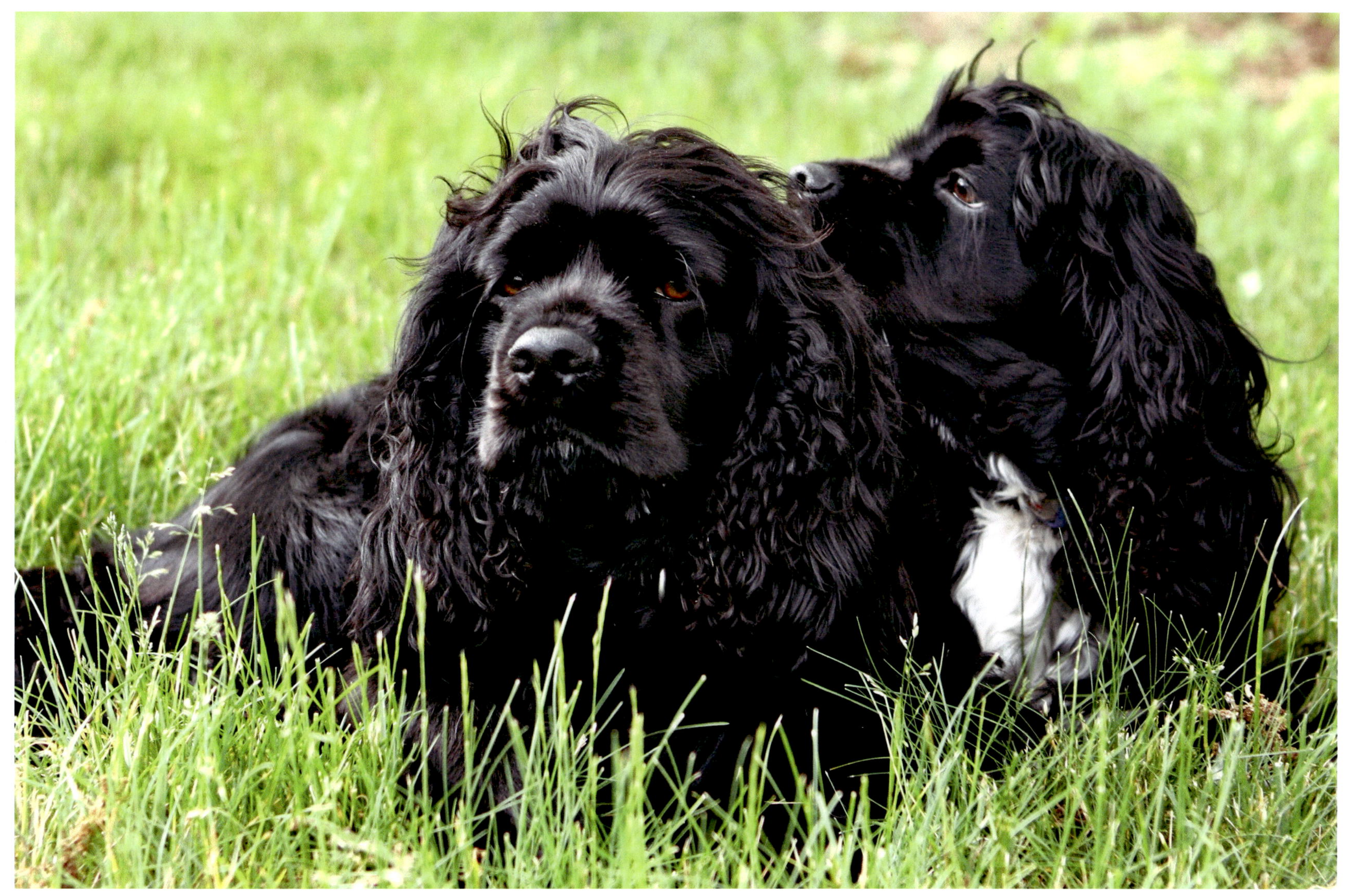

Scout and **Lily** (above), cocker spaniels

Amos (opposite), Cavalier King Charles spaniel

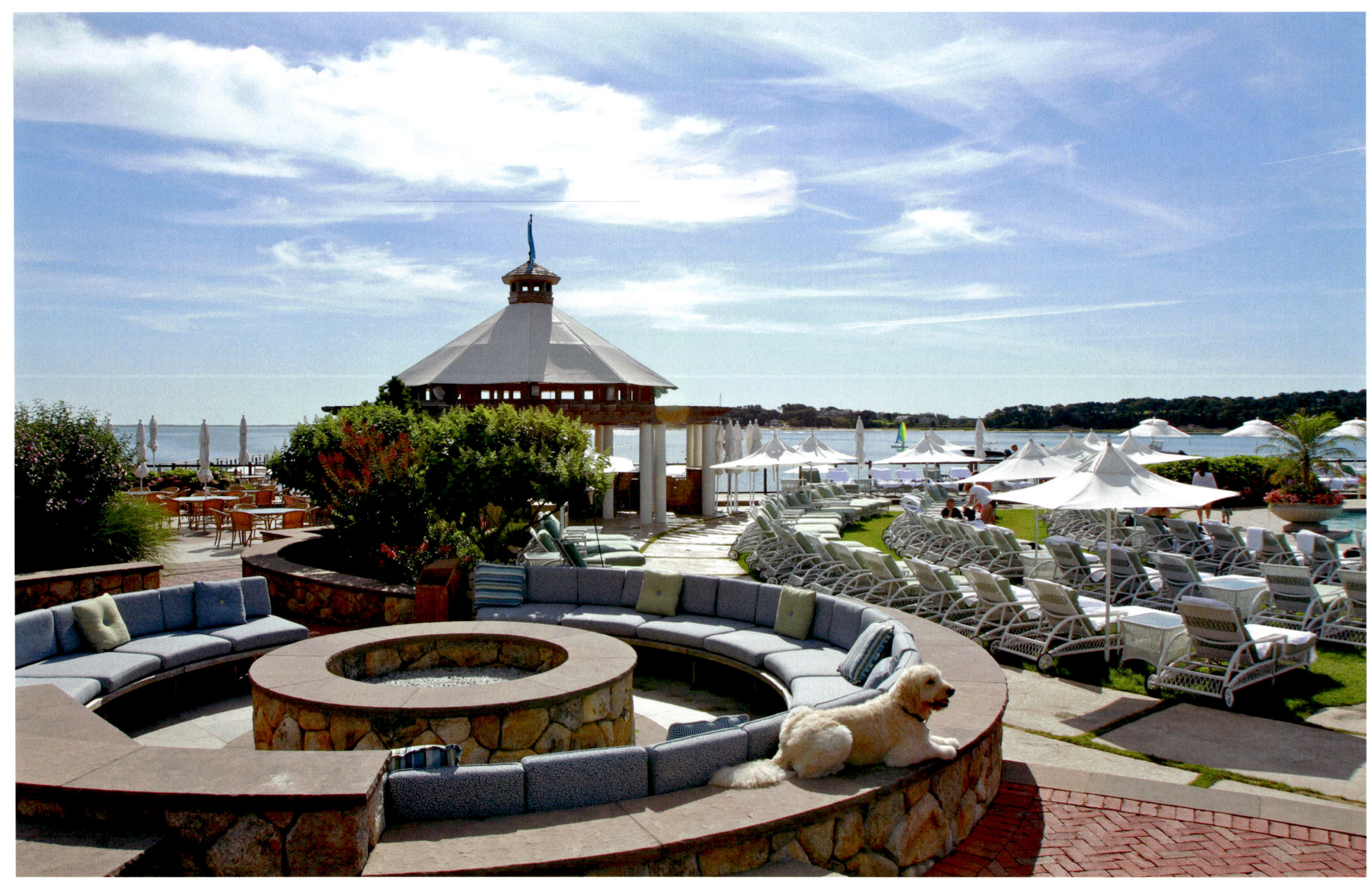

Shanti, labradoodle, Wequassett Inn

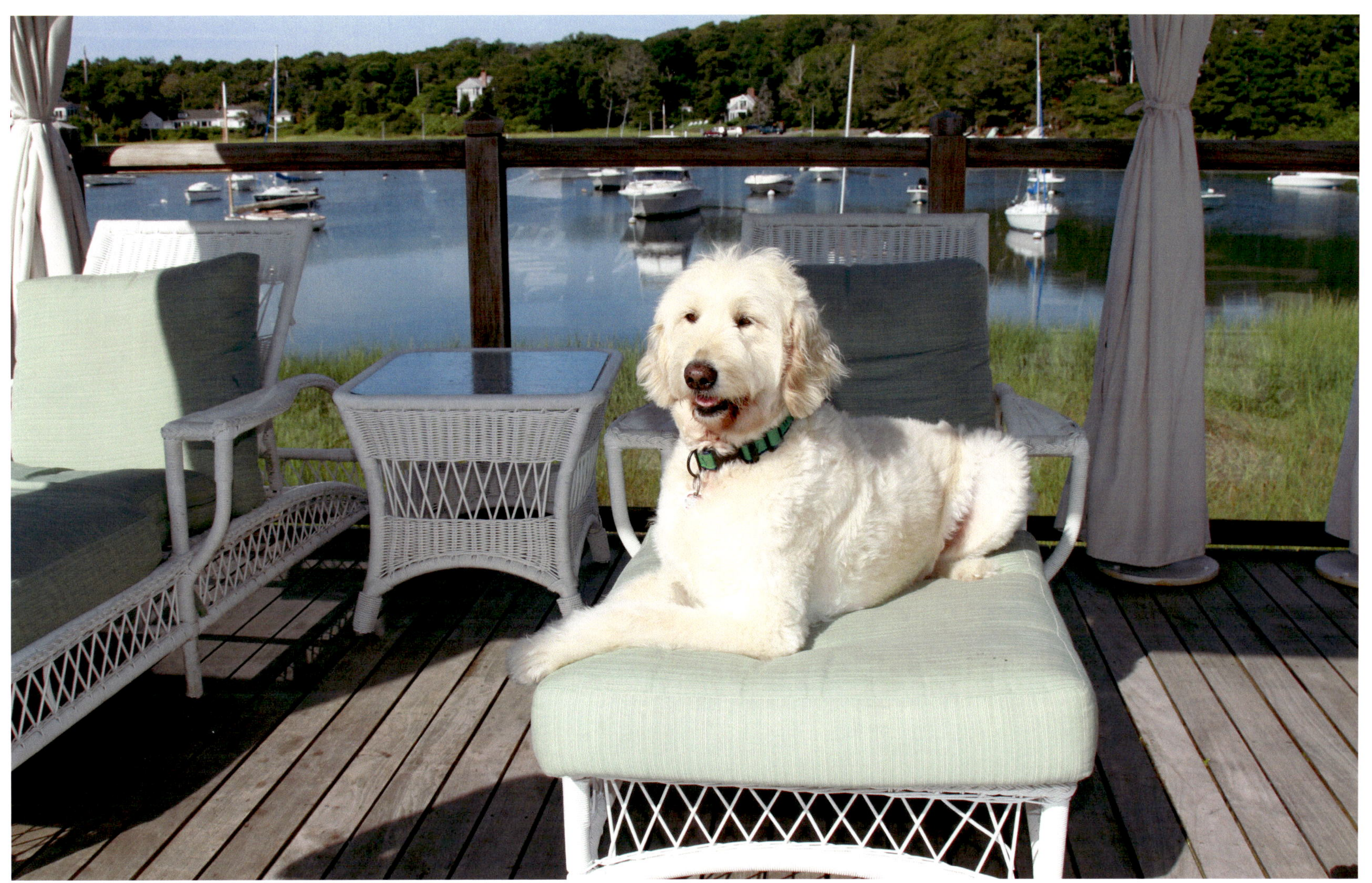

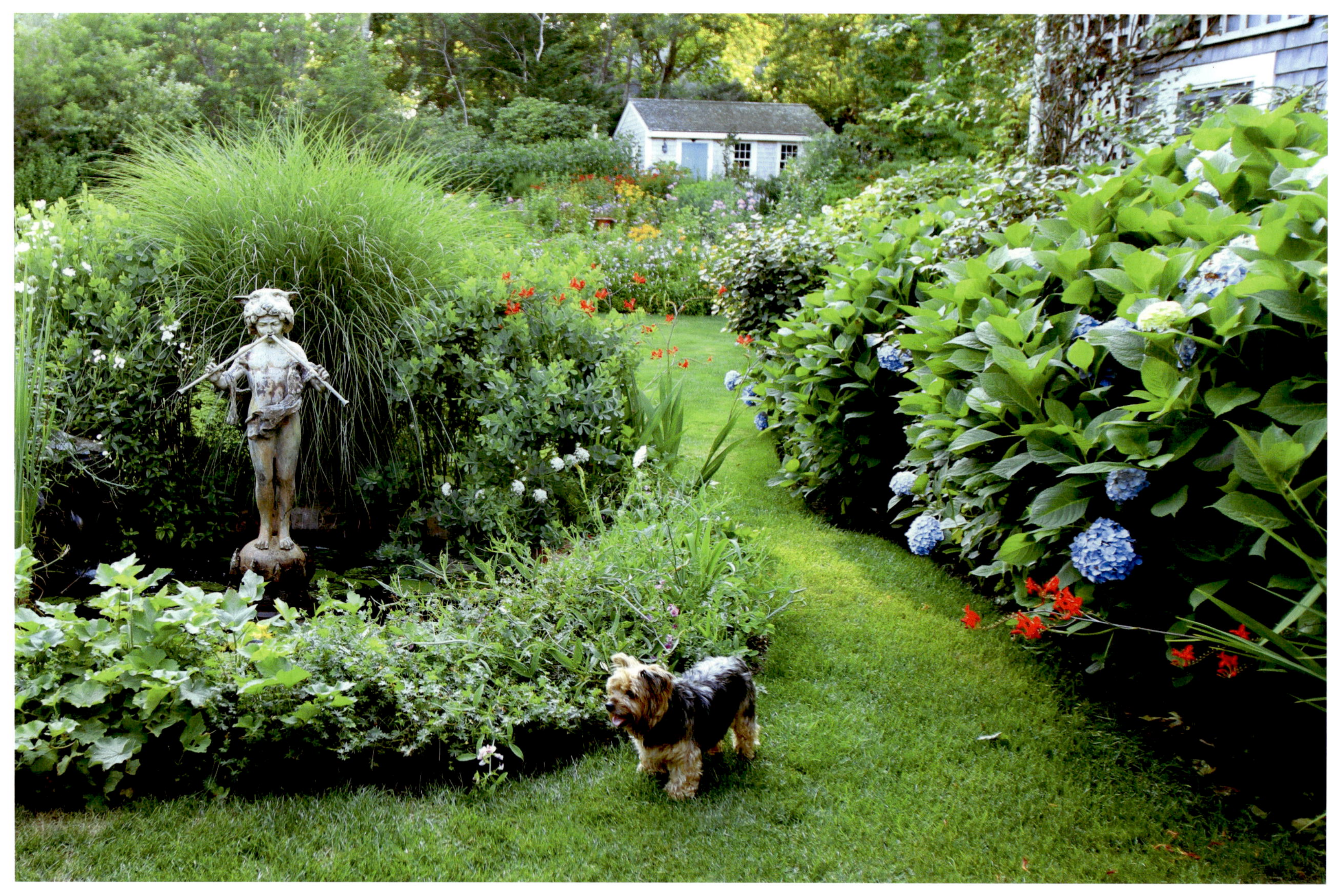

Penny, Yorkshire terrier, Inn on Little Pleasant Bay

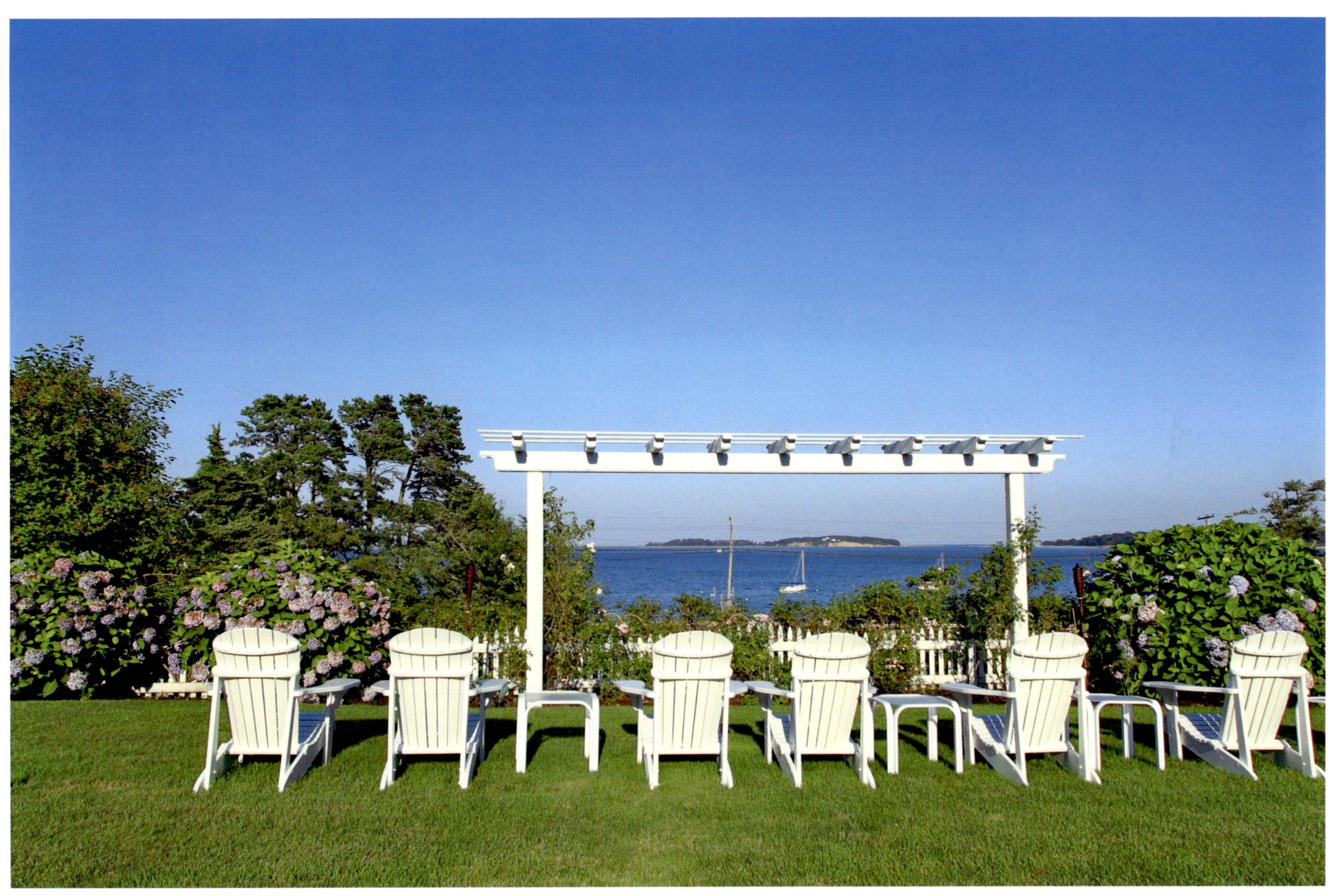

Inn on Little Pleasant Bay

Maggie, goldendoodle

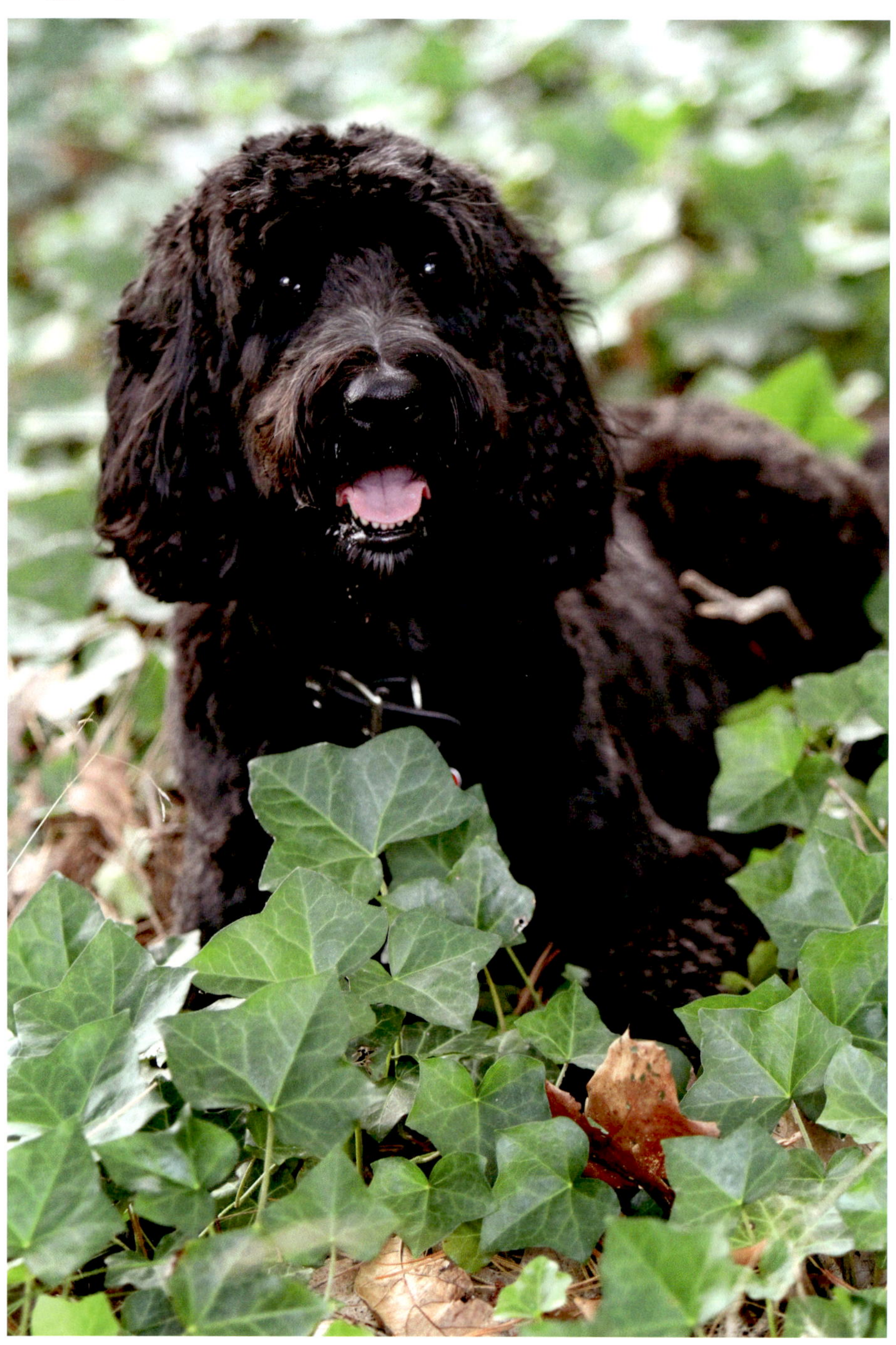

How dull a garden seems to me
without a dog disrupting its calmness,
breaking the hard-edged symmetry
by lying across its paths, rolling on the
panels of lawn, enjoying the aspect
at the top of a knoll, sniffing the air,
nosing the flowers.

— Page Dickey,
Dogs in Their Gardens

Smokey, Yorkipoo

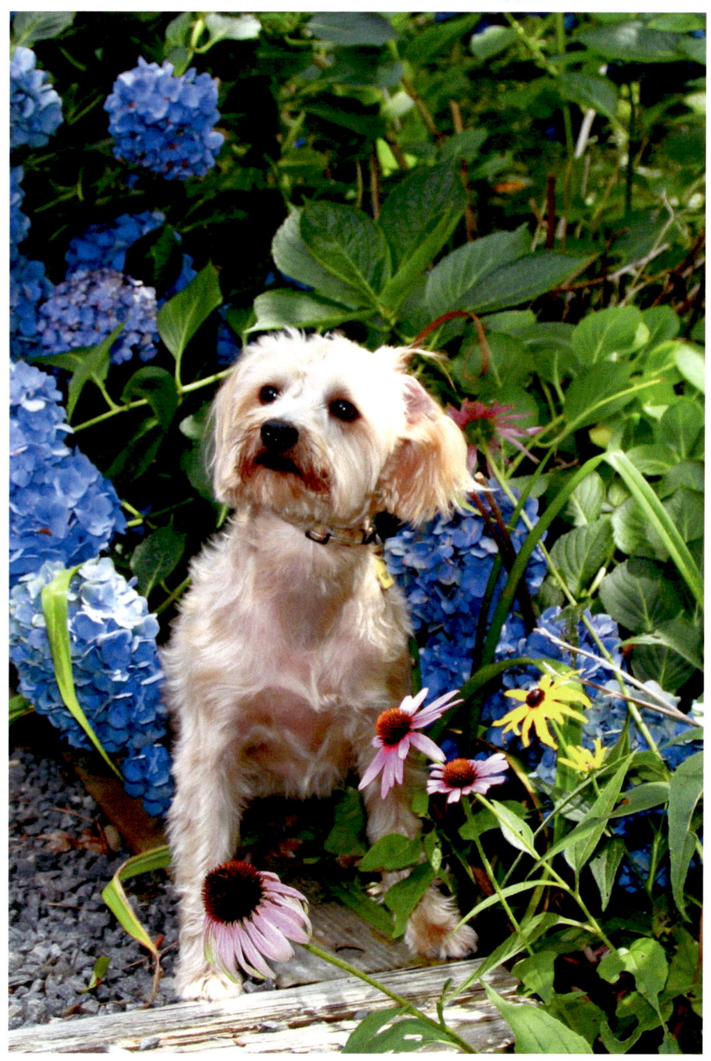

Maggie, Corgi mix

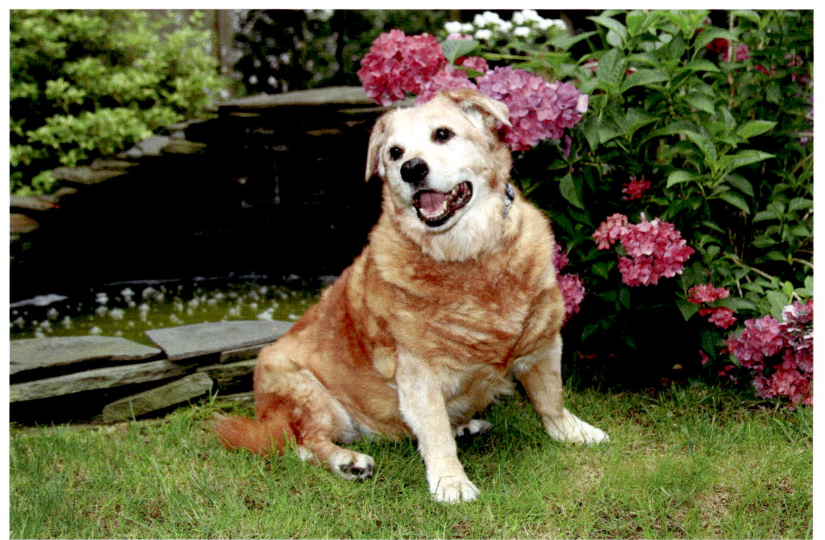

Moose, Labrador retriever

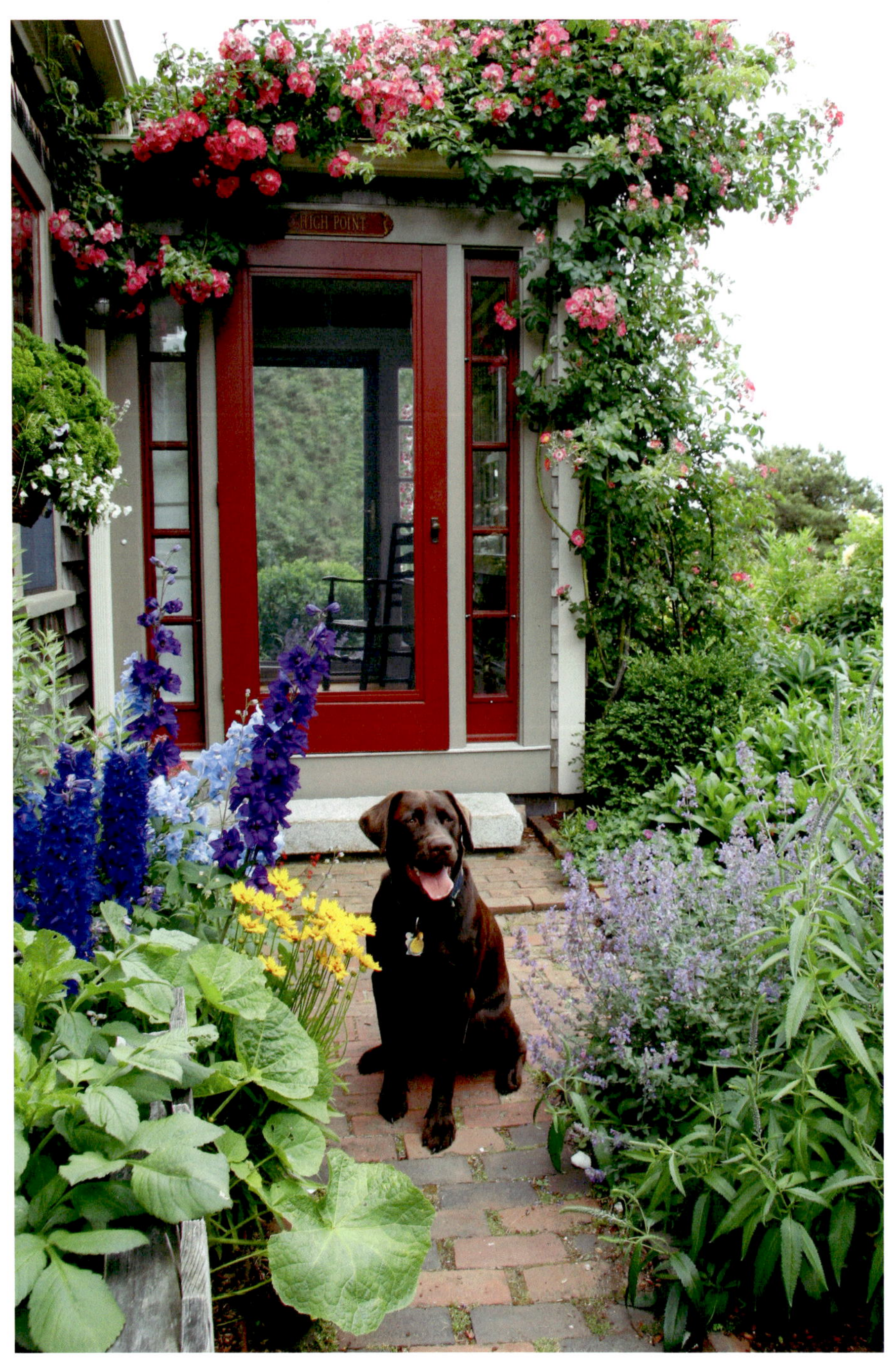

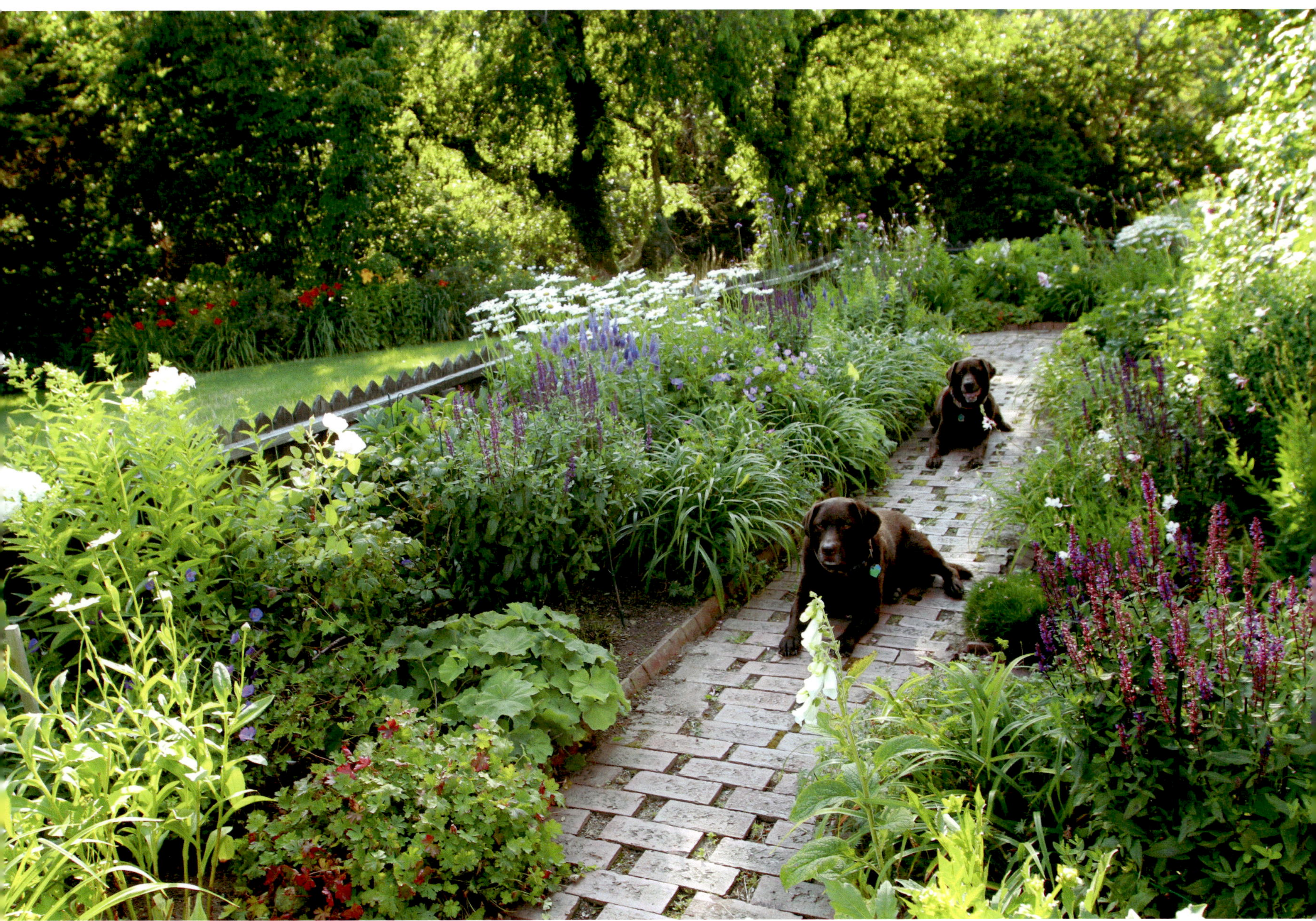

Moose and **Bear**, Labrador retrievers

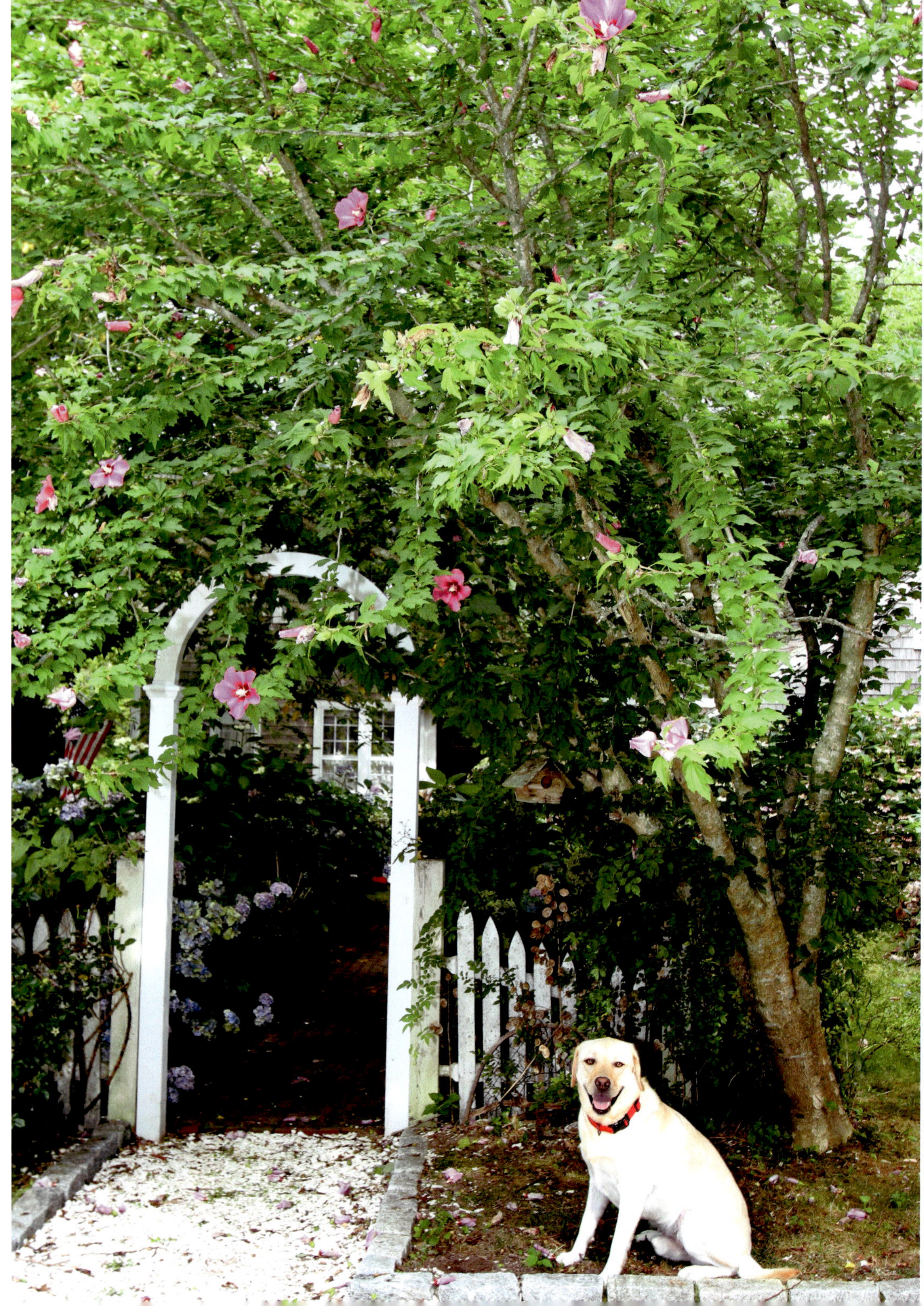

Chester (opposite), Labrador retriever

Annie (below), basset hound, Strong Island, Chatham

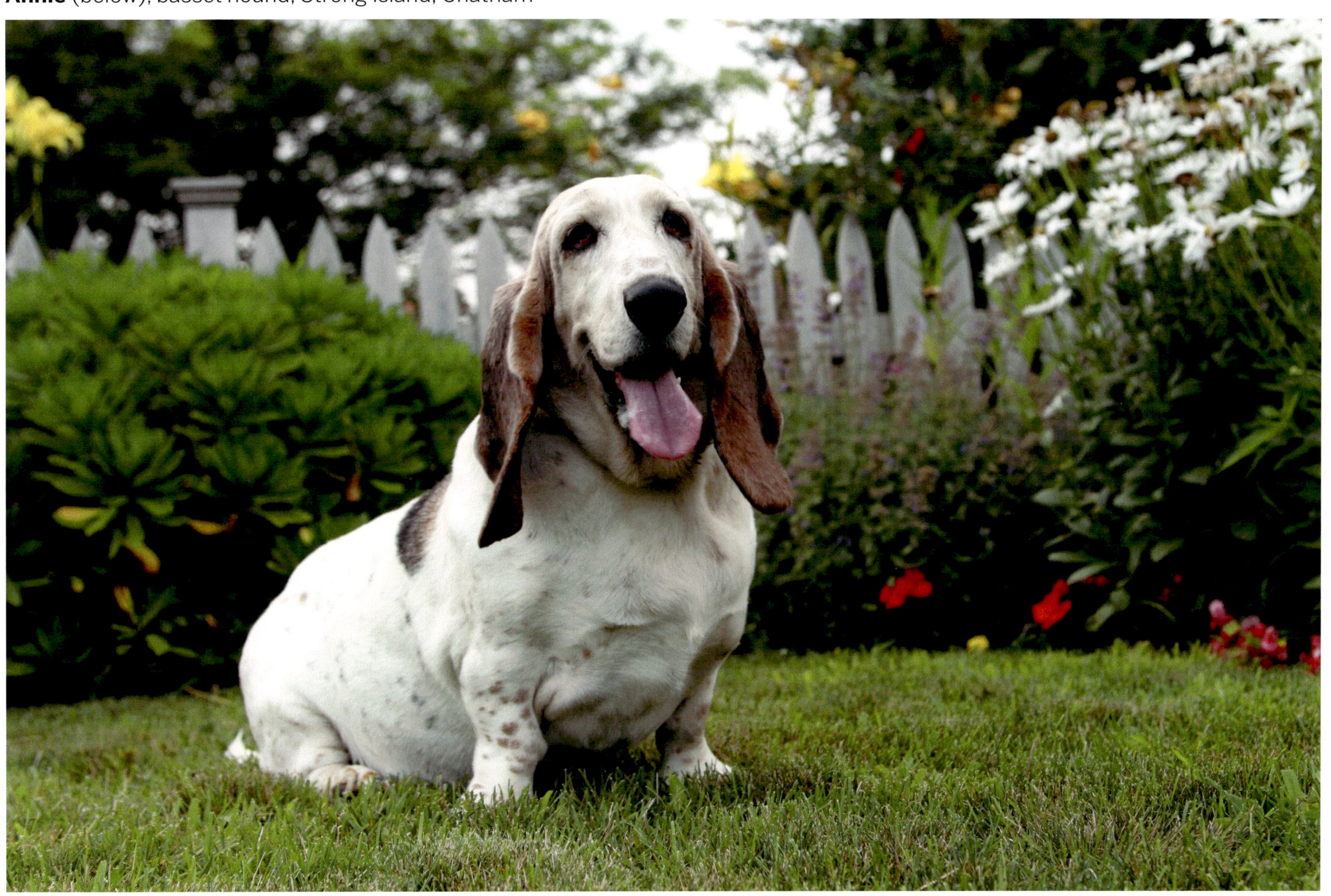

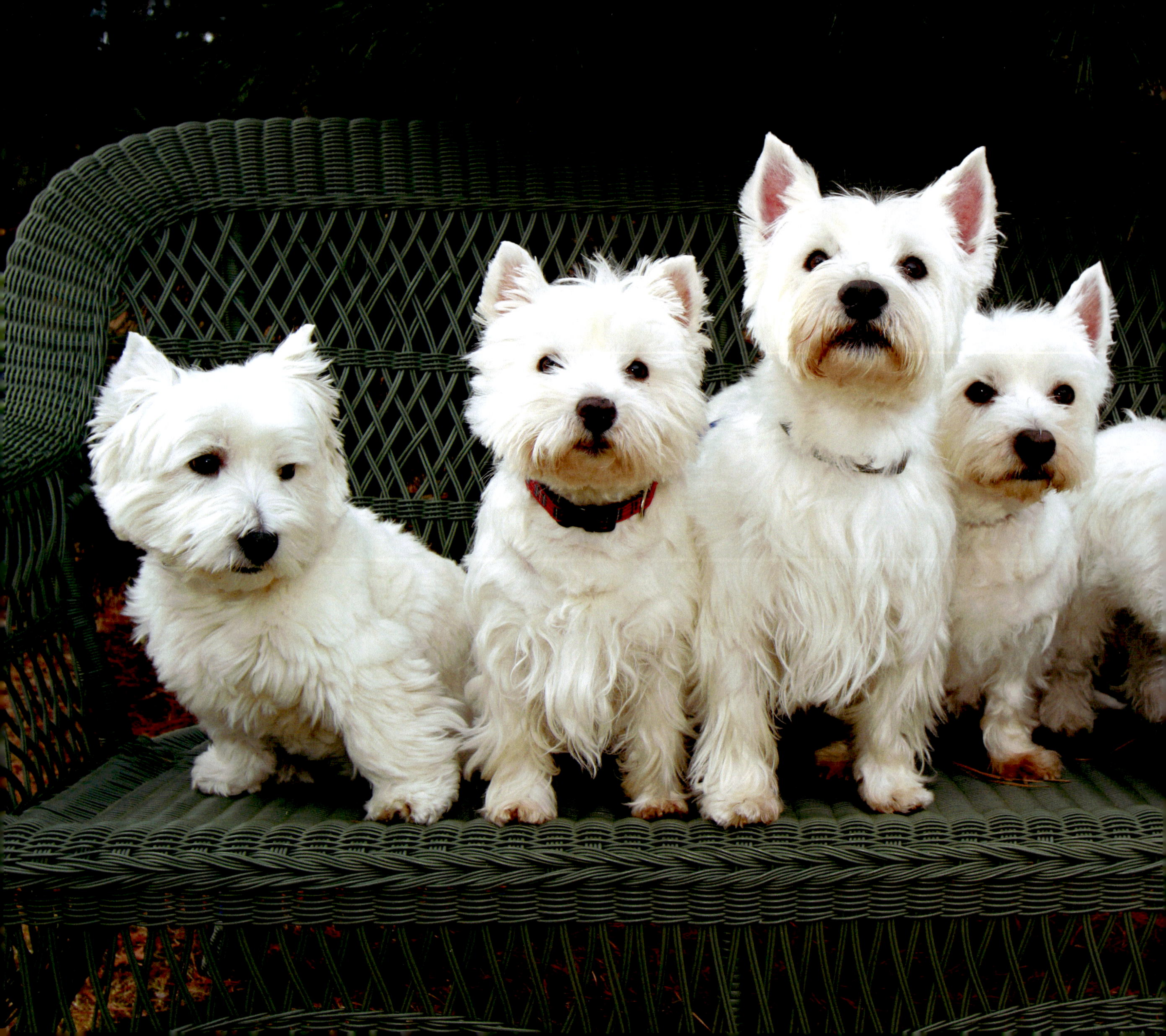

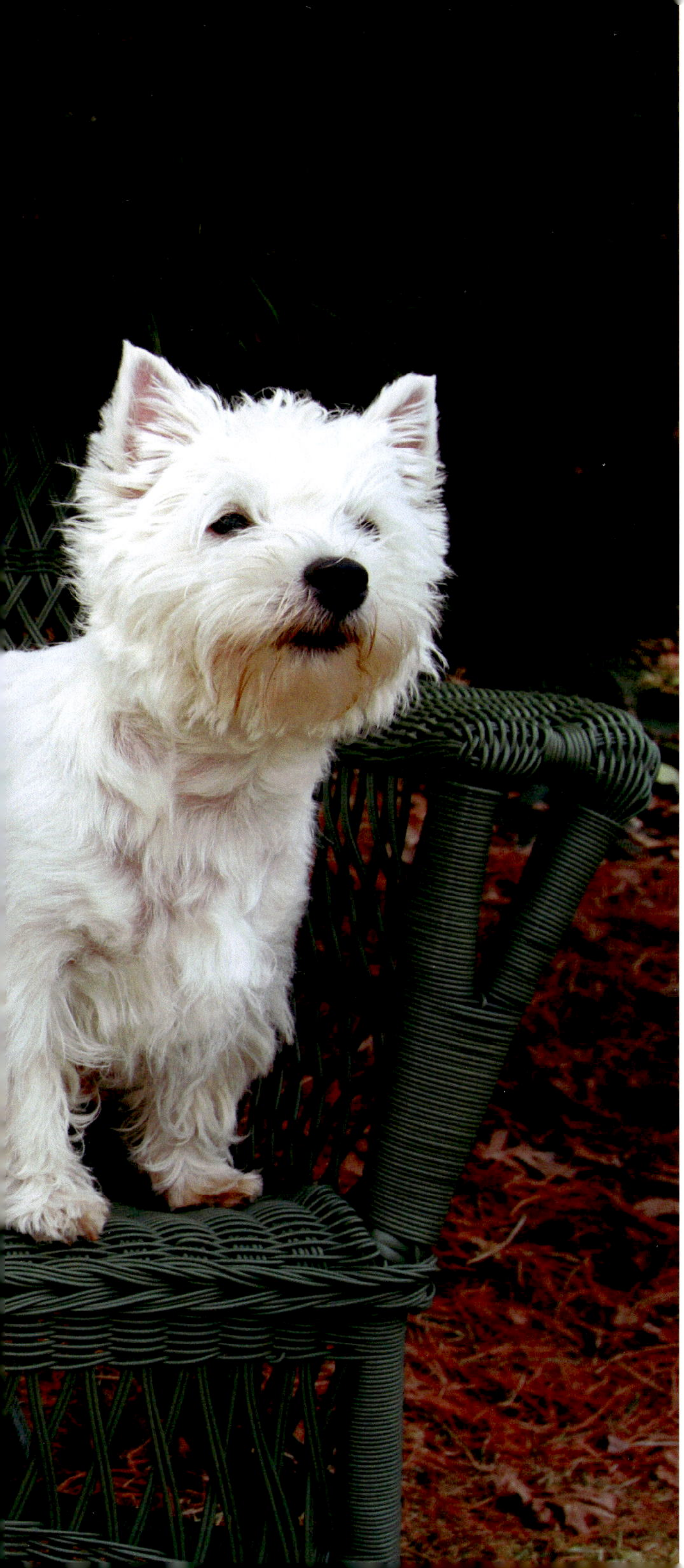

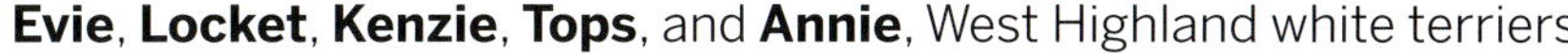

Evie, **Locket**, **Kenzie**, **Tops**, and **Annie**, West Highland white terriers

Licks are Pump's way of making contact, her hand outstretched for me. She greets me home with licks at my face as I bend to pet her; I get waking licks on my hand as I nap in a chair; she licks my legs thoroughly clean of salt after a run; sitting beside me, she pins my hand with her front leg and pushes open my fist to lick the soft warm flesh of my palm. I adore her licks.

— Alexandra Horowitz,
Inside of a Dog

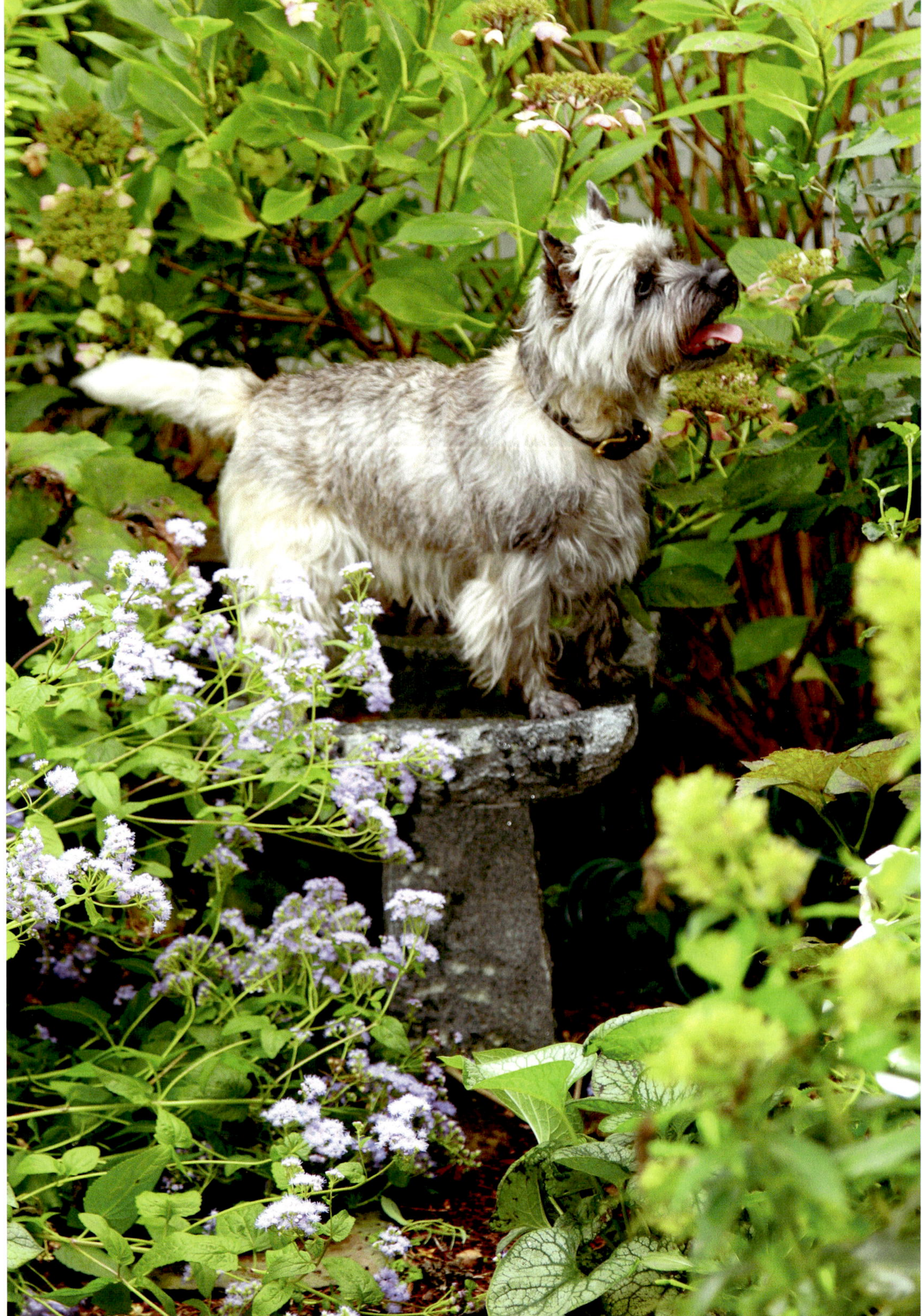

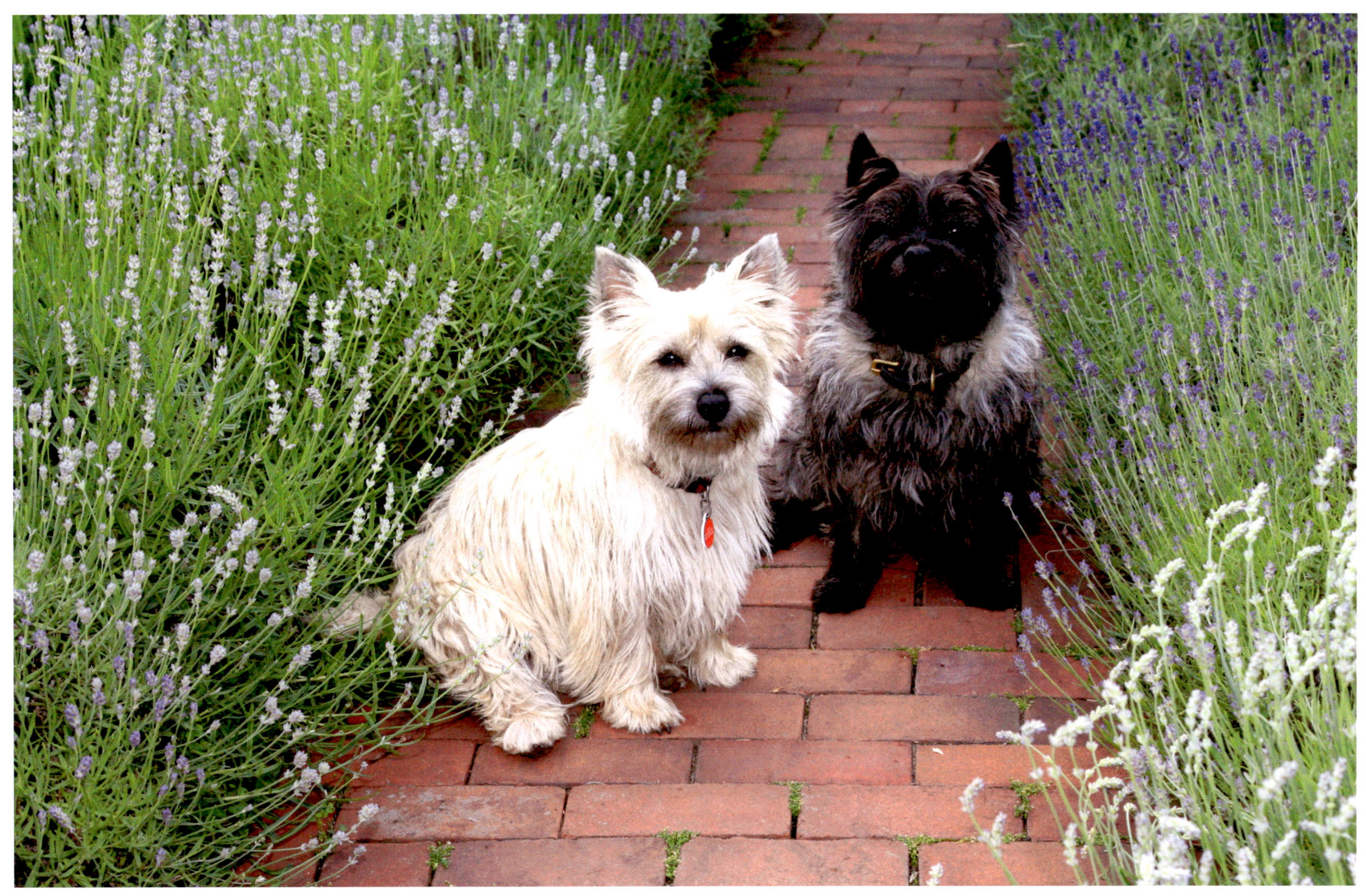

Dylan and **Conor** (above), Cairn terriers

Dylan (opposite)

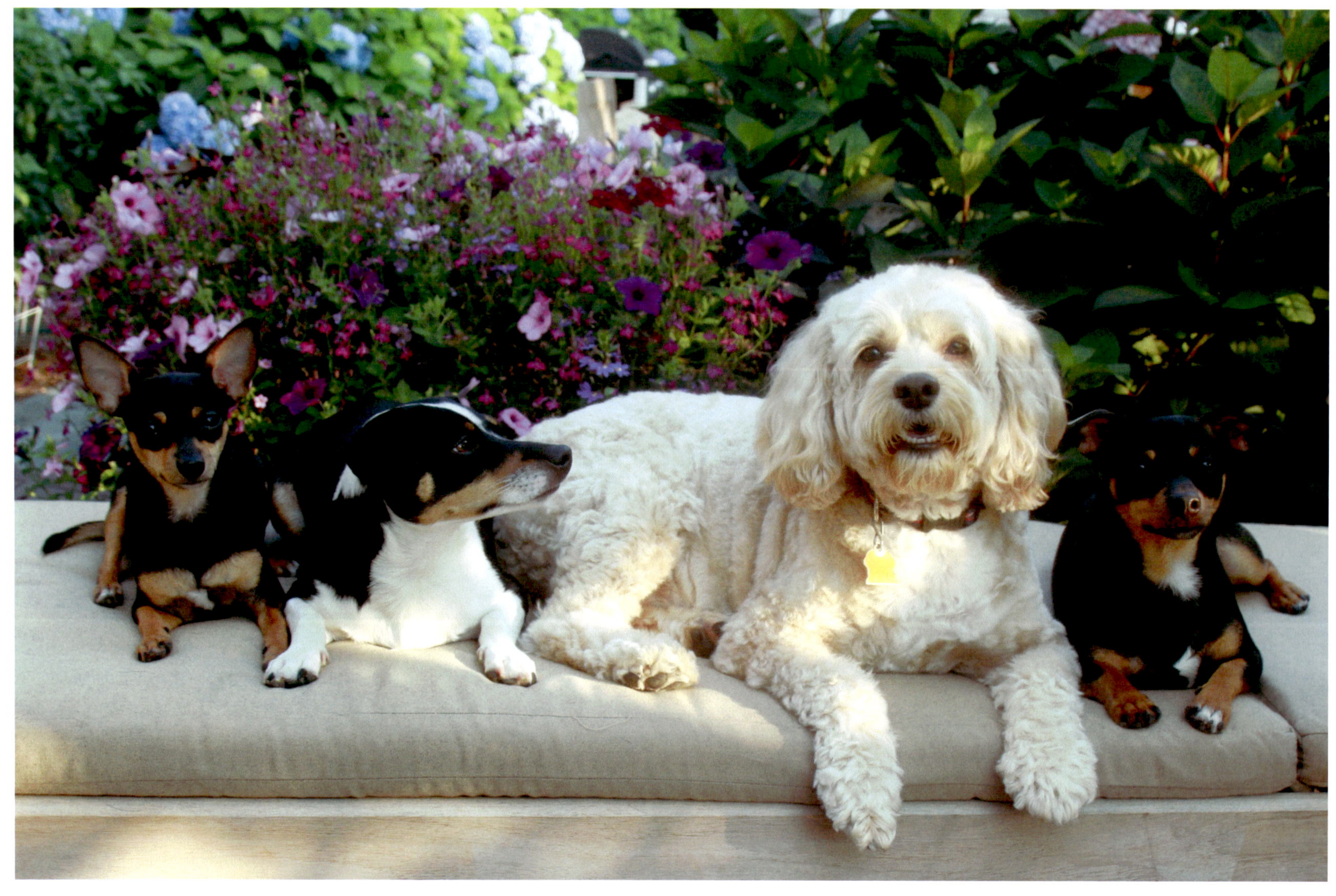

Ruby, **Roscoe**, and **Rudy**, Chihuahuas, and **Zeus**, cockapoo

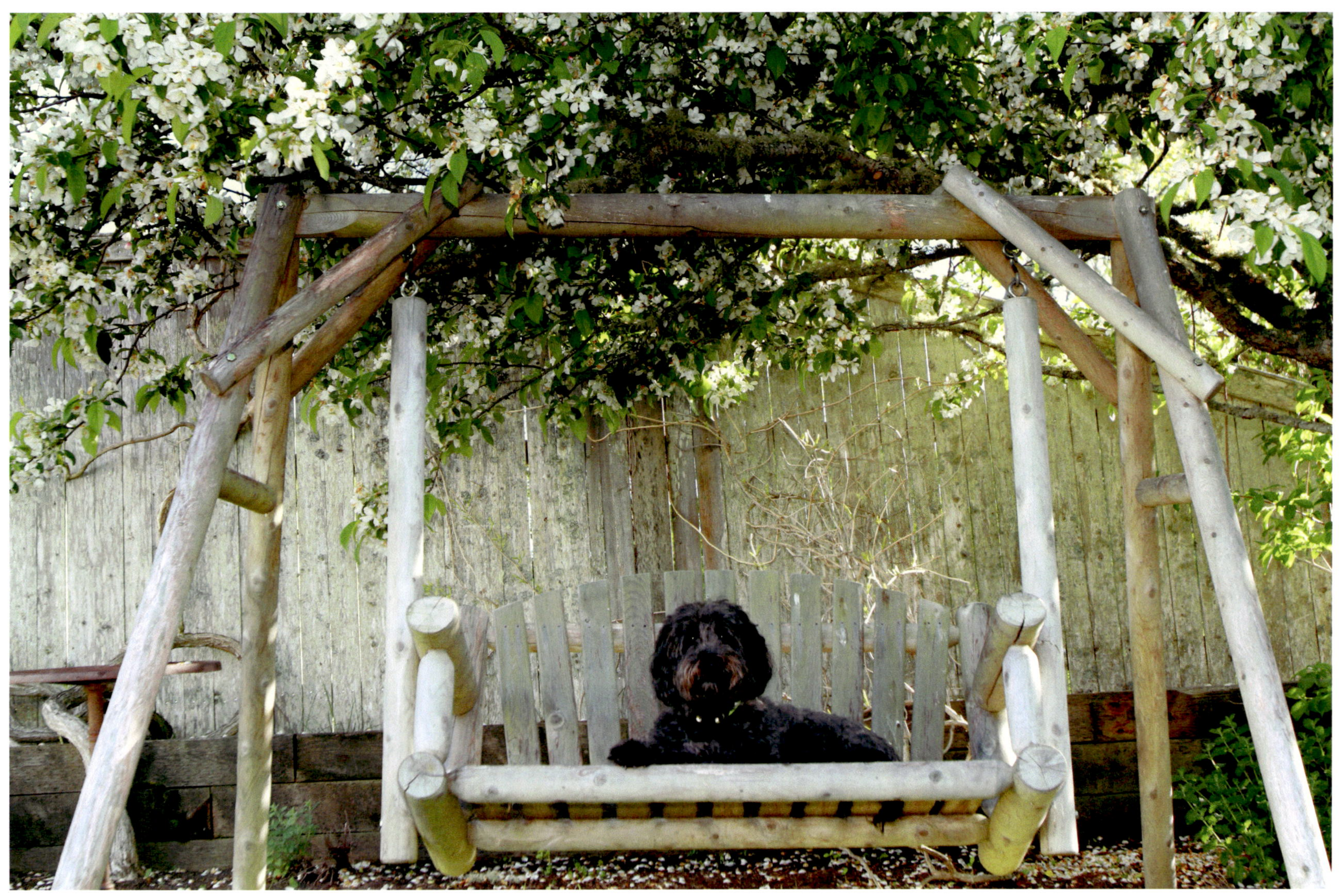

Oscar, goldendoodle

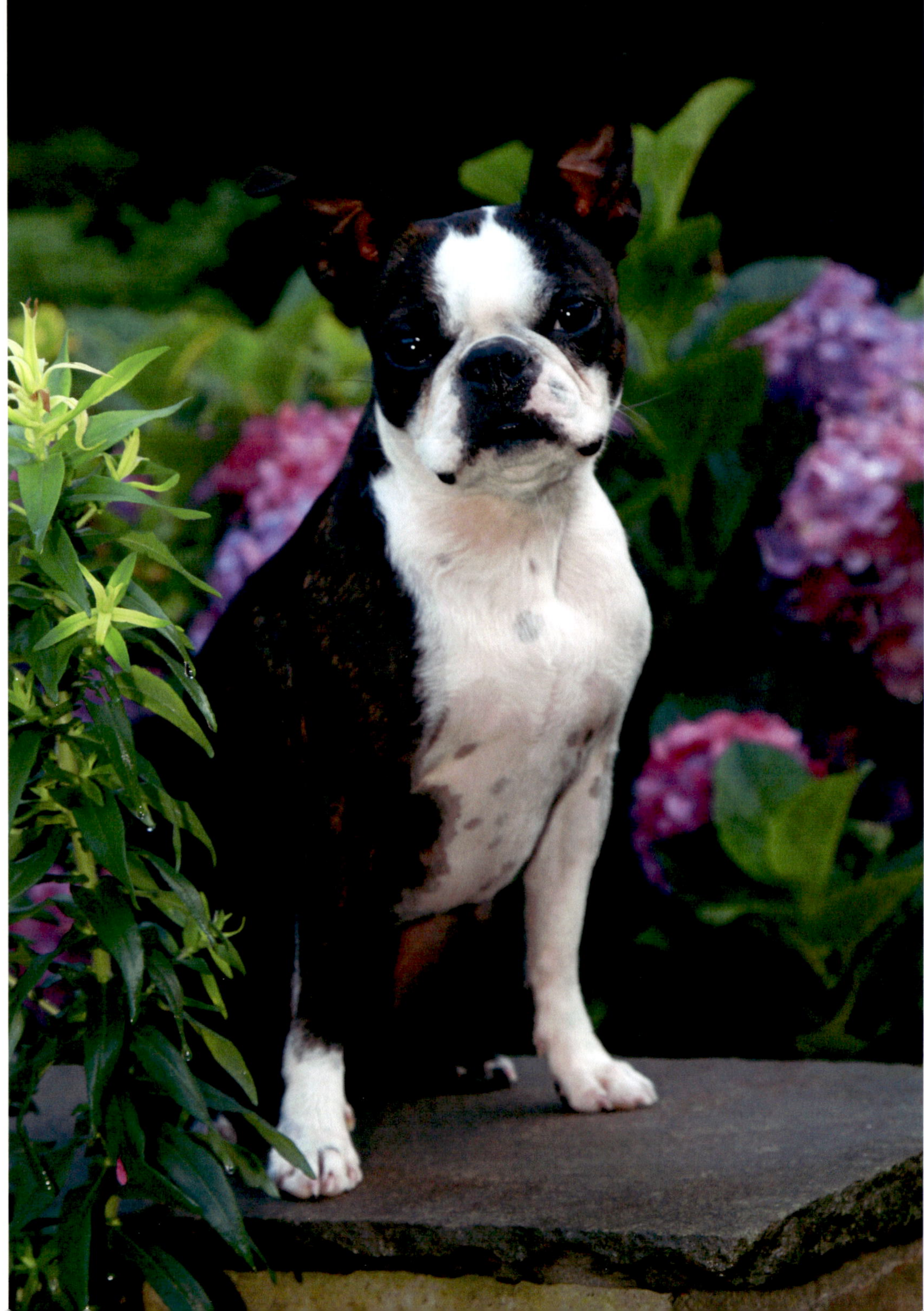

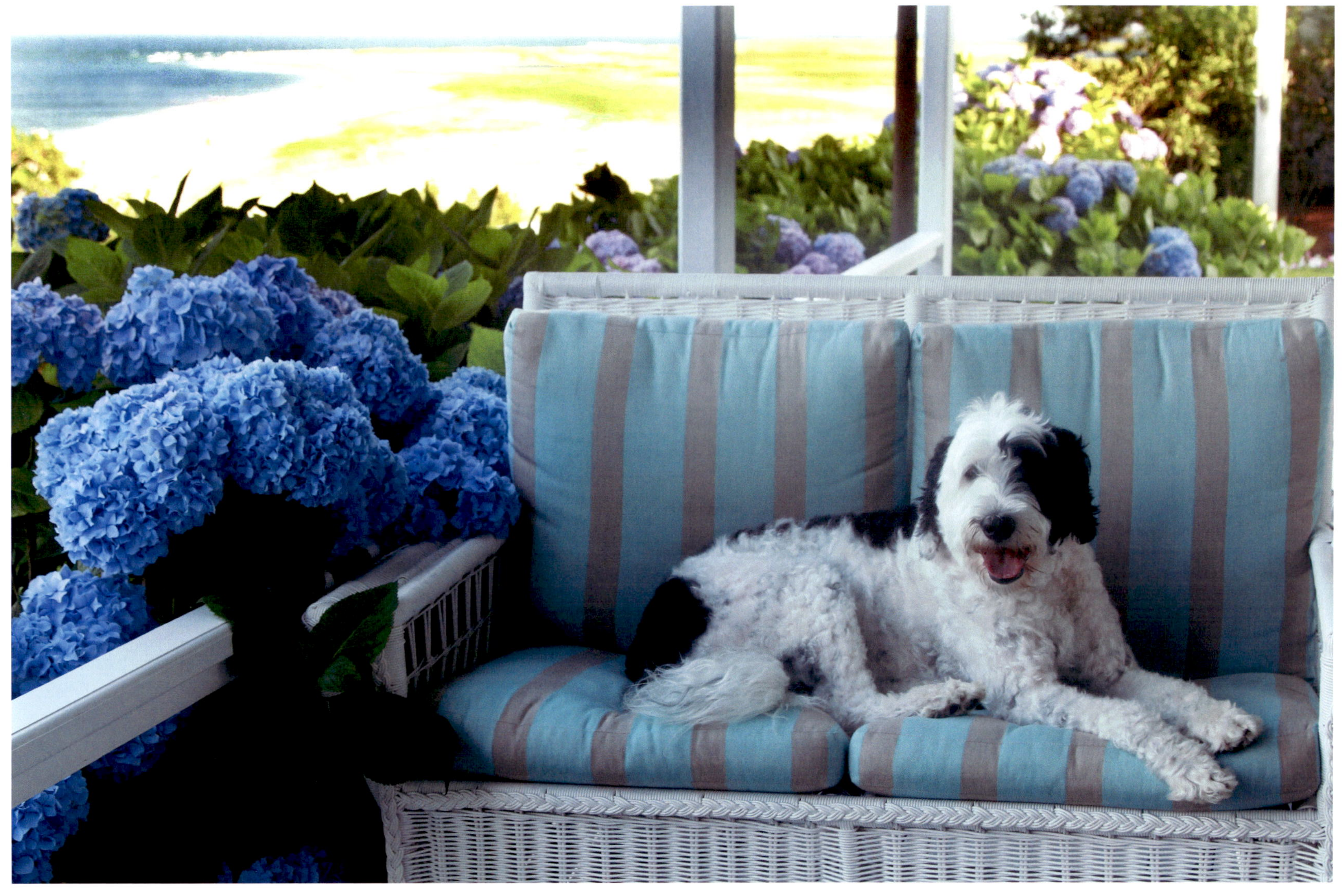

Adam from Chatham (above), Portuguese water dog

Izzy (opposite), Boston terrier

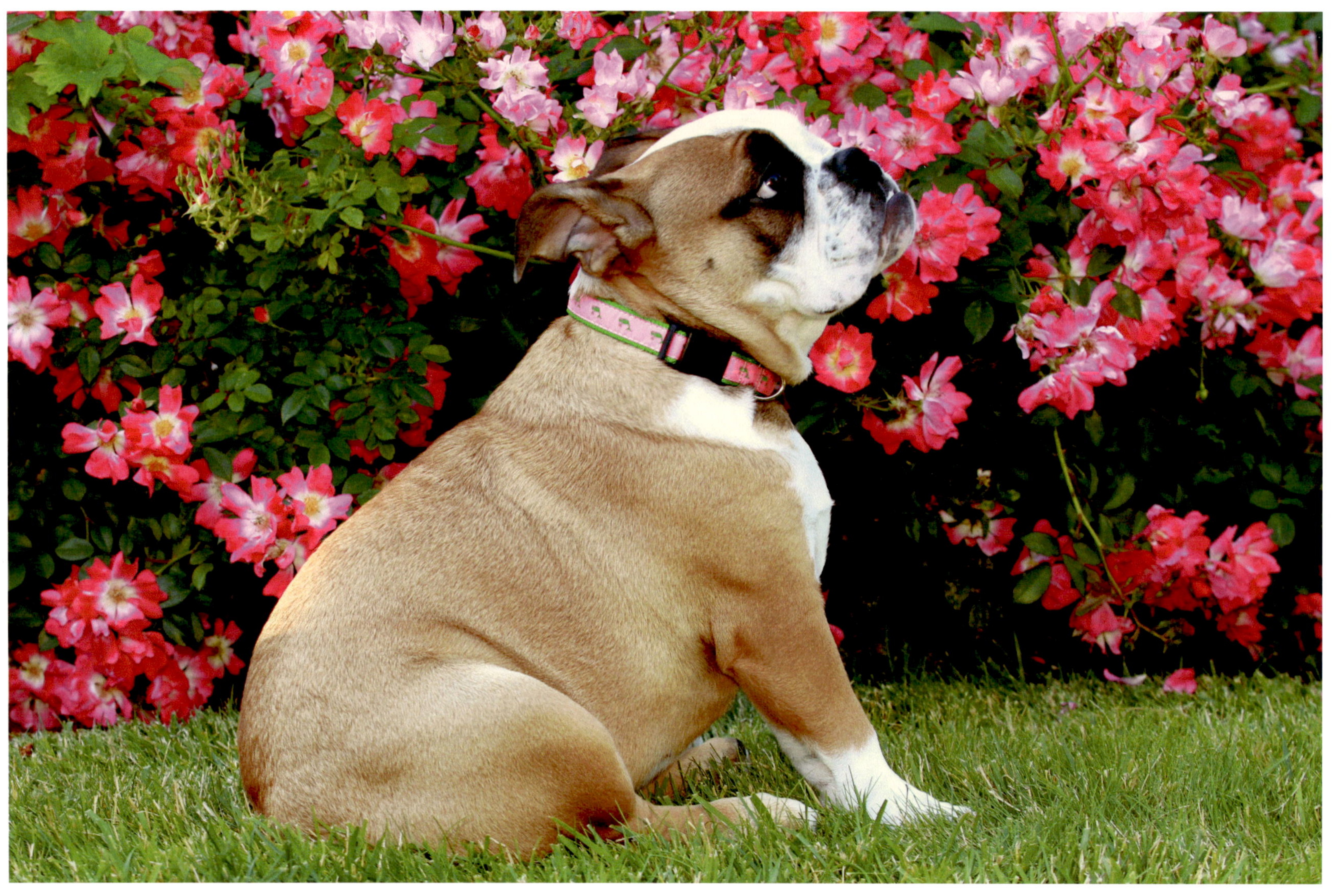

Lilli P., bulldog

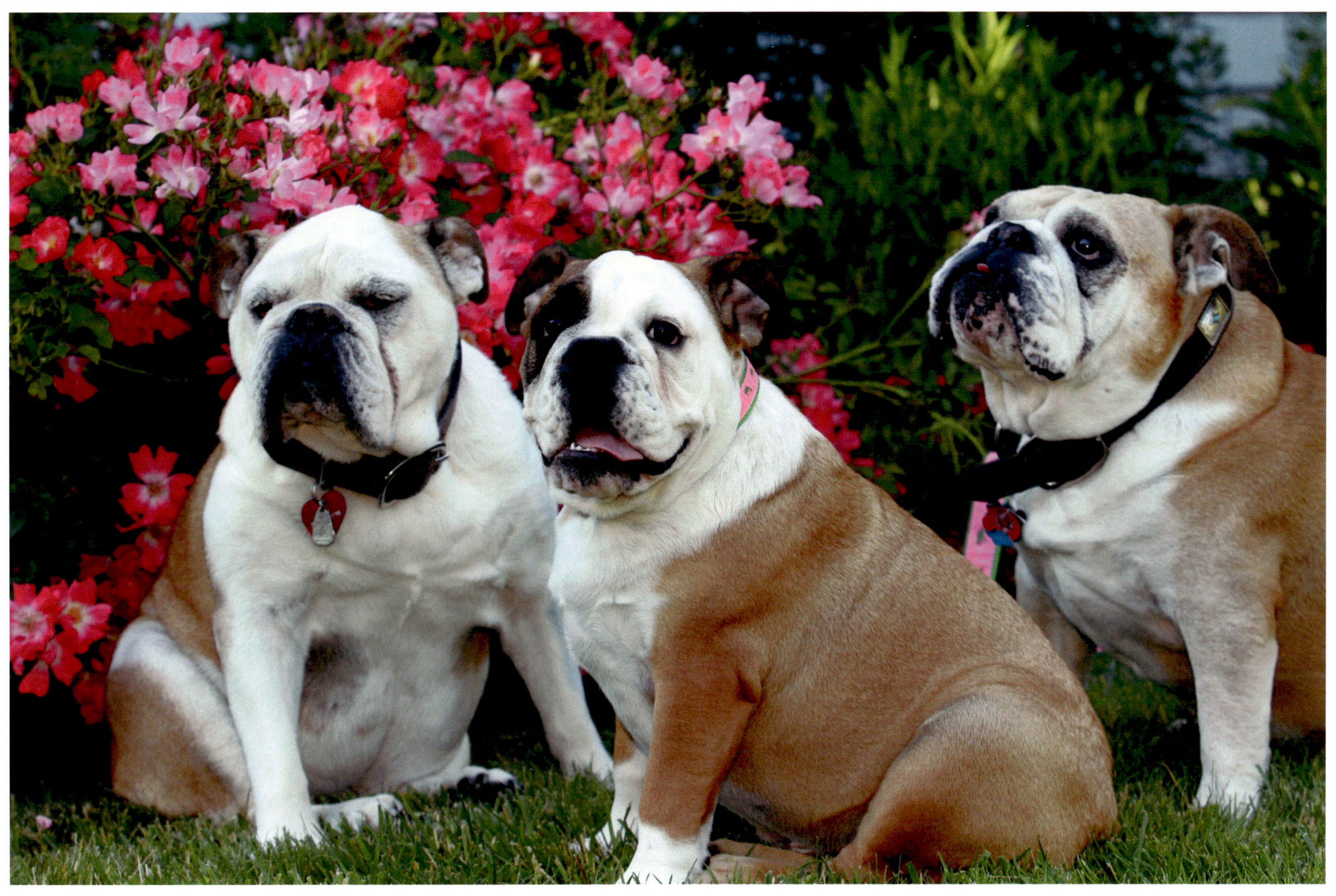

Bellarossa, **Lilli P.**, and **Barthalamew**, bulldogs

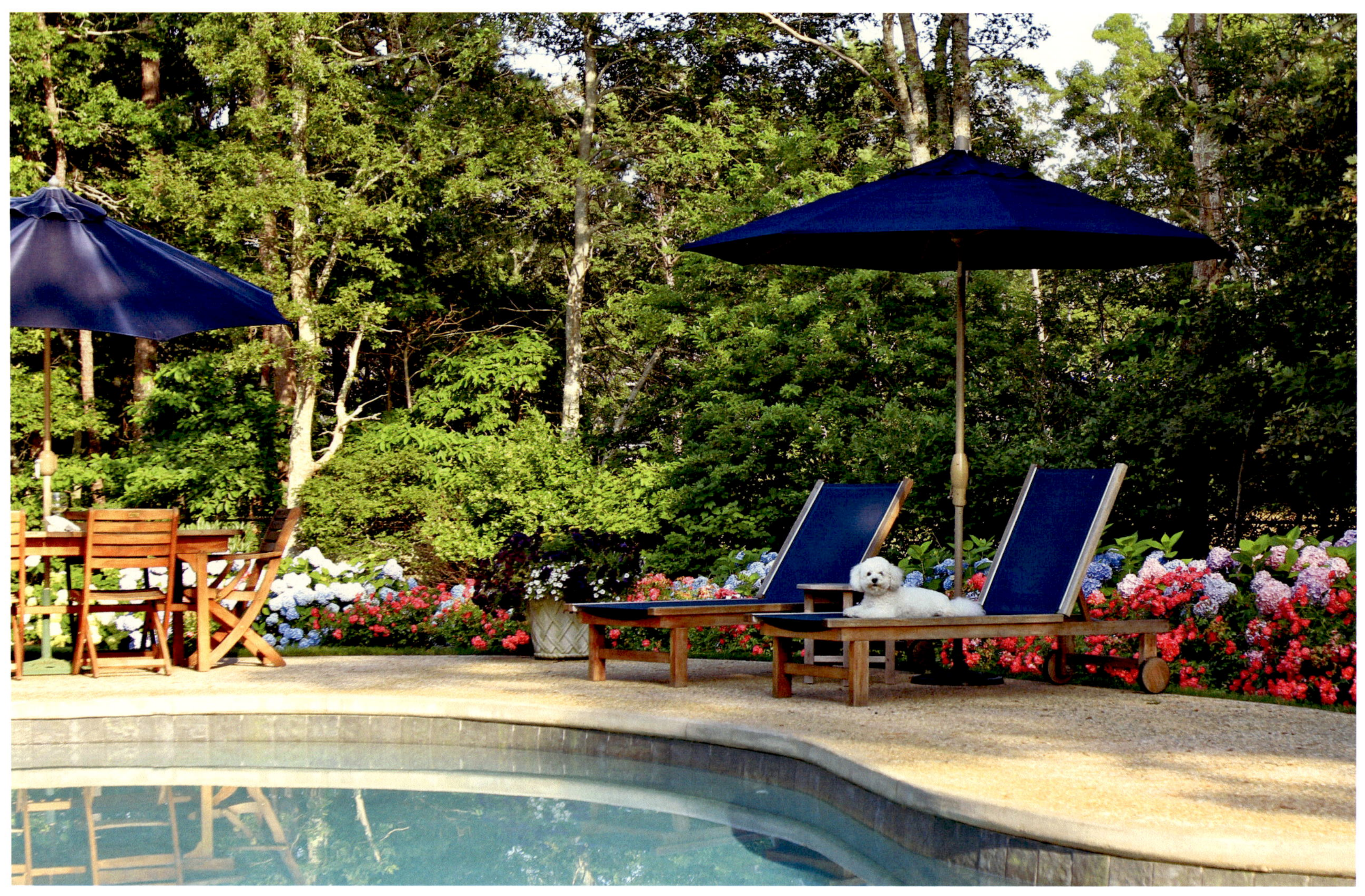

Lulu, bichon frise

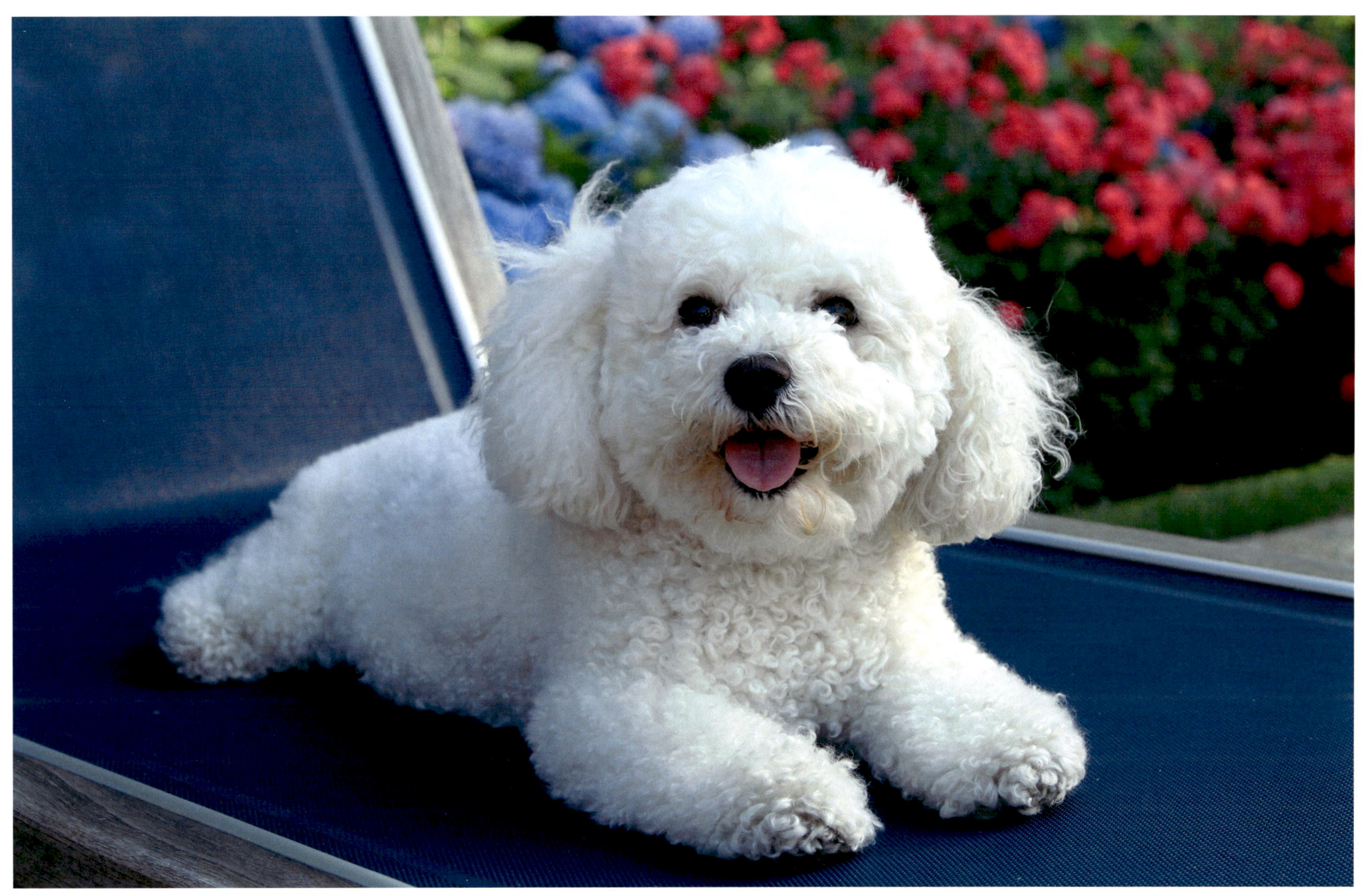

Angus, Scottish terrier, and **James**, Slovakian rough-haired pointer

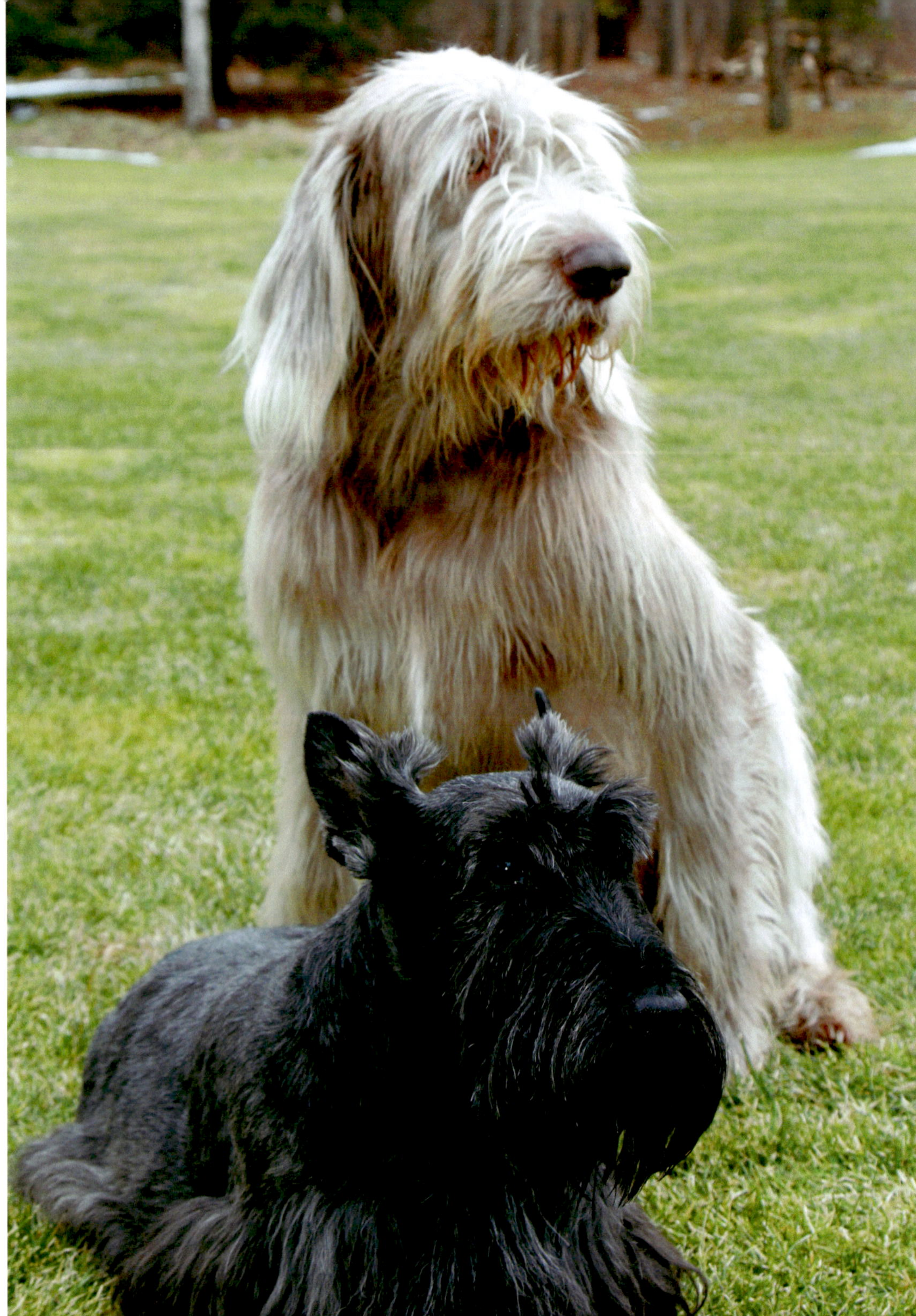

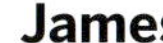
James

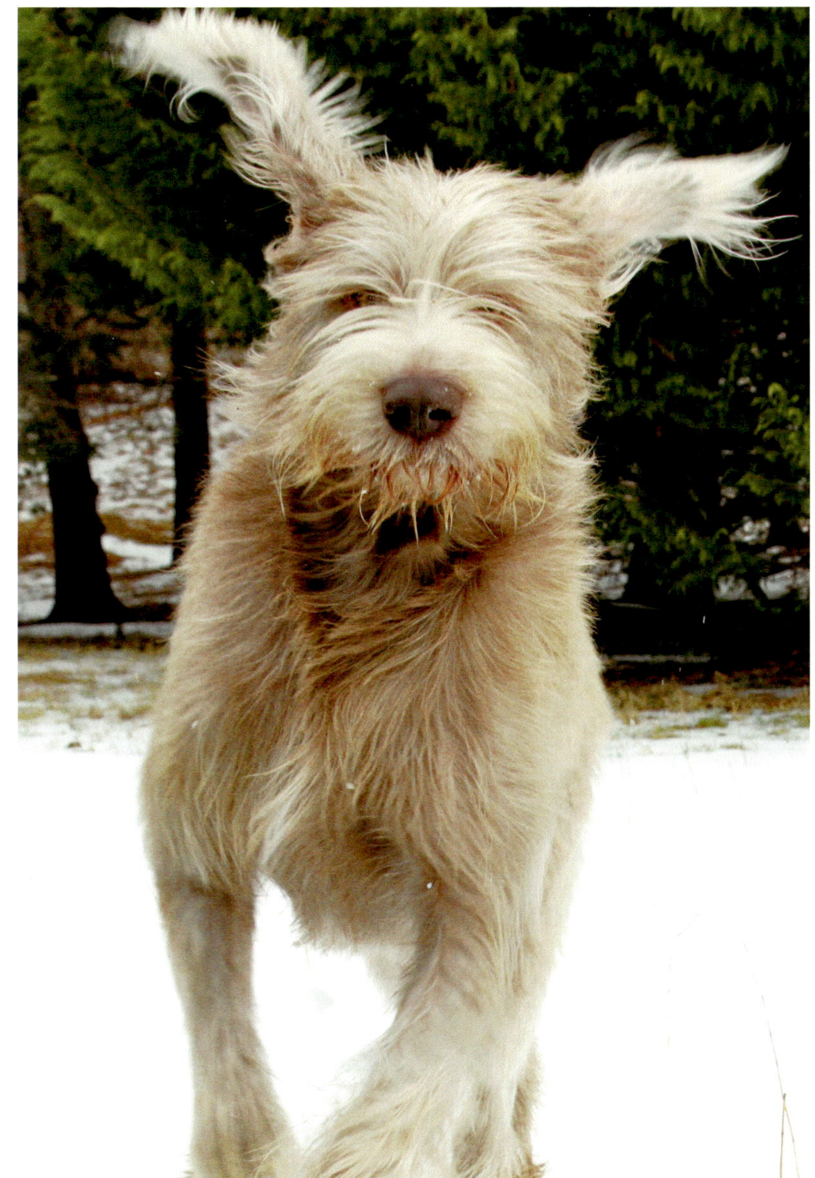

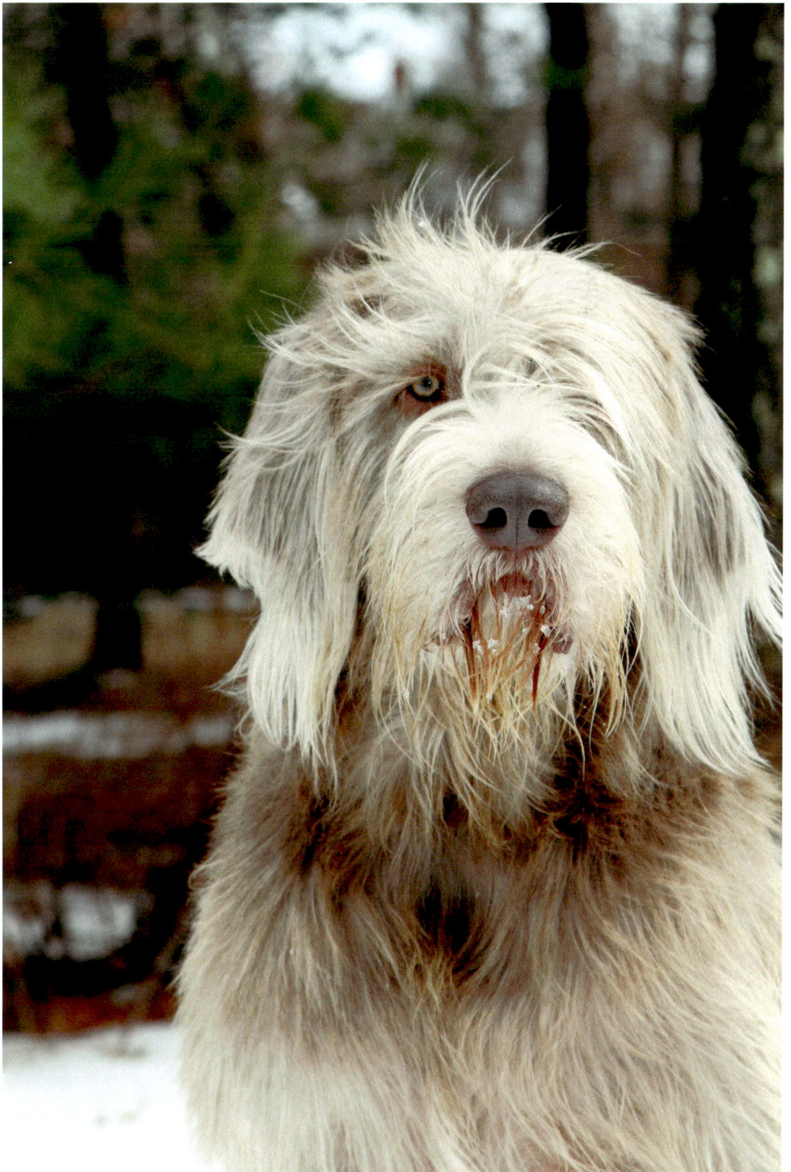

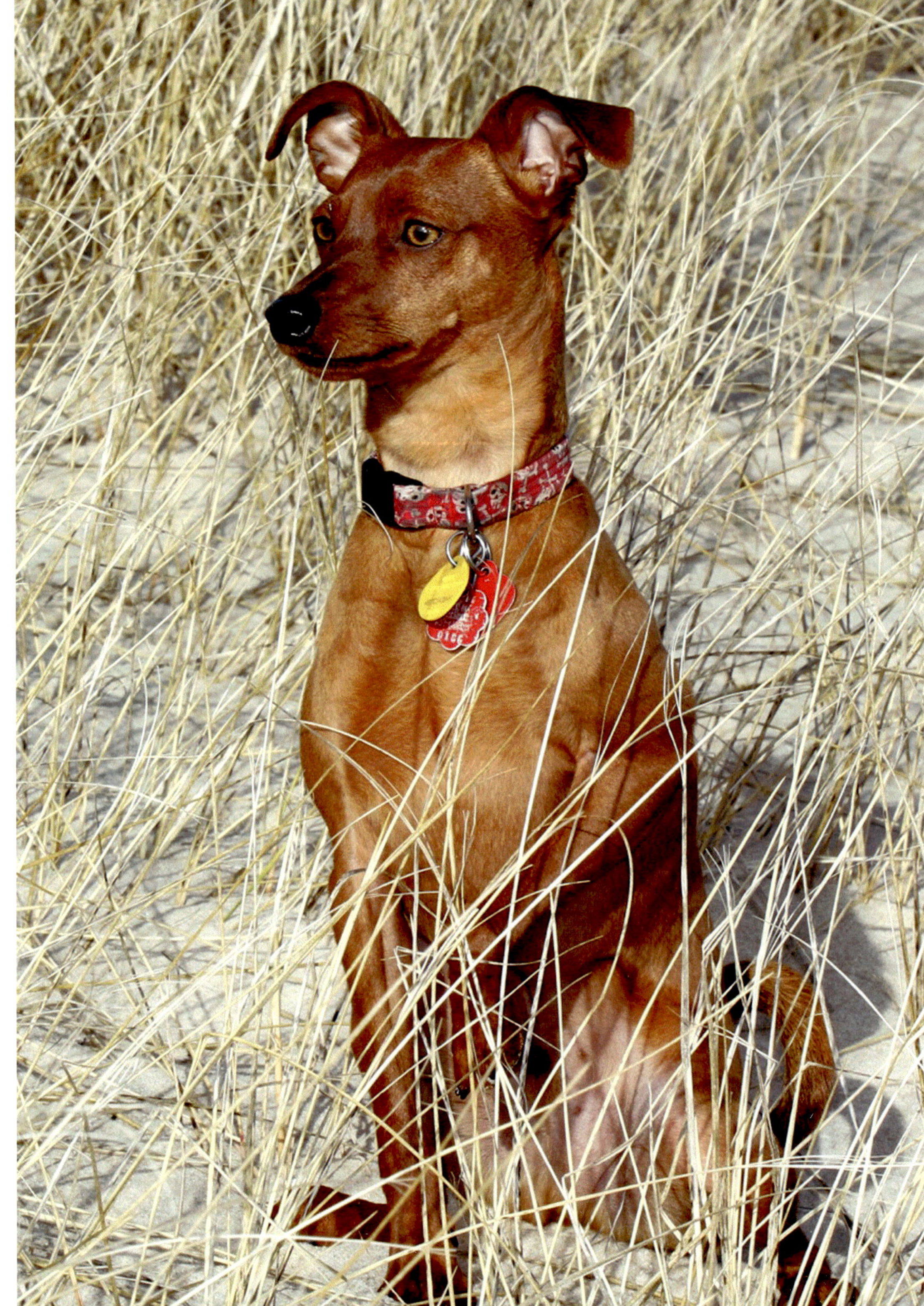

Teddy, miniature pinscher, Lighthouse Beach

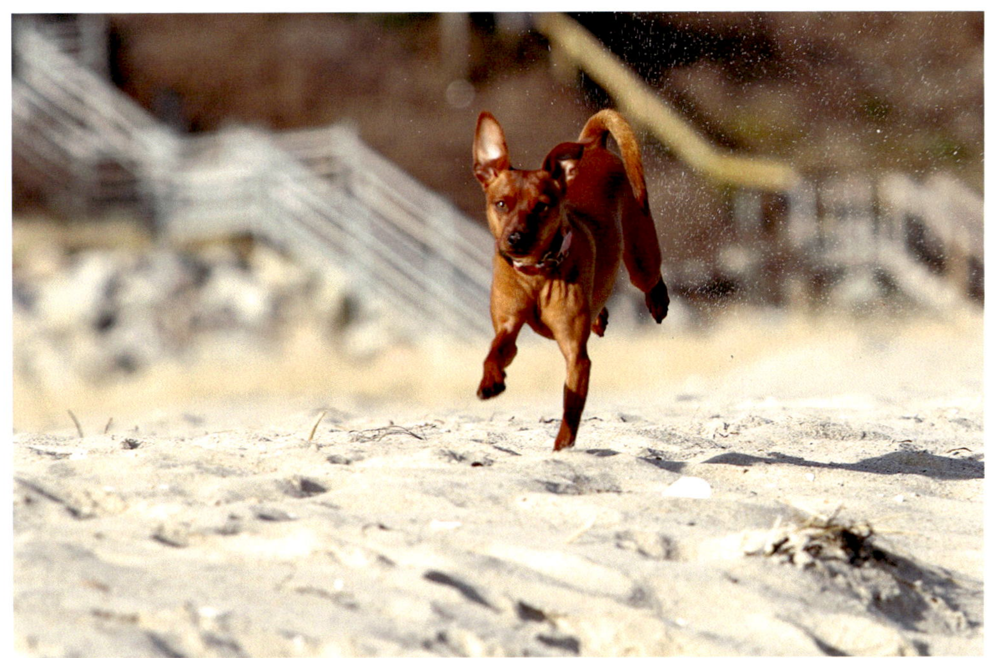

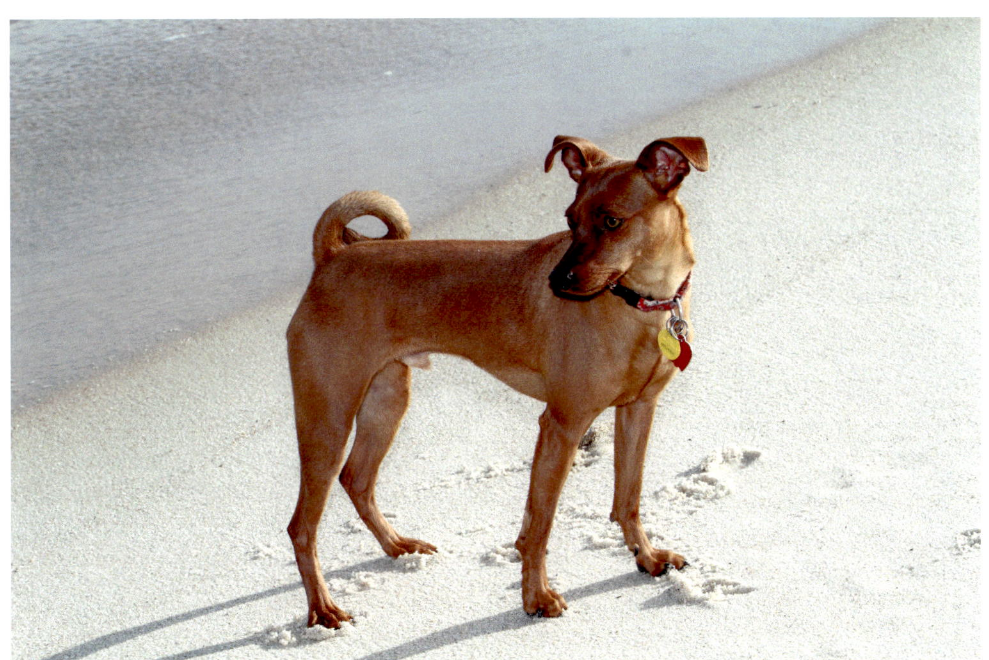

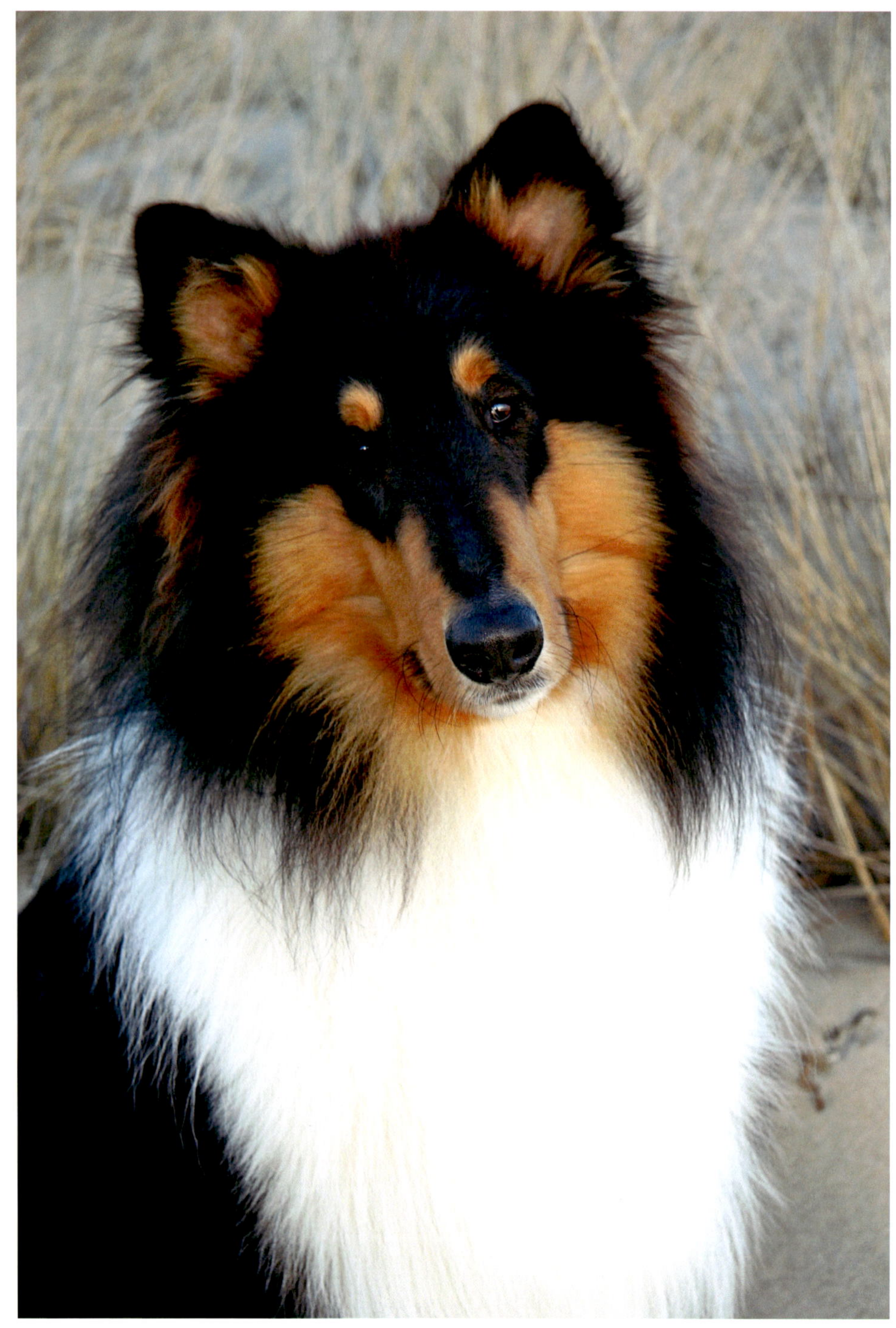

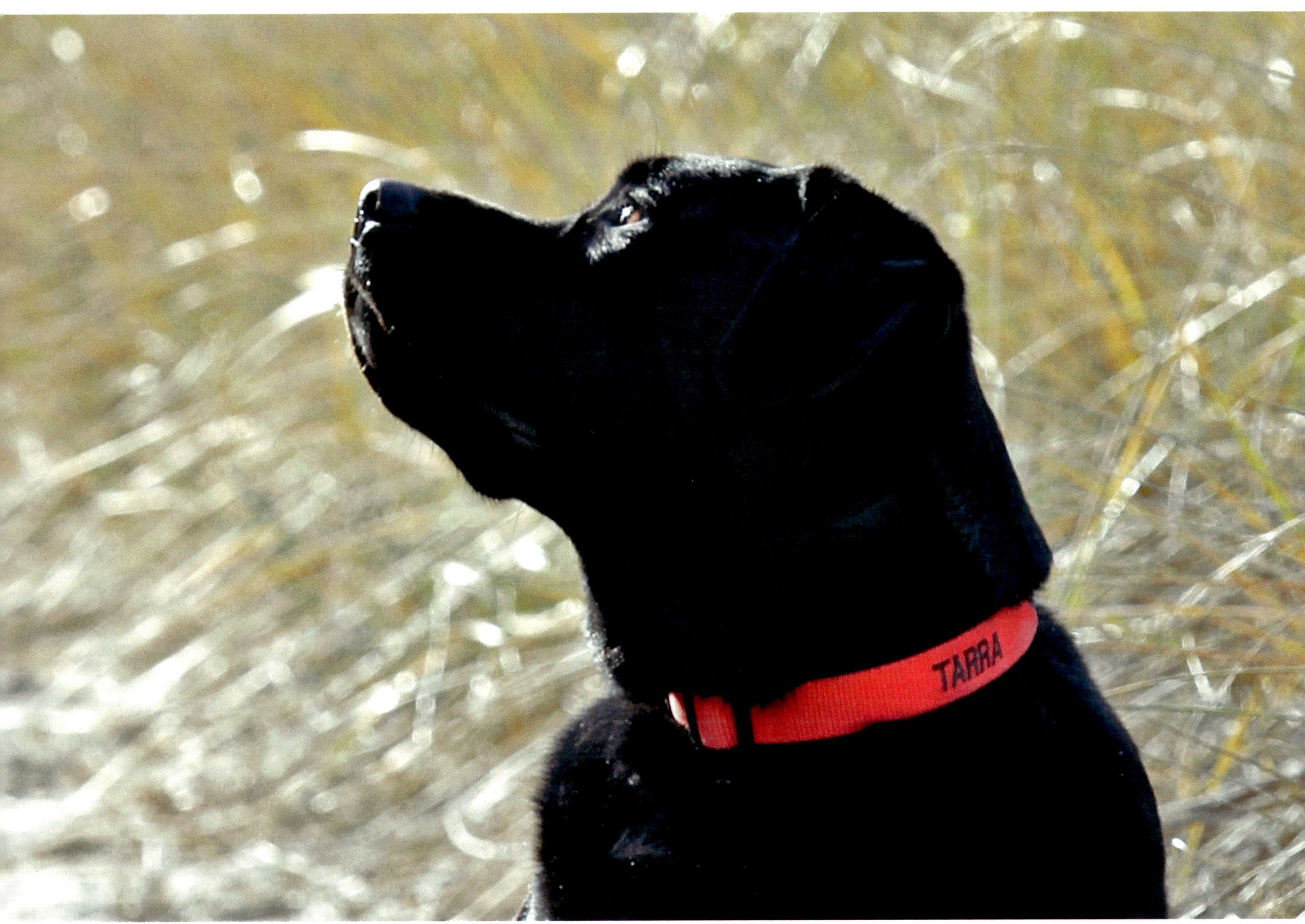

Tarra (above), Labrador retriever, Ridgevale Beach

Beckett (opposite), collie, Harding's Beach

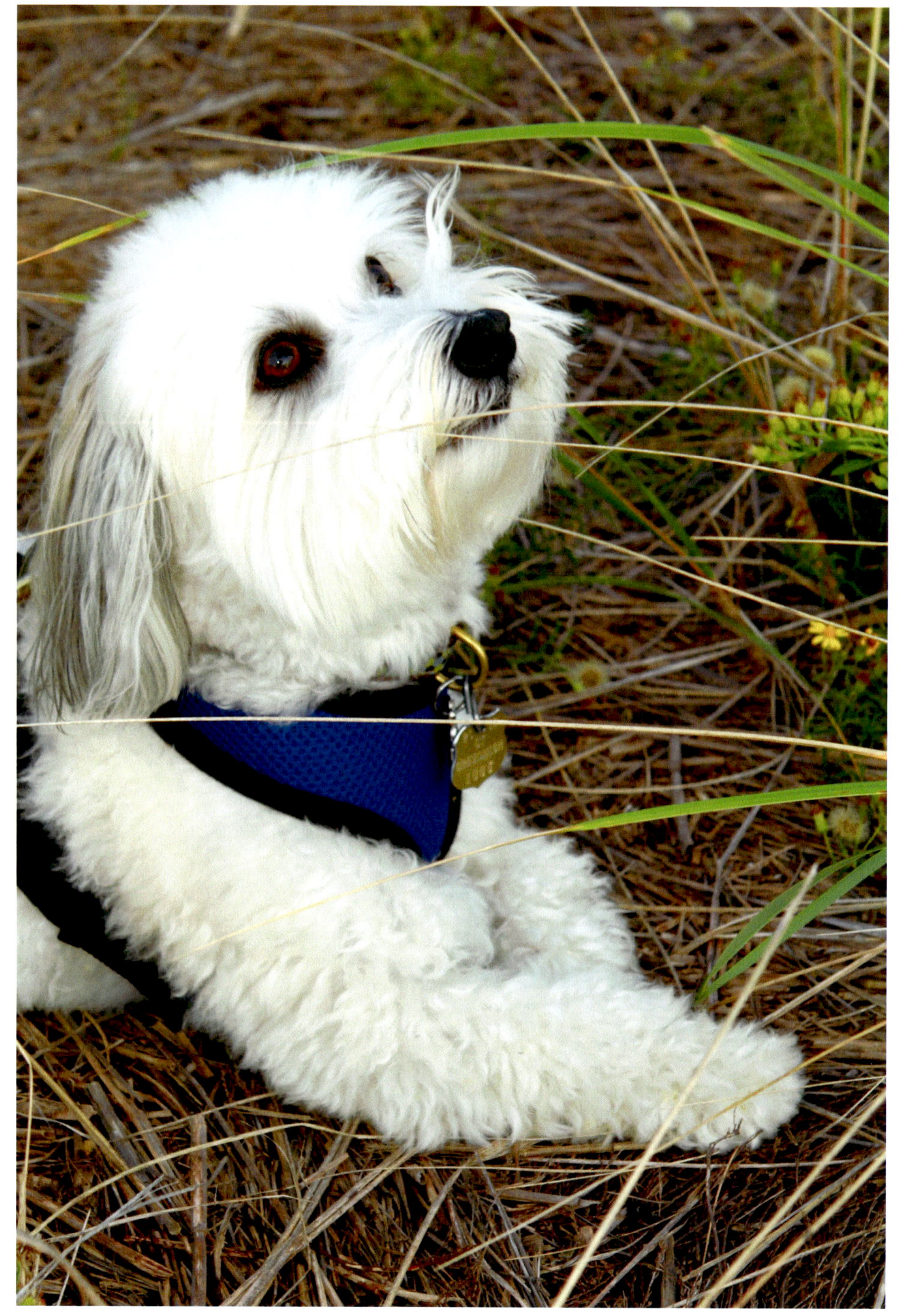

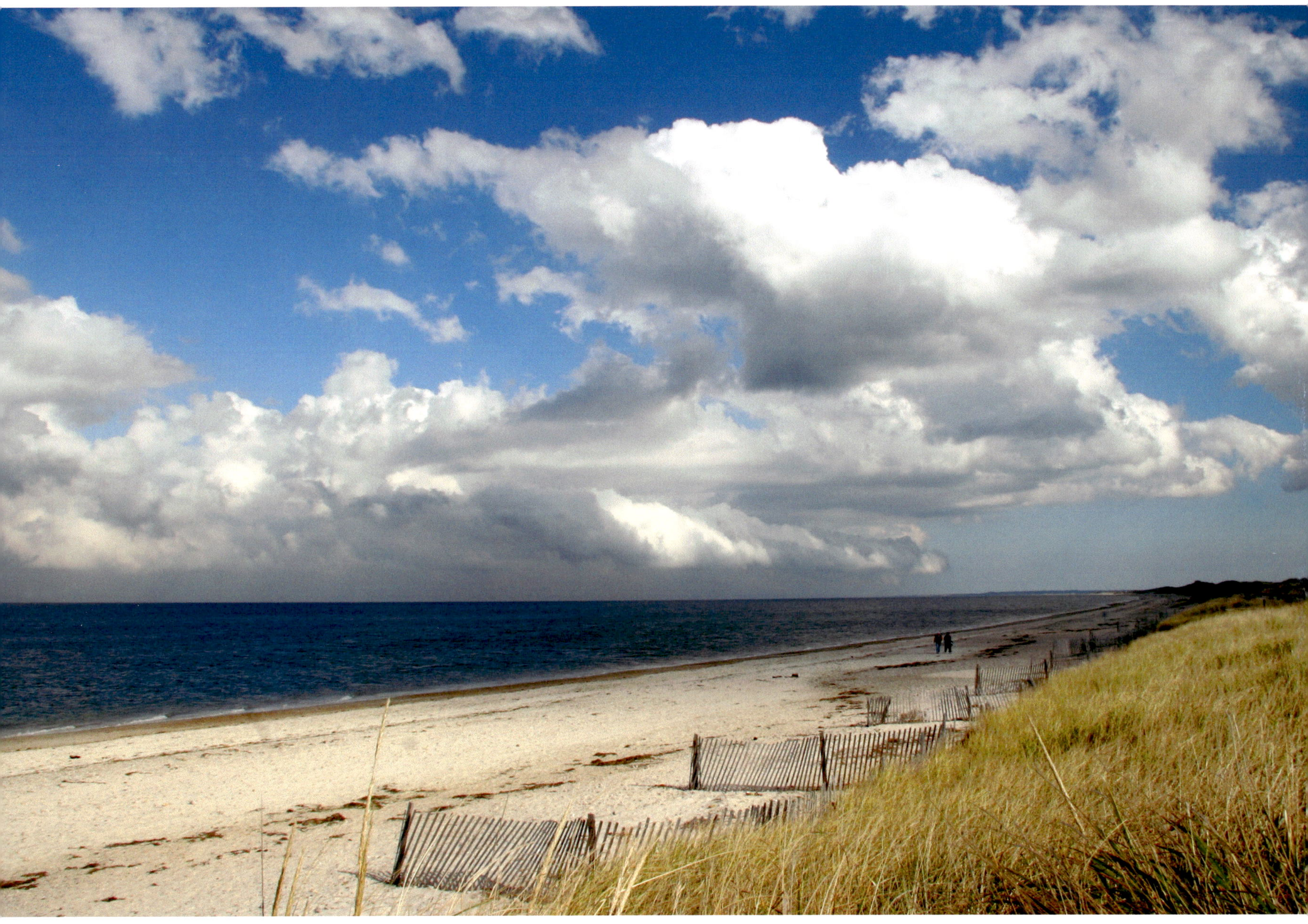

Sandy Neck Beach (above)

Dash (opposite), Havanese, Outermost Harbor

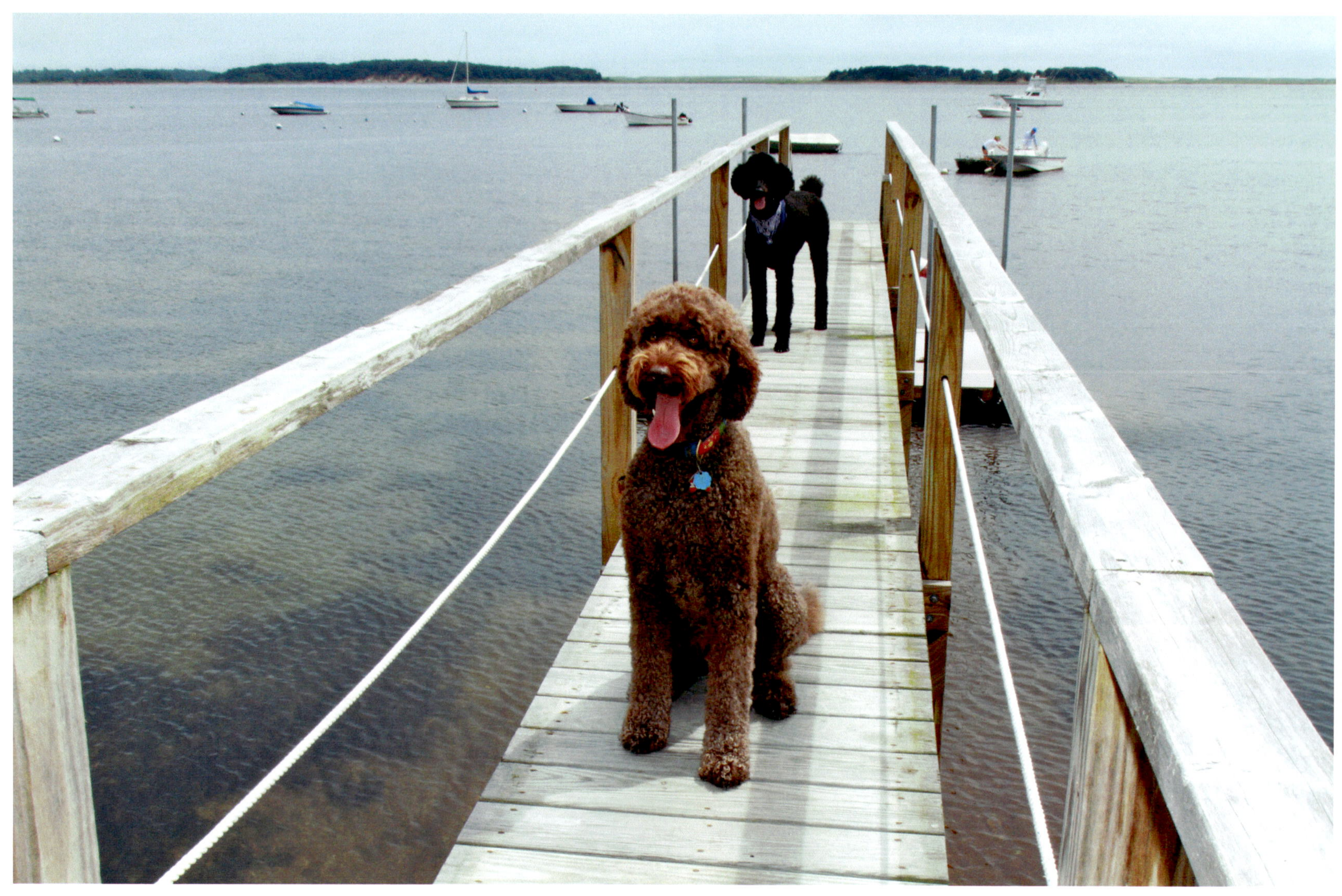

Wilbur, Australian labradoodle, and **Bandit**, standard poodle, Little Pleasant Bay

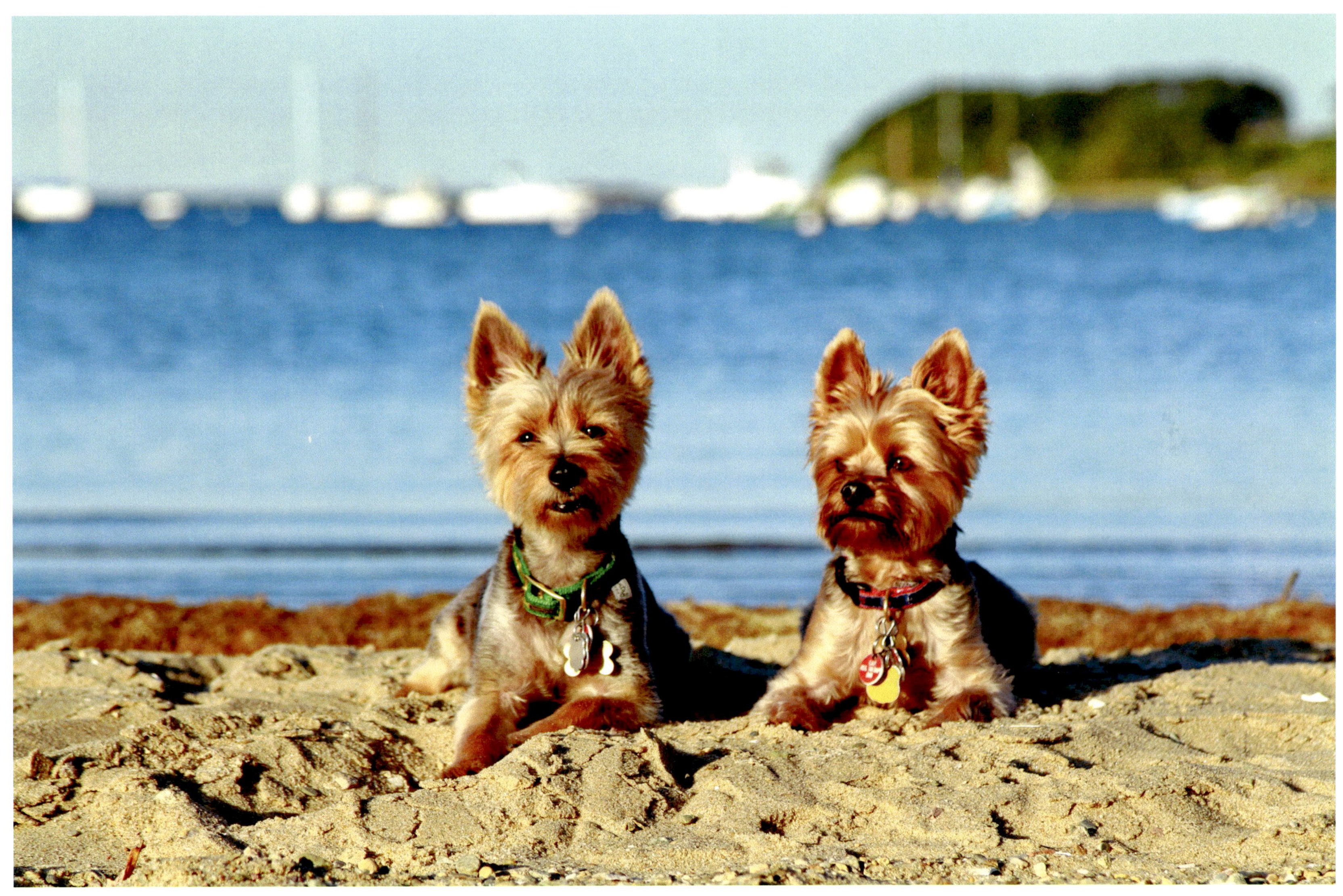

Fenway, silky terrier, and **Monomoy**, Yorkshire terrier, Pleasant Bay

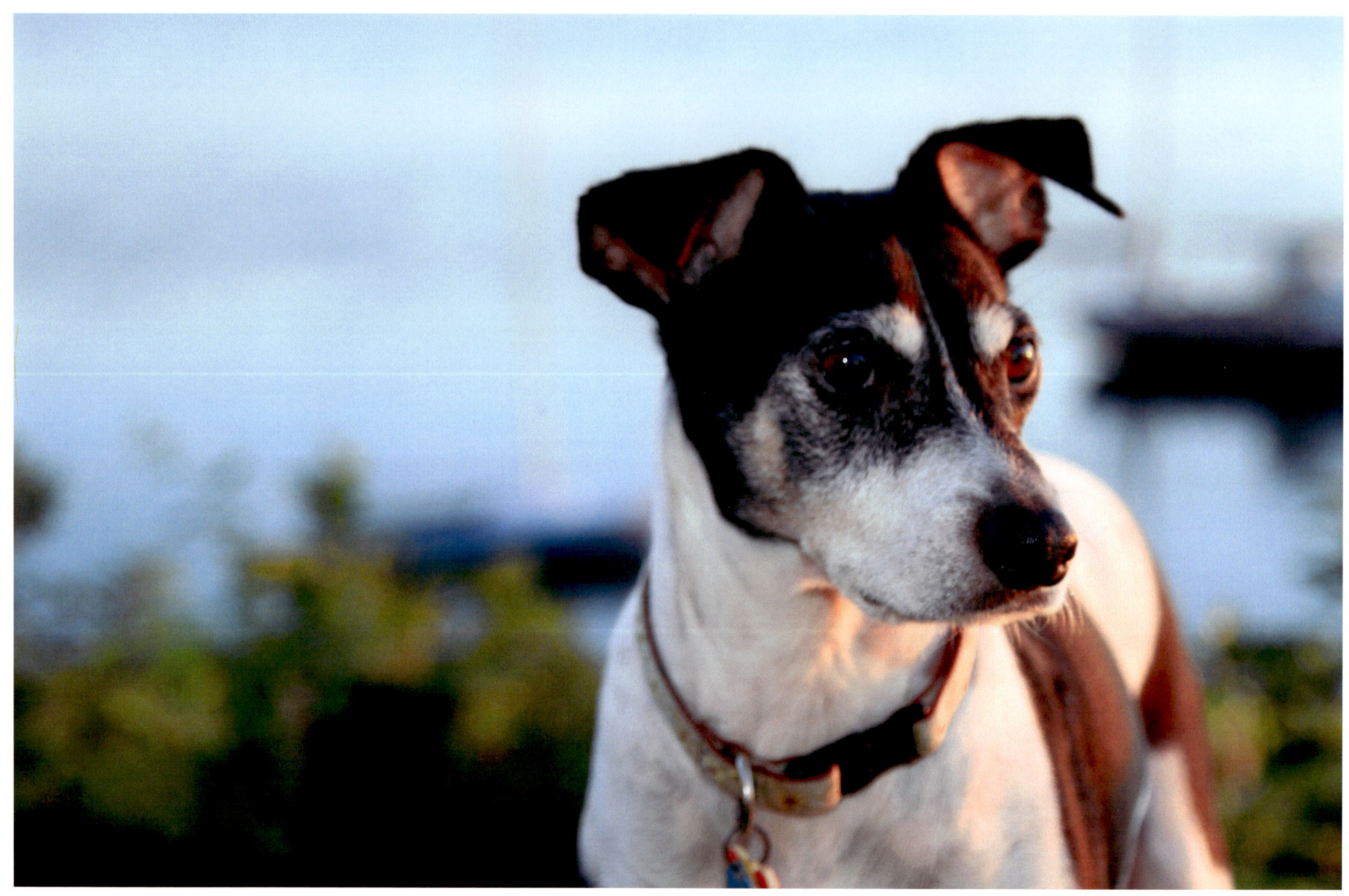

Polly, rat terrier, Oyster River

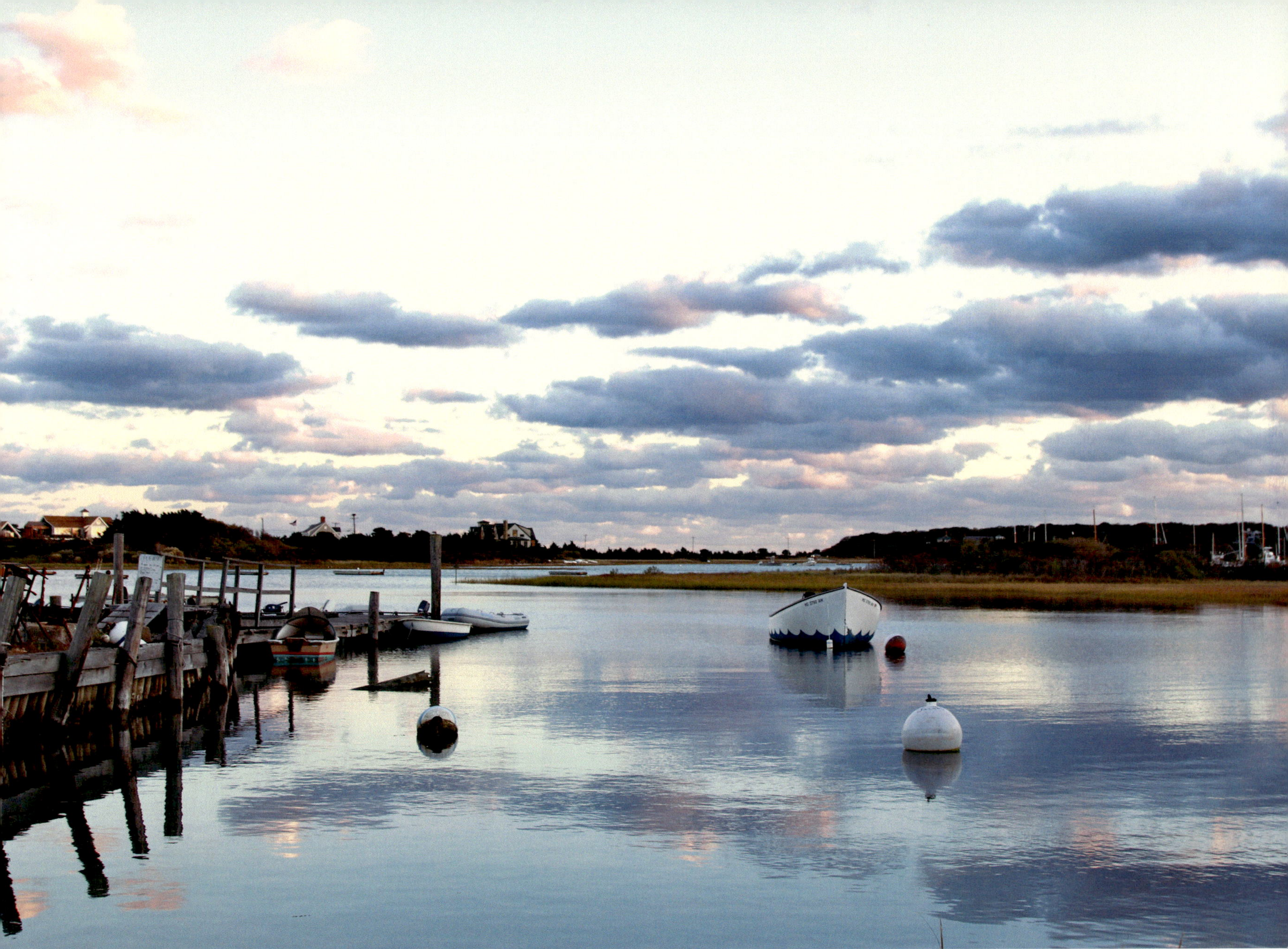

Stage Harbor

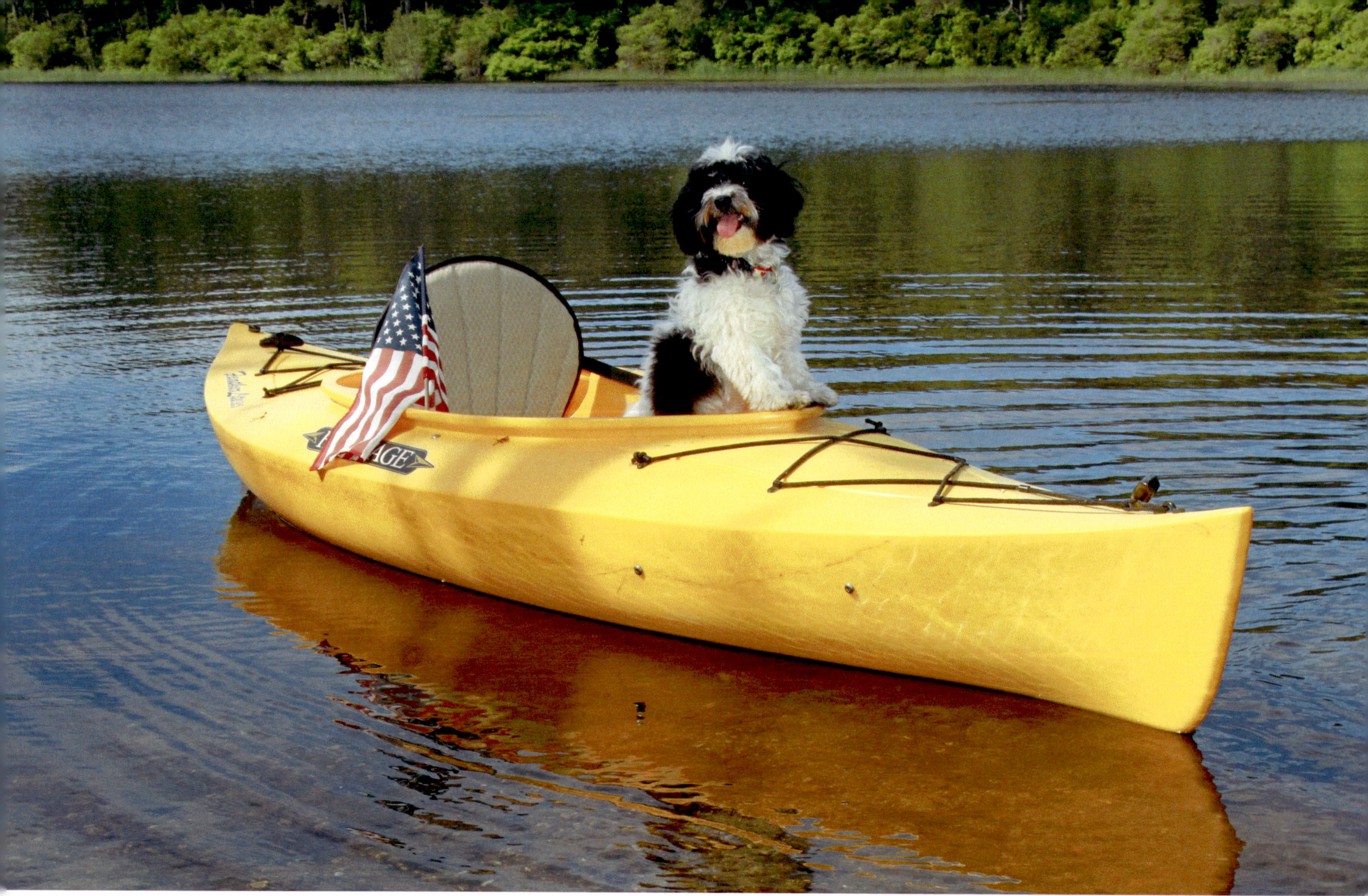

Zoey, Havanese, Pickerel Pond

Schosi, Jack Russell terrier mix, Arey's Pond

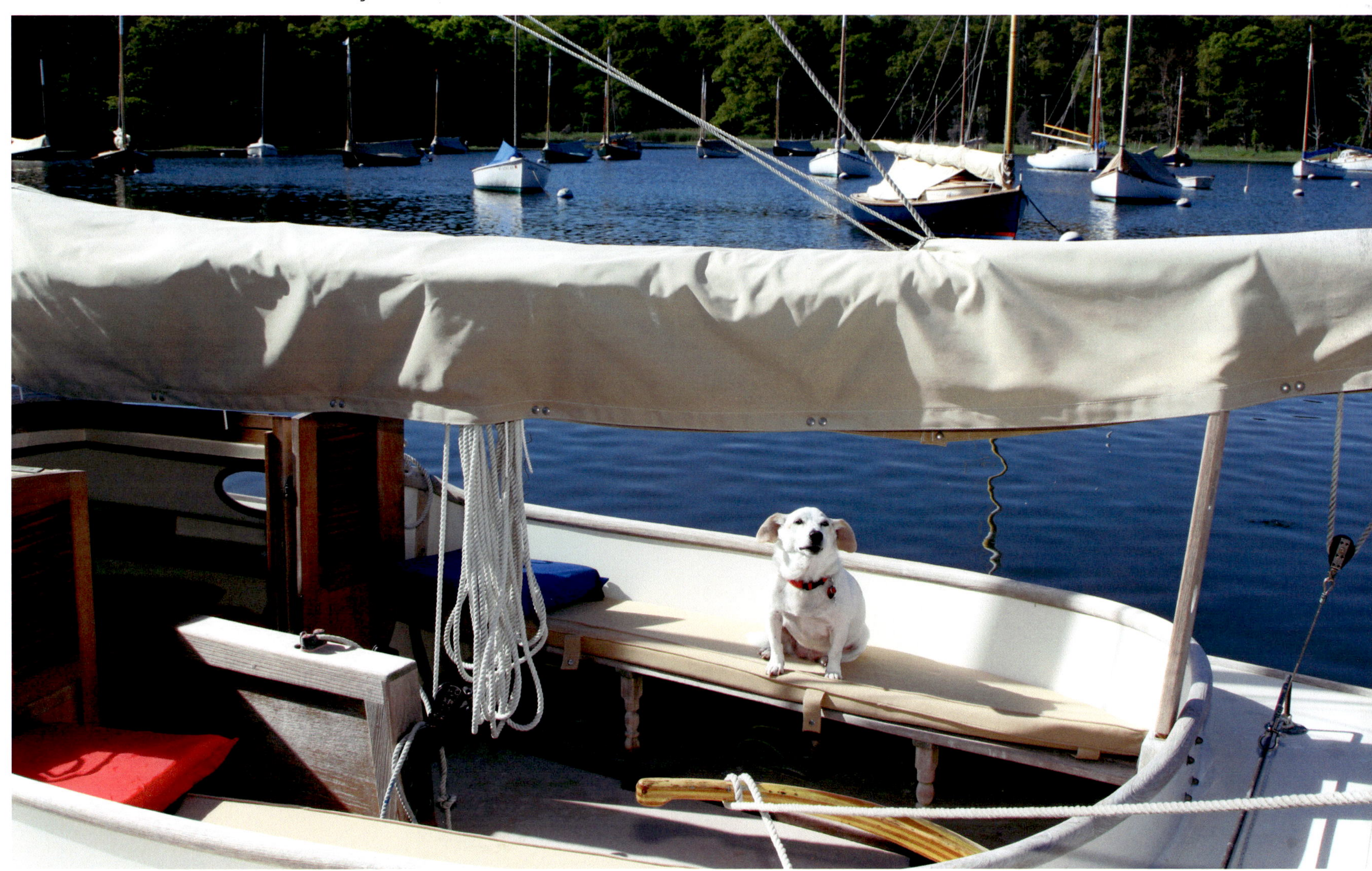

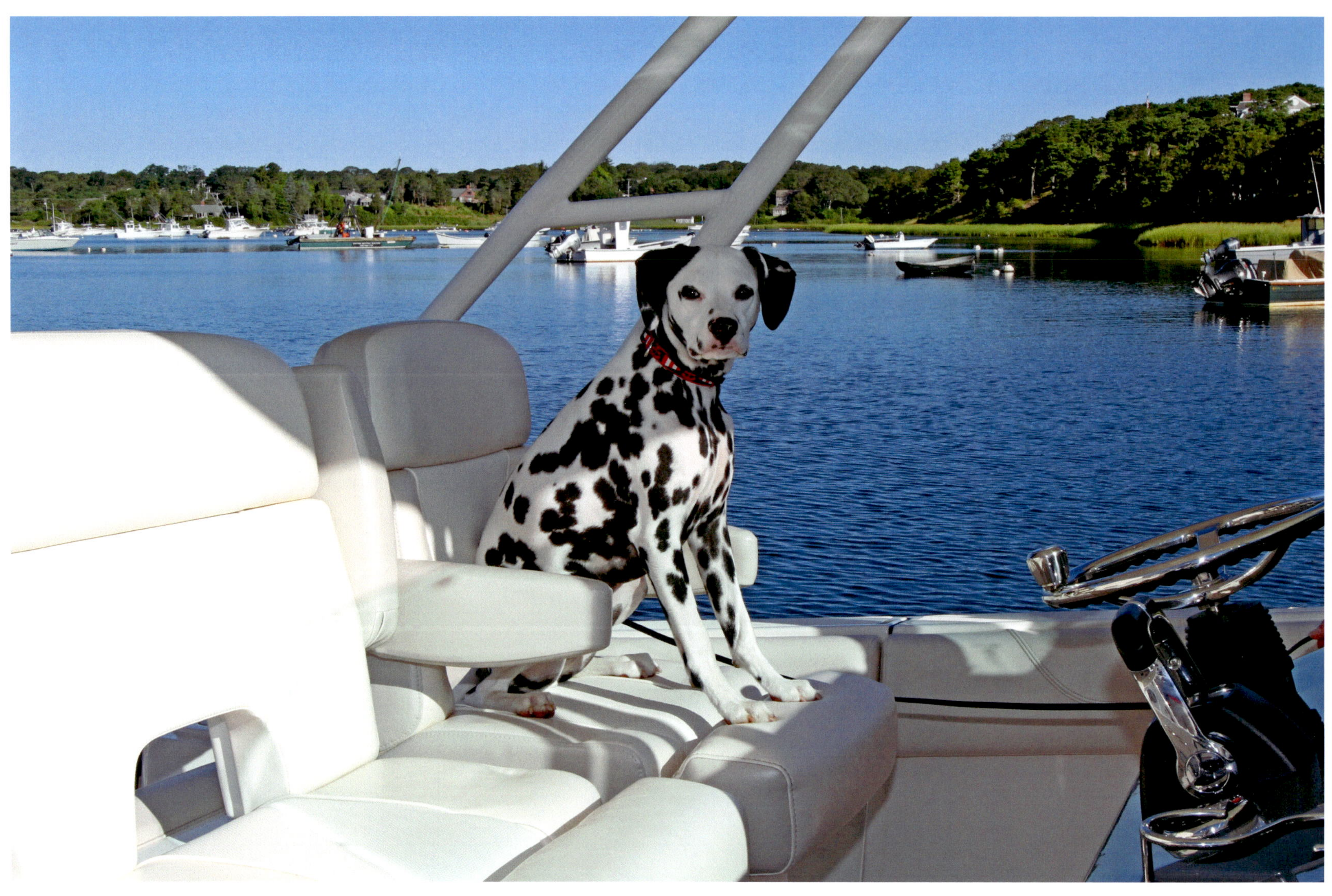

Stormy, Dalmatian, Ryder's Cove

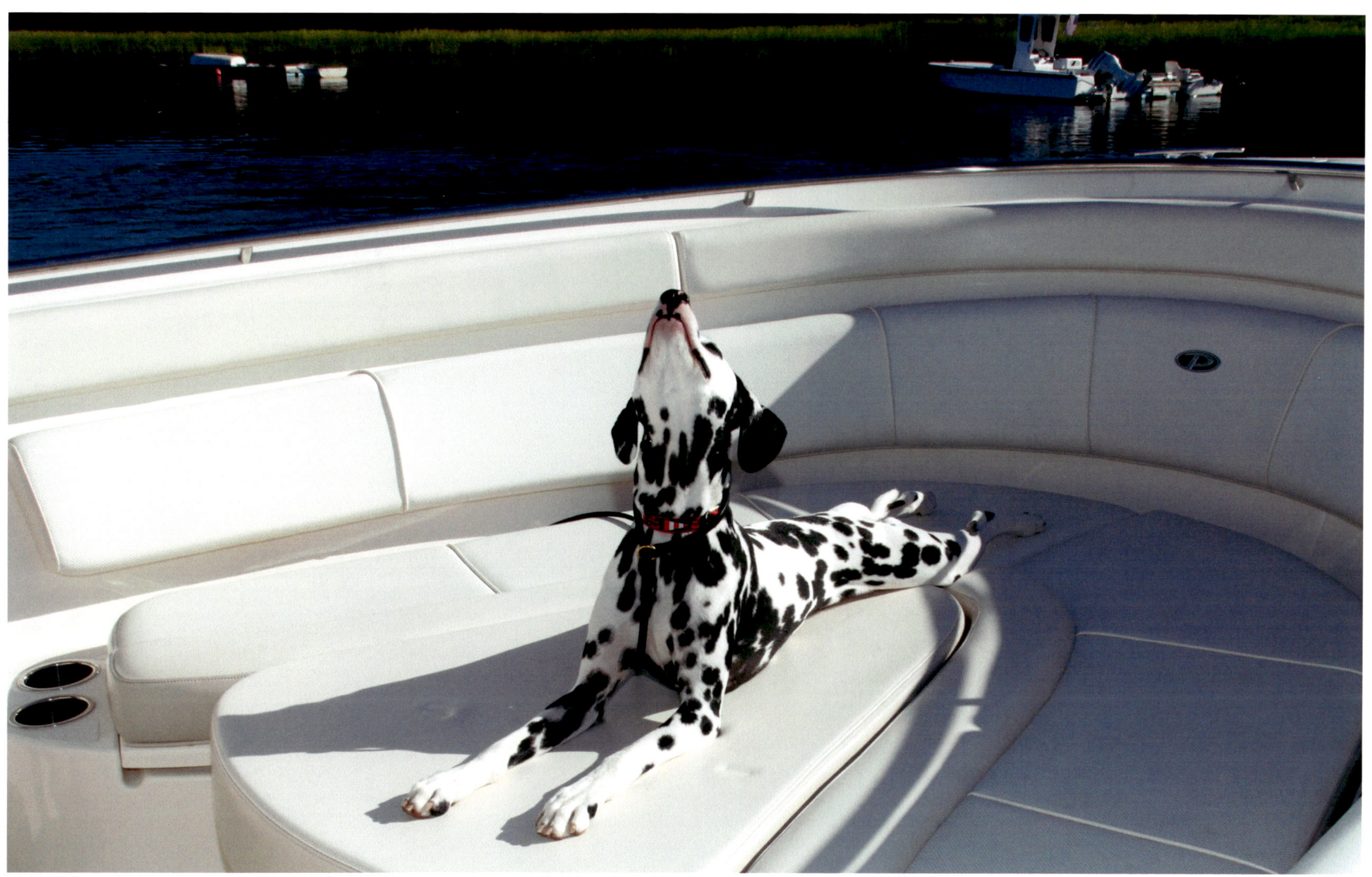

Oliver, Papillon, in the Brewster Bookstore

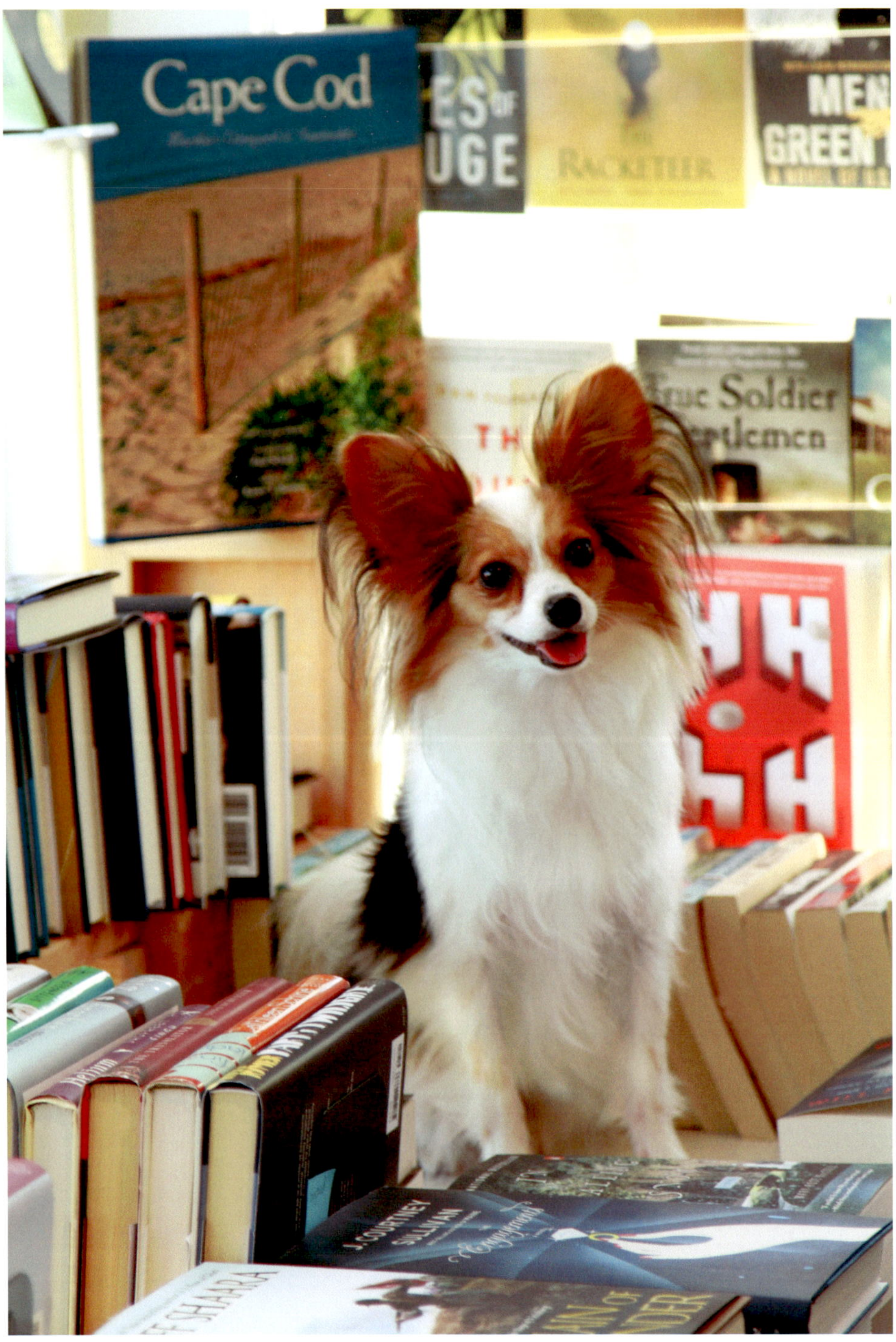

Danger, miniature pinscher

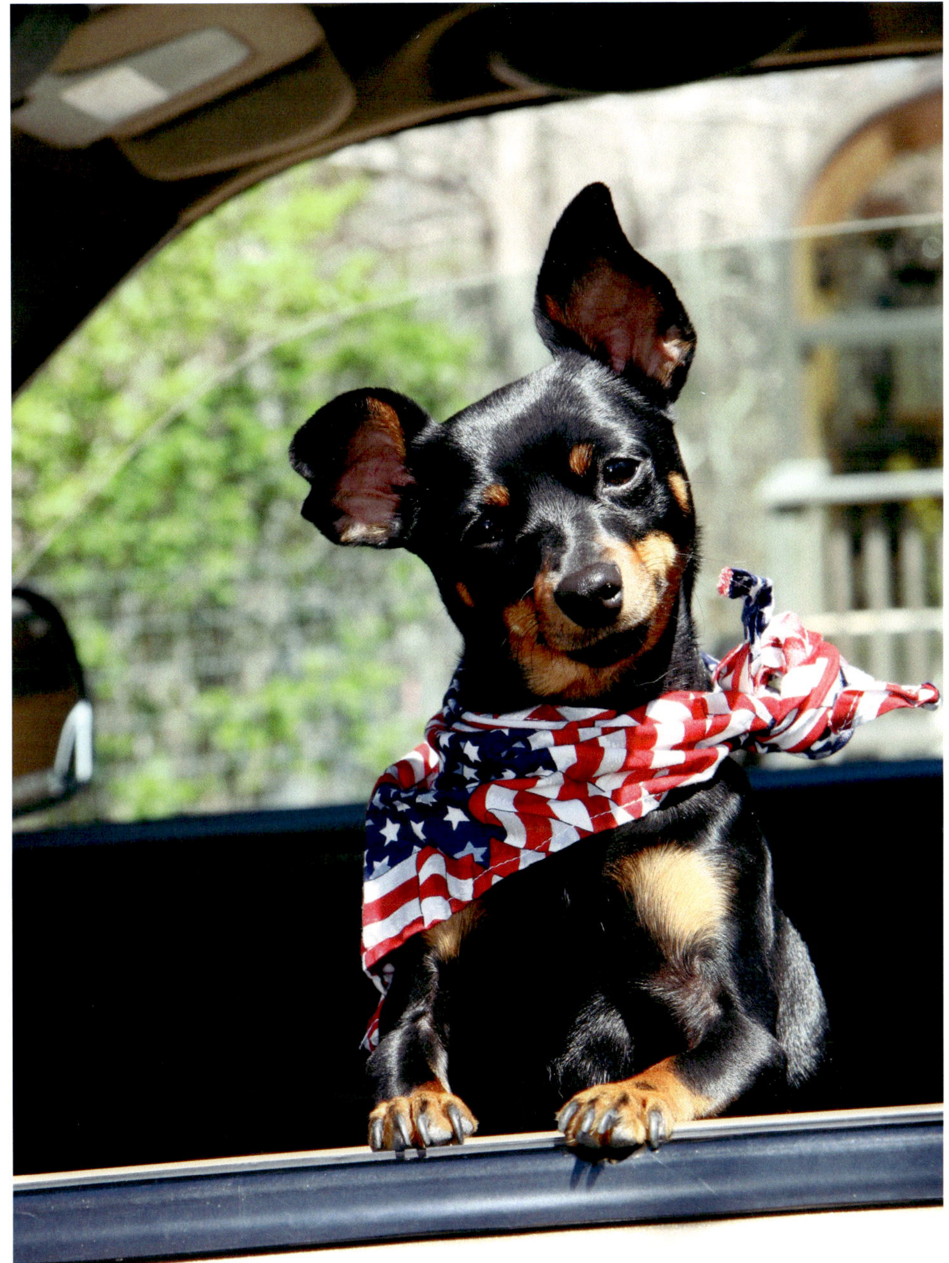

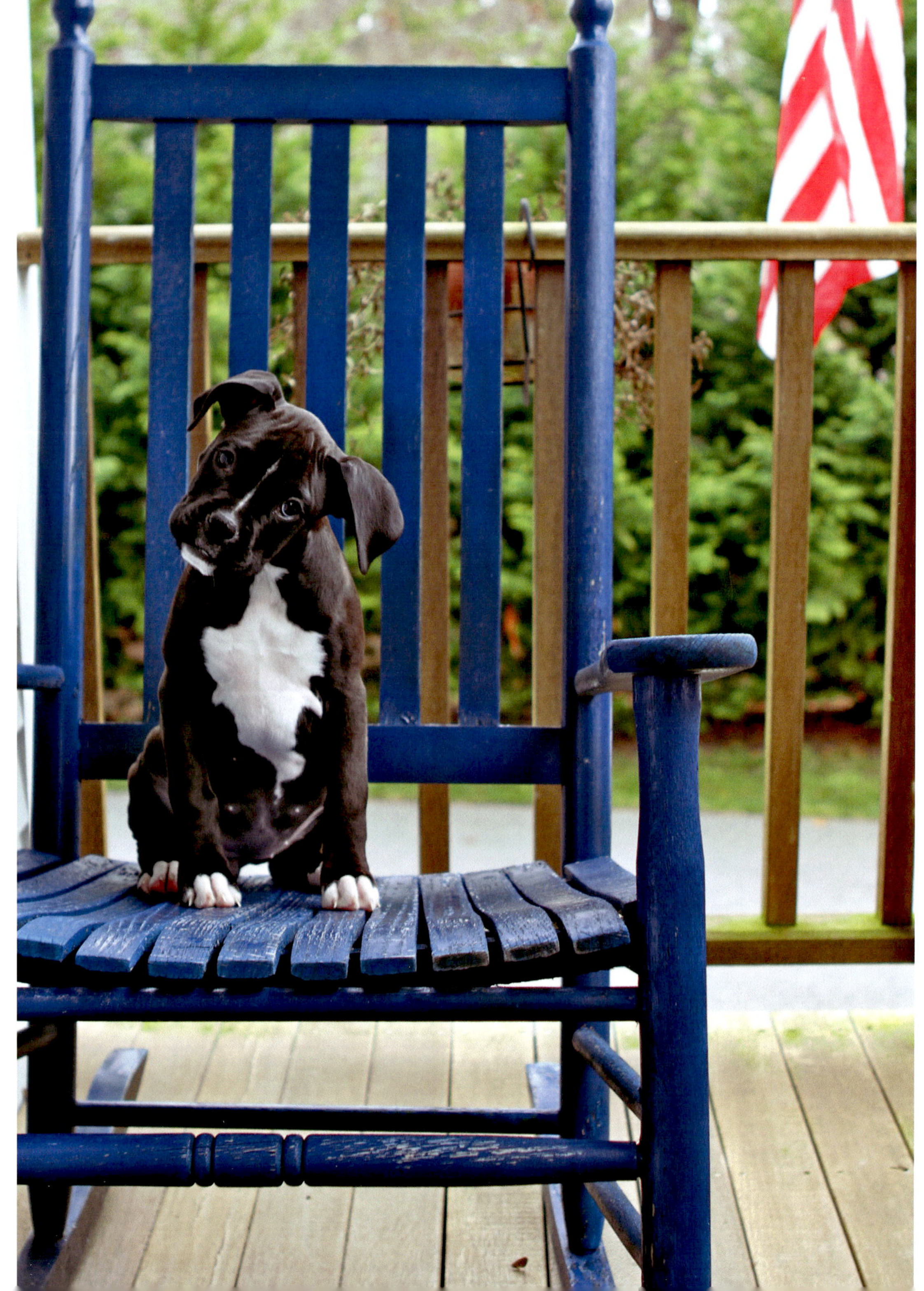

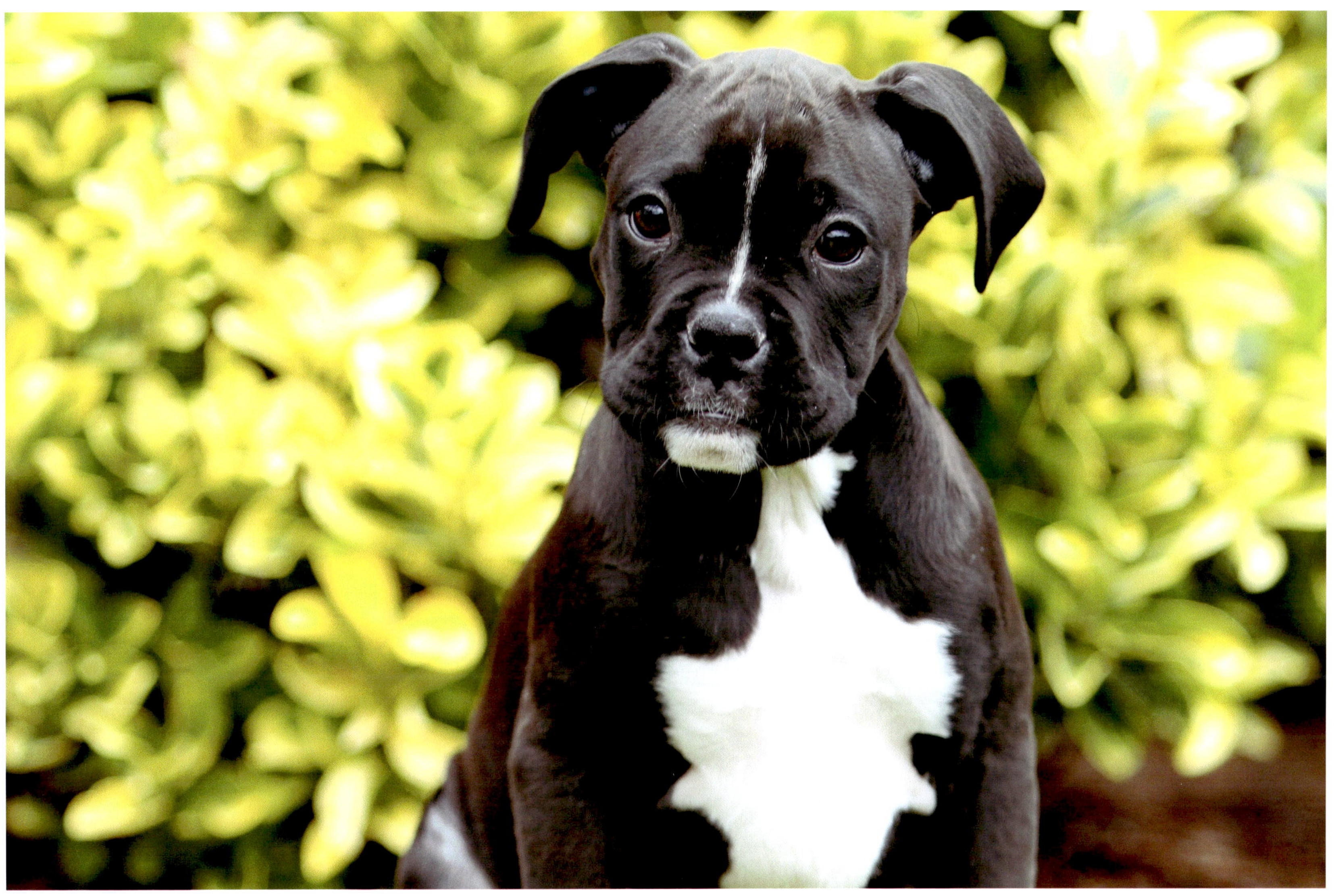

Nike, sealed brindle boxer

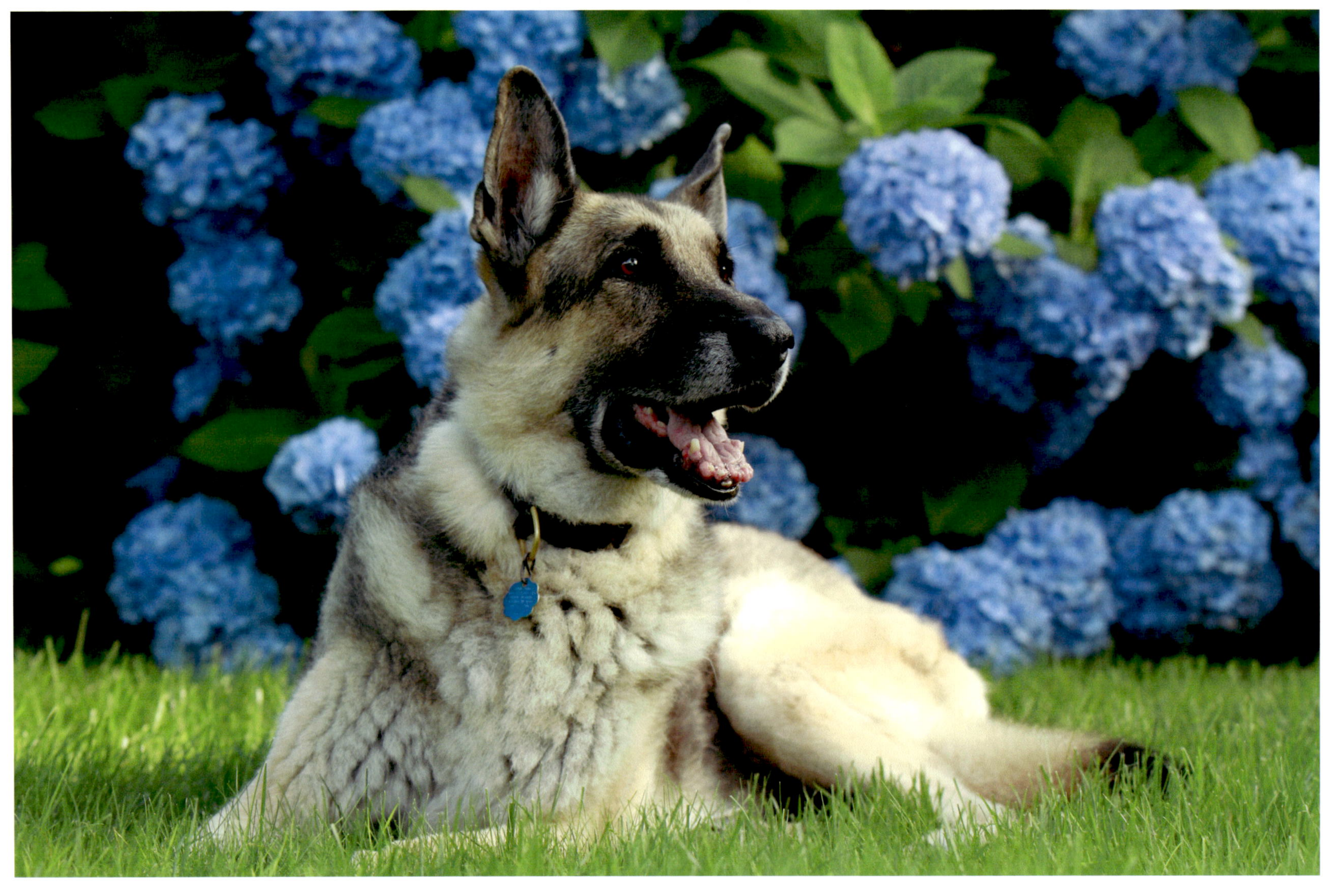

Buckley (above), German shepherd

Noelle, **Trooper**, and **Stogie**, (opposite), British cream golden retrievers

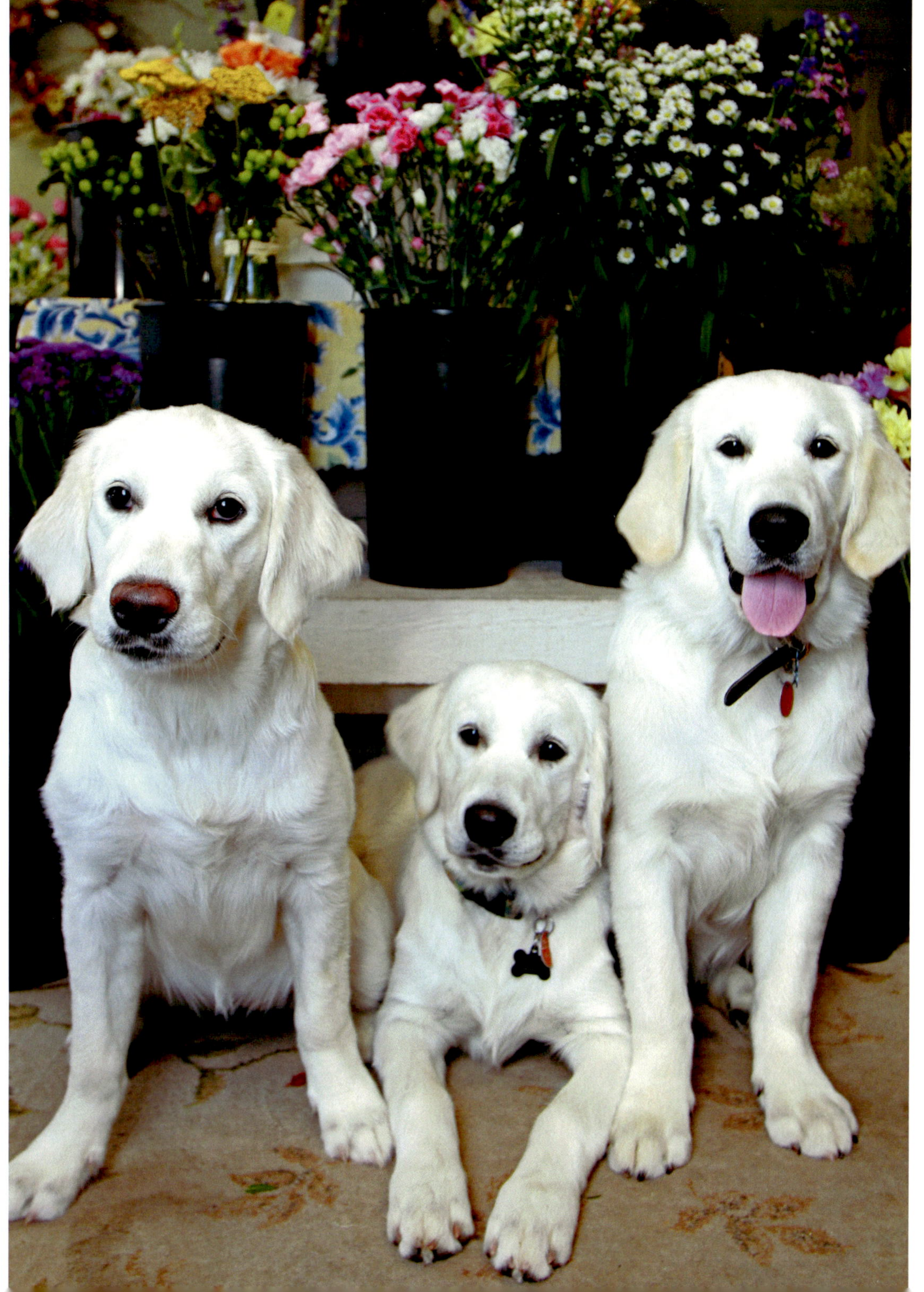

Hank, Labrador retriever

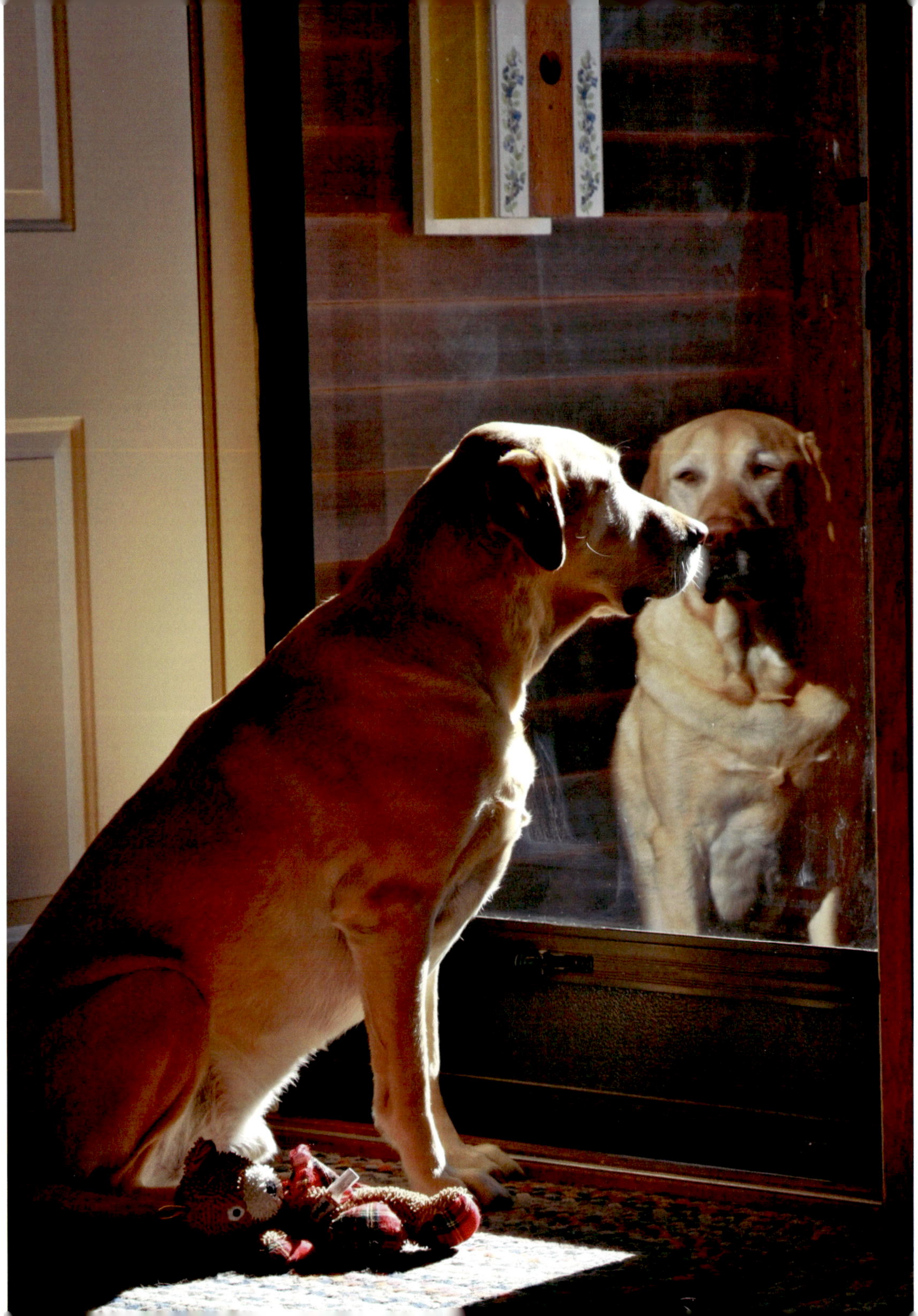

Such short little lives our pets have to spend with us, and they spend most of it waiting for us to come home each day.

— John Grogan, *Marley and Me*

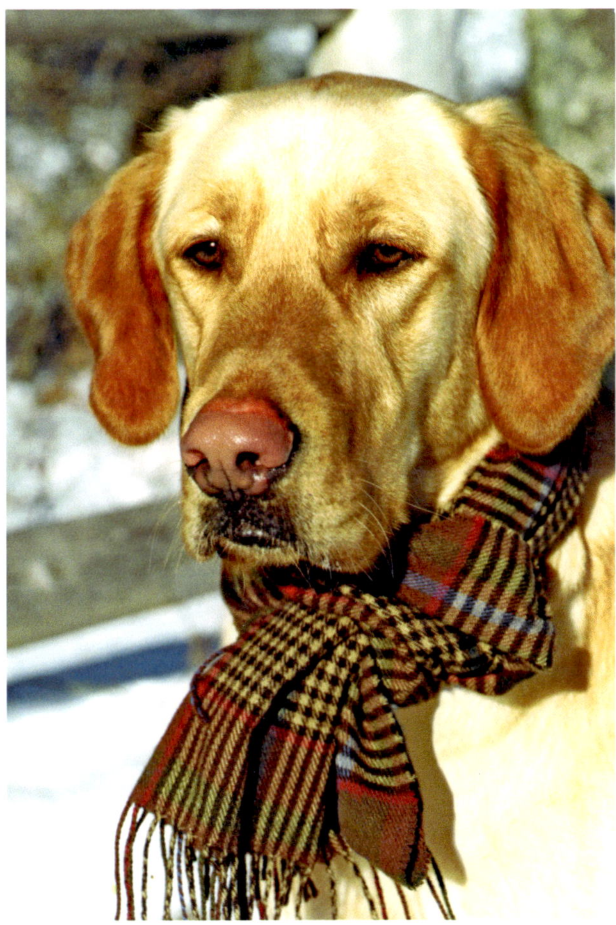

Jack, golden retriever mix

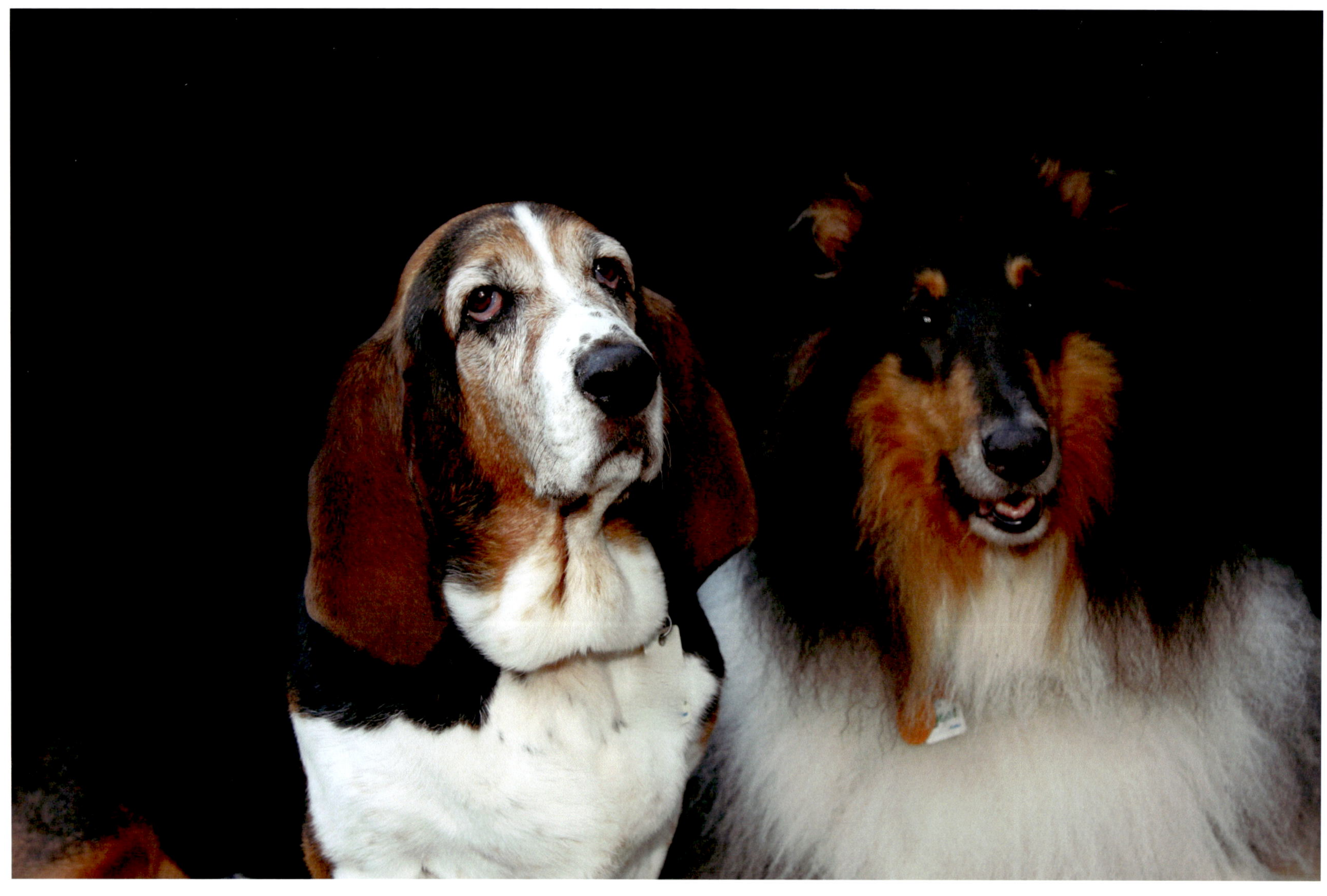

Snickers, bassett hound, and **Beckett**, collie (above)

Jake, Boston terrier, and **Sophie**, toy Yorkshire terrier (opposite)

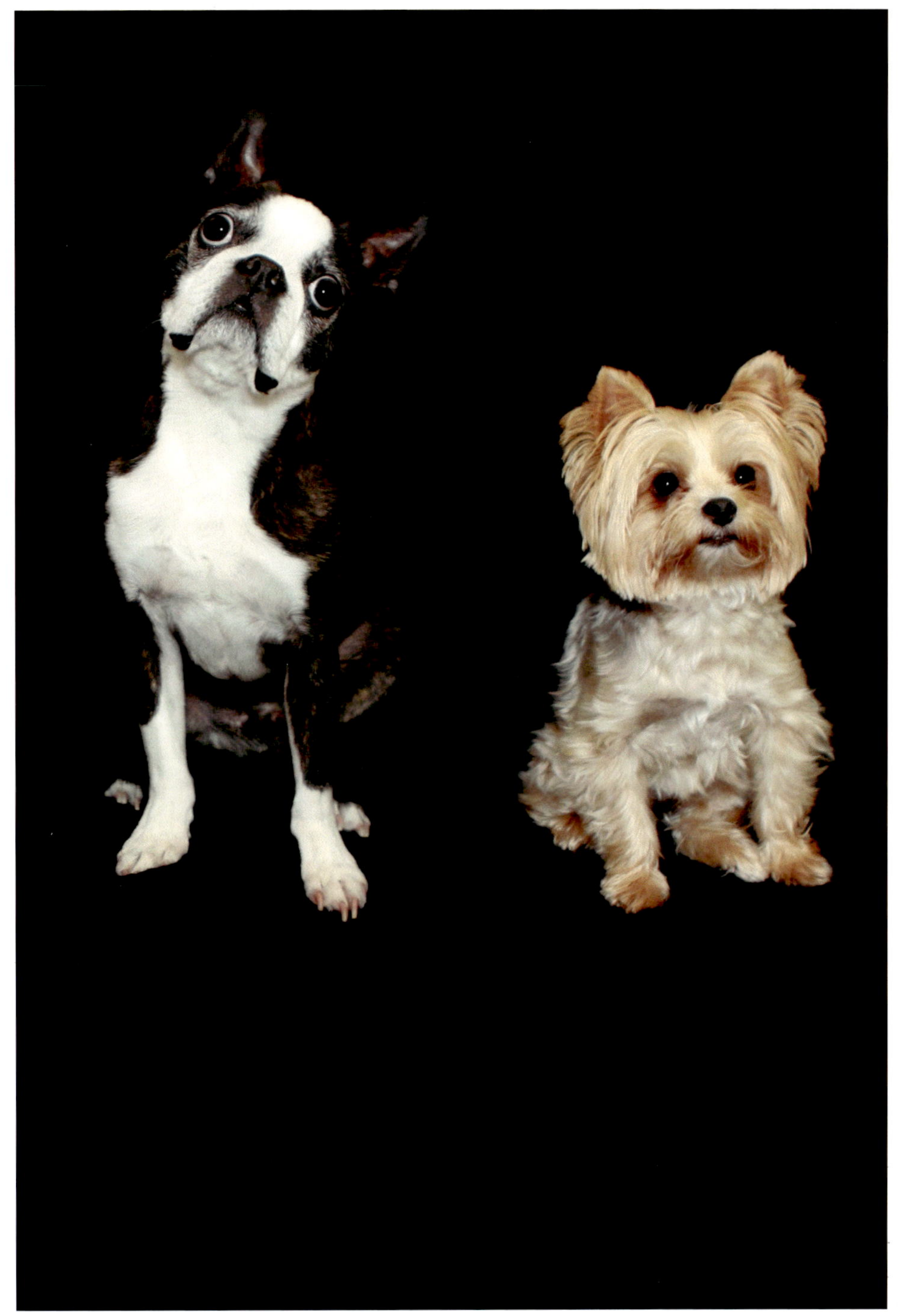

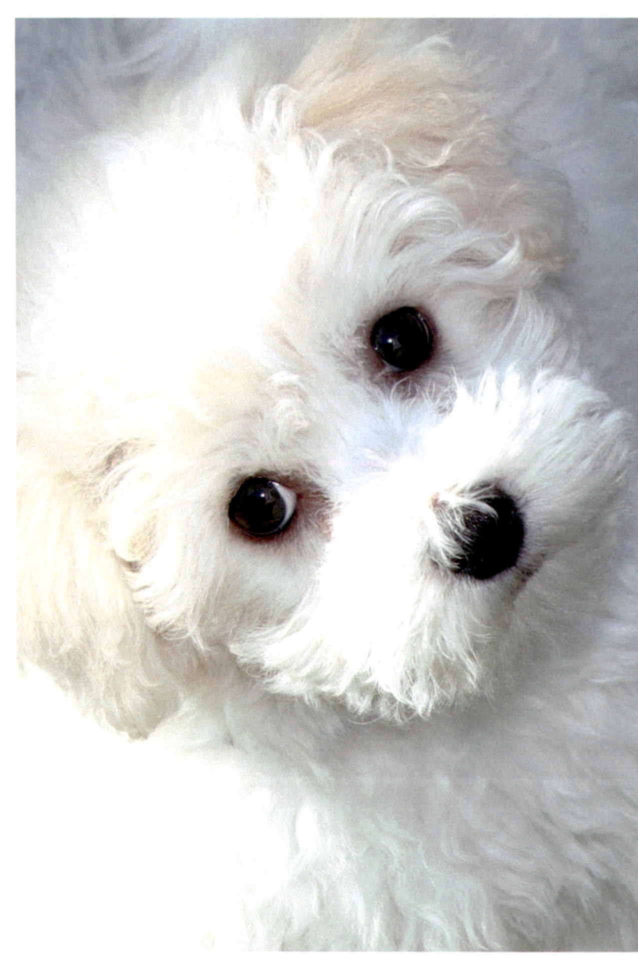

A puppy is a puppy is a puppy.
He's probably in a basket with a bunch
of other puppies.

Then he's a little older and he's nothing
but a bundle of longing.

He doesn't even understand it.

Then someone picks him up and says,
"I want this one."

— Mary Oliver, *Dog Songs*

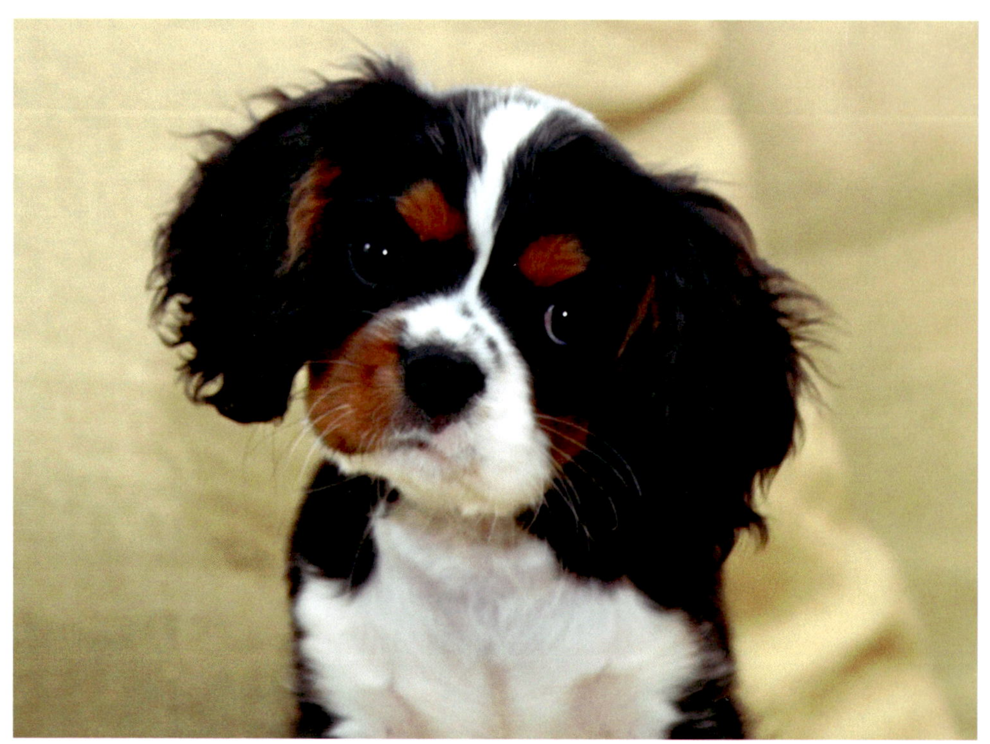

Ziva (above), bichon frise

Murphy (right), Cavalier King Charles spaniel

Stormy (opposite, top), Dalmatian

Lilli (opposite, bottom), schipperke

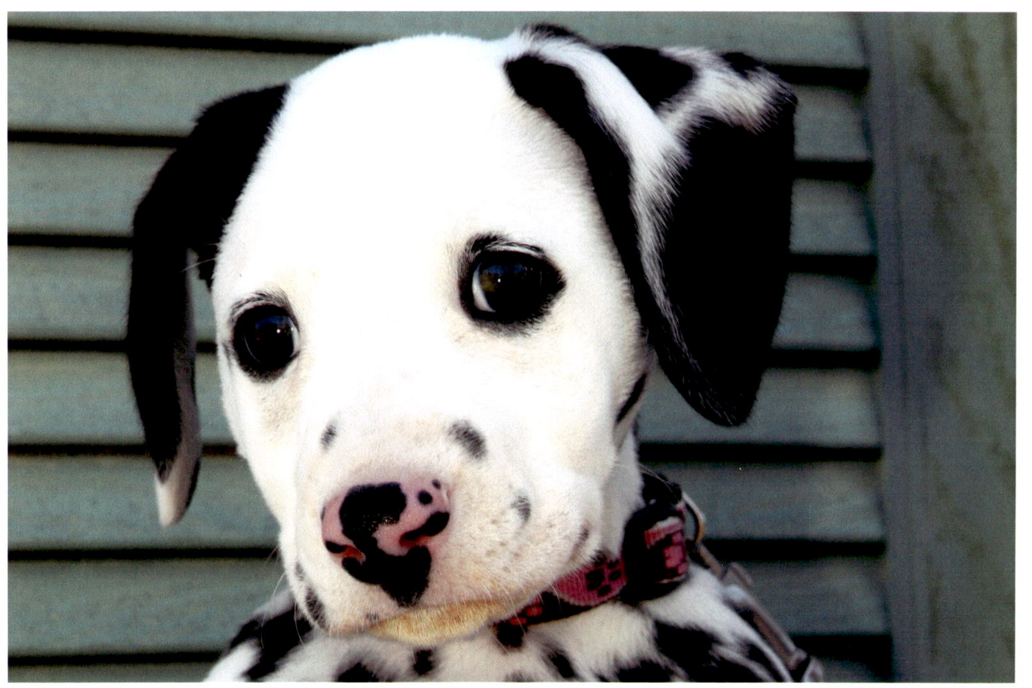

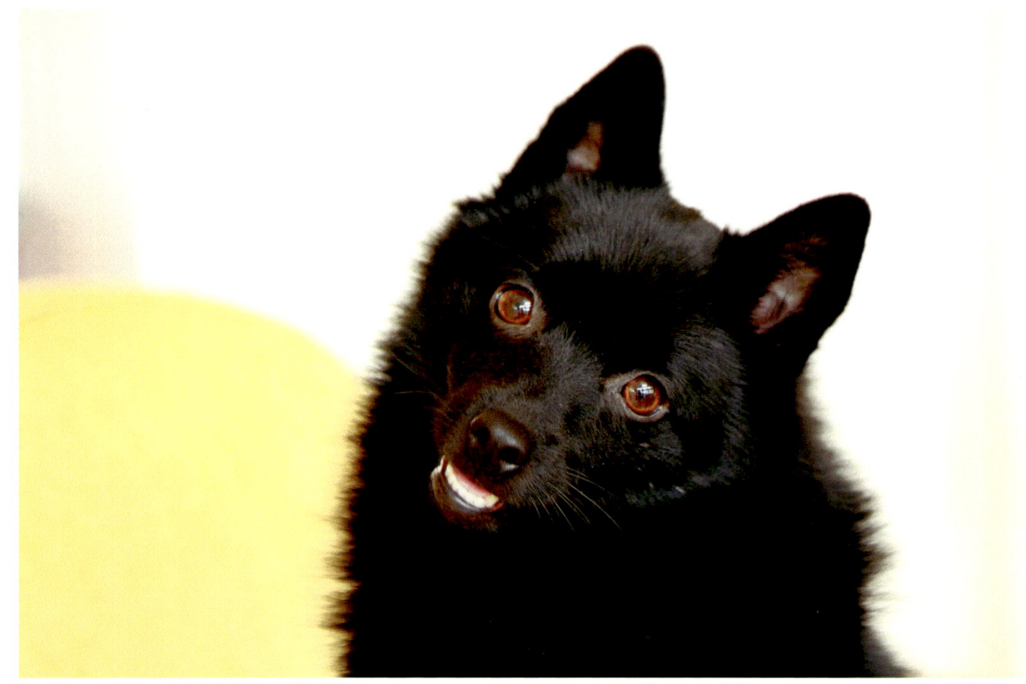

Henry (below) and **Chester** (bottom), Labrador retrievers

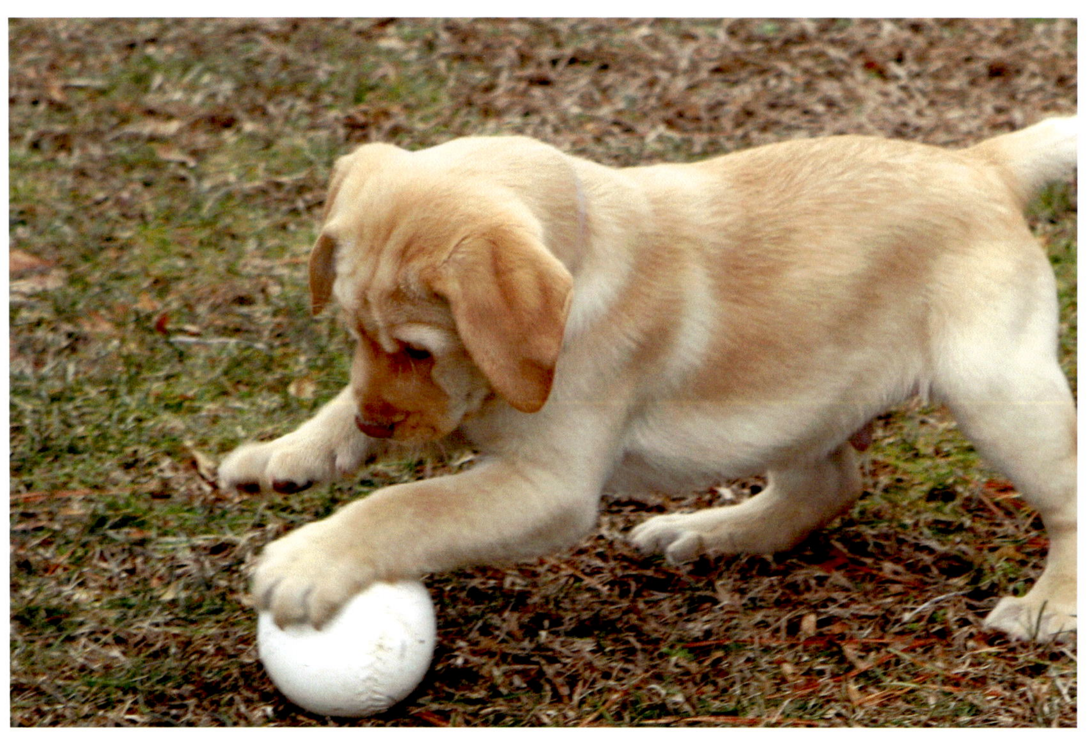

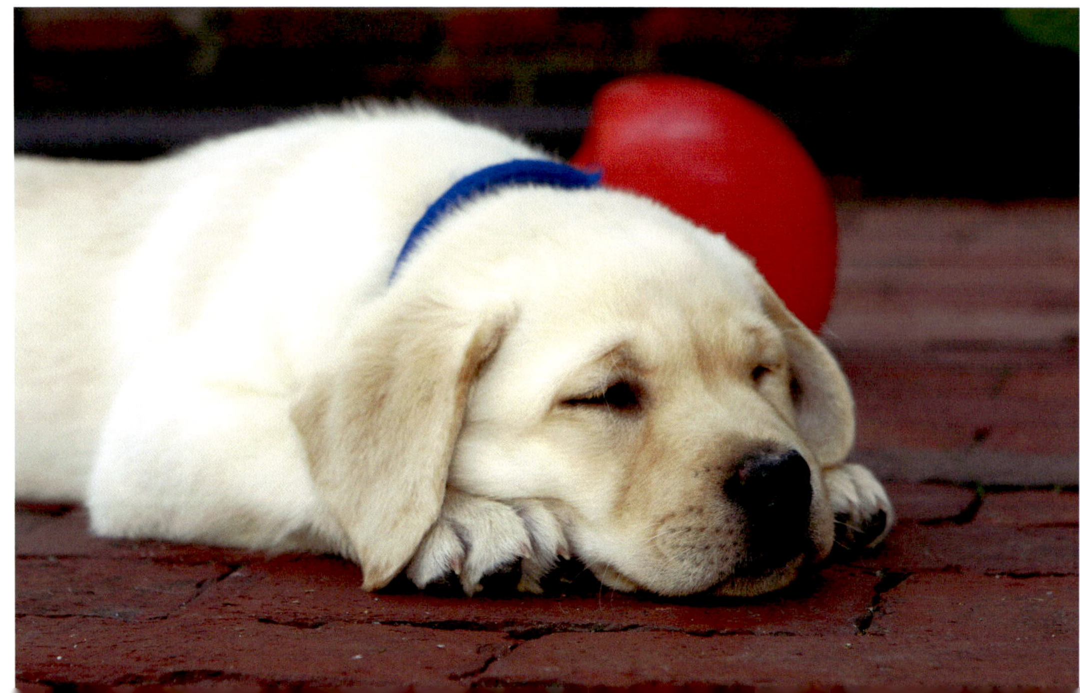

Gus (below) and **Hunter** and **Molly** (bottom), Labrador retrievers

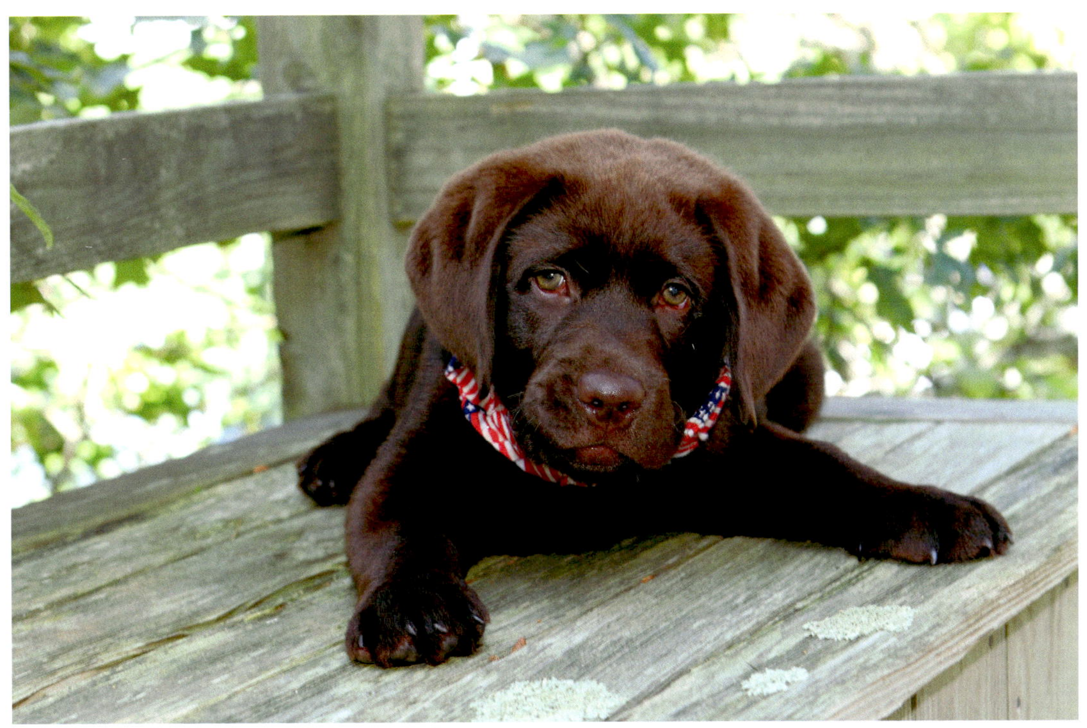

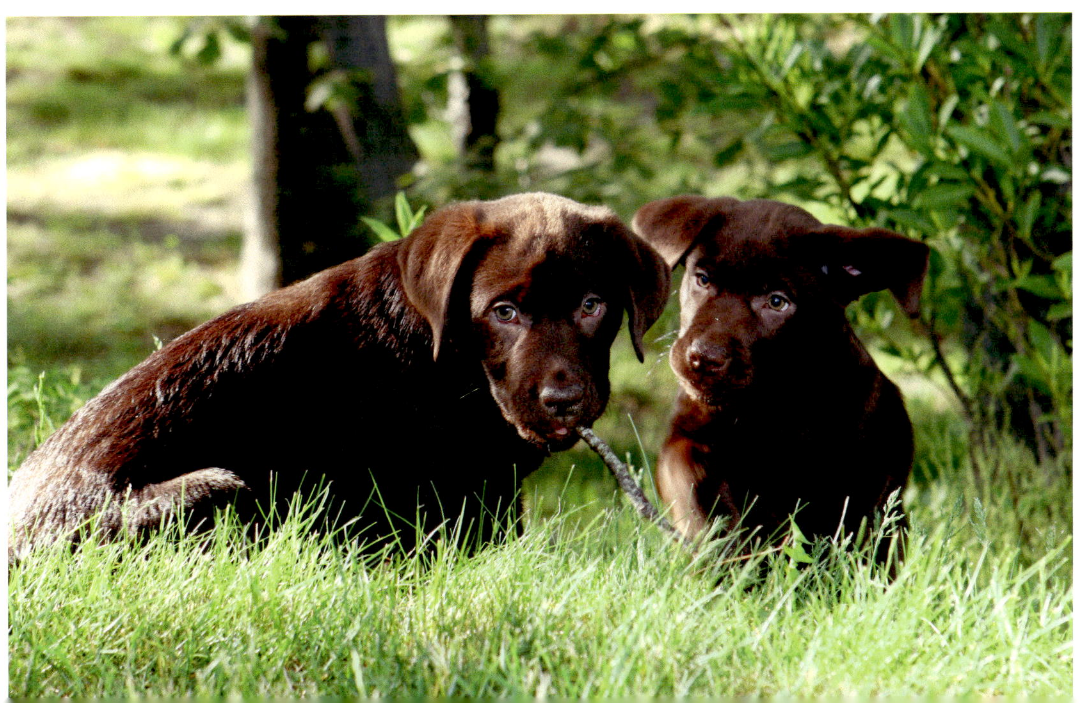

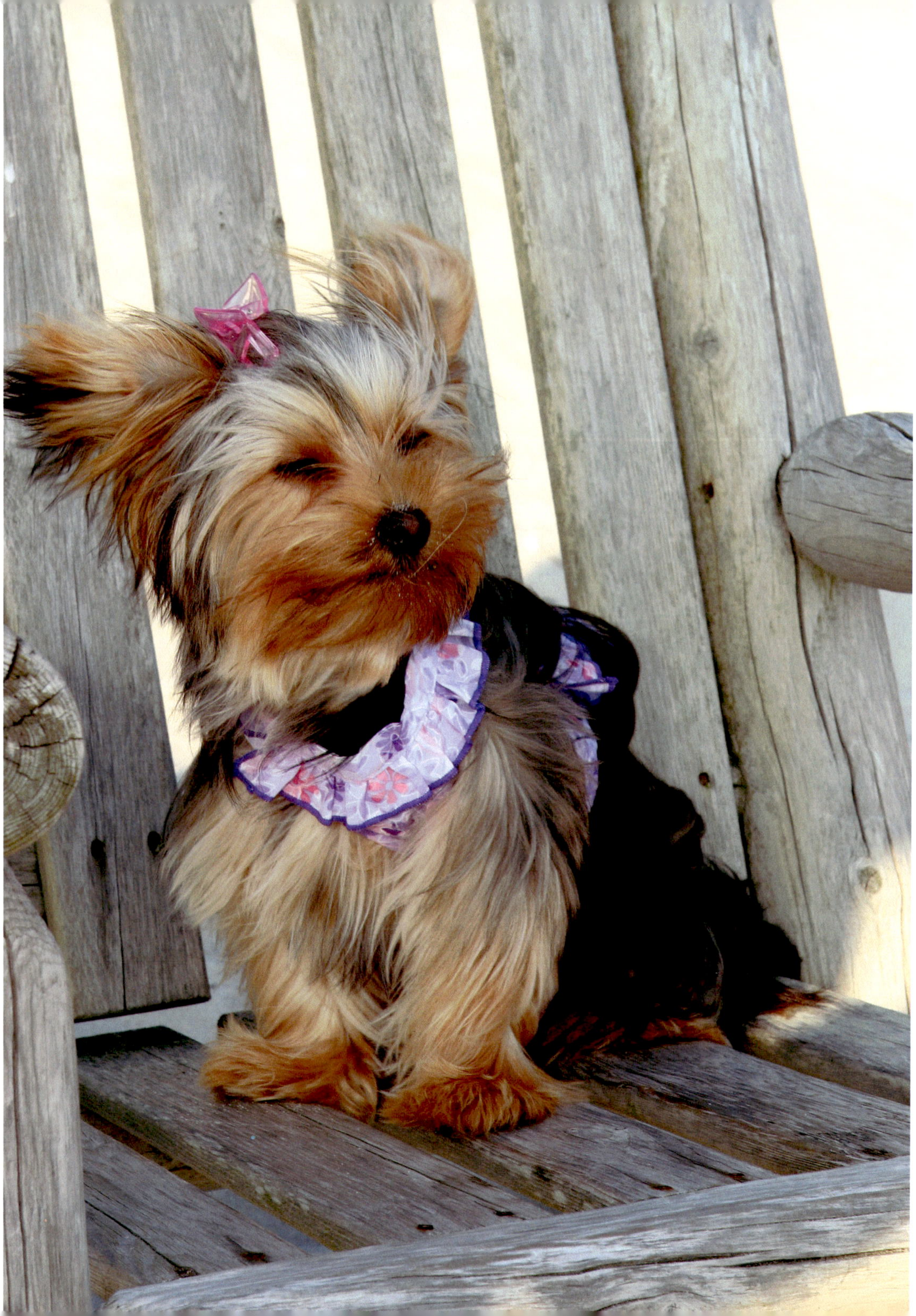

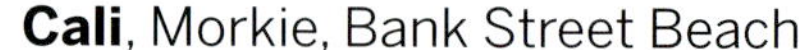

Cali, Morkie, Bank Street Beach

Forest Gump (below), pug; **Nellie** (bottom), Newfoundland

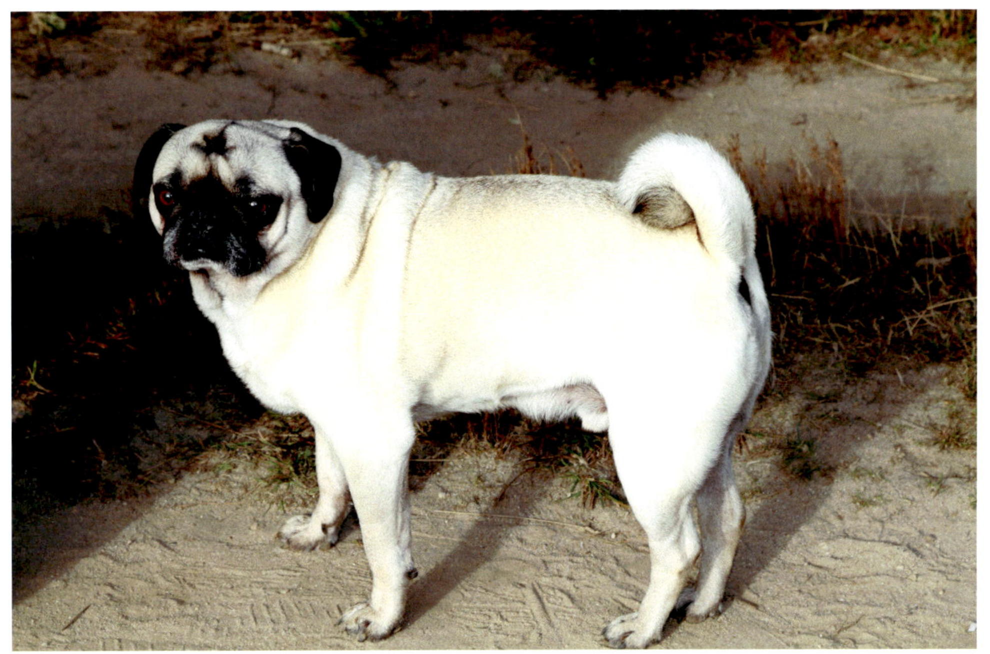

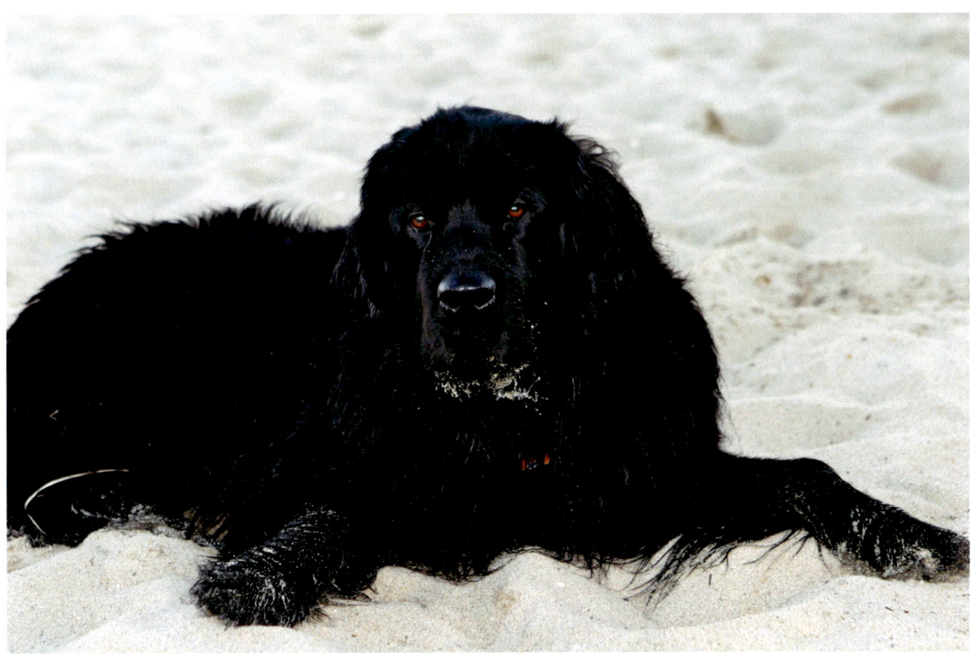

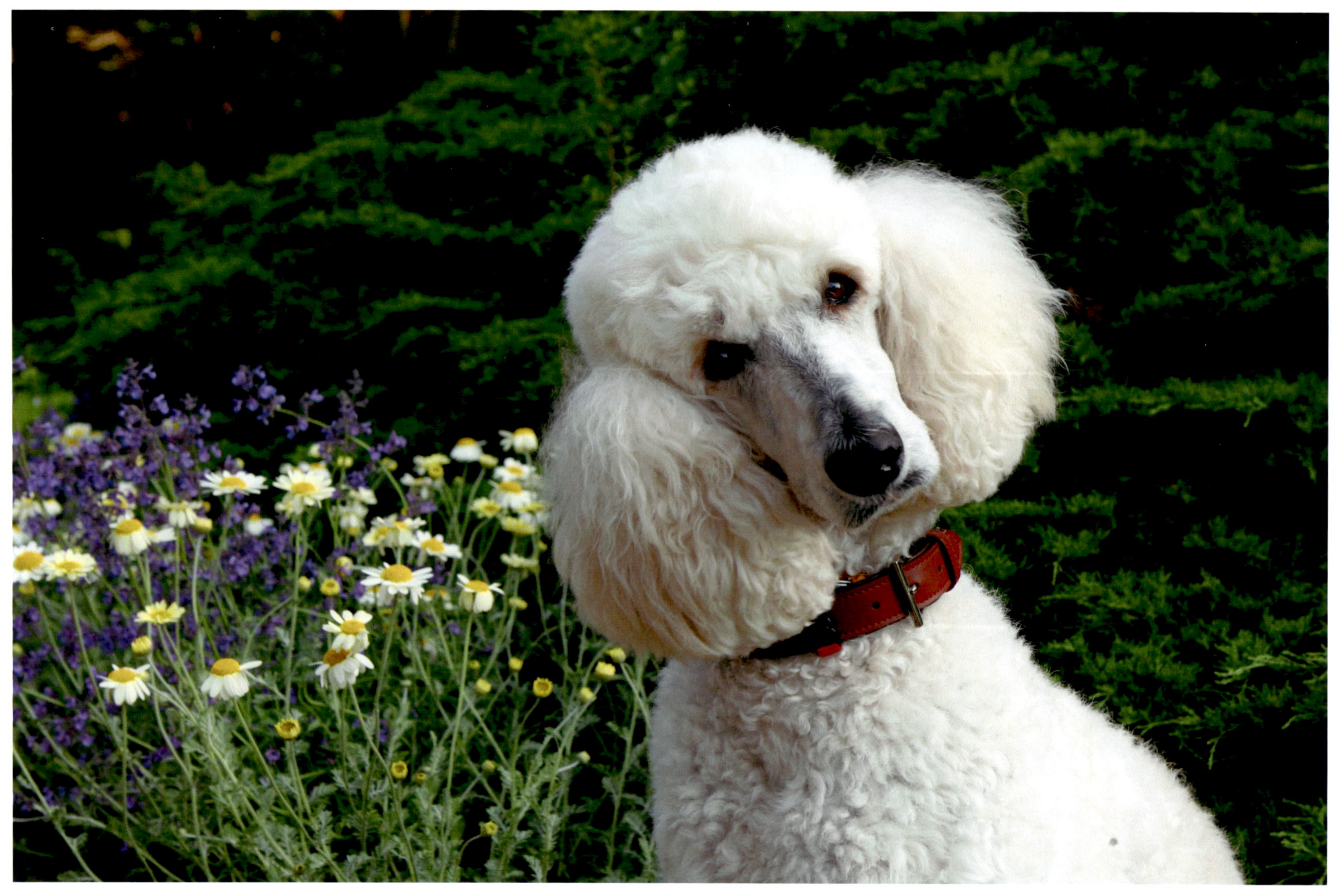

Maisey, standard poodle

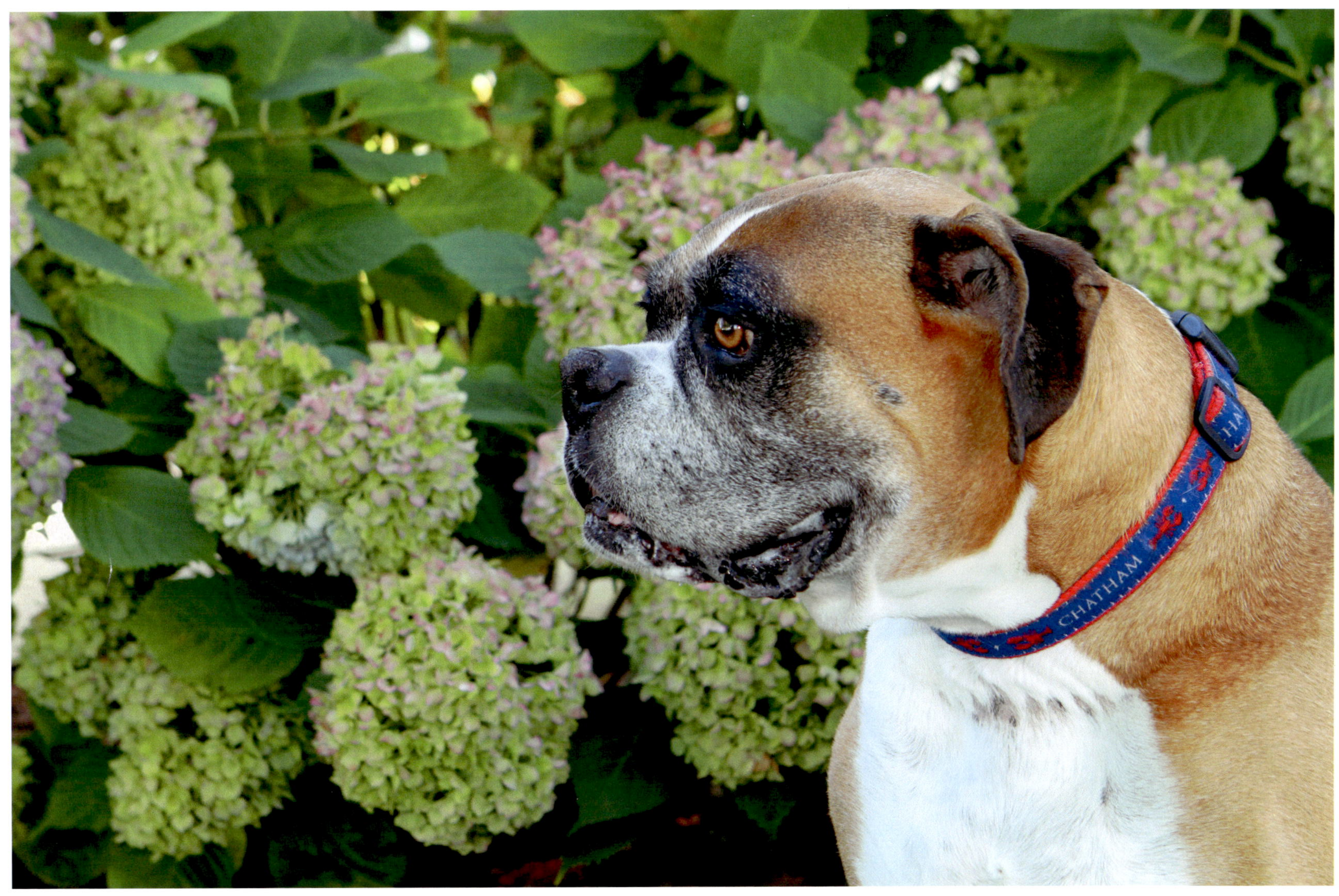

Riley, boxer

Brooklyn, French bulldog, Scargo Lake

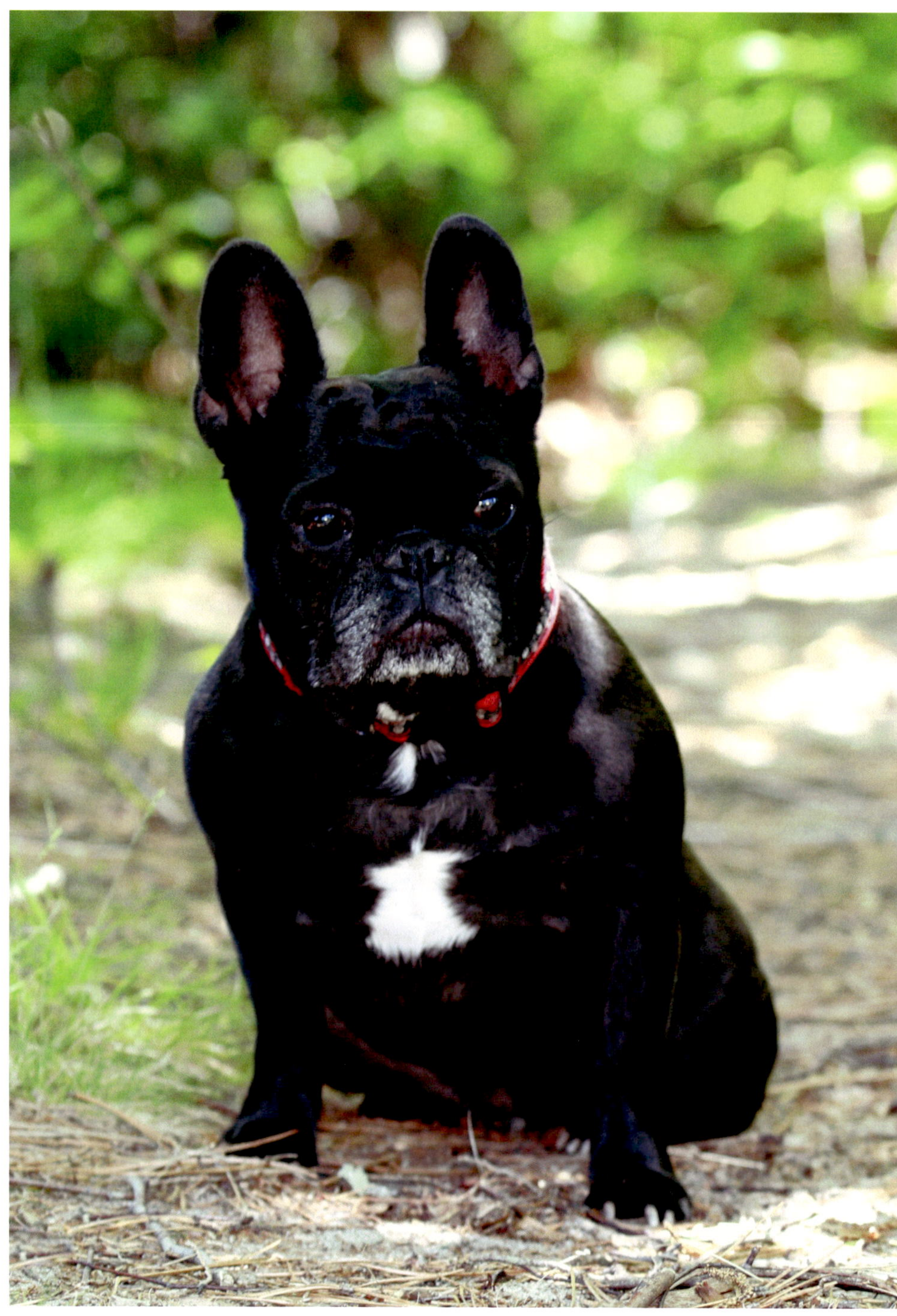

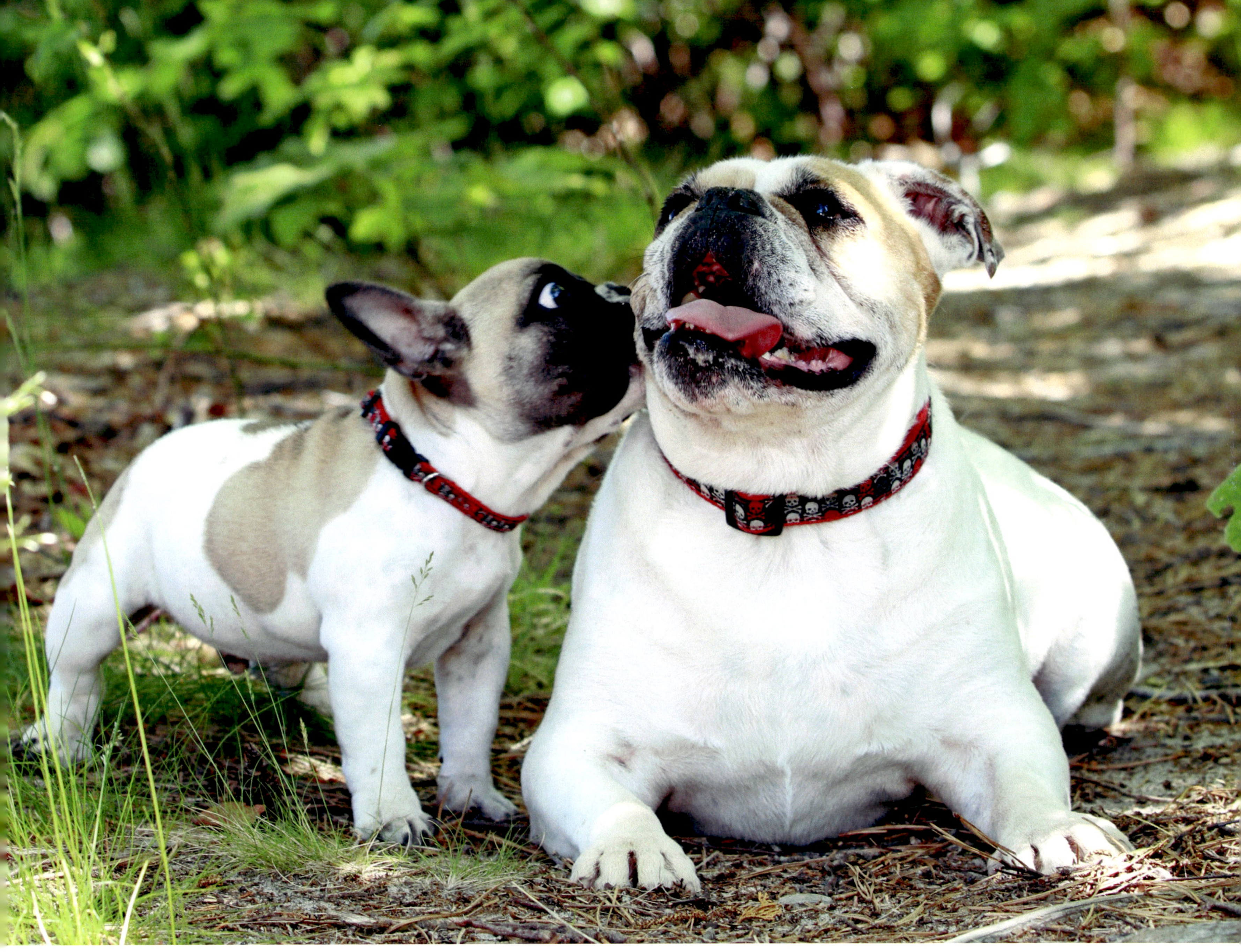

Manny, French bulldog, and **Bronx**, bulldog, Scargo lake

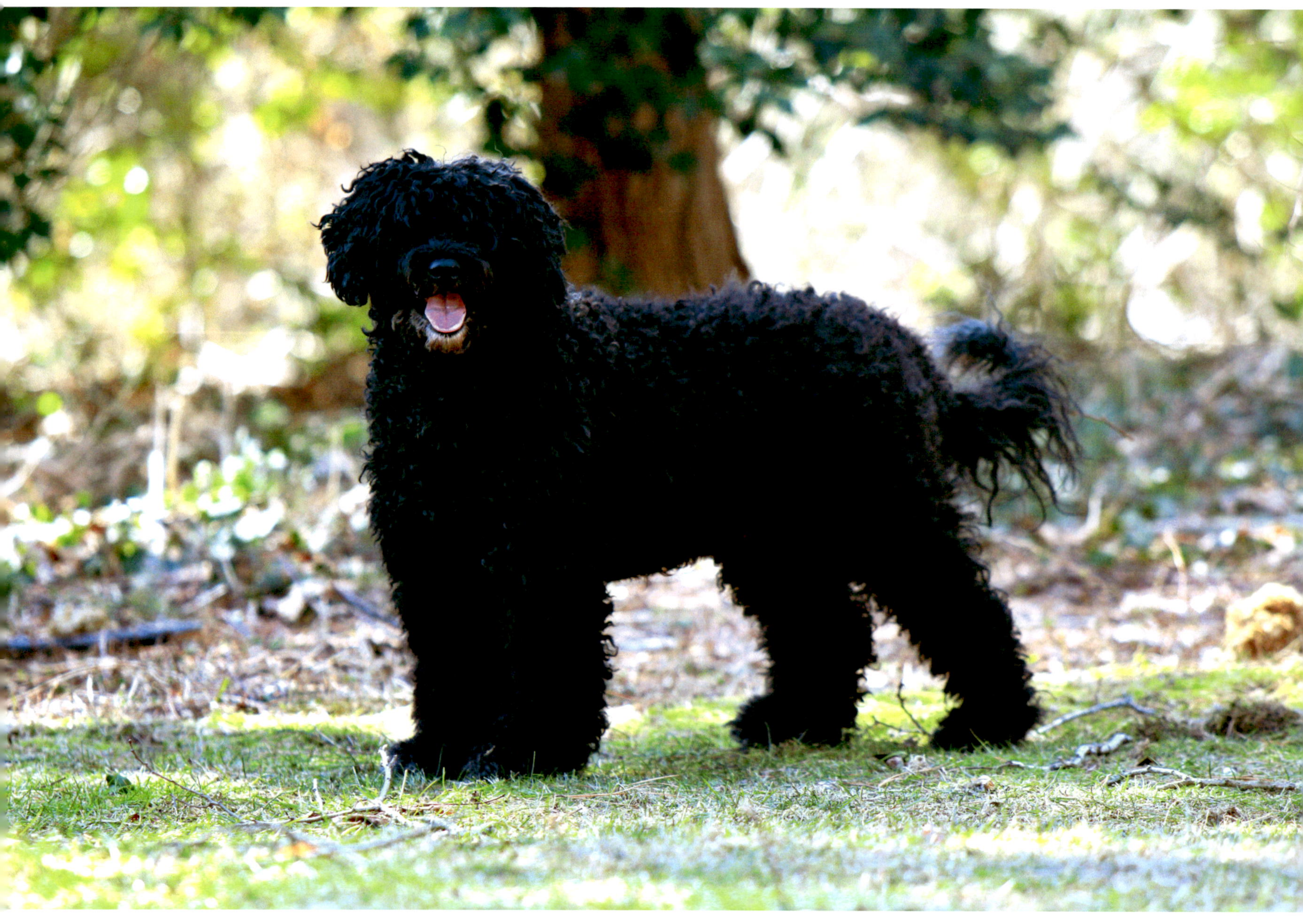

Indy, Portuguese water dog

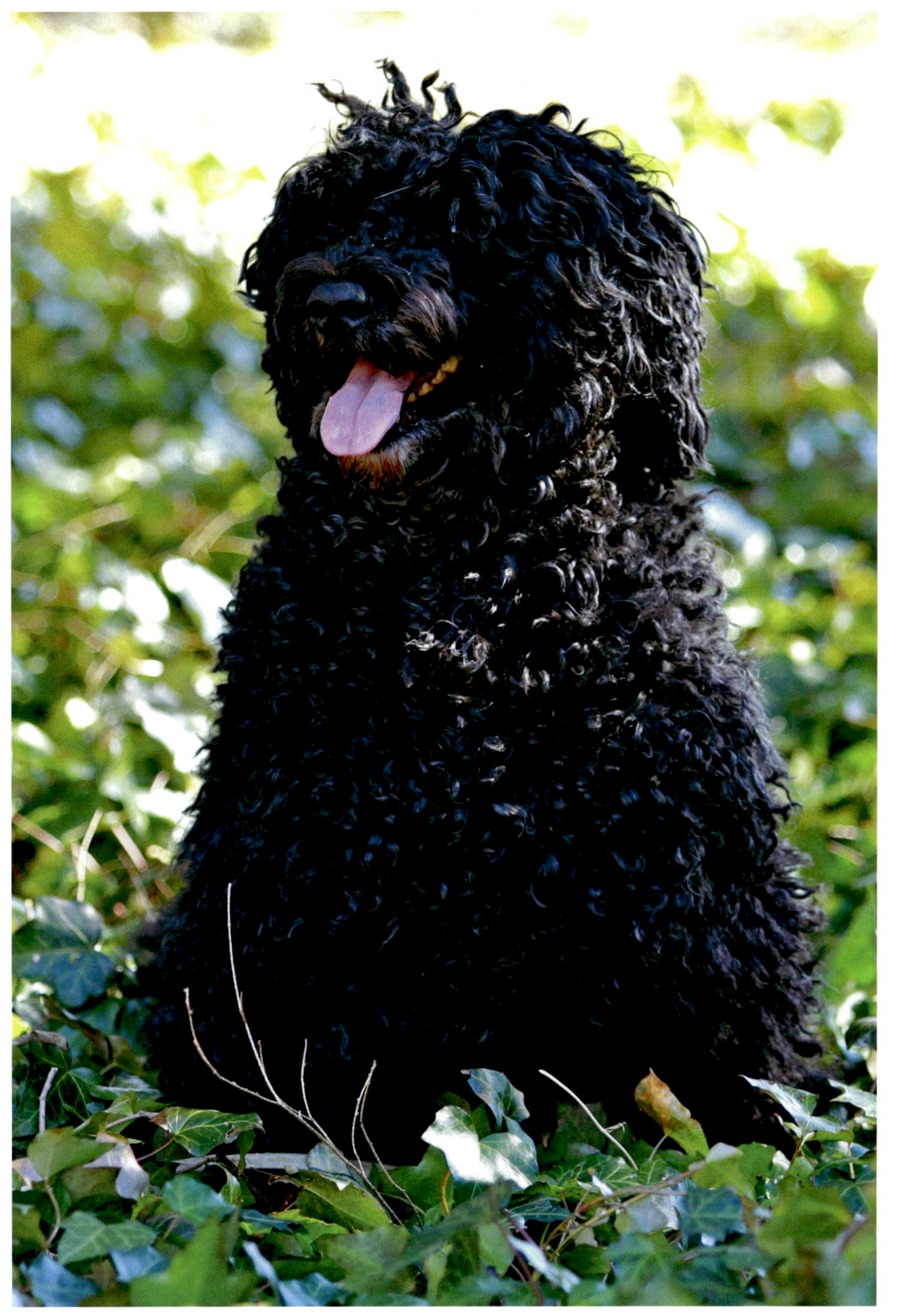

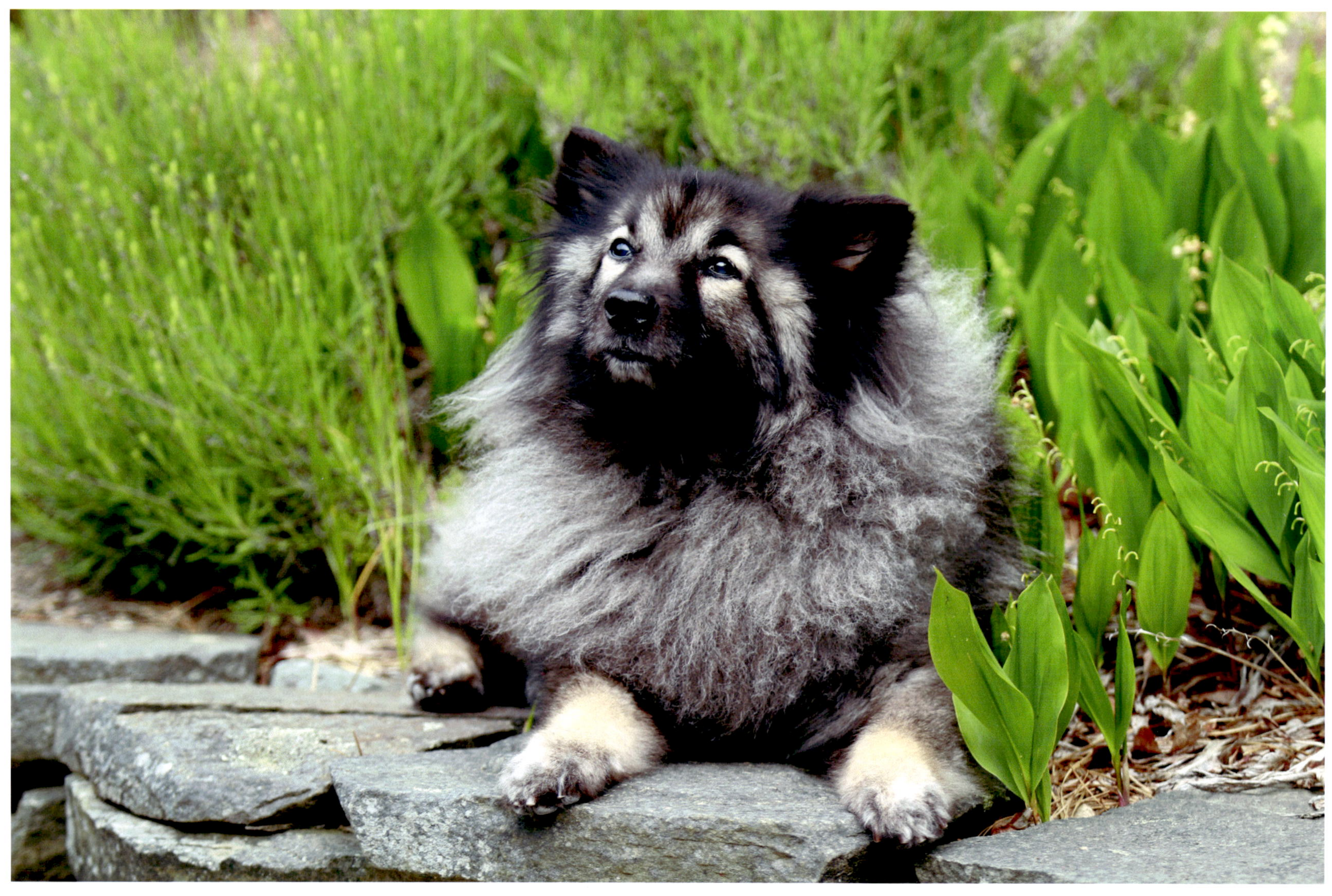

Boo (above), Keeshond

Maddie (opposite), Labrador retriever

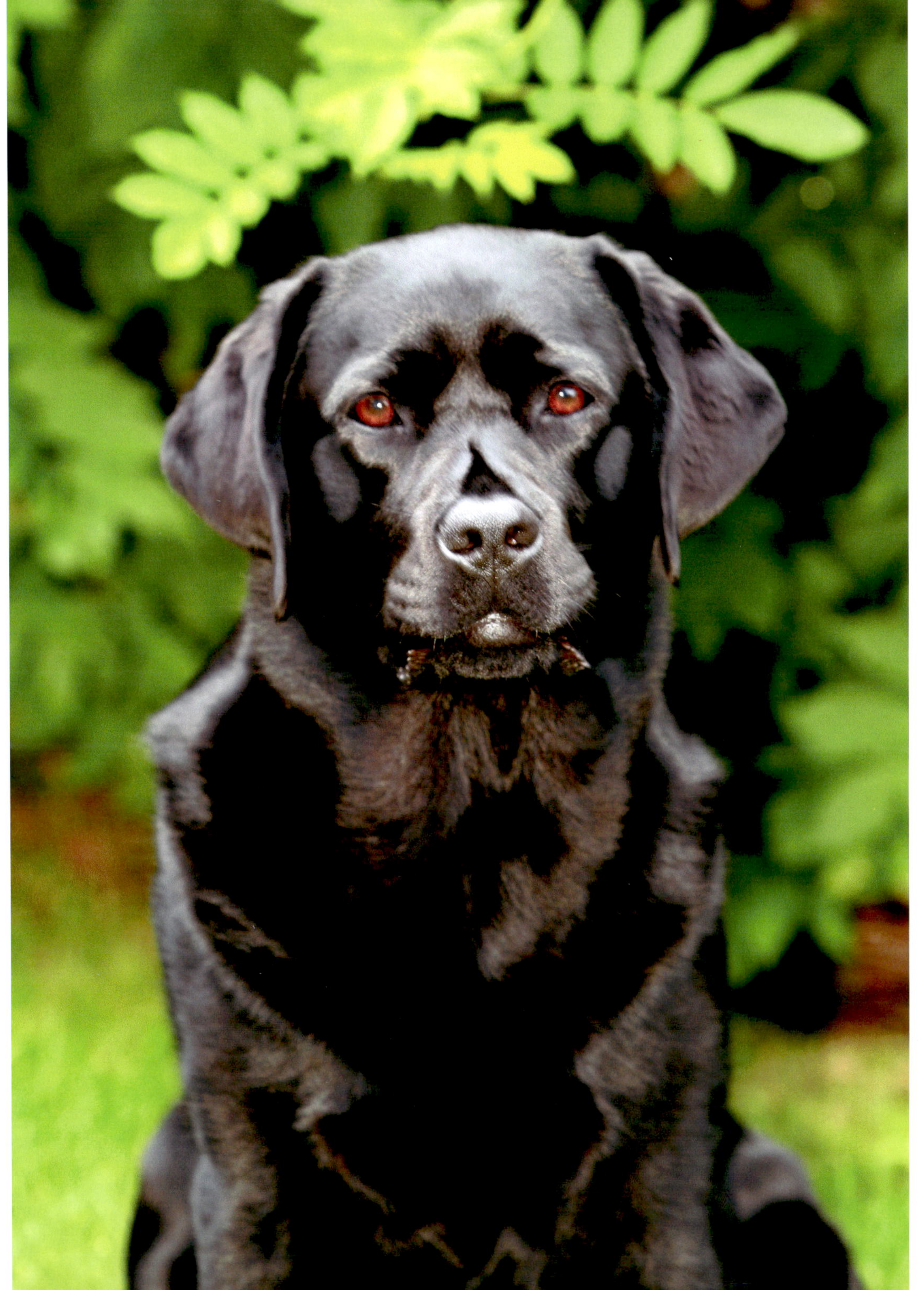

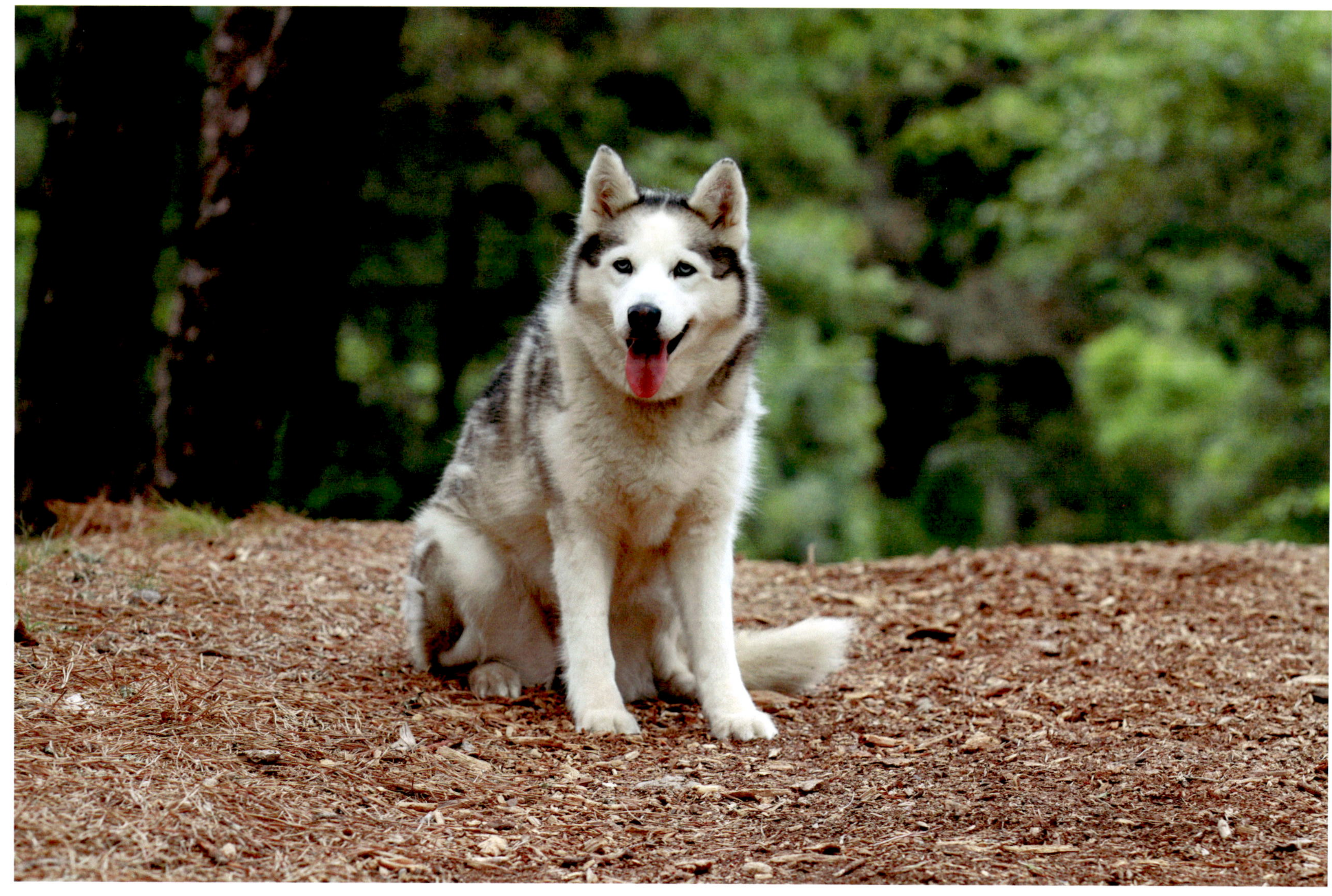

Makayla (above), Siberian husky, Strong Island

Lord Nibbler (opposite), Australian shepherd mix, Forest Beach

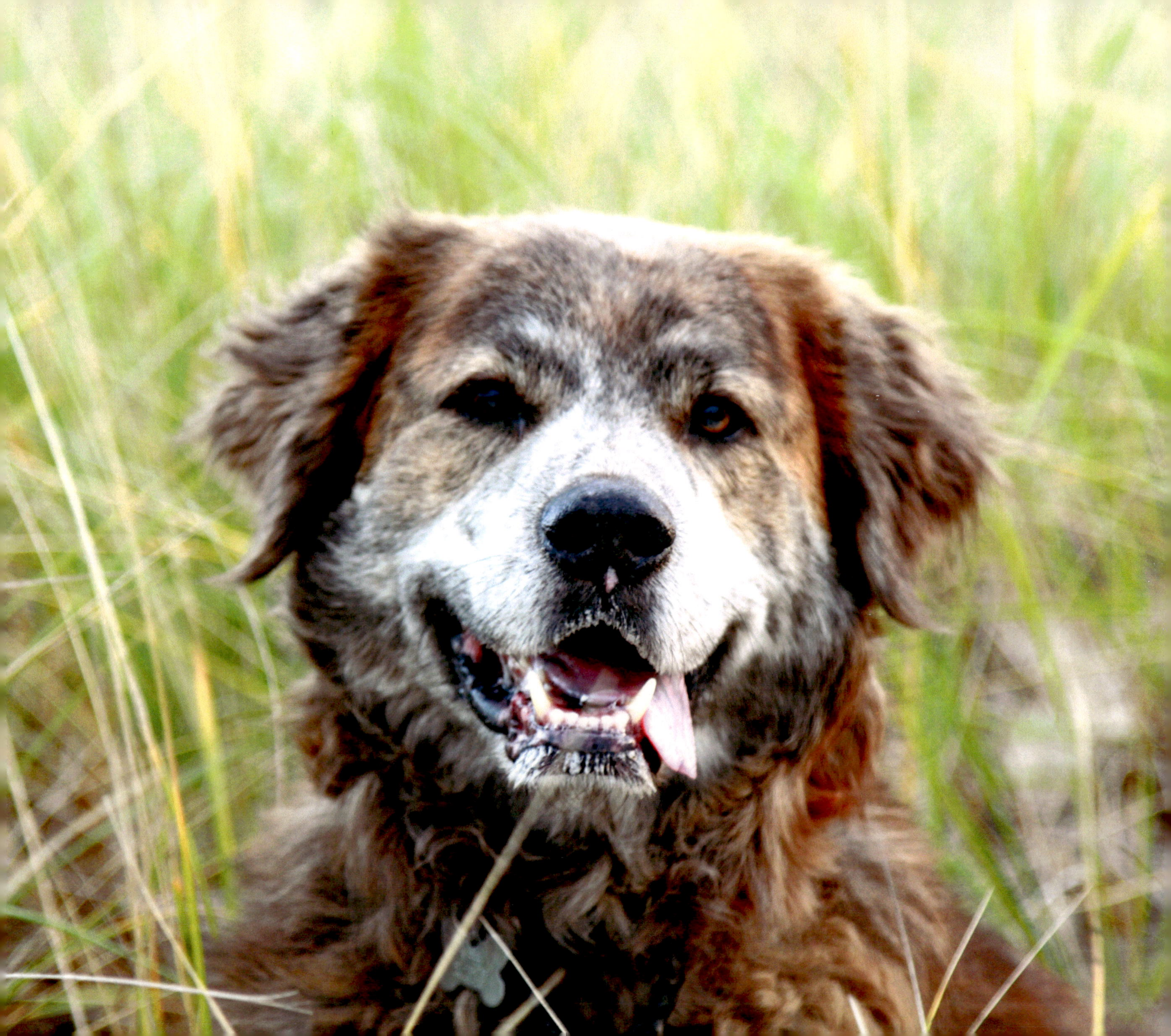

Rocky, border collie mix

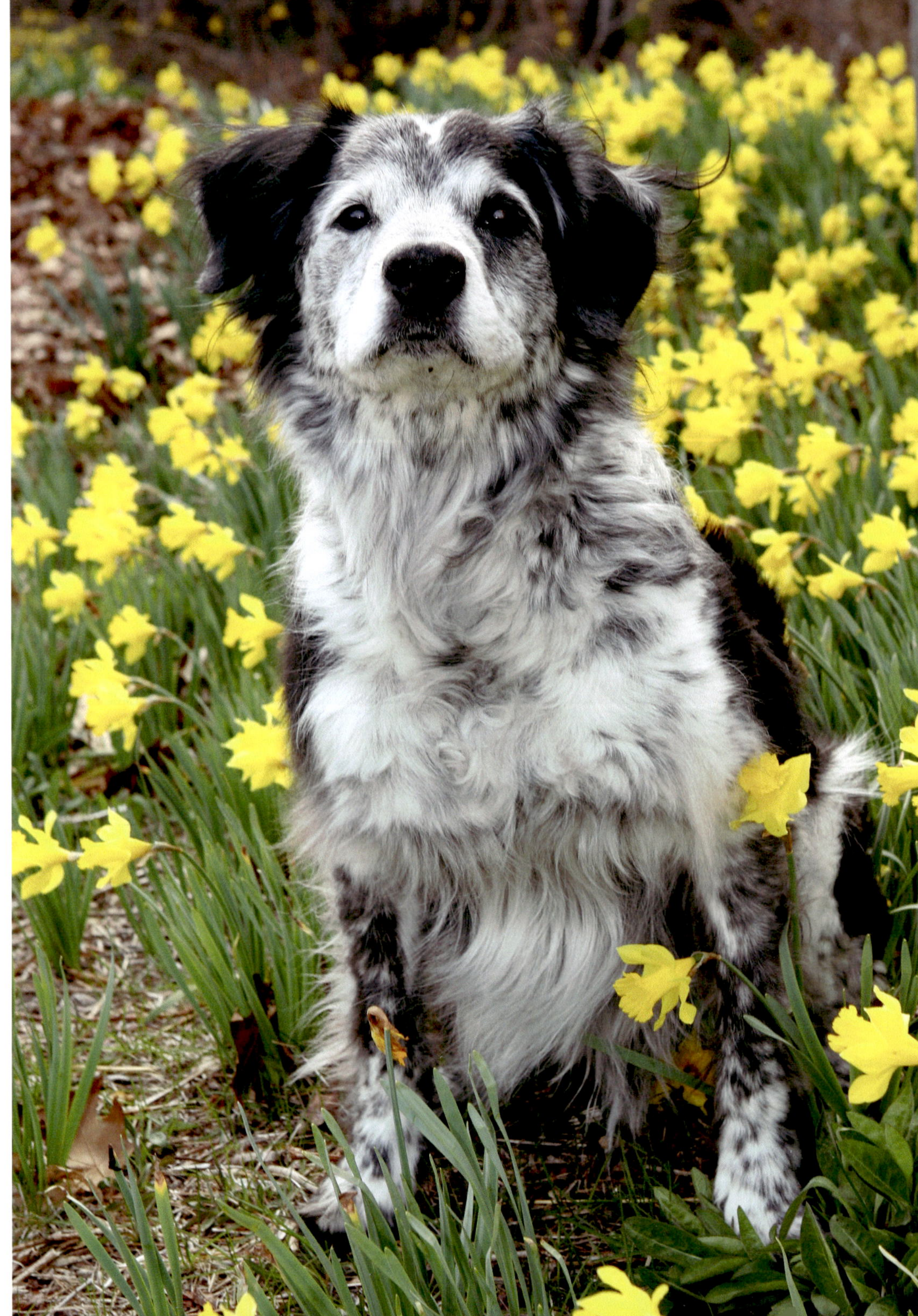

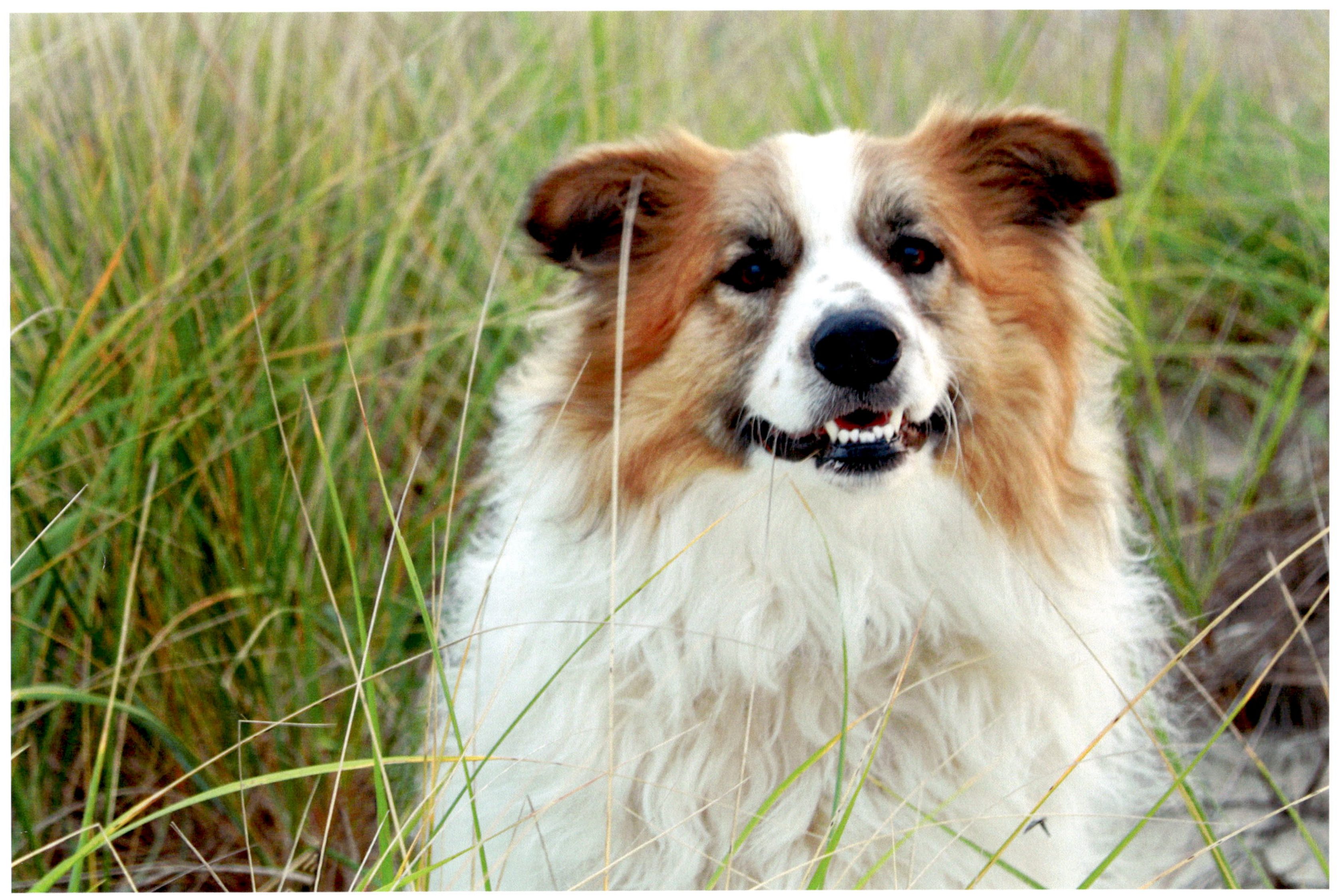

Jaeger, Great Pyrenees mix, Forest Beach

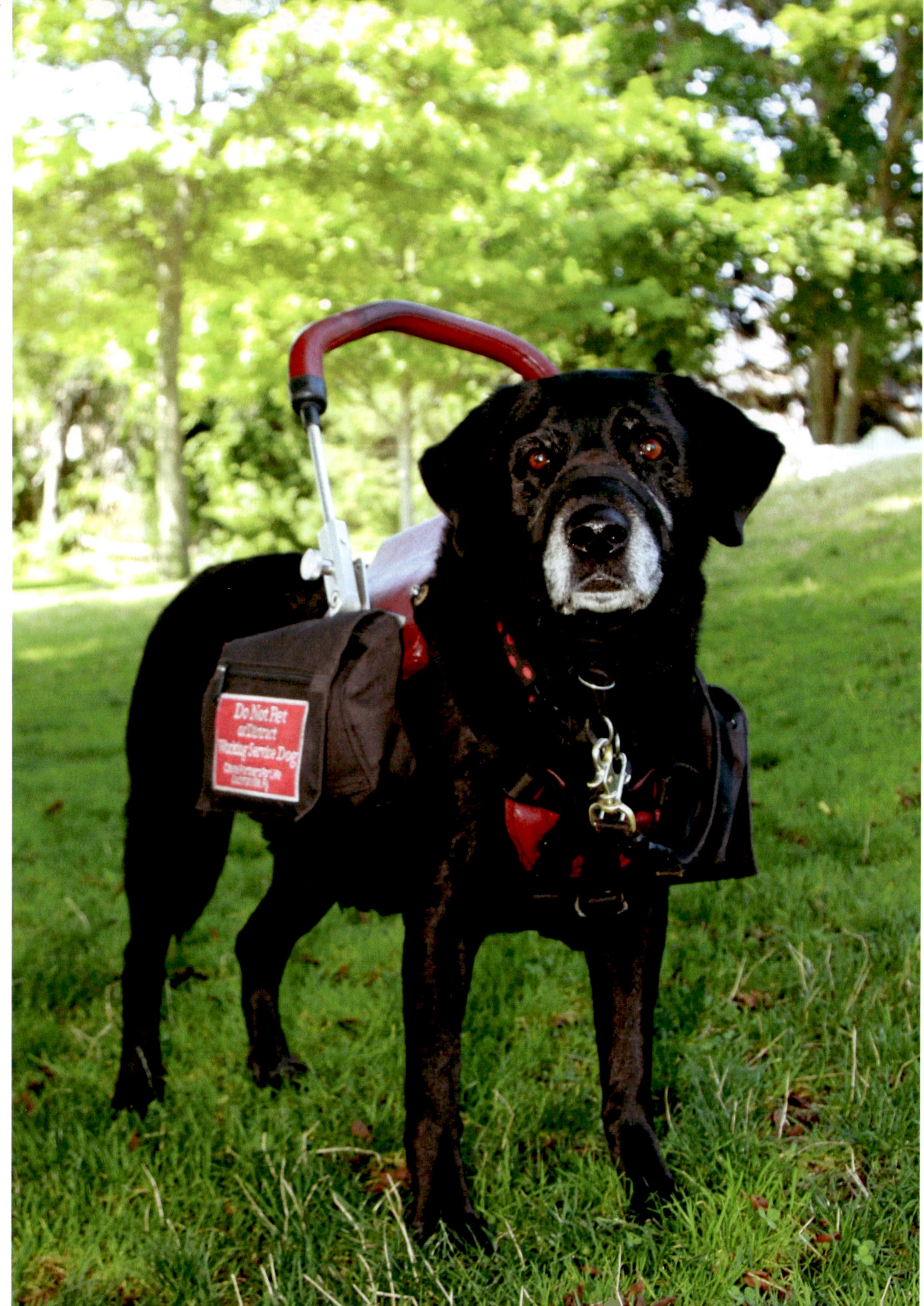
Do Not Pet

Chewbacca, collie (right)

Adele (opposite), Labrador retriever

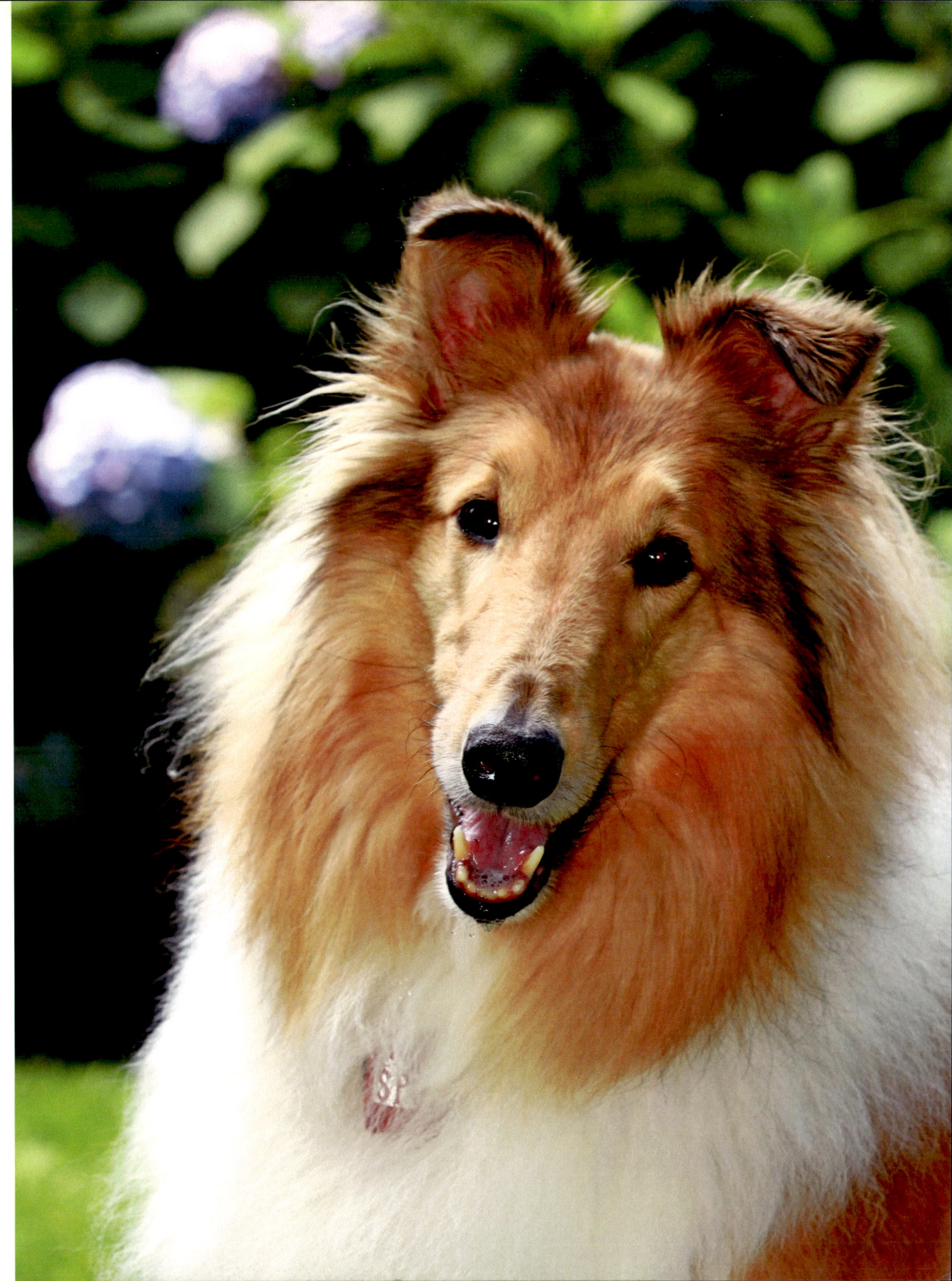

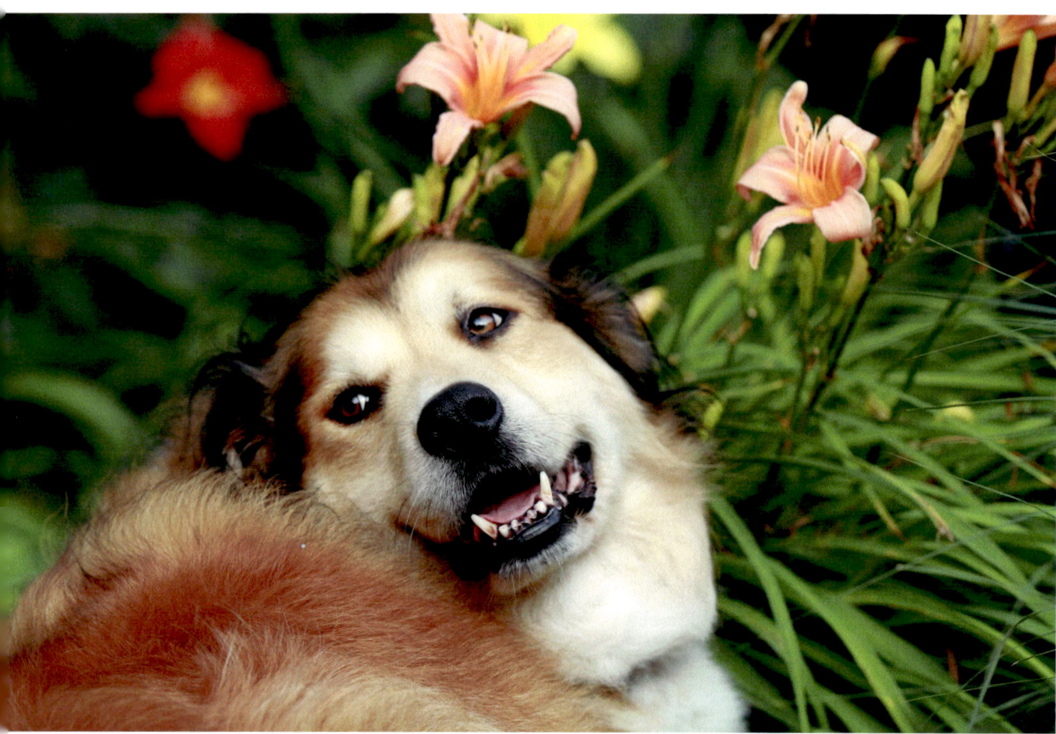

Whiskey, Great Pyrenees mix

Oliver (below), Papillon

Whiskey and **Oliver** (opposite)

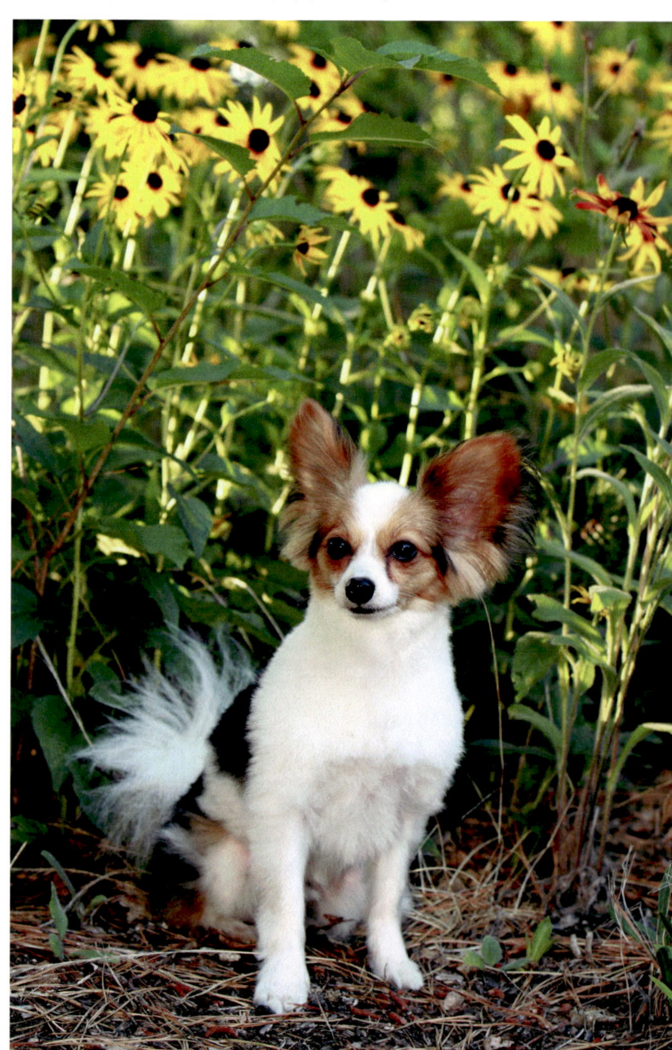

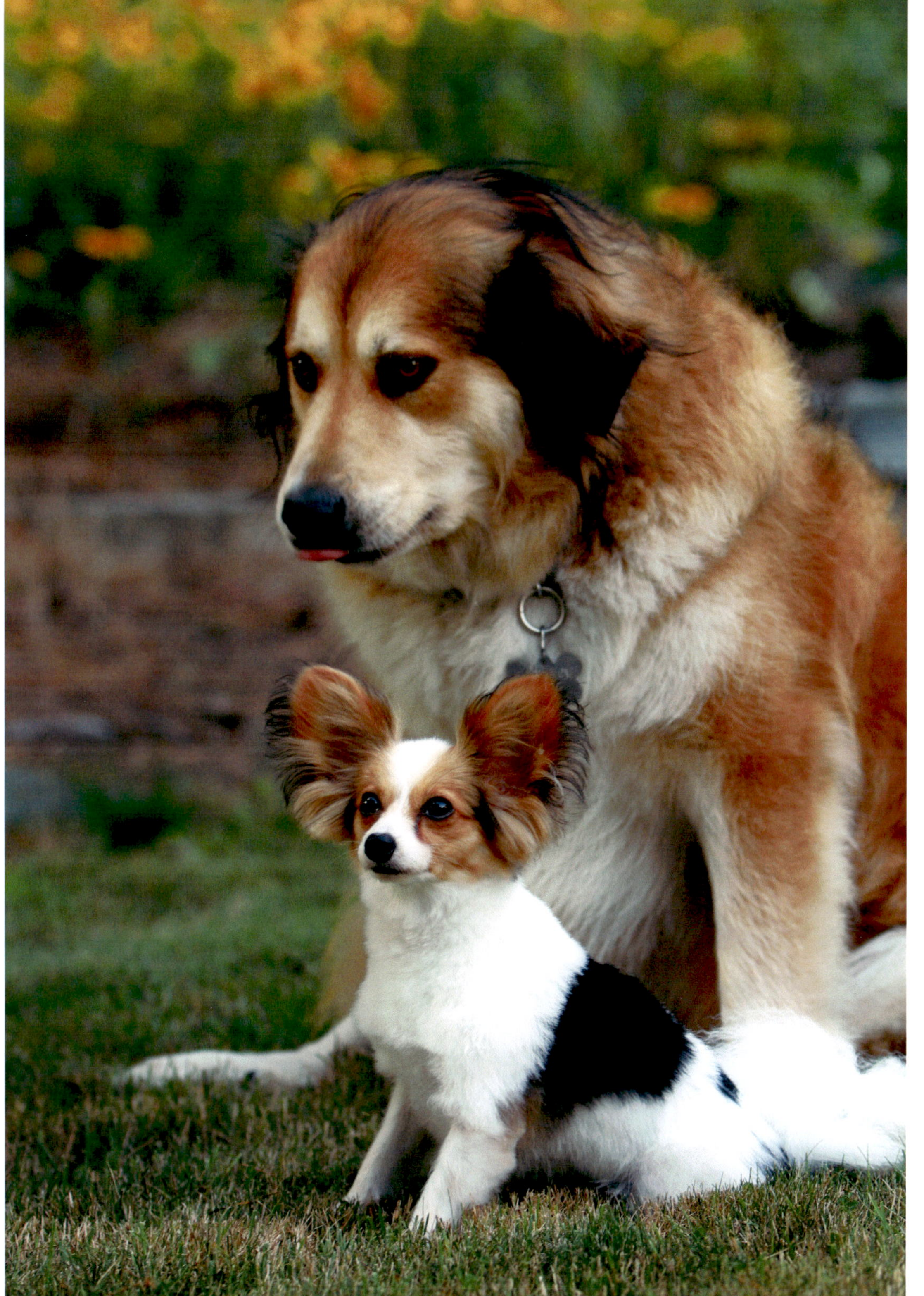

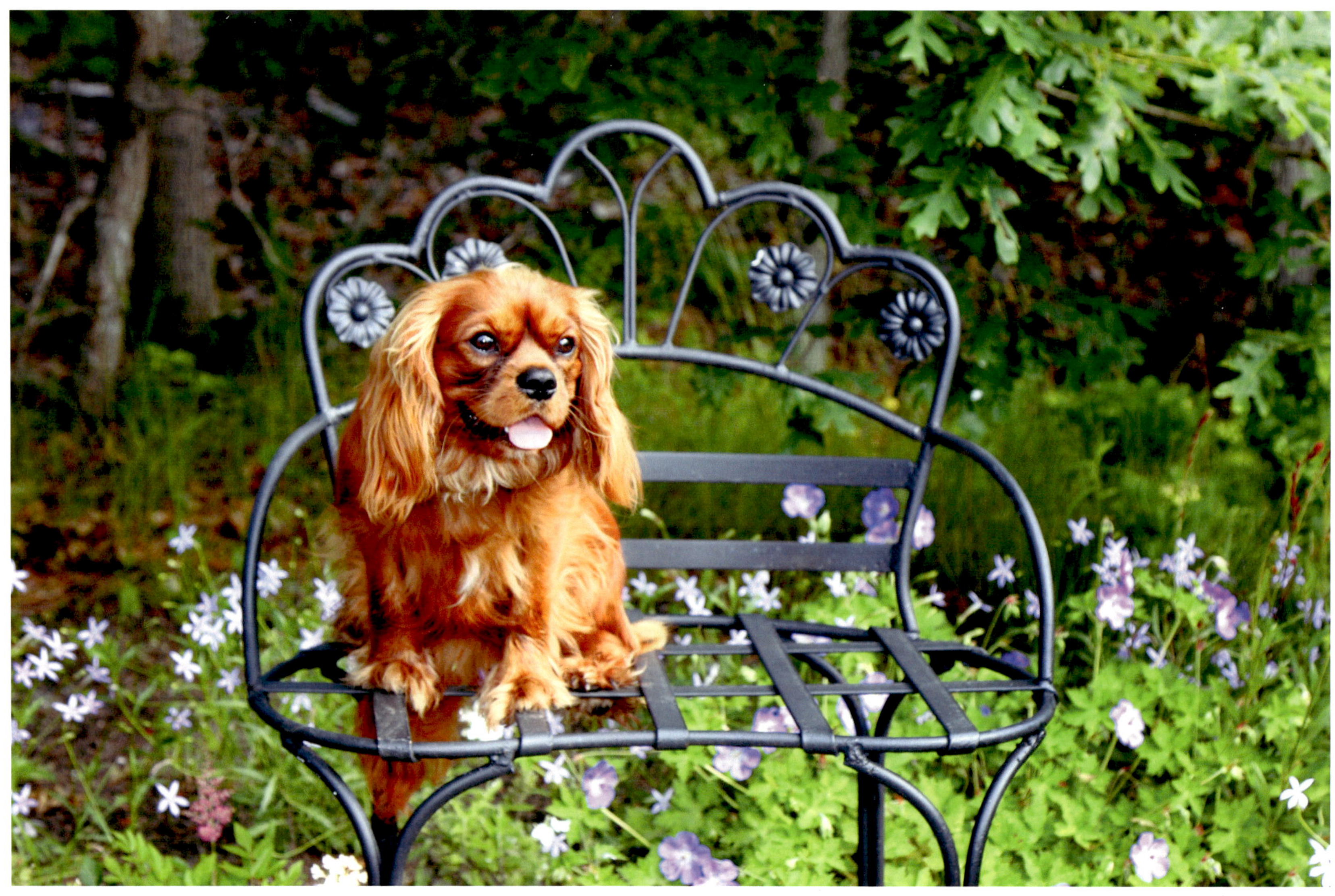

Beau, Cavalier King Charles spaniel

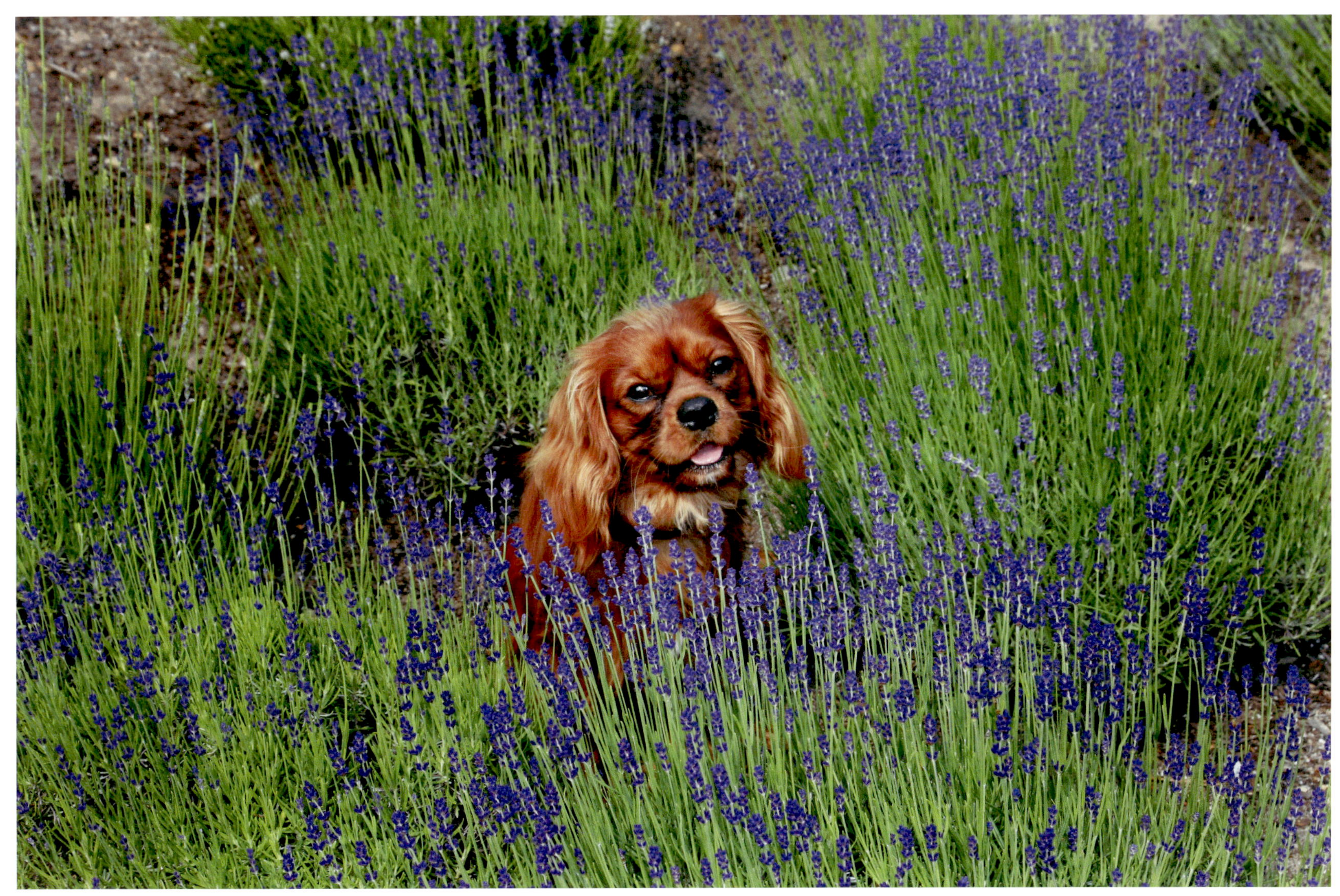

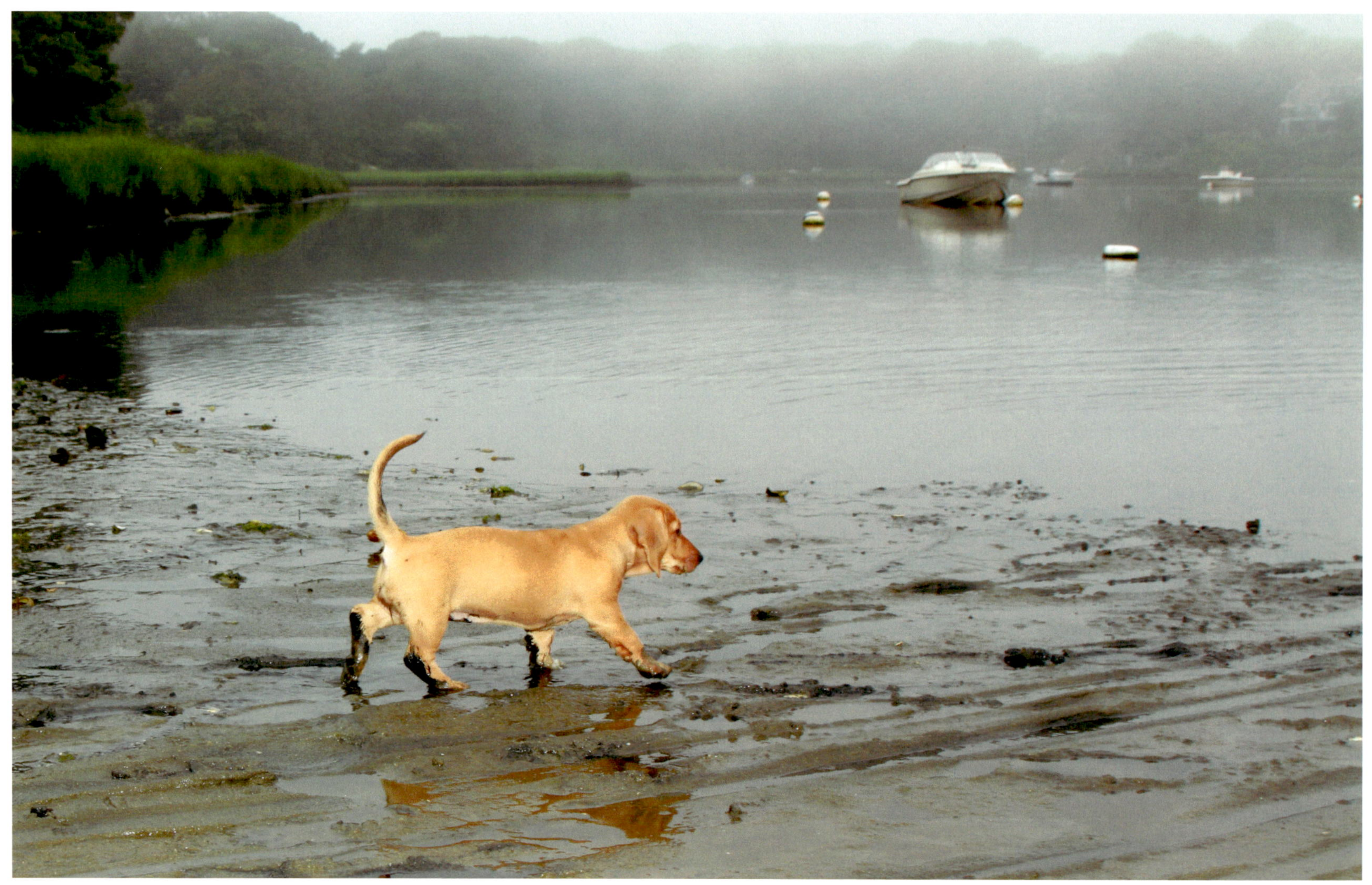

Masie, Dachshund mix, Taylor's Pond

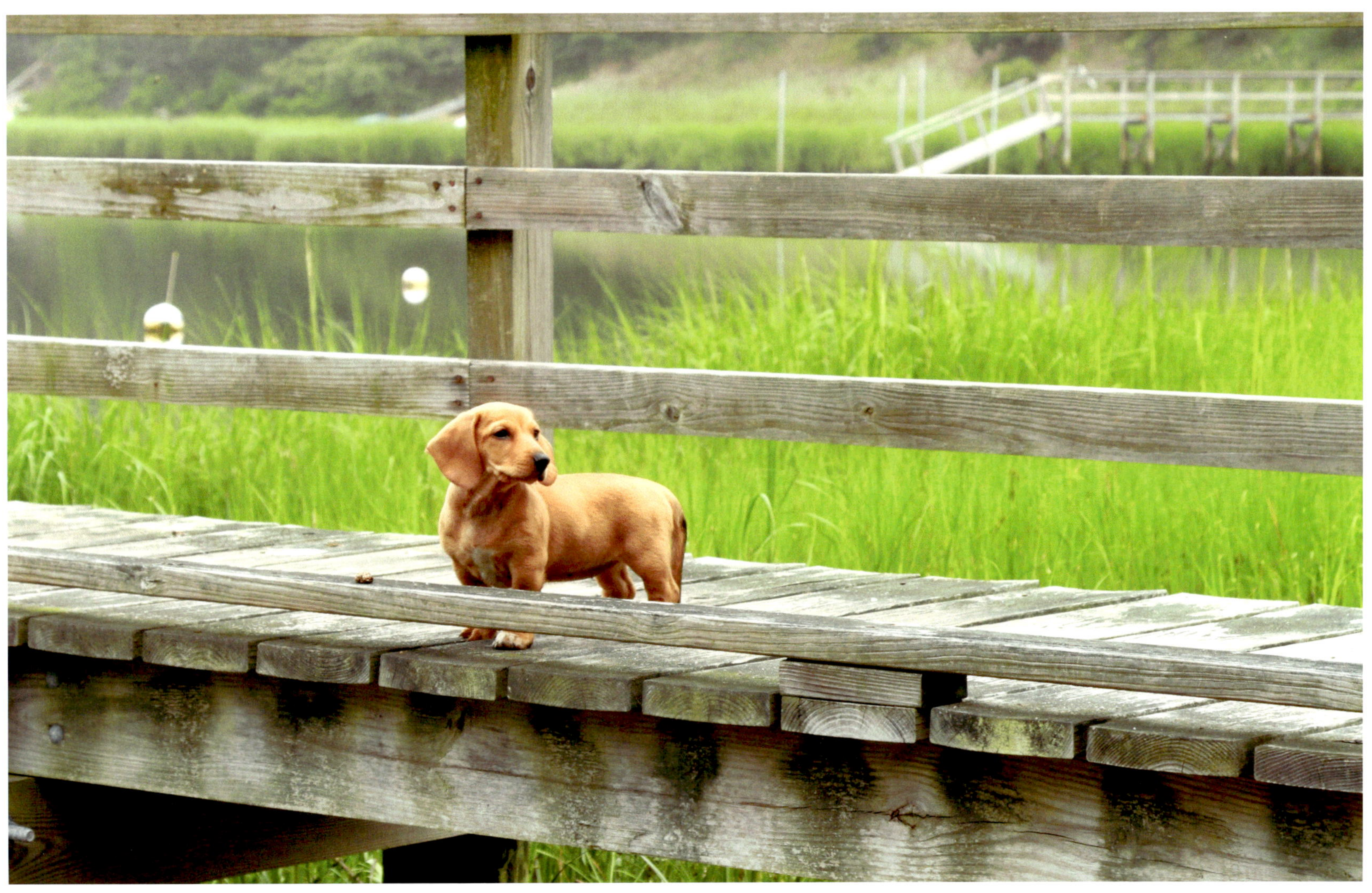

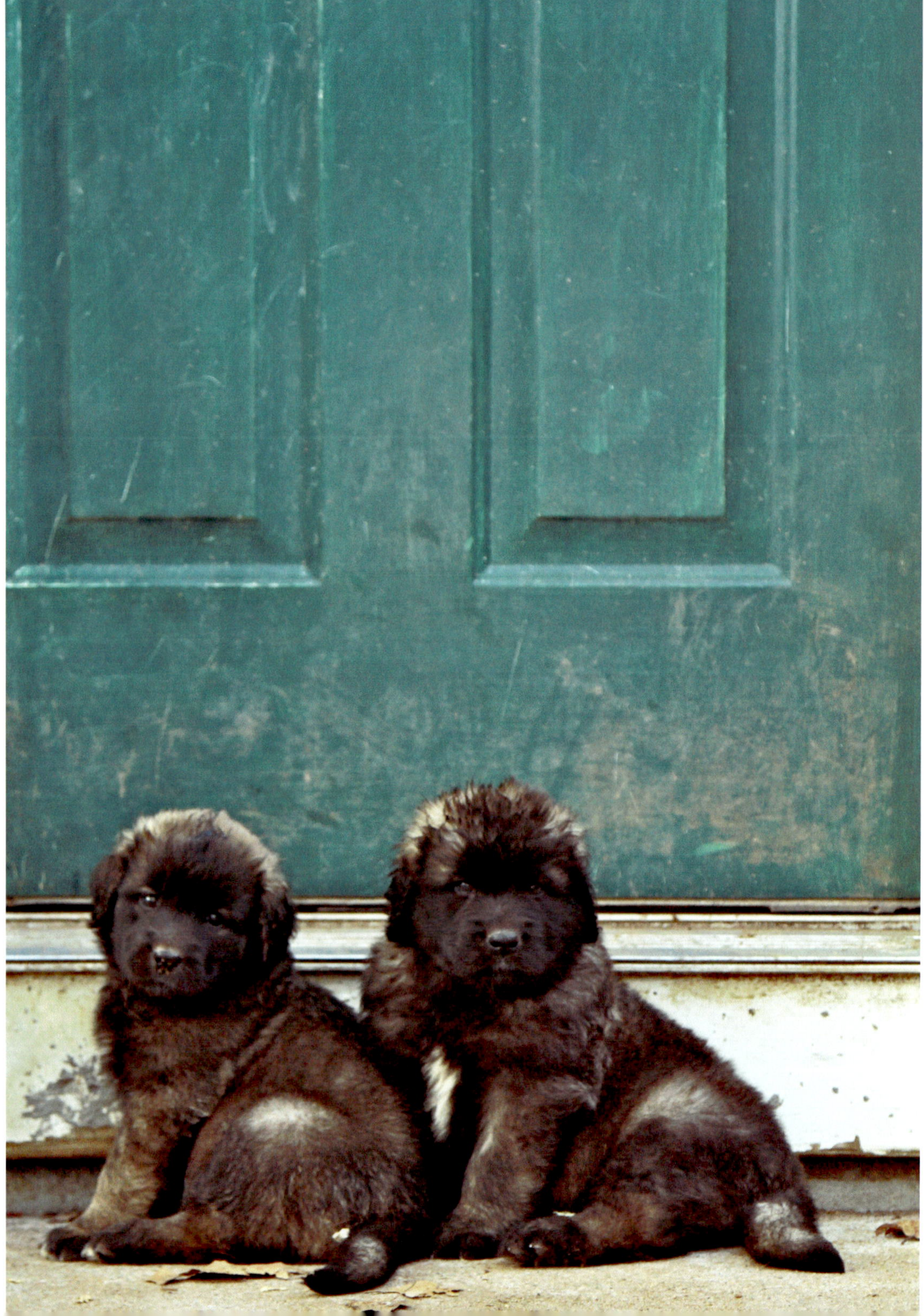

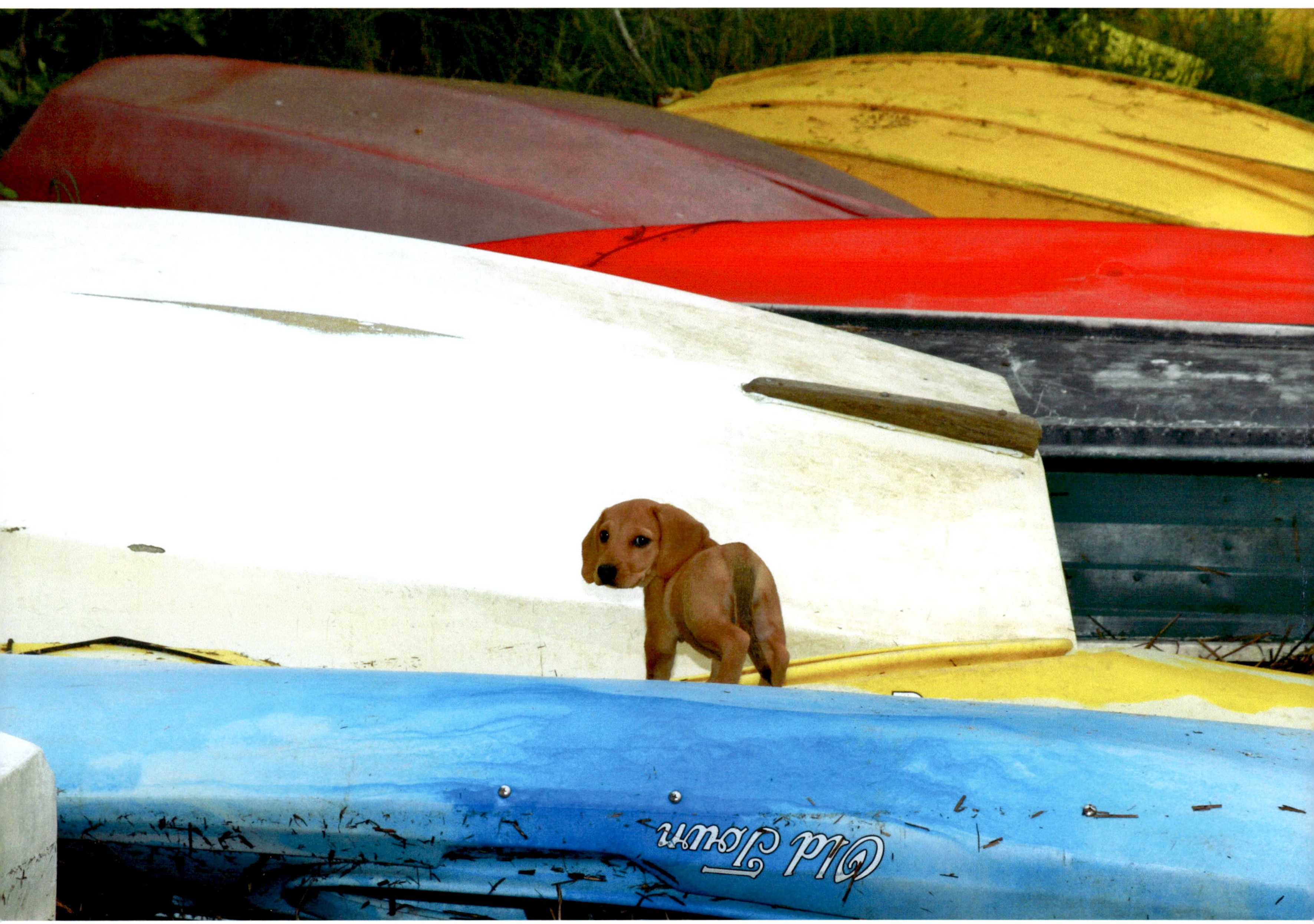

Masie (above), Taylor's Pond

Brownie and **Dudley** (opposite), Leonbergers

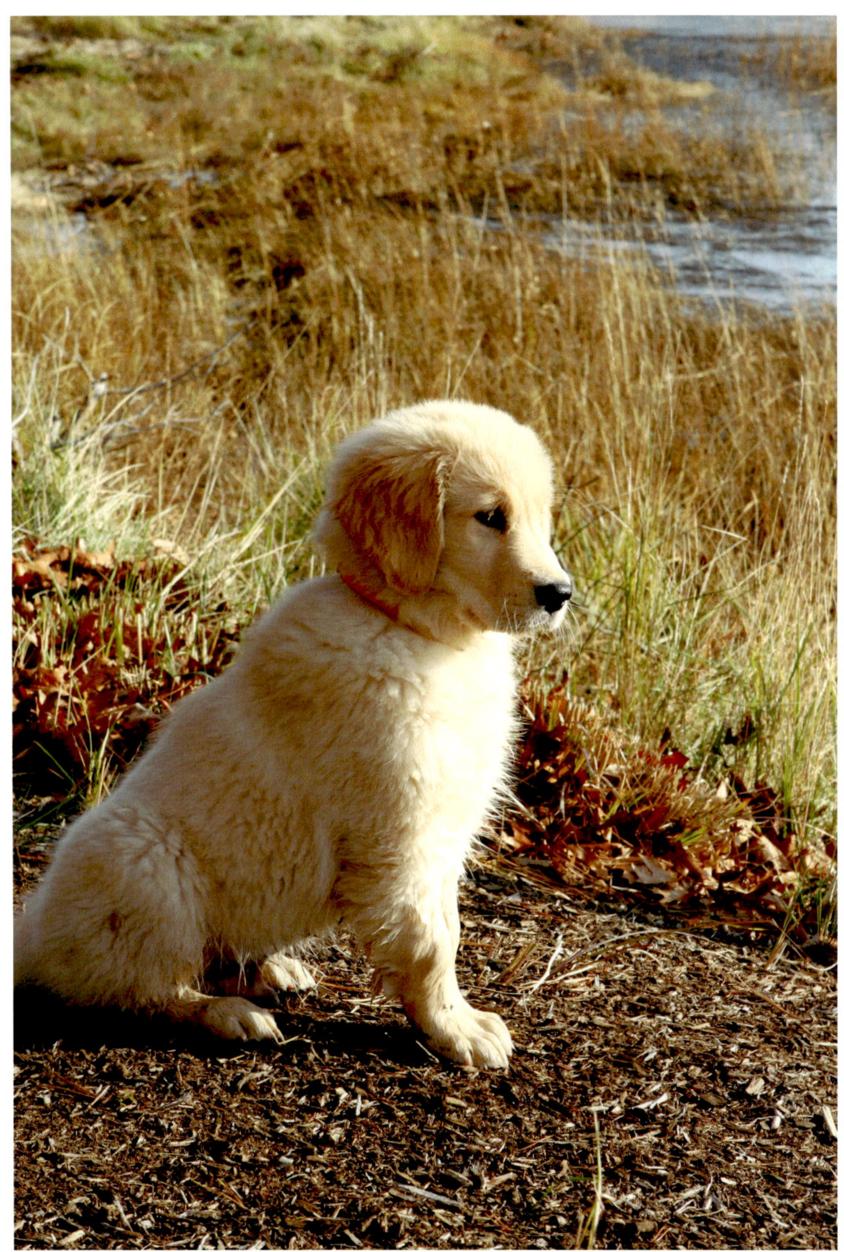

Wrigley, golden retriever, Ryder's Cove

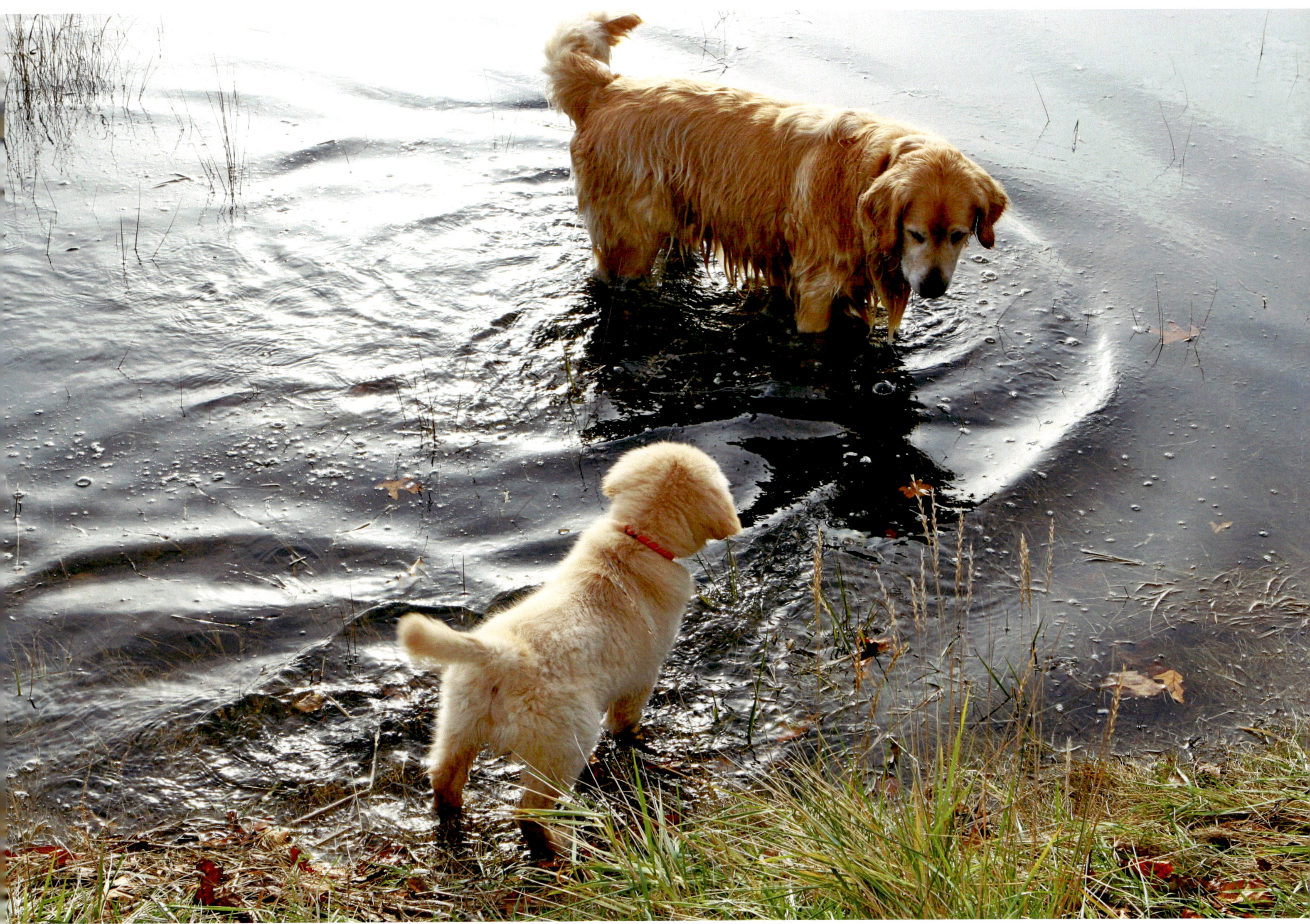

Wrigley and **Raffles**, golden retrievers, Ryder's Cove

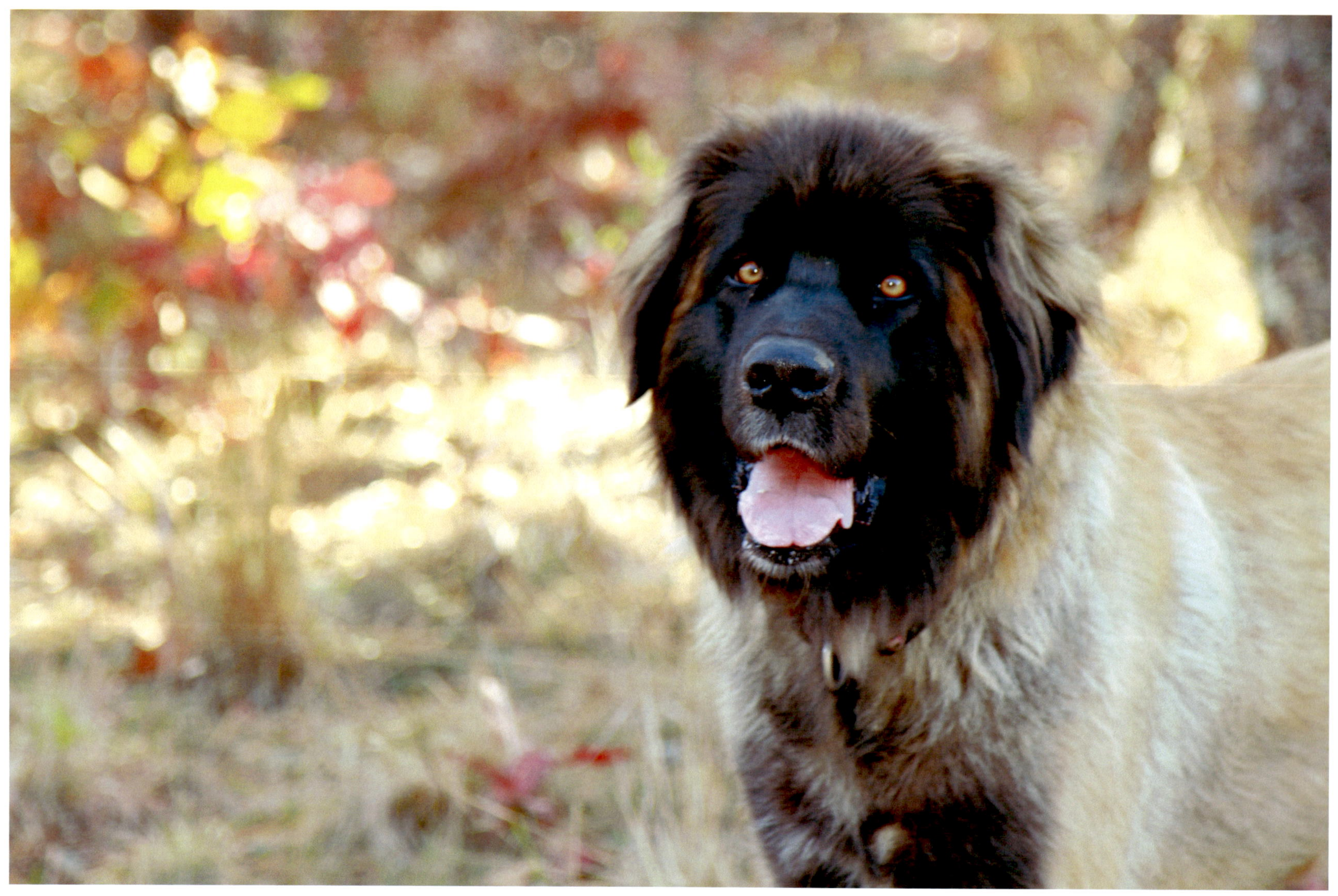

Opal, Leonberger

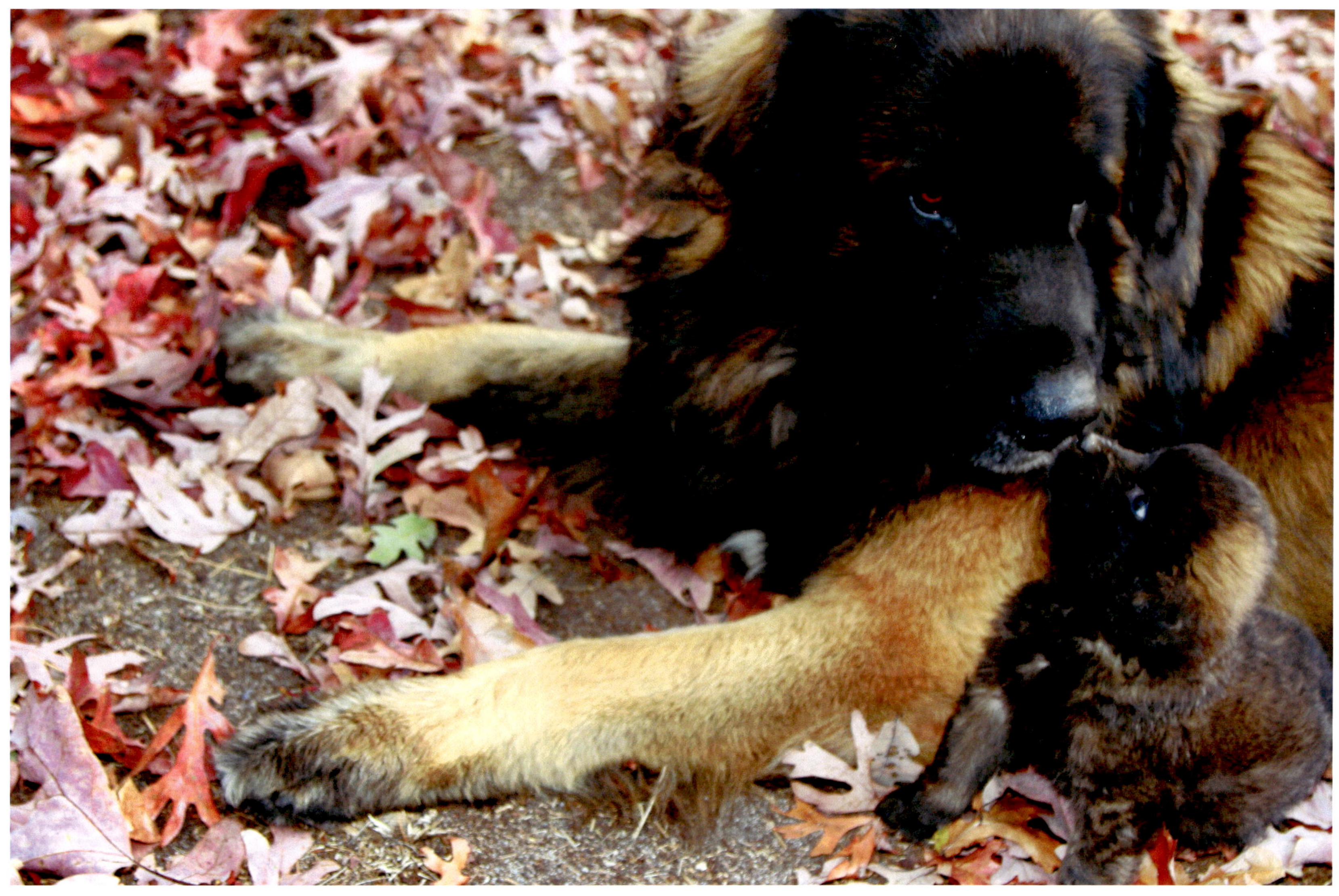

Rocco and **Brownie**, Leonbergers

Gunner, Weimaraner, and **Chico**, Chihuahua

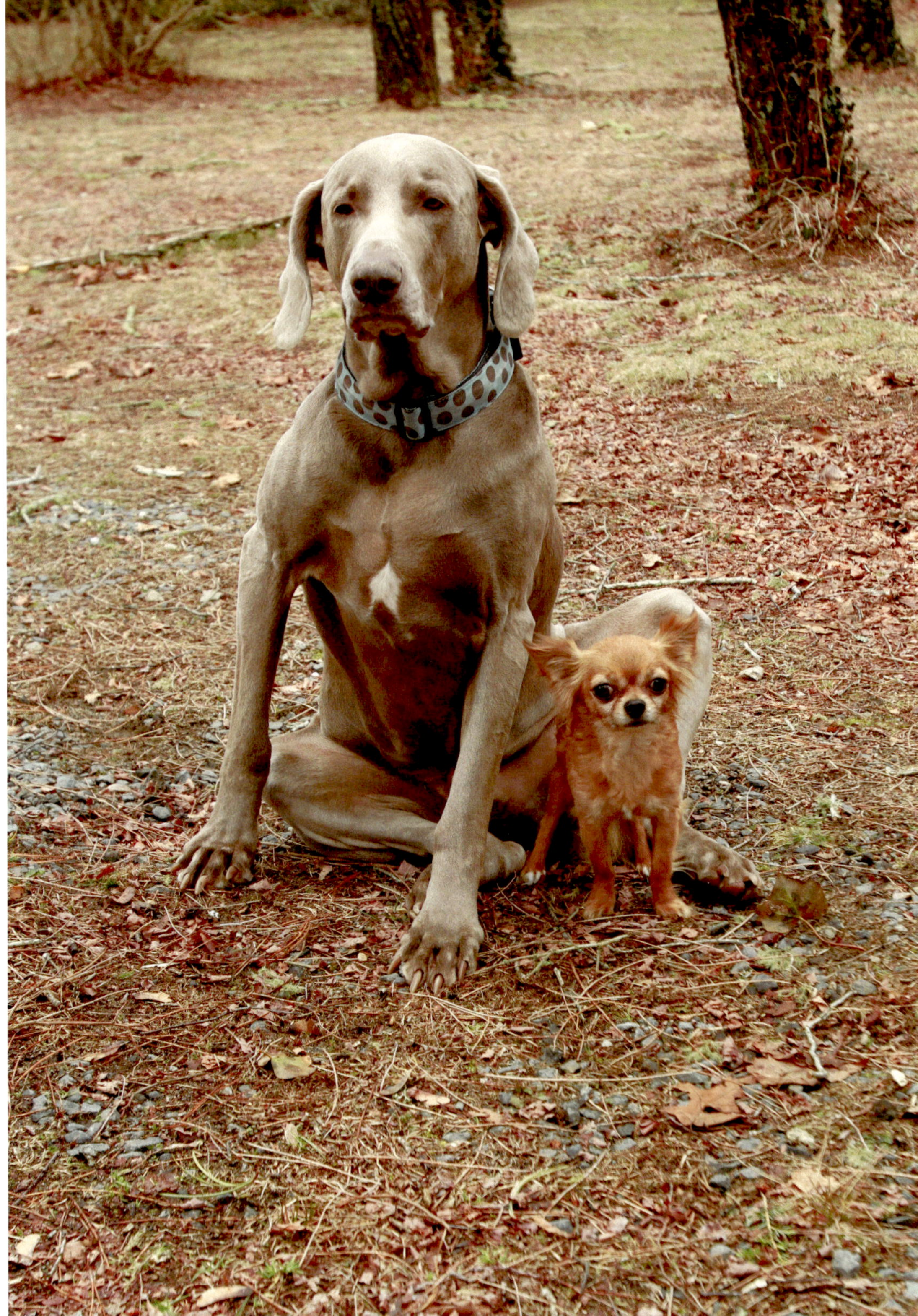

Gunner

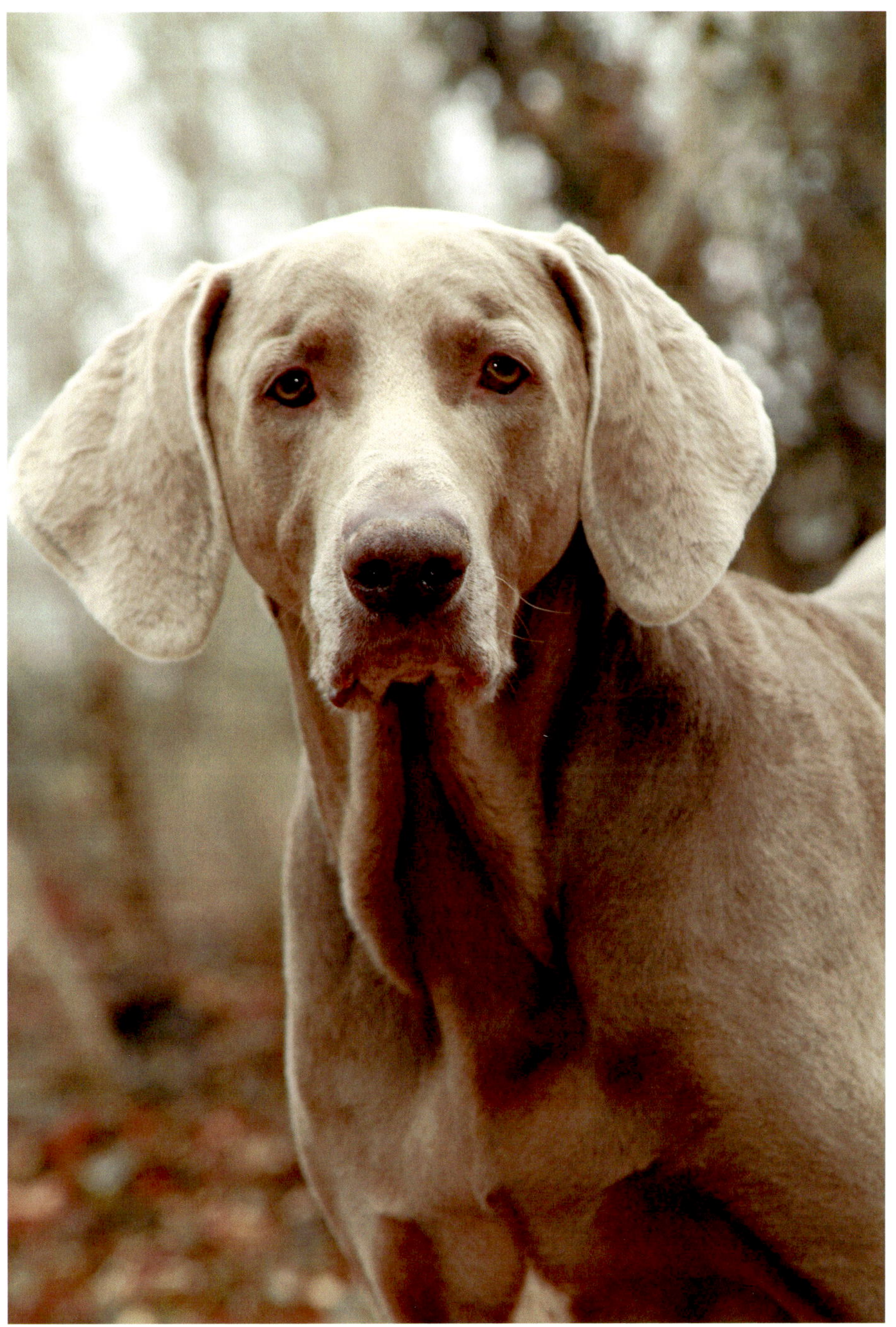

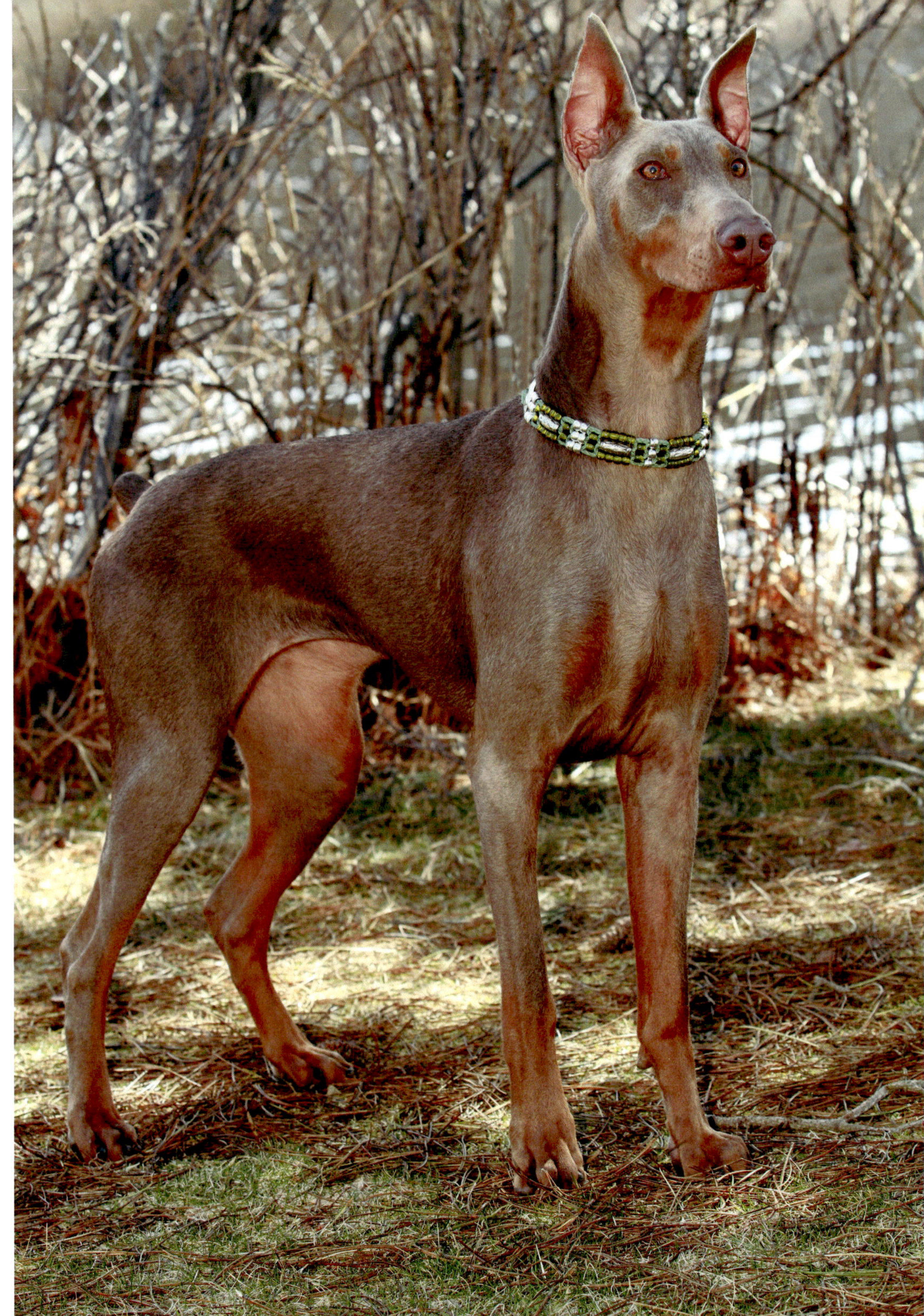

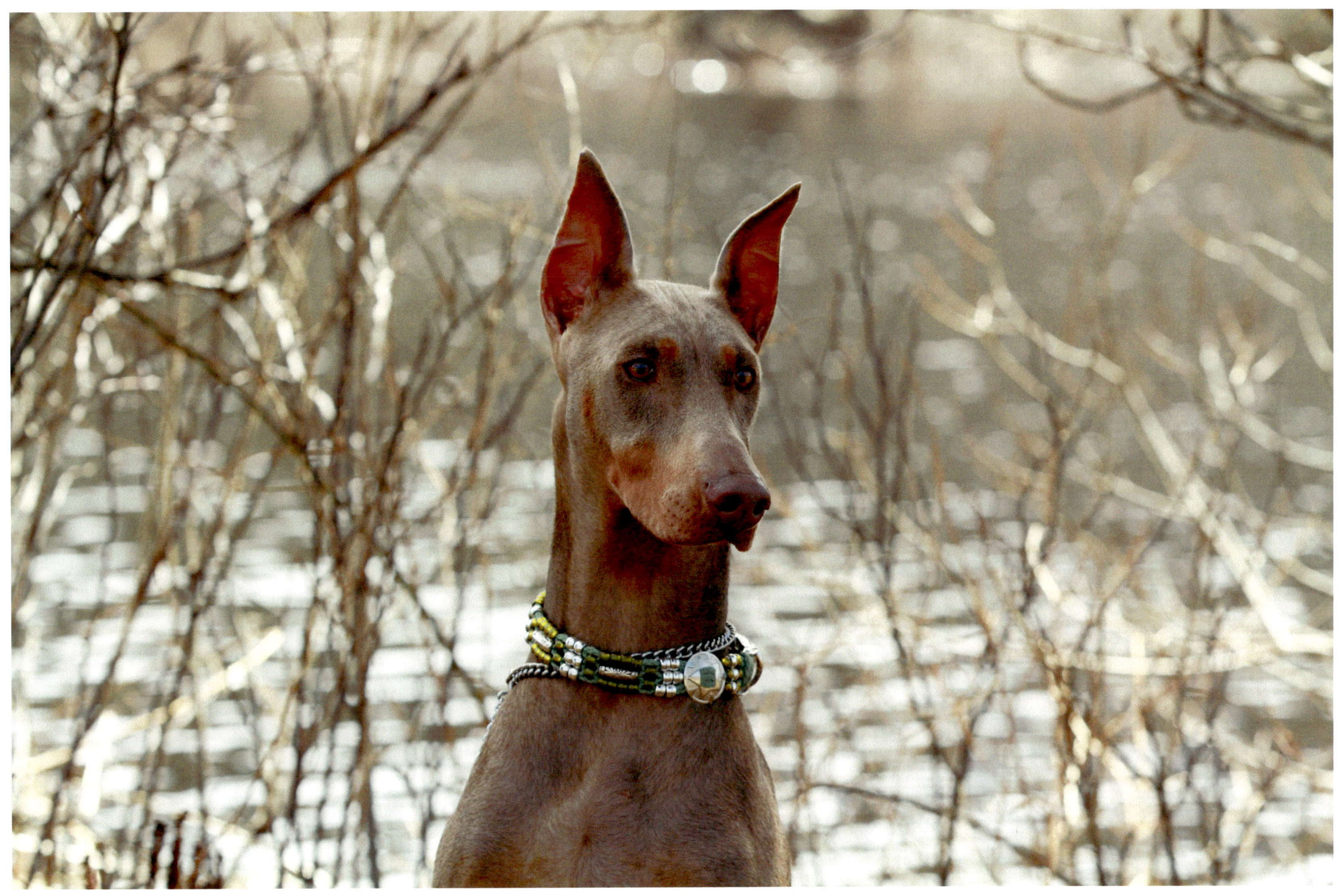

Quinn, Doberman pinscher, Pilgrim Lake

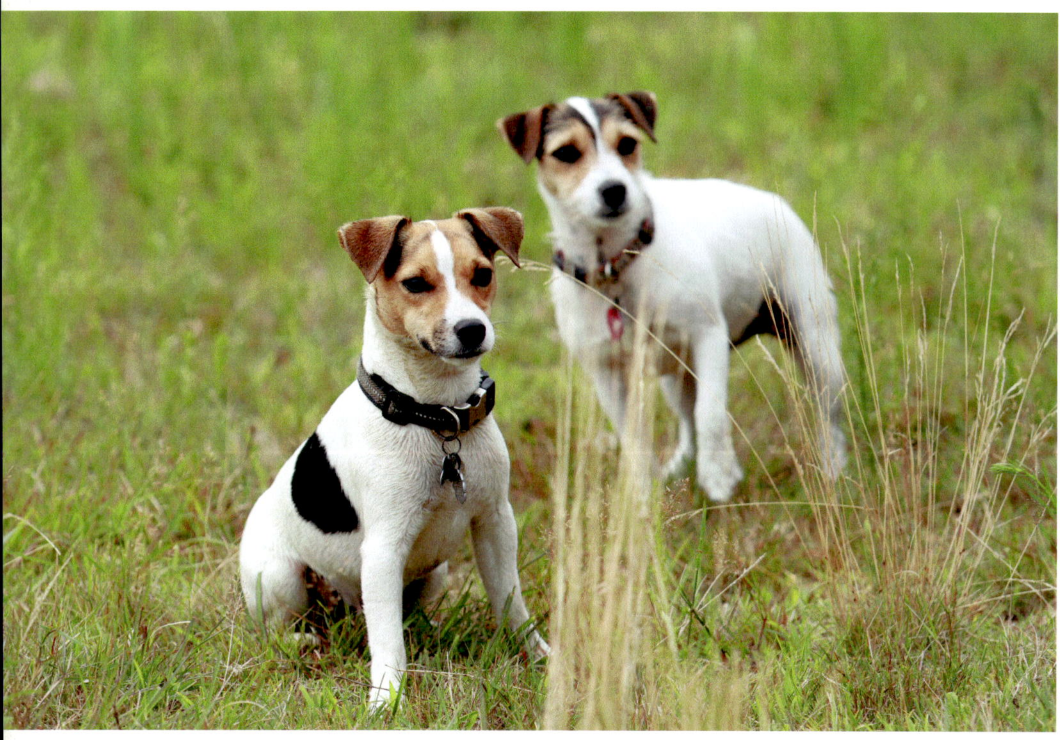

Dan and **Lucy** (above), Jack Russell terriers, Strong Island

Dan (right and opposite)

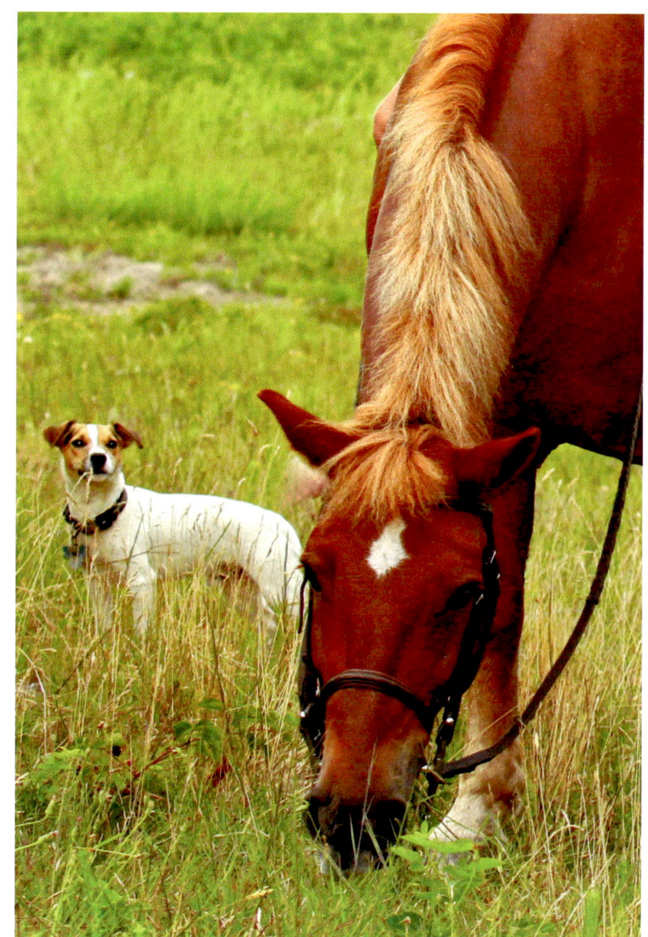

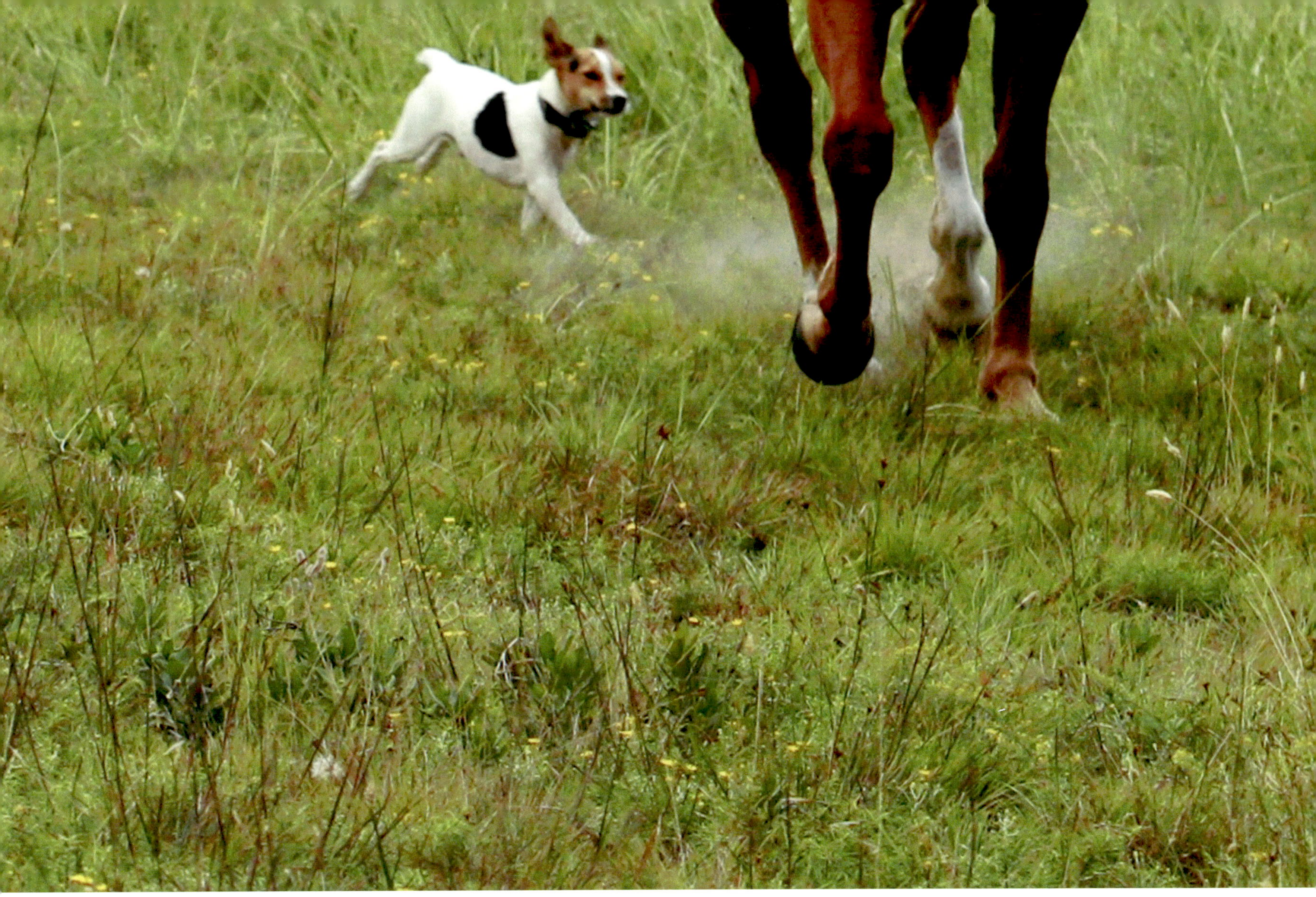

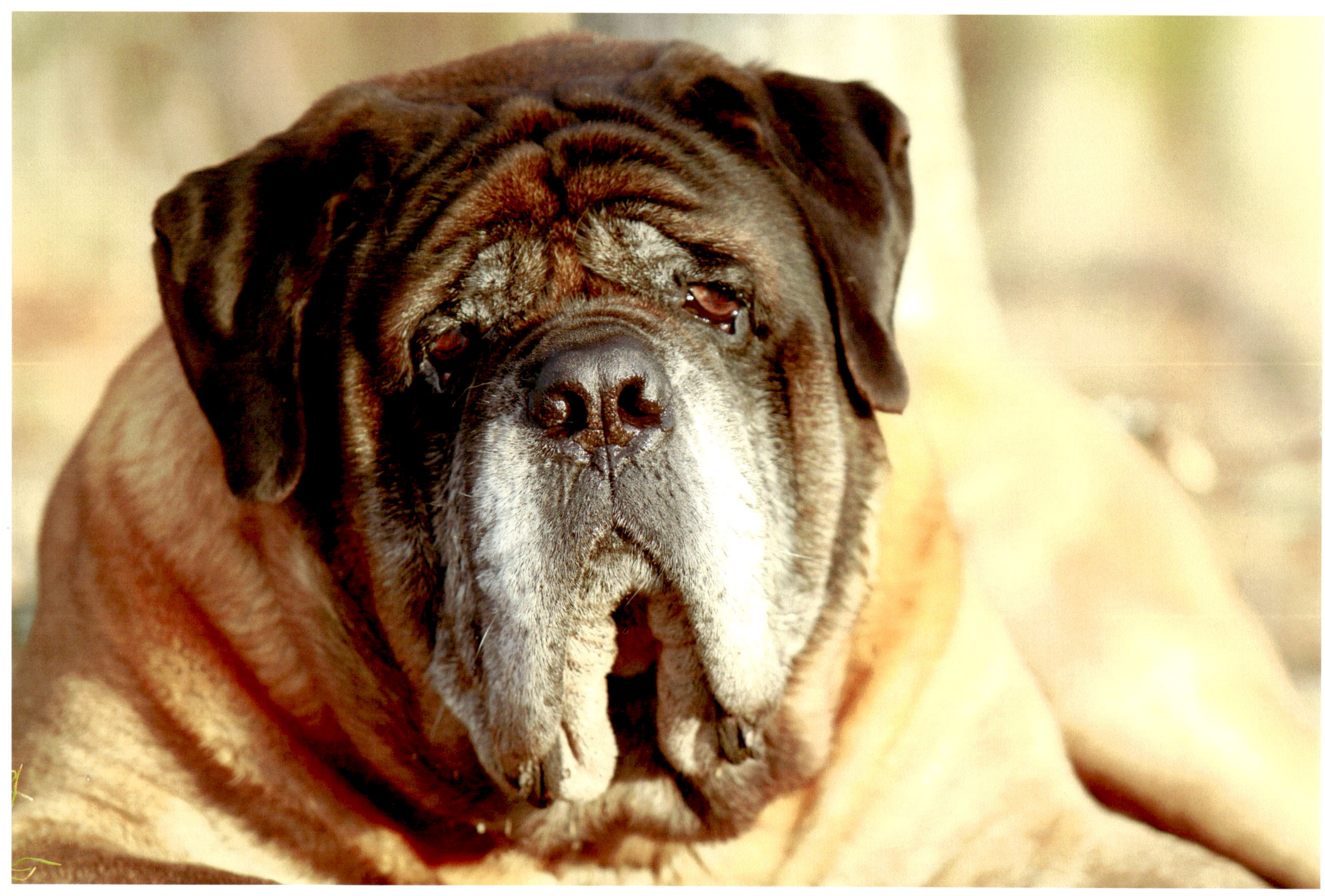

Beamer, English mastiff

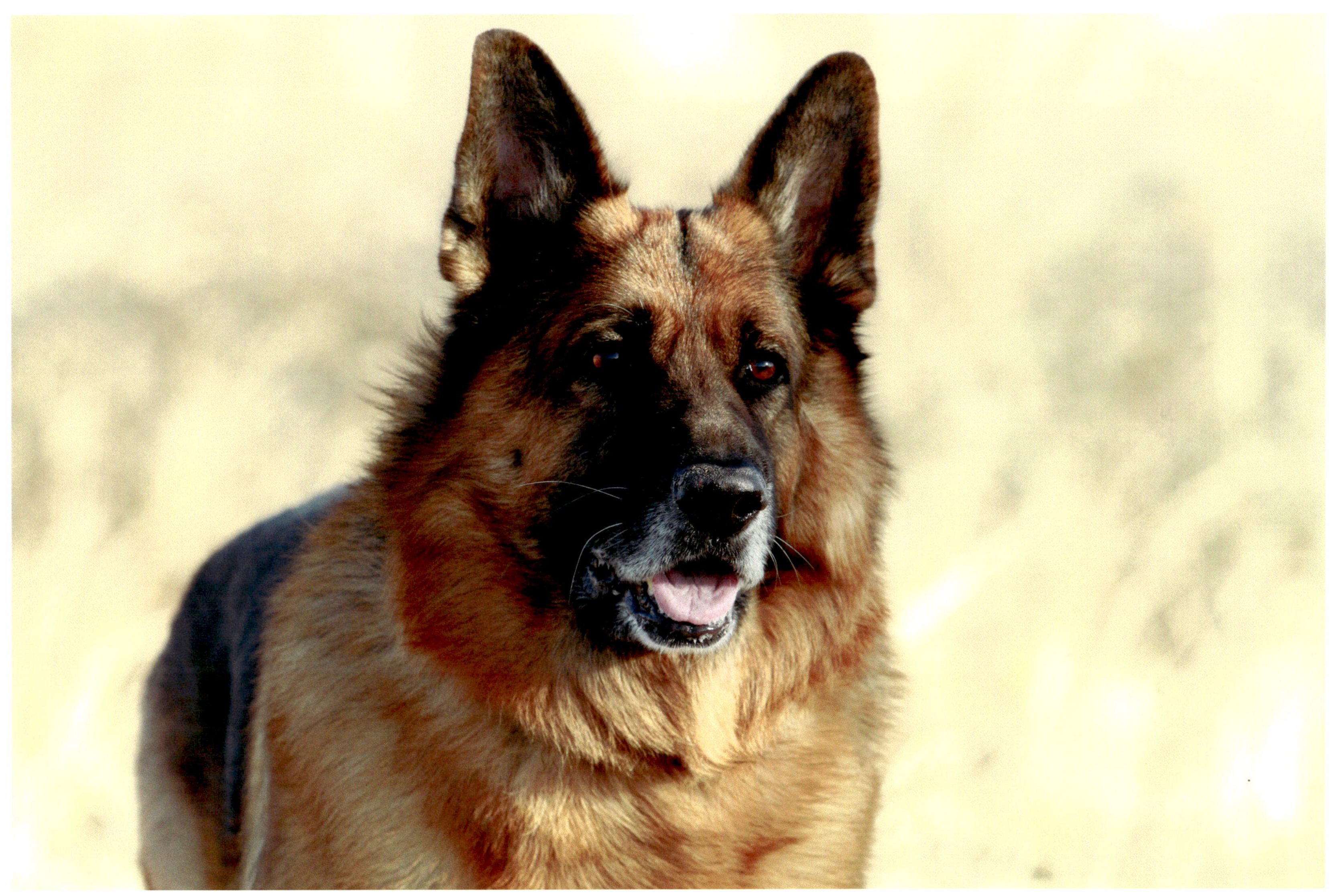

C.J., Belgian long-haired shephard

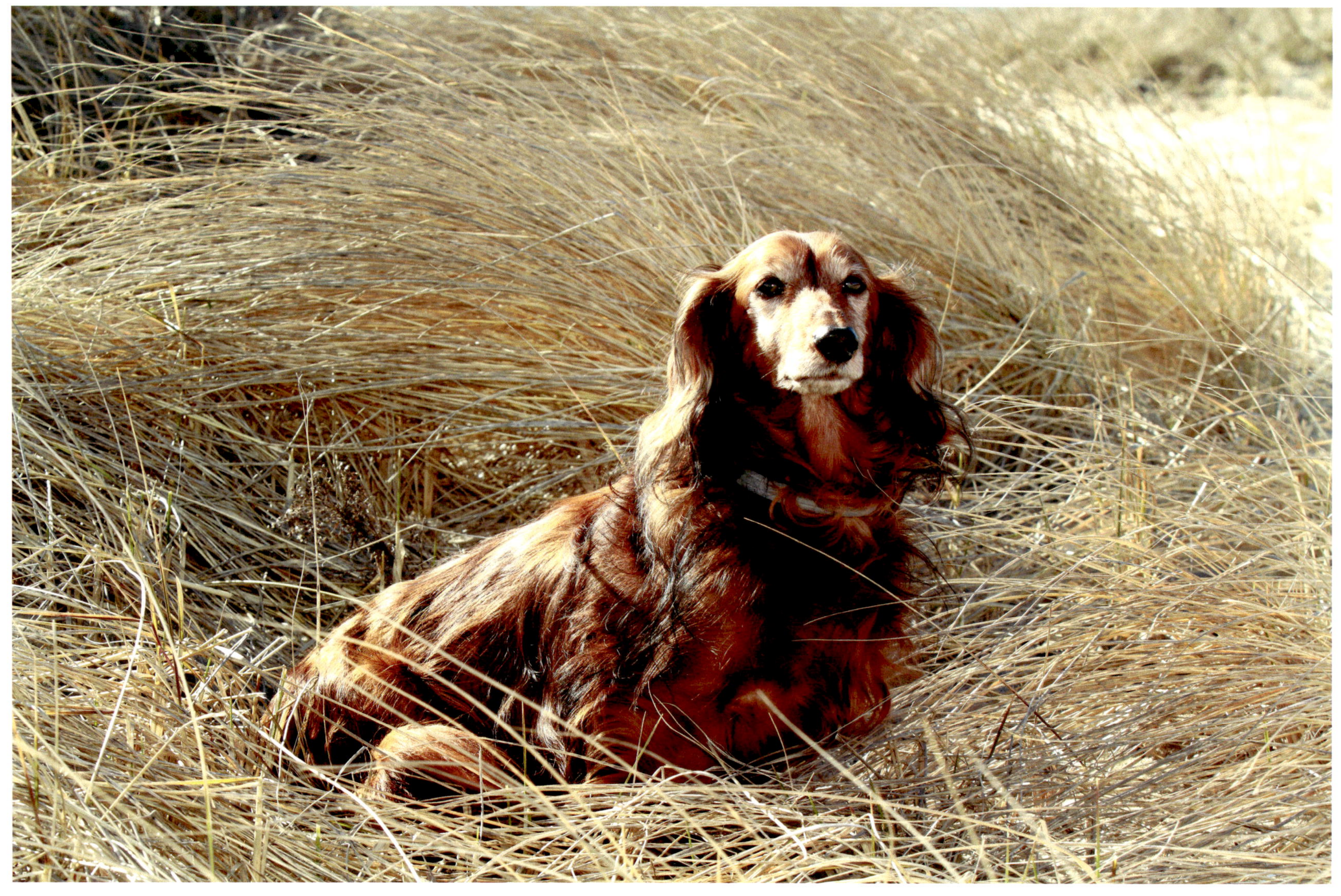

Percy, dwarf long-haired dachshund

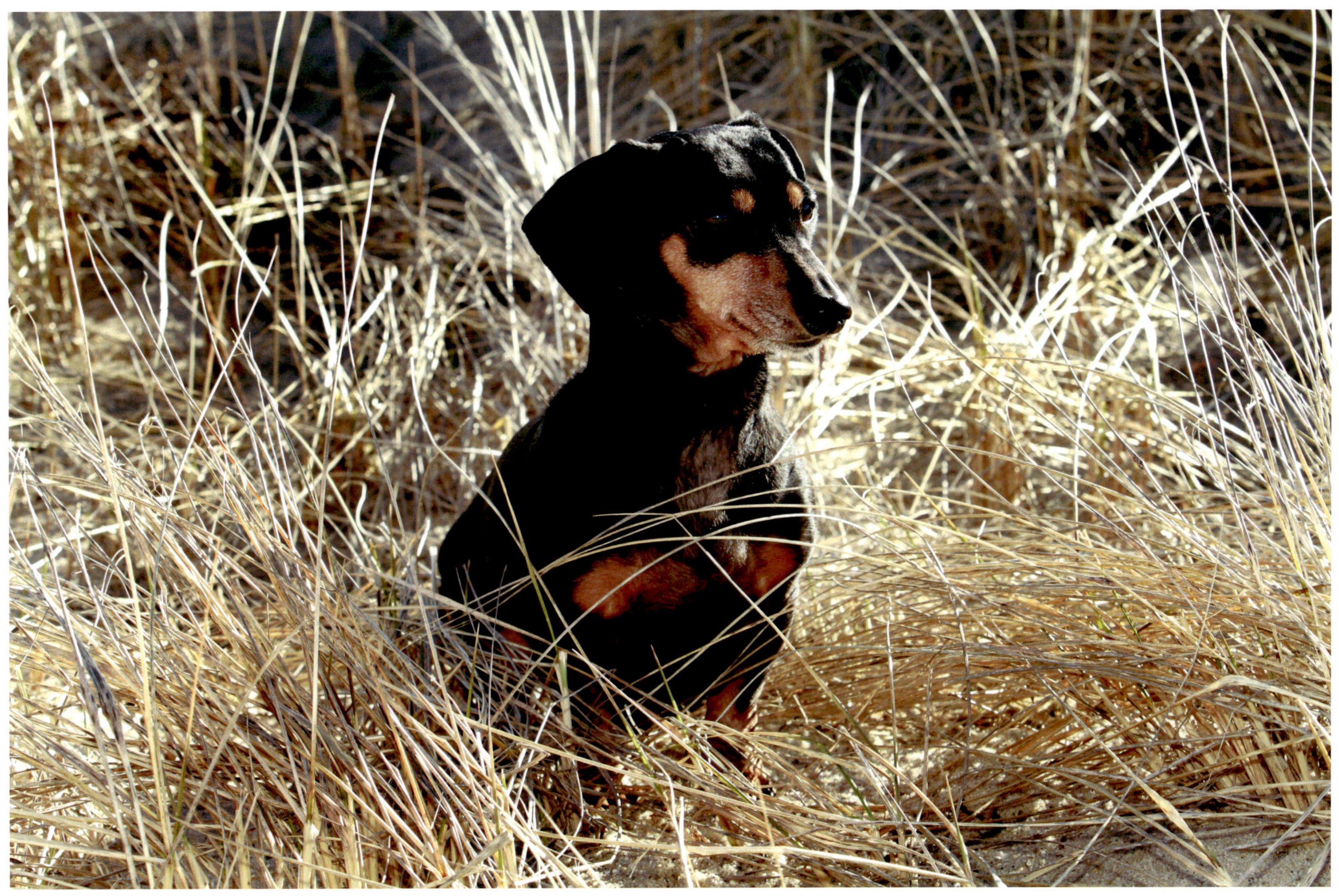

Suzie, miniature smooth dachshund

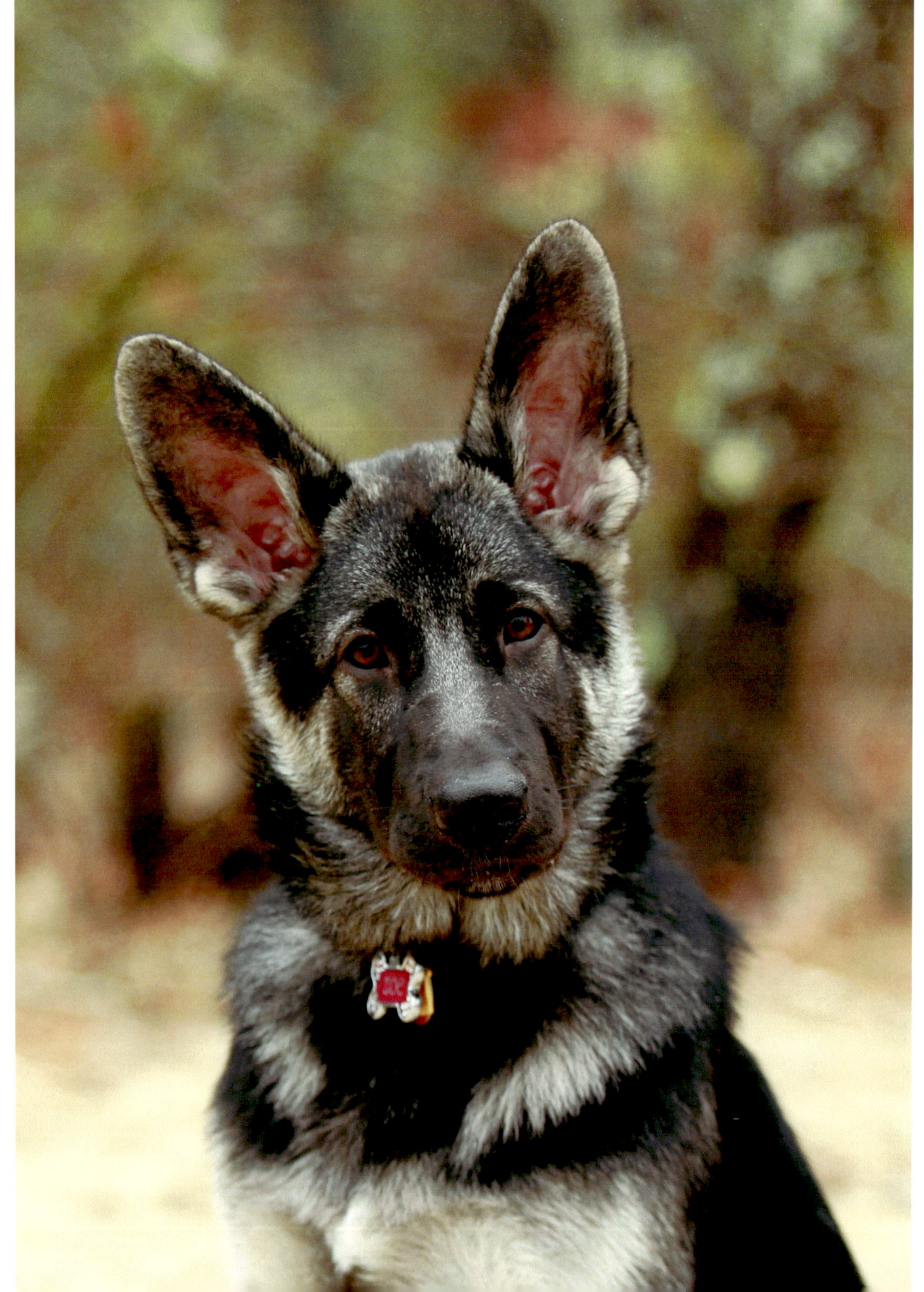

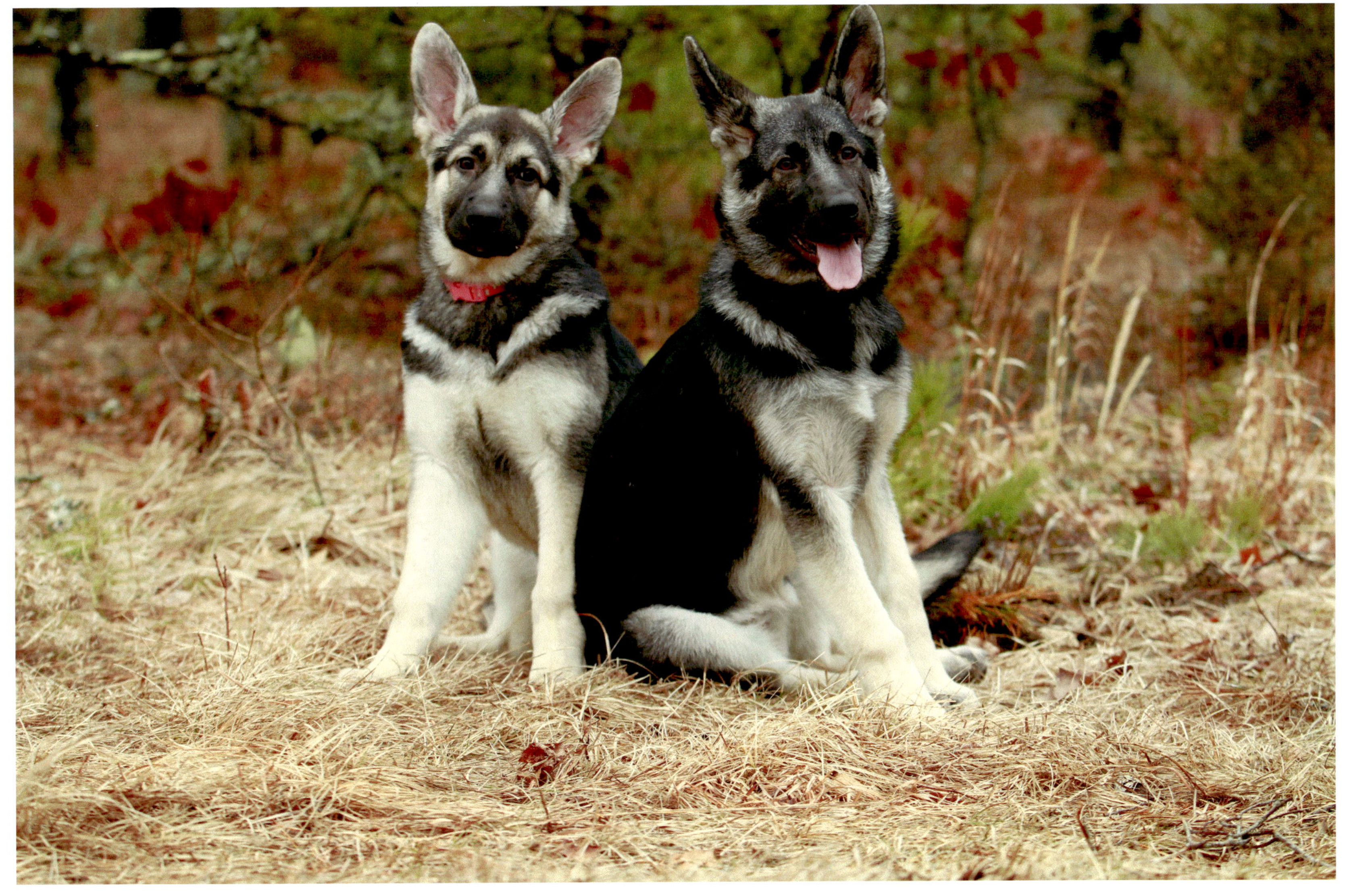

Shandy and **Zoe** (above), German shepherds, Thompson's Field

Zoe (opposite)

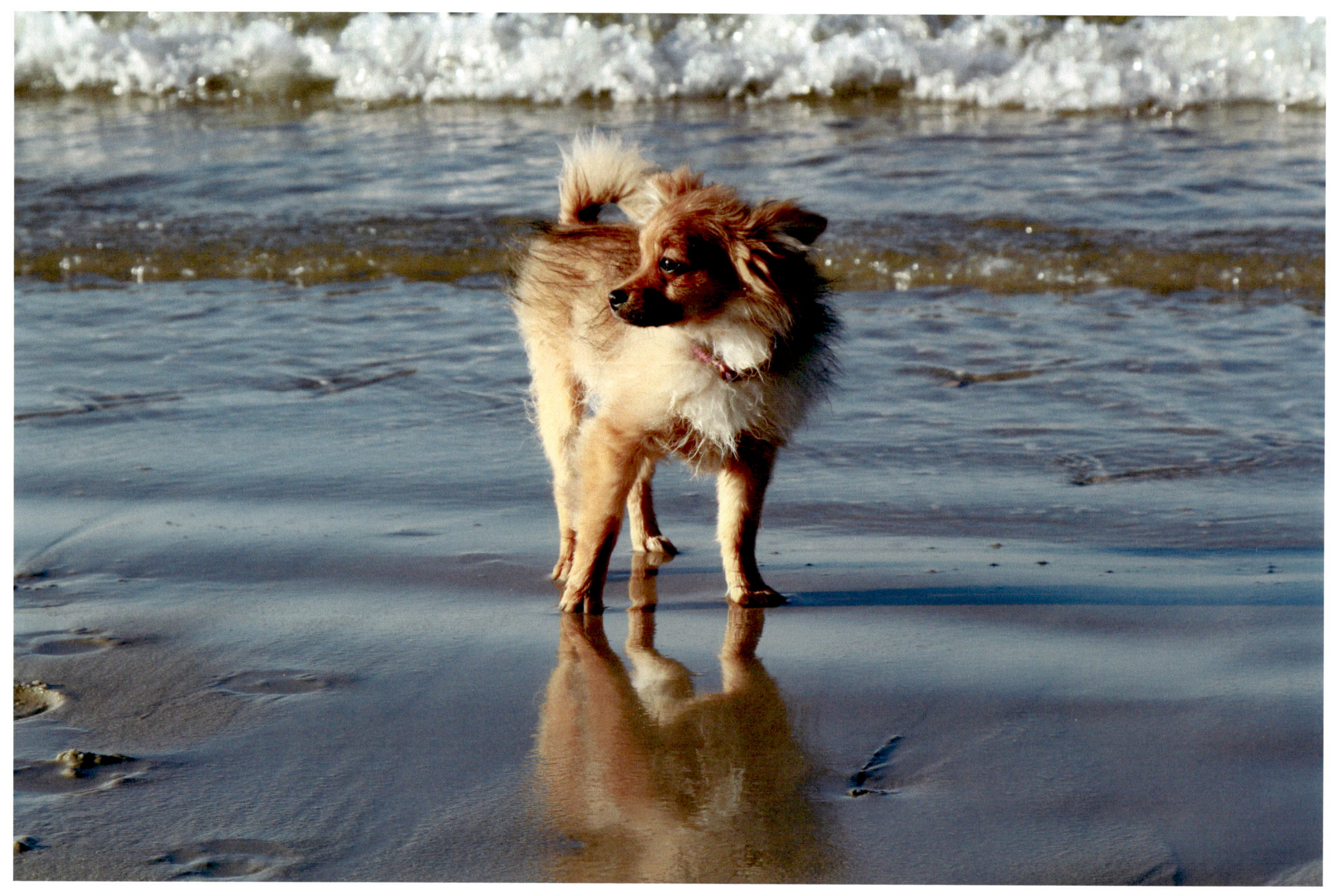

Ruby, Pomeranian, Bank Street Beach

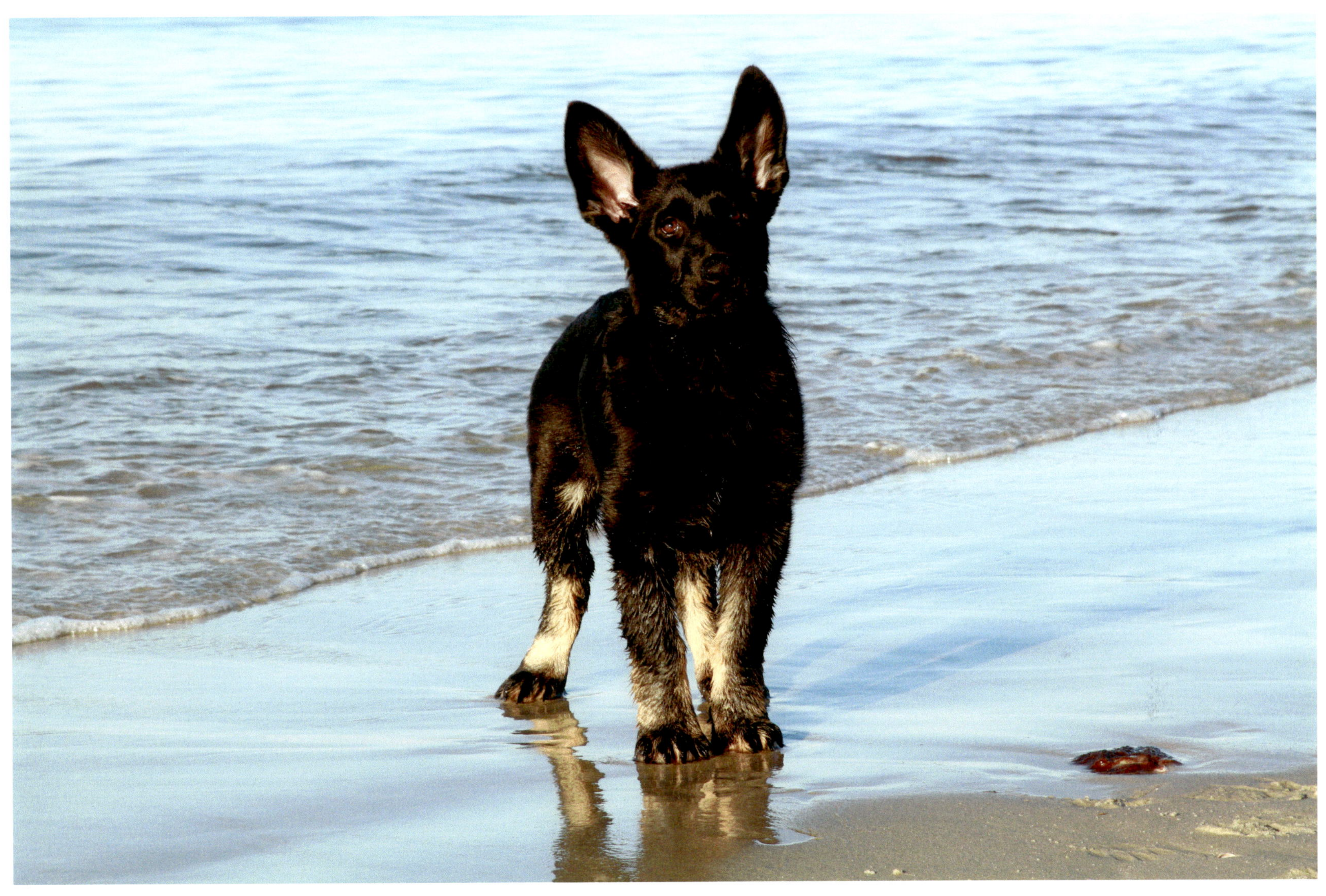

Caymus, German shepherd, Bank Street Beach

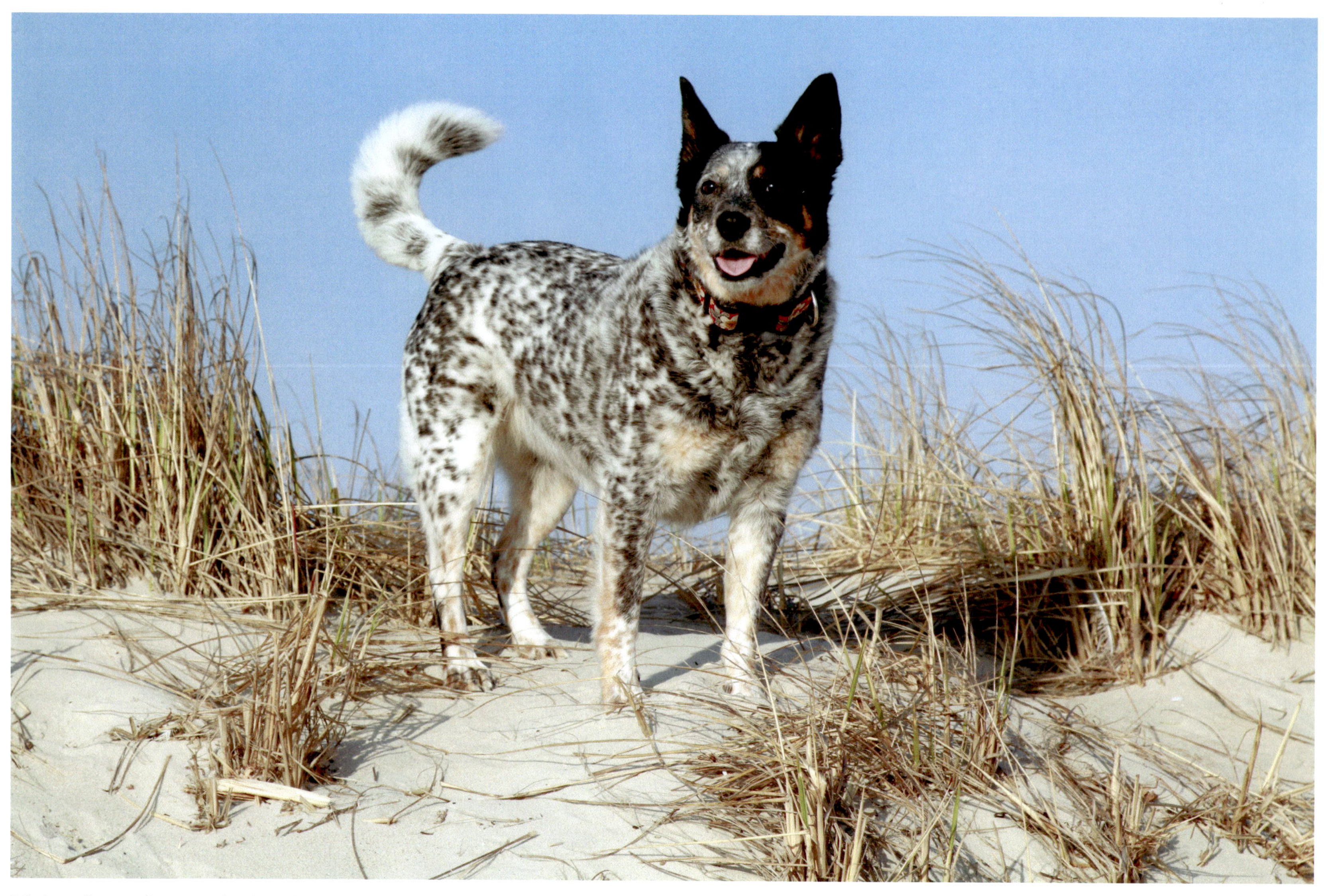

Maisy, Australian cattle dog, Bank Street Beach

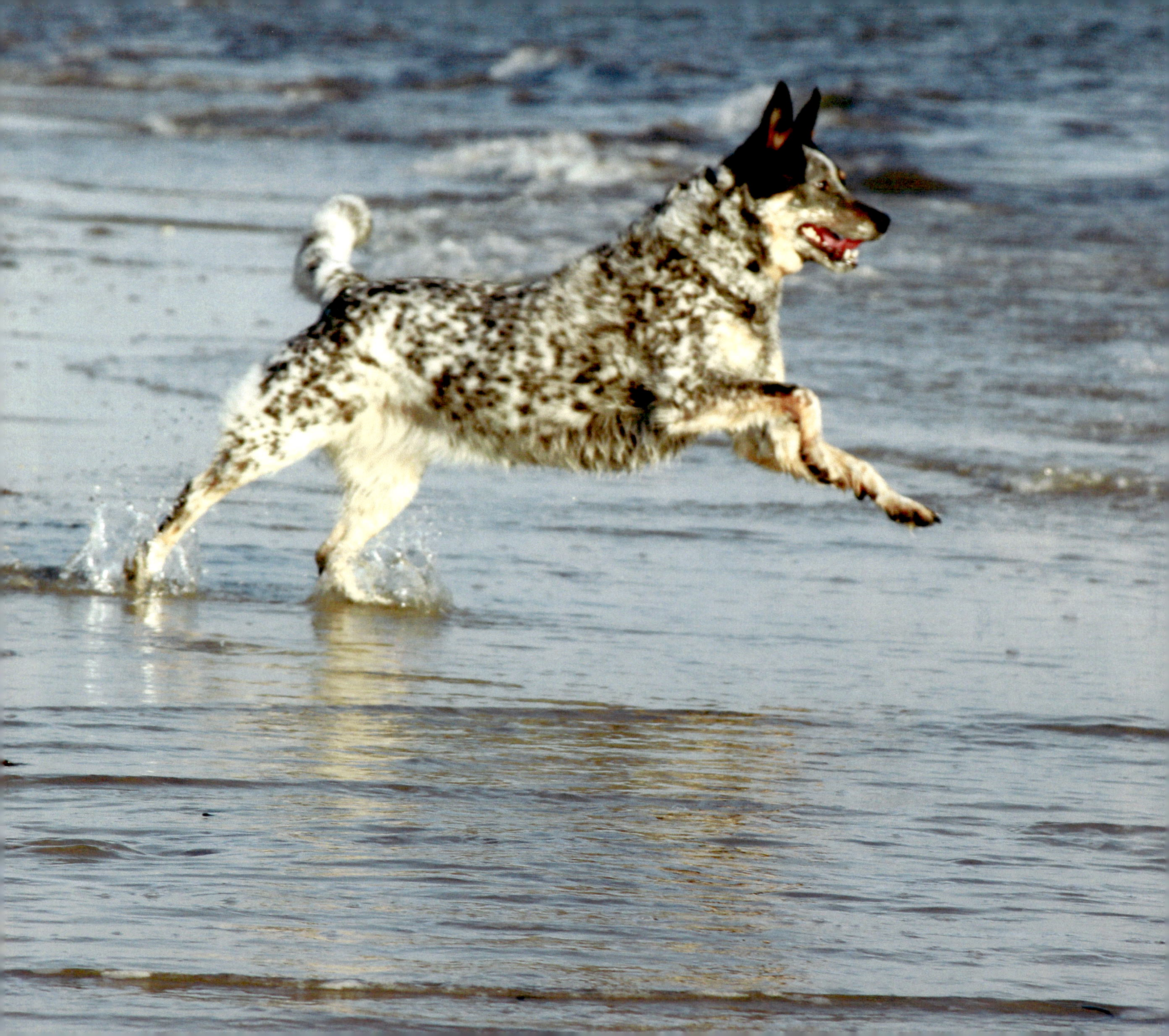

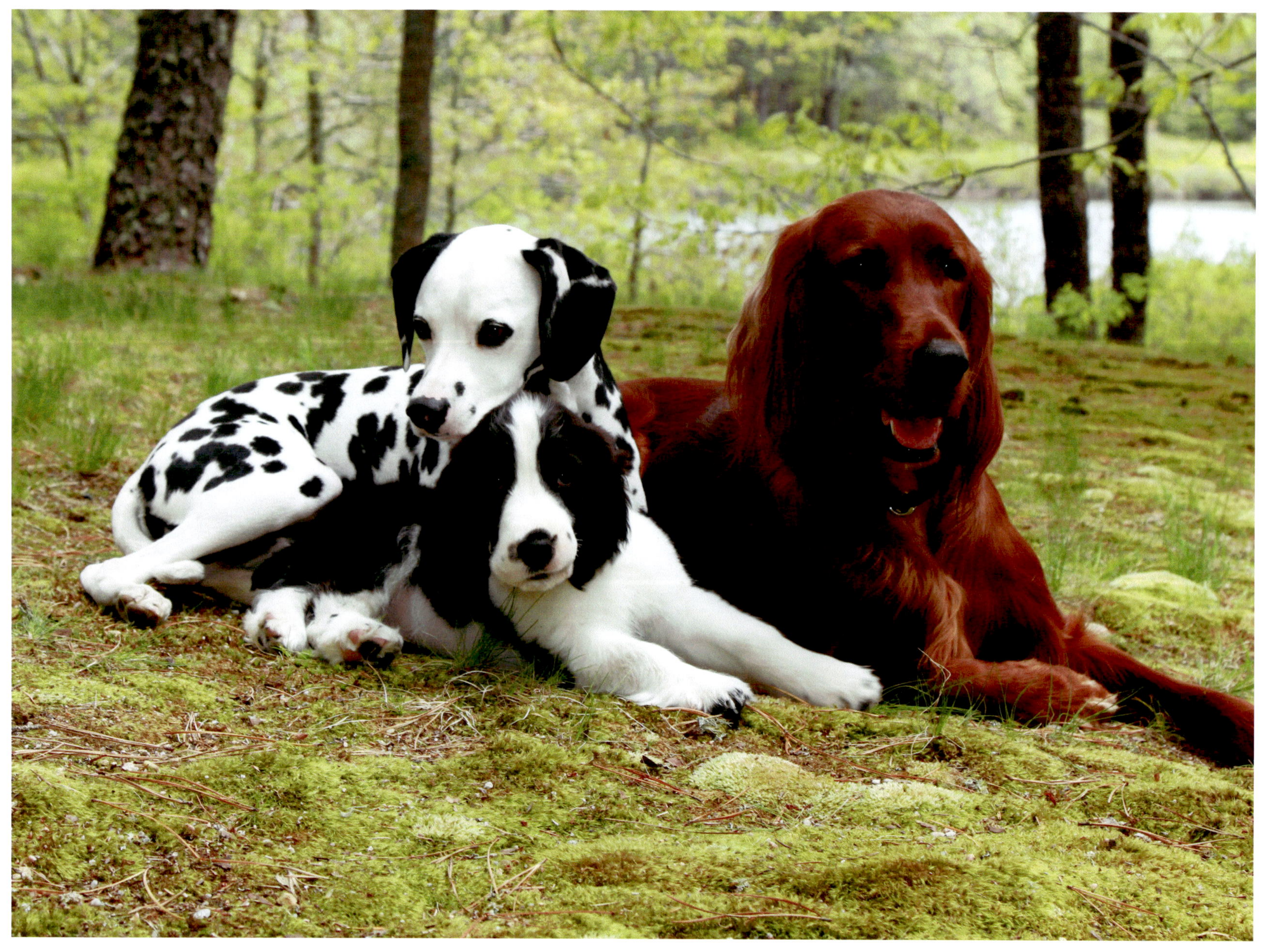

Stormy, Dalmatian, **Oliver**, springer spaniel, and **Georgia**, Irish setter, Shoal Pond

Maggie May, Rhodesian ridgeback mix, Kent's Point

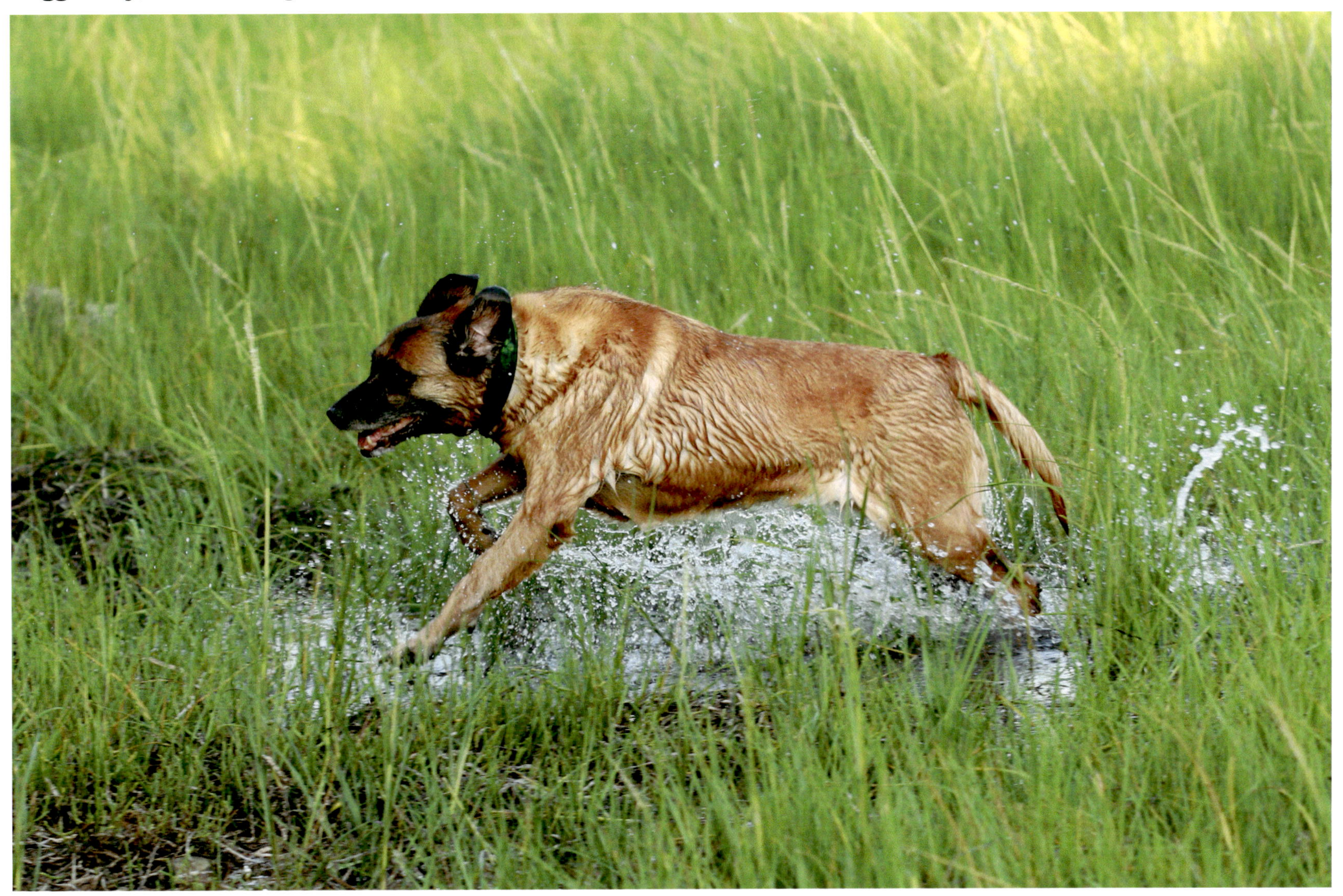

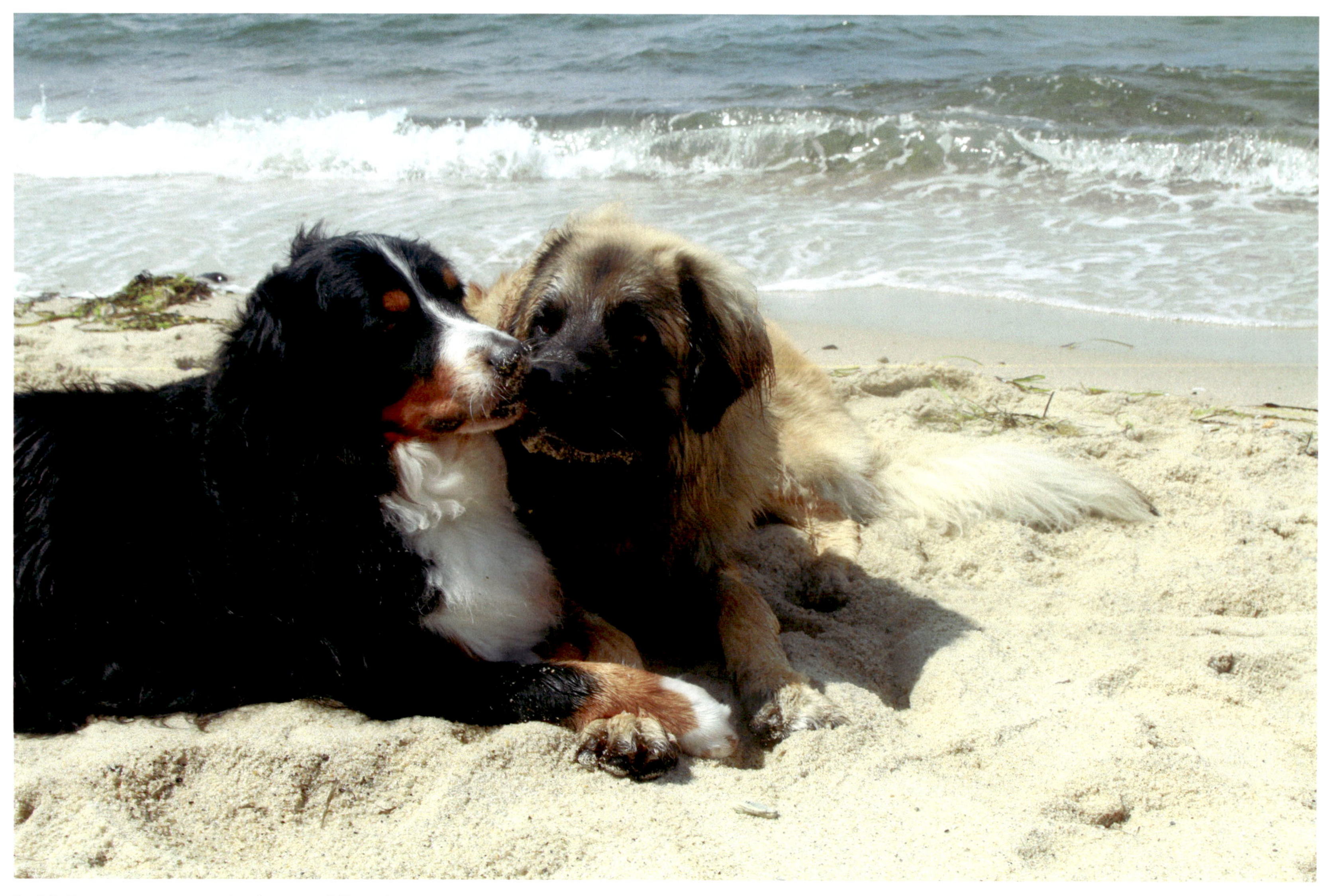

Loki, Bernese mountain dog, and **Bamboo**, Leonberger, Cape Cod Bay

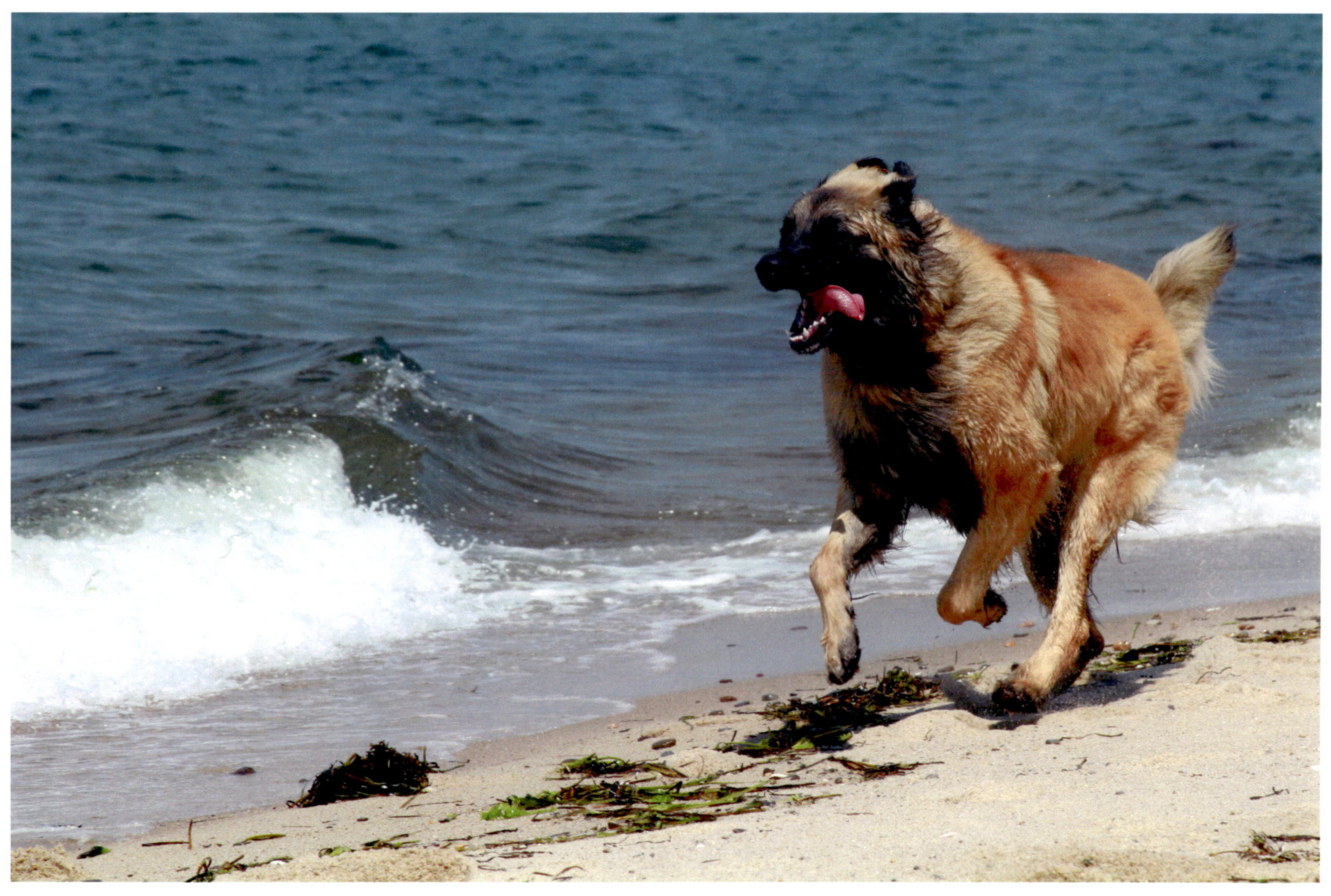

Bamboo

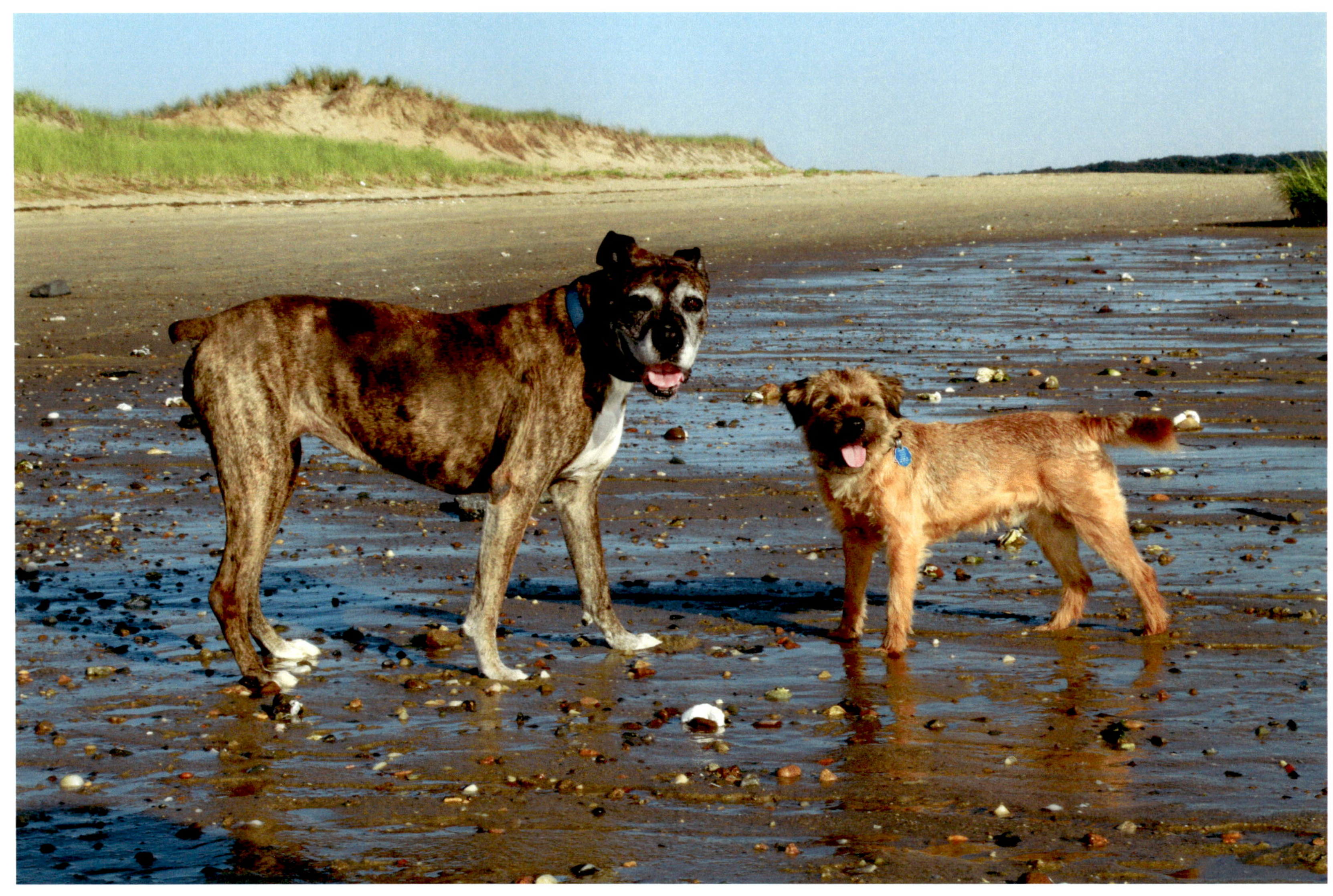

Brindy, boxer, and **Charlie**, Border terrier, Lieutenant Island

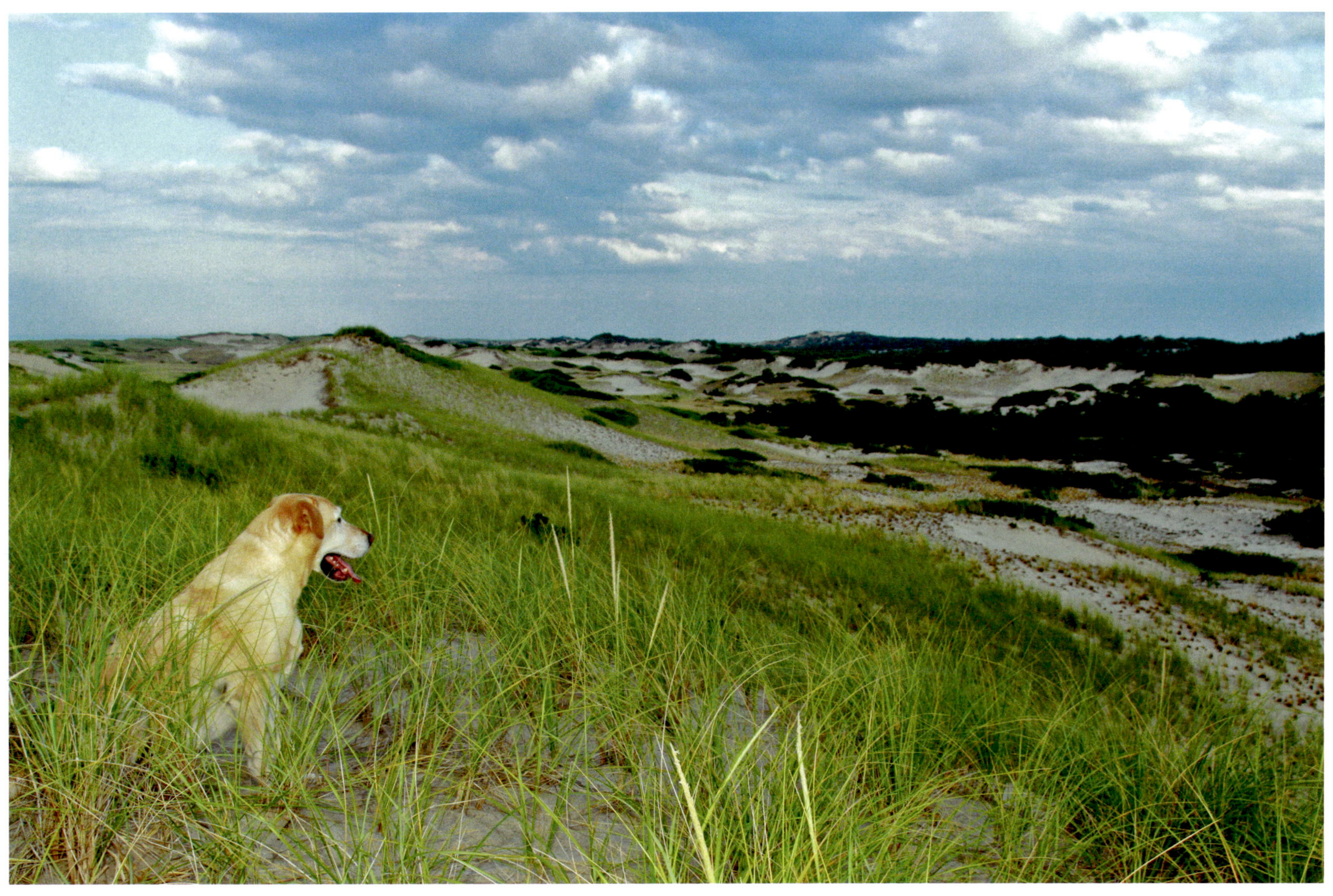

Hank, Labrador retriever, Race Point Beach

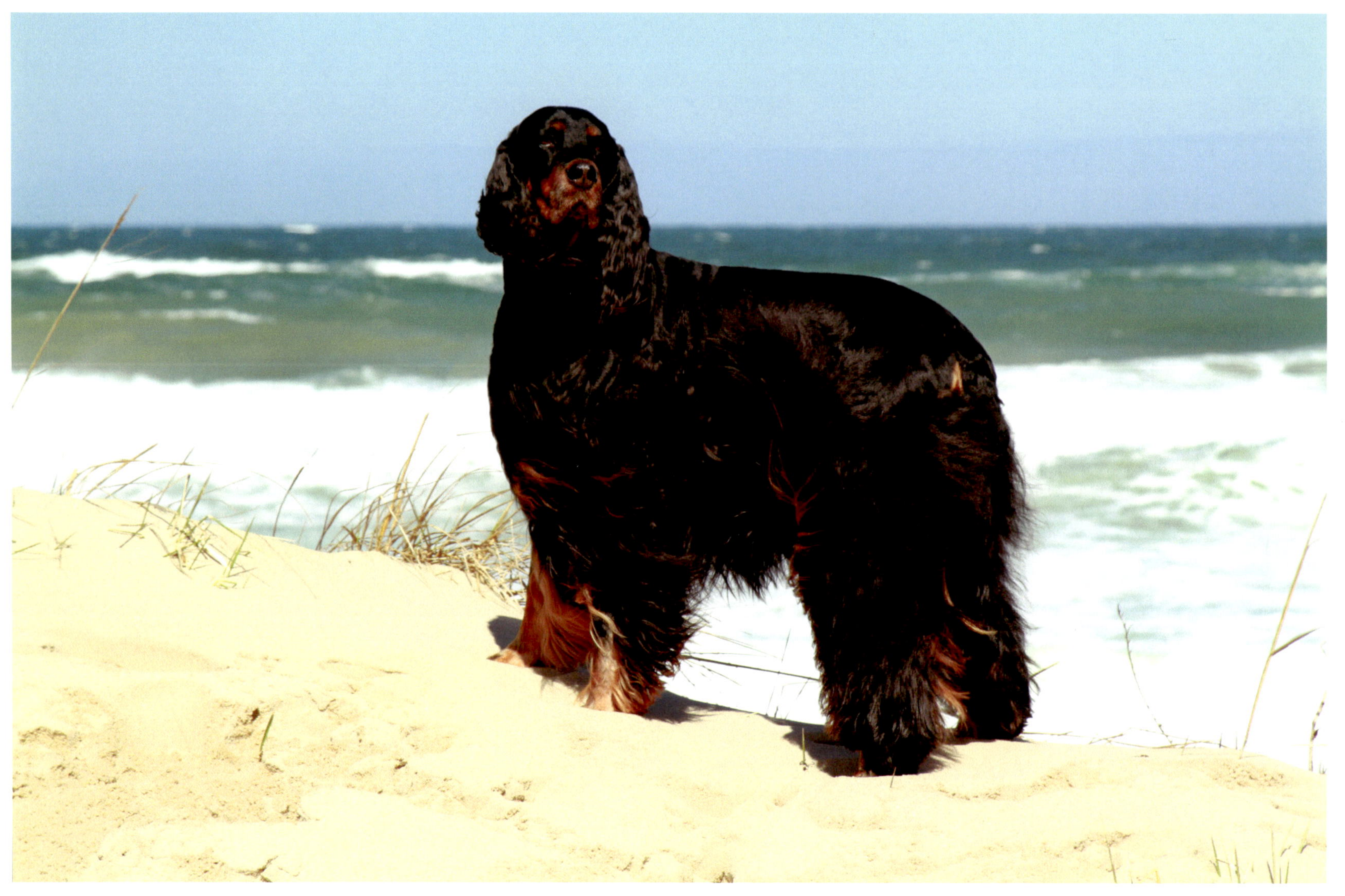

Kendelle, Gordon setter, Head of the Meadow Beach

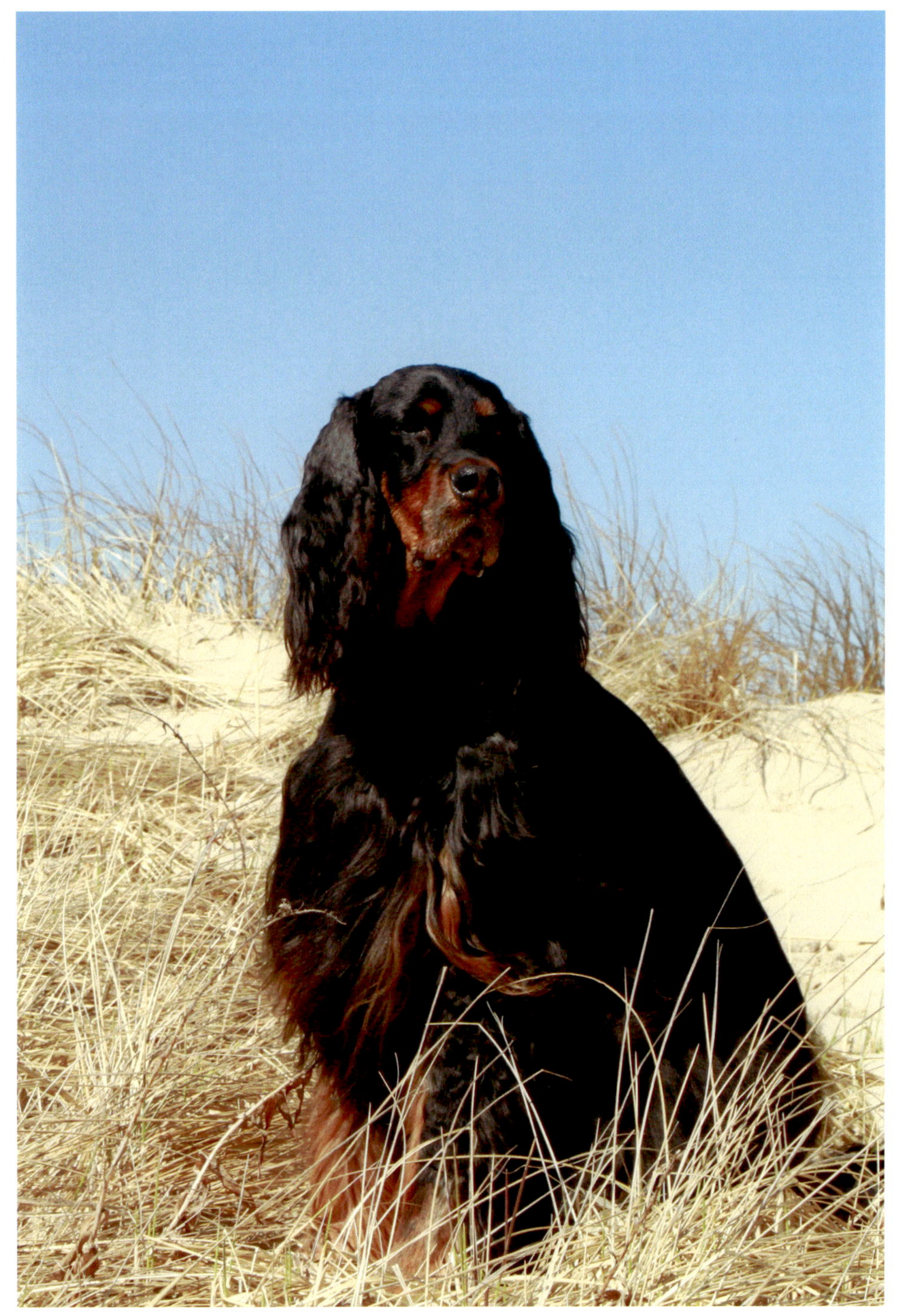

Nikia (below) and **Nikia** and **Sasha** (bottom), Samoyeds, Harding's Beach

Sasha (opposite)

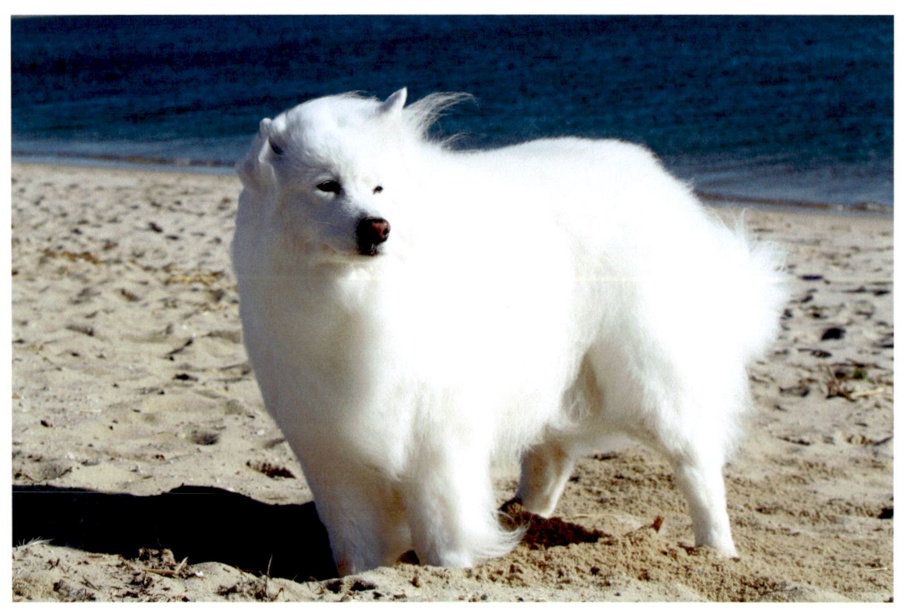

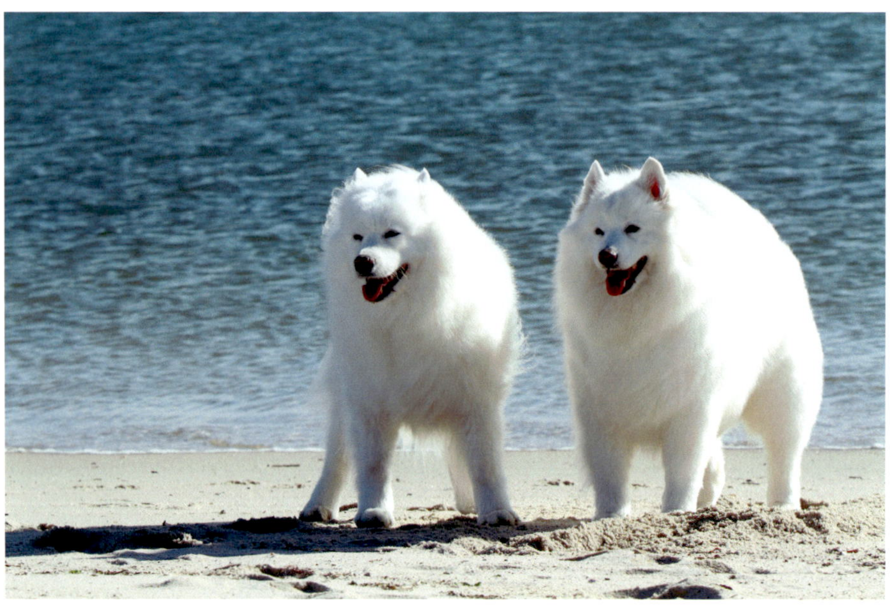

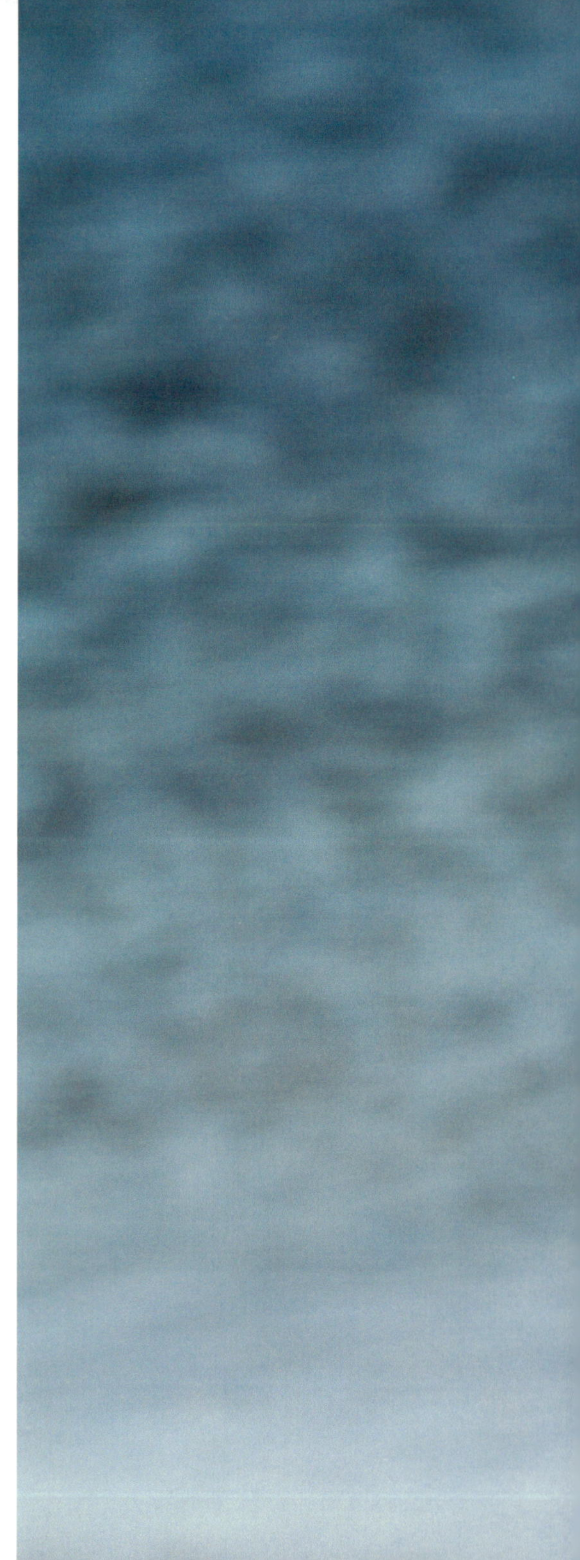

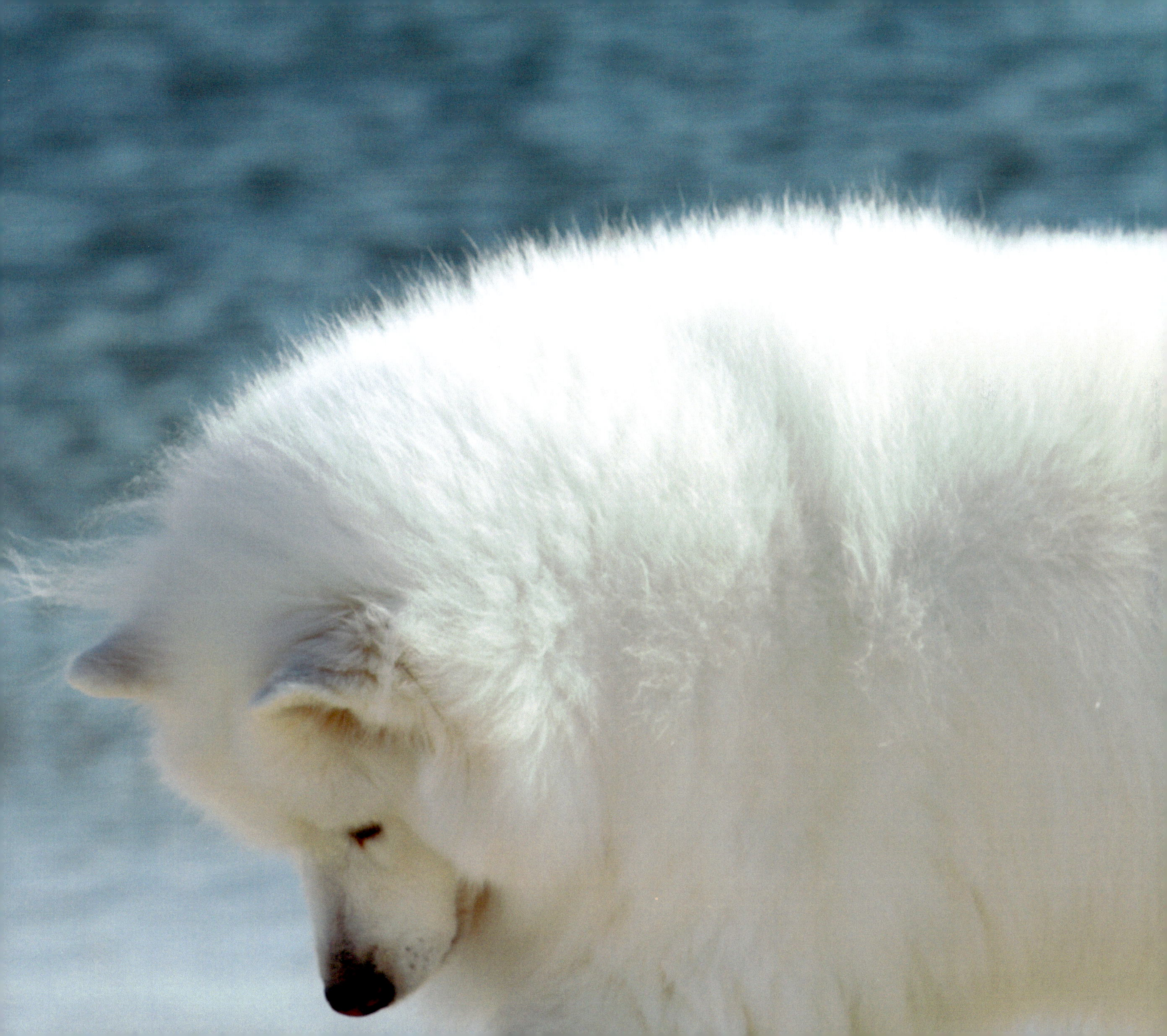

Bird dogs plead with you to imagine the great things you could be doing together. Their delight is a lesson in the bliss of living.

—Thomas McGuane,
The Only Honest Way to Eat Poultry

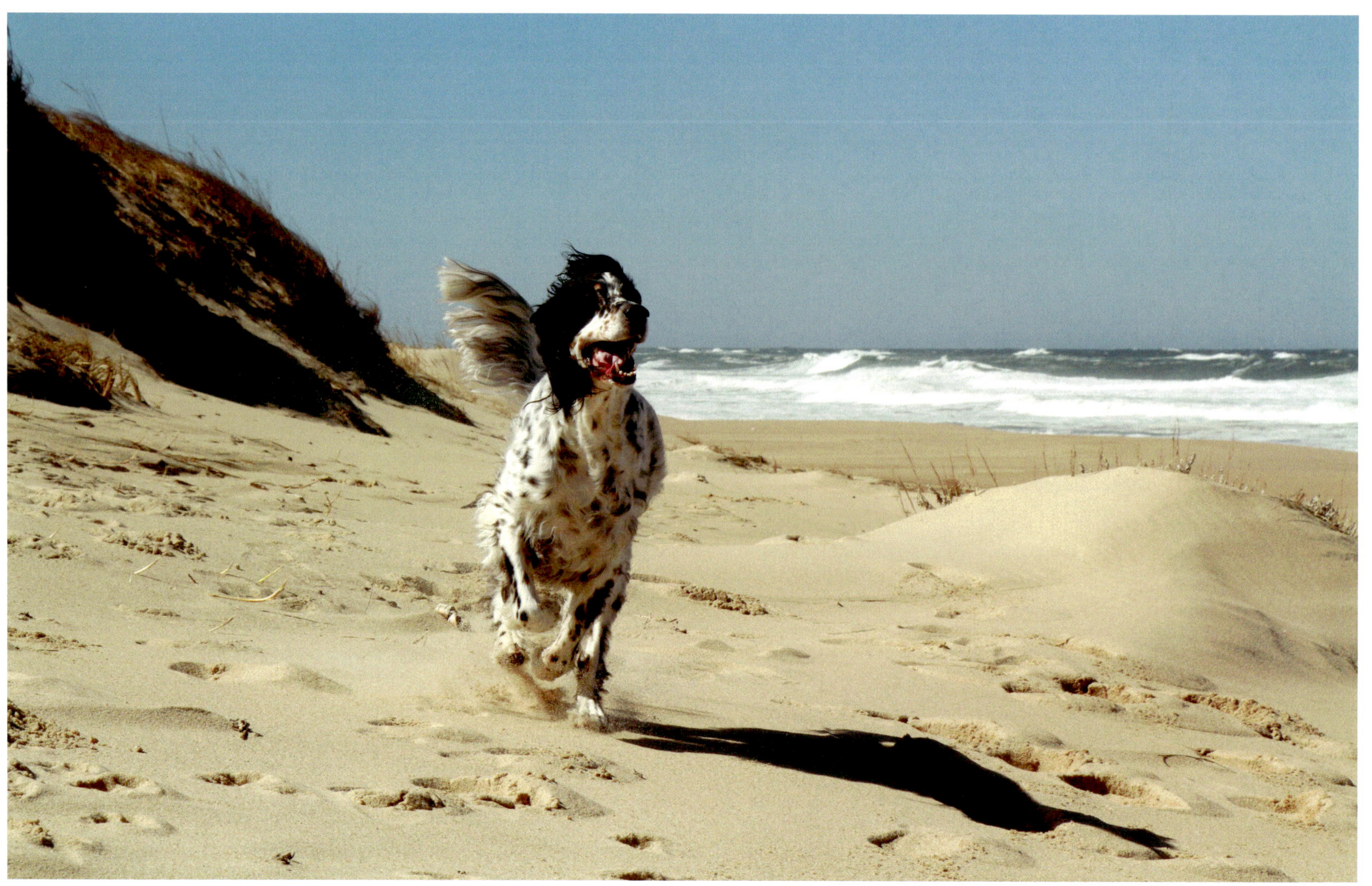

Monty, Llewellin setter, Head of the Meadow Beach

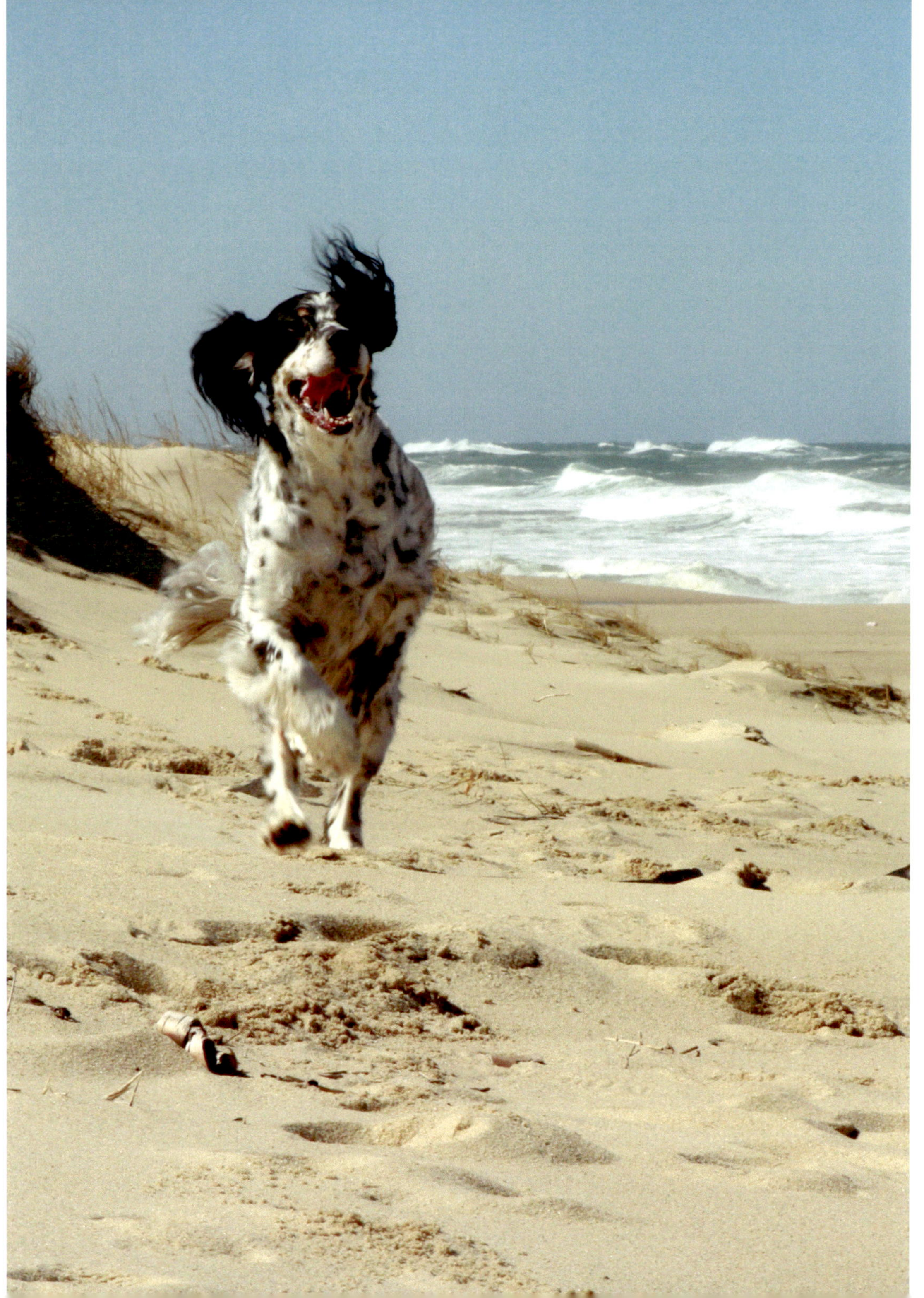

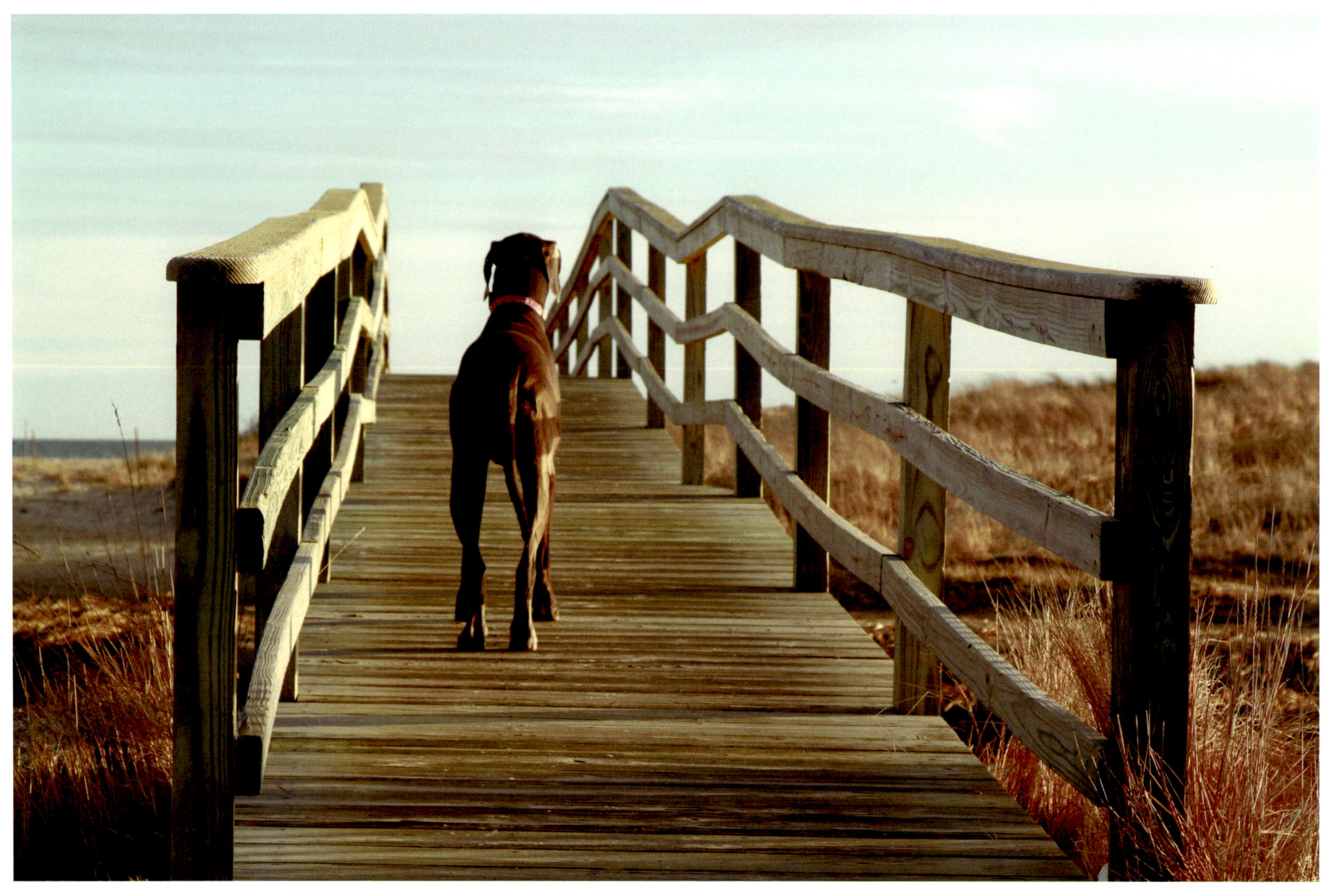

Bella Blu, Great Dane, Ridgevale Beach

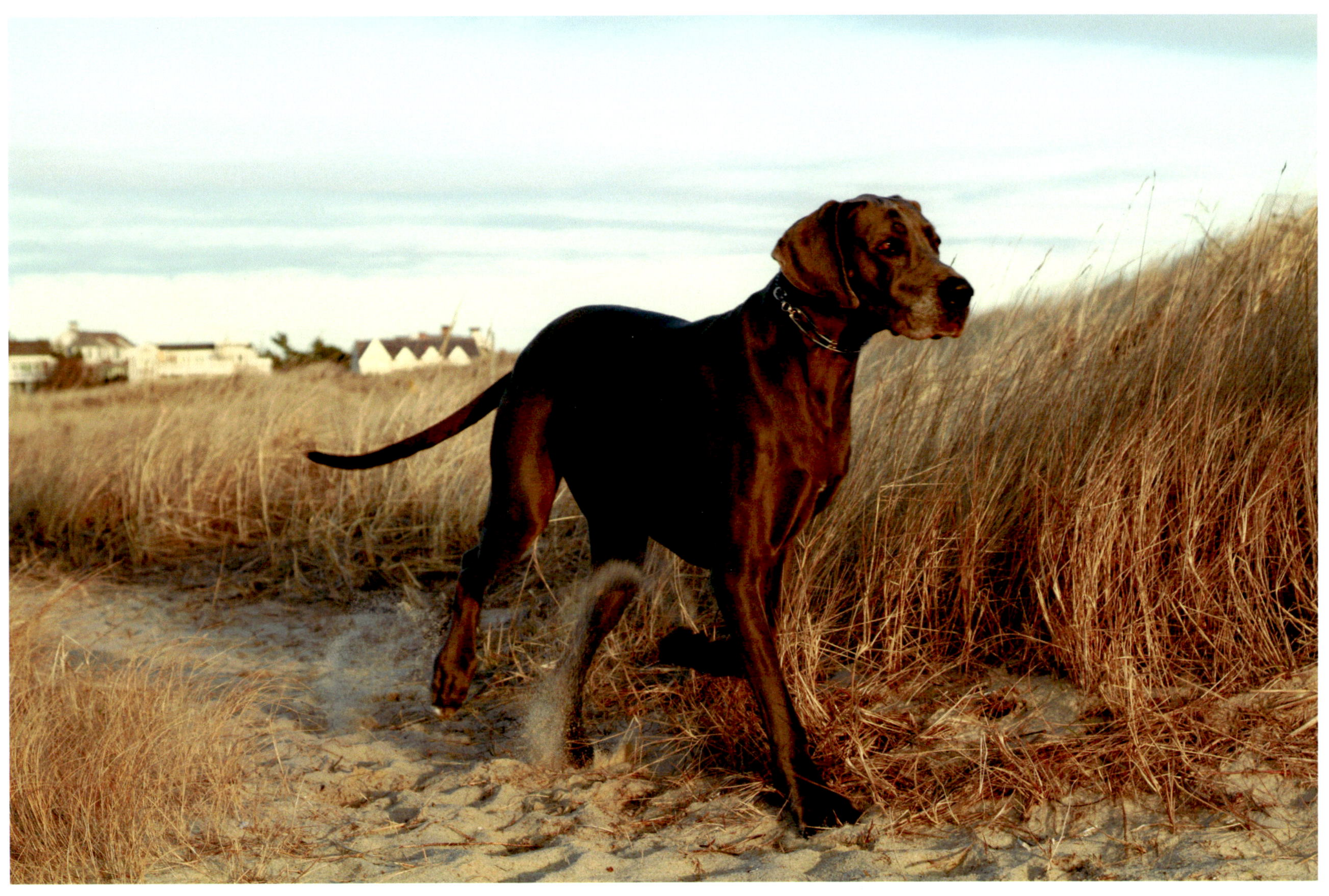

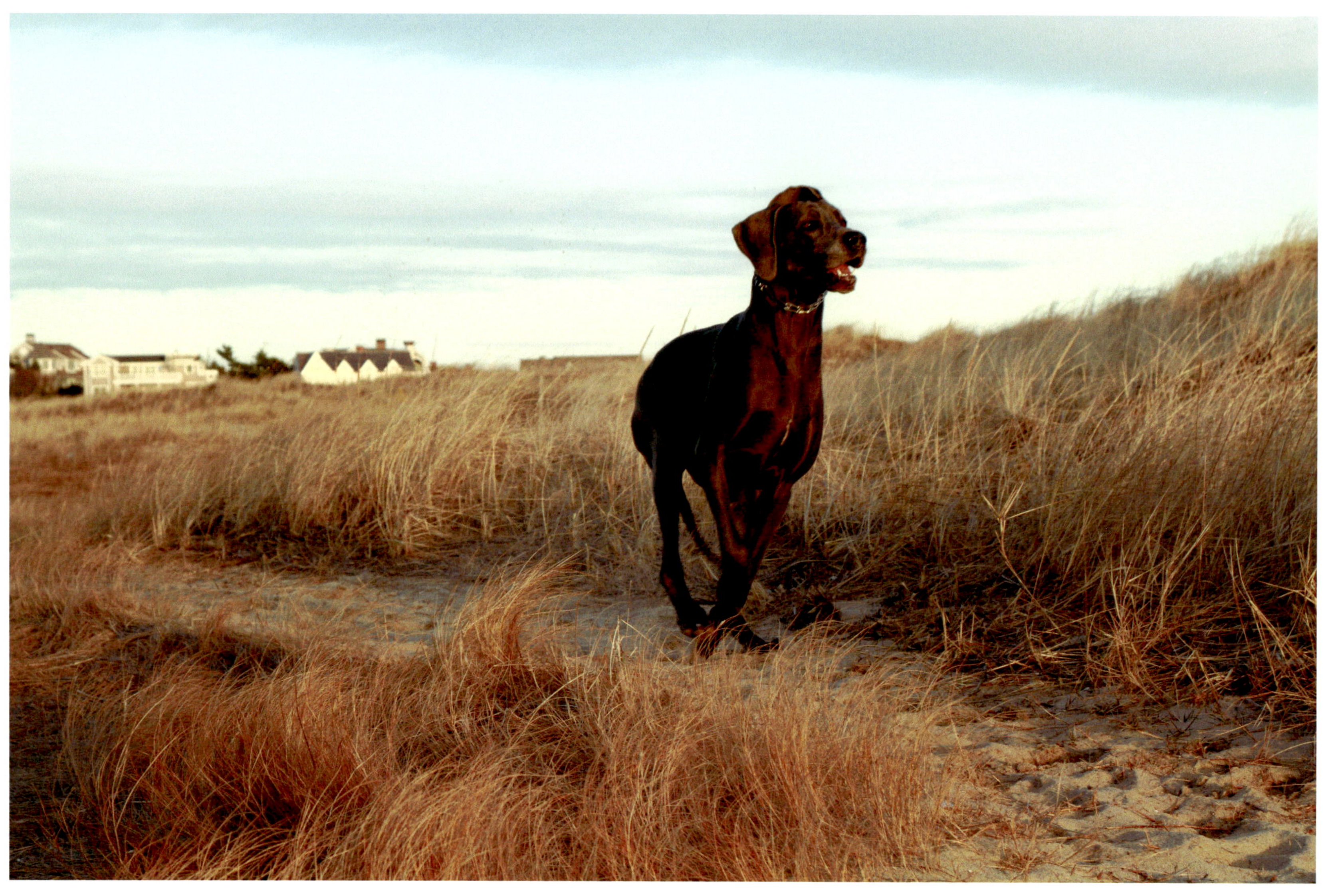

Bella Blu, Great Dane, Ridgevale Beach

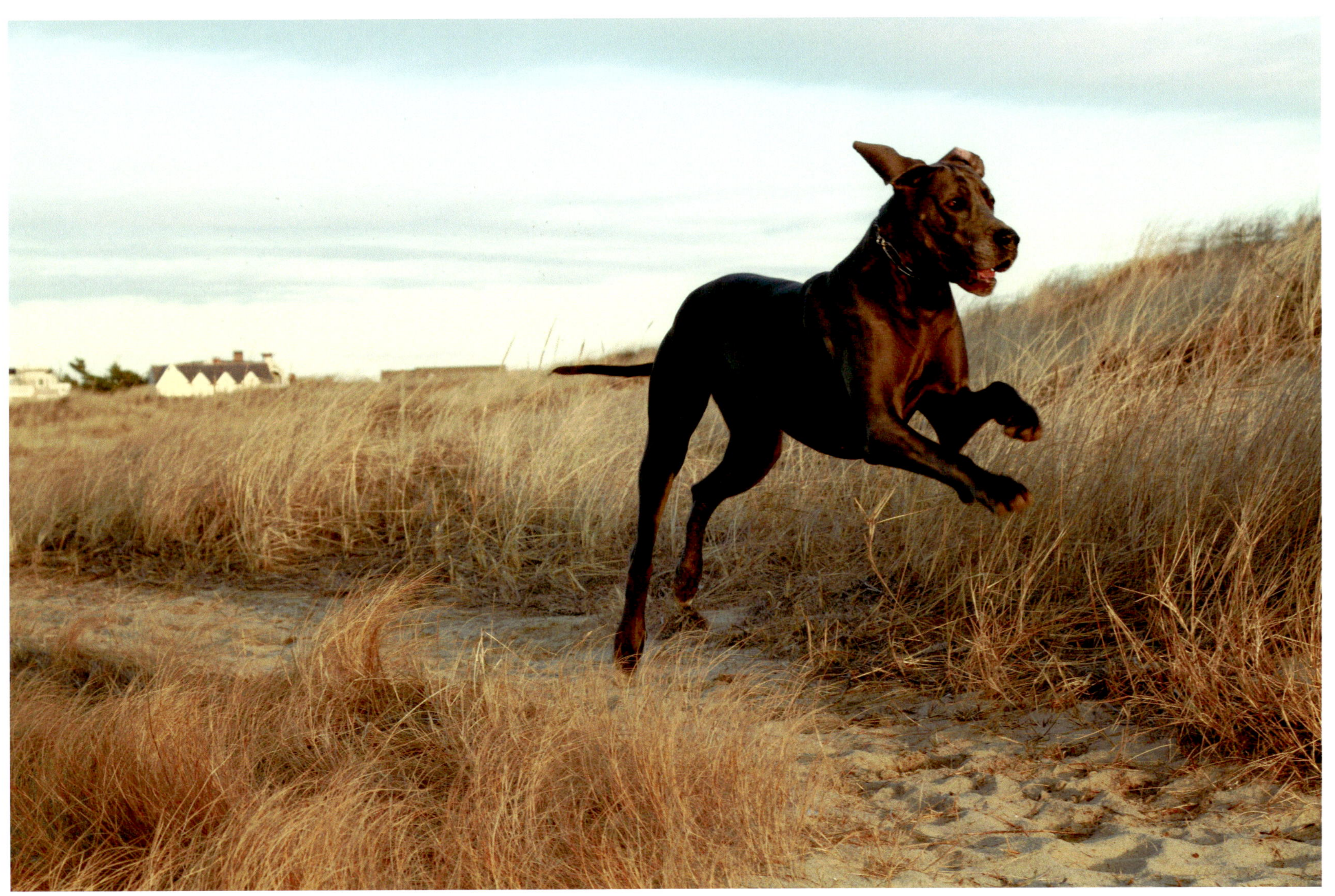

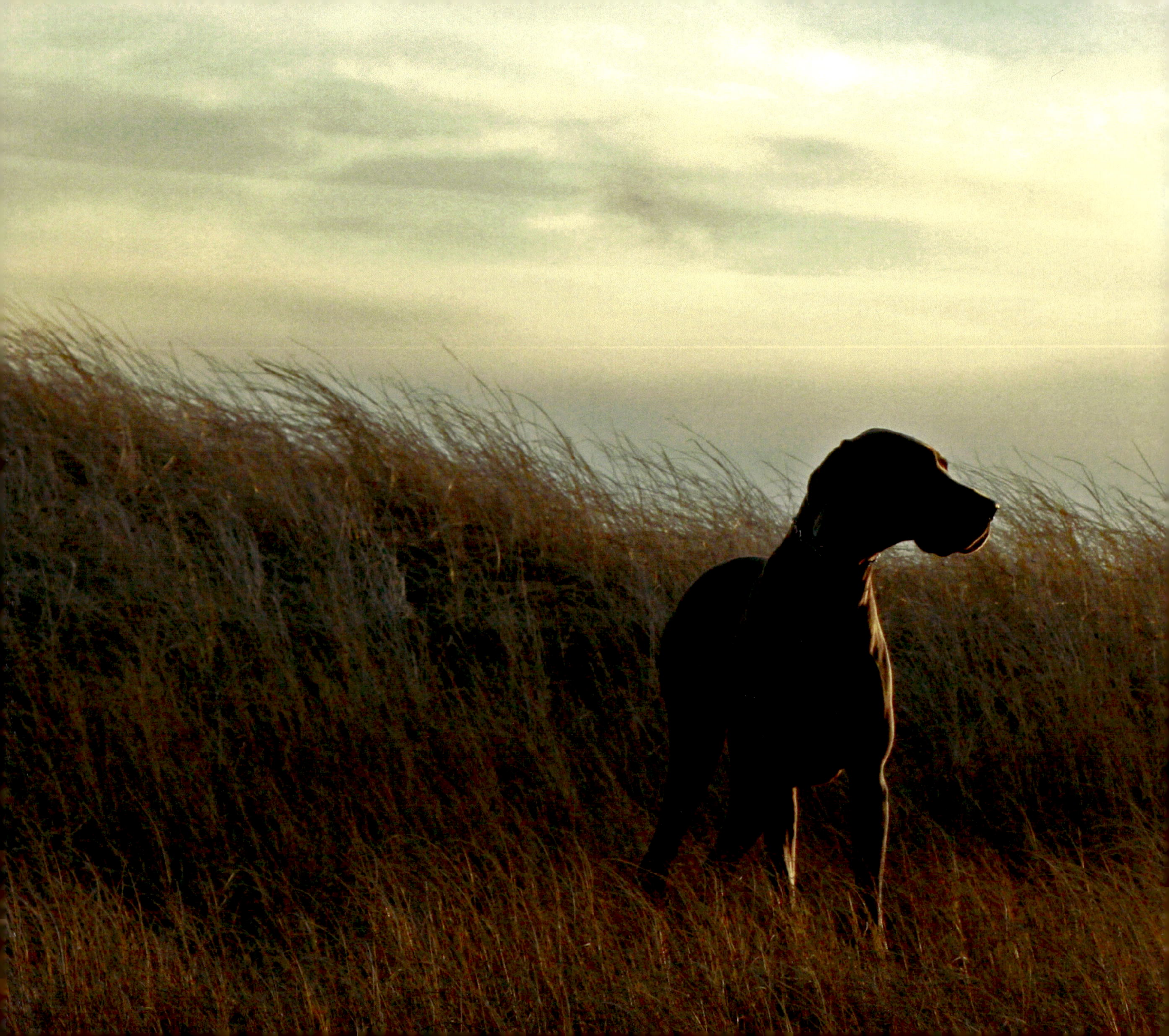

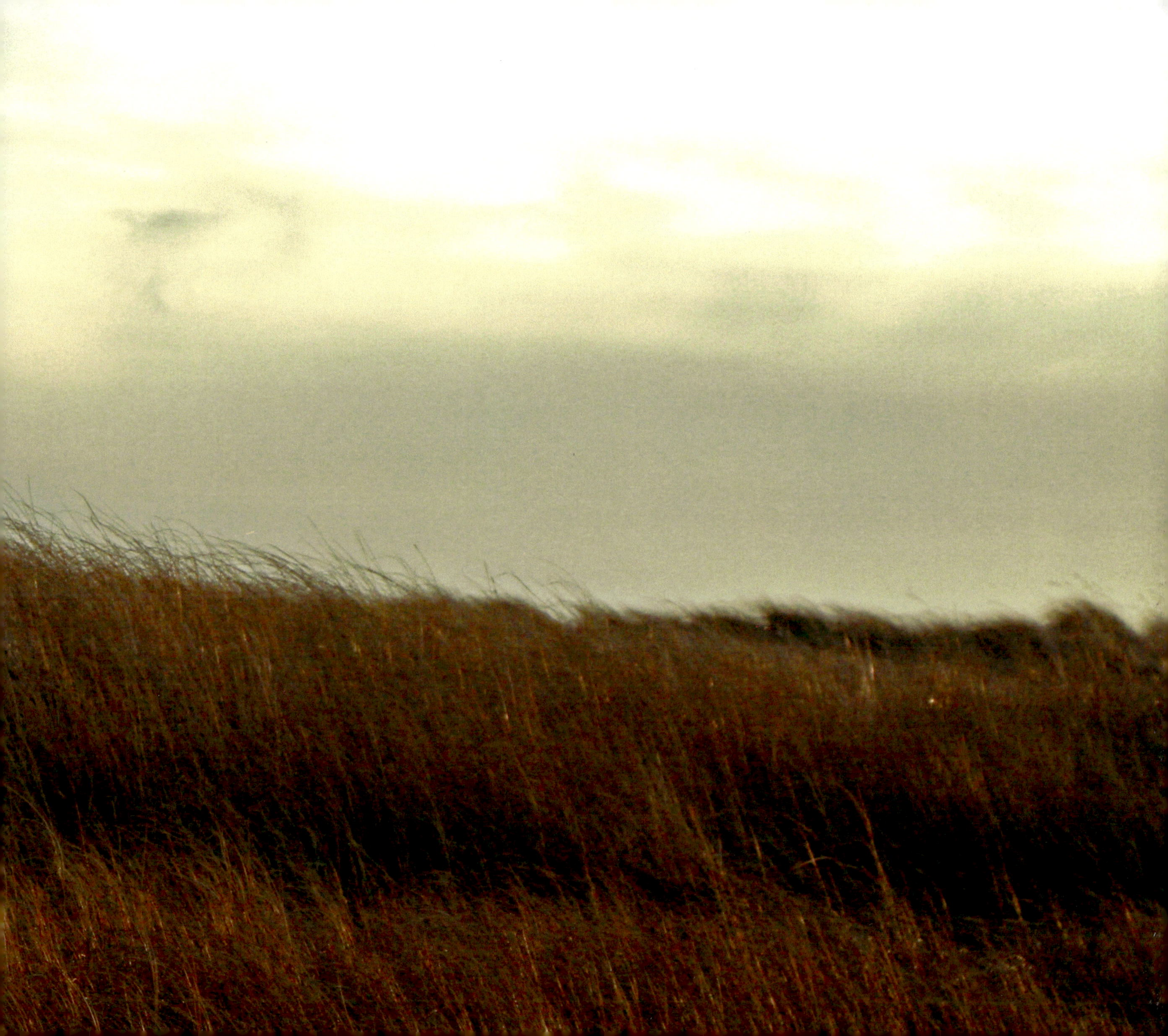

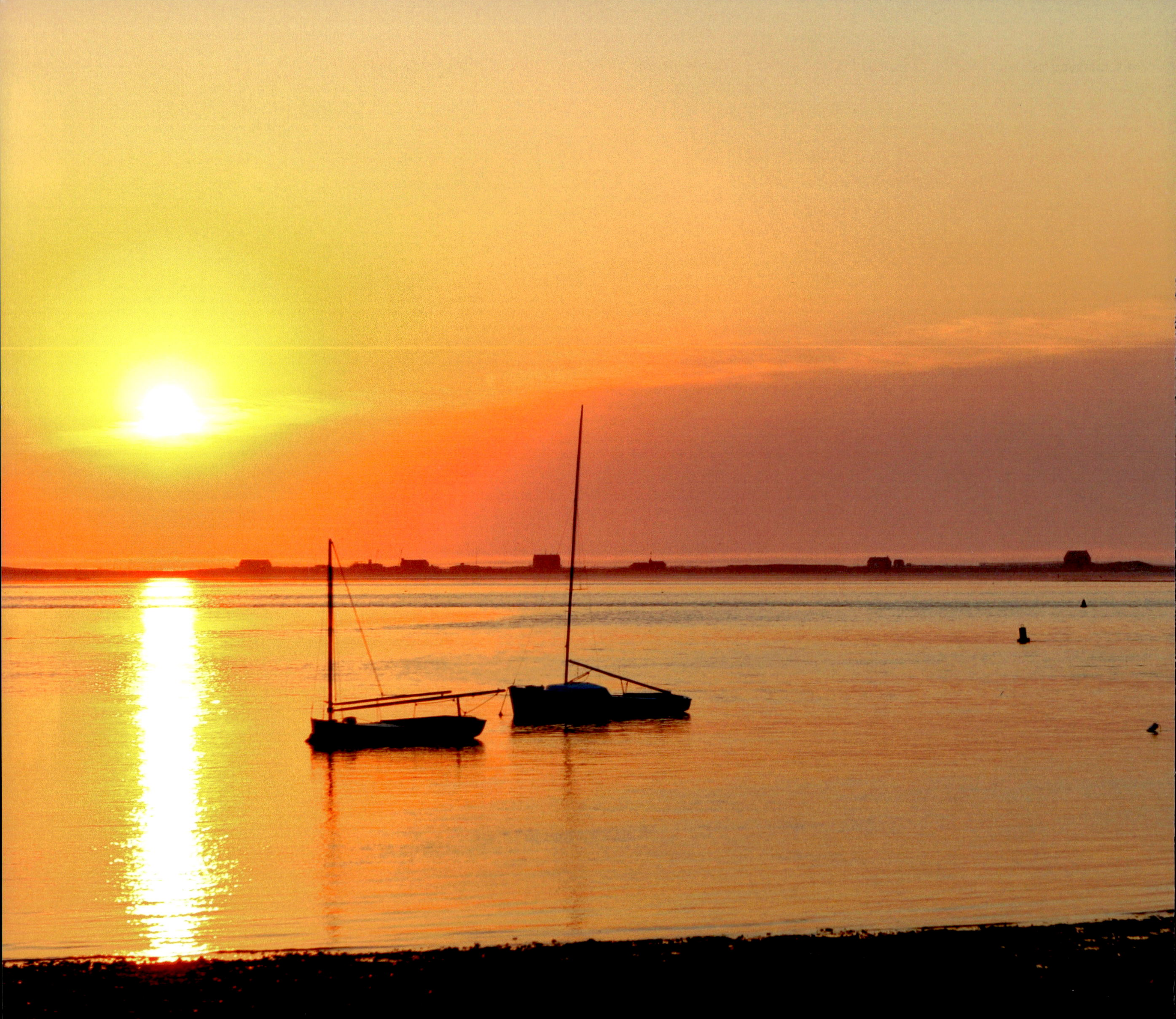

Acknowledgments

I am indebted to the following people, whose expertise and contributions were essential to this book:

Chris Hardy believed in my passion for creating an elegant pictorial book about dogs on Cape Cod and made it possible for me to bring it to fruition. Constance Sullivan shared my enthusiasm for the project and for dogs. She was essential in helping me shape a vision for the book, as well as realize its creation and production. Kate Dewitt greatly enhanced the book with her elegant design and typographic treatment. Marcy Ford gave me significant assistance with her technical skills. My husband Adrian supported me wholeheartedly and with great patience through endless hours of photo shoots and bleary-eyed nights at the computer. Lastly, I am especially grateful to the people who graciously allowed me to photograph their dogs, and to the dogs whose pictures grace these pages.

This labor of love has made me cherish dogs even more, having experienced the unconditional love and pride that exist between these people and their beloved companions.

— Kim Roderiques

Copyright

Dogs on Cape Cod was edited and produced by Constance Sullivan and designed and typeset by Kate DeWitt

All images by Kim Roderiques

Printed in China
First Printing, 2014
Library of Congress Control Number: 2014954406

ISBN: 9780692300893
First published in the United States of America in 2015 by Hummingbird Books, North Salem, New York

Bella Blu (previous spread), Great Dane, Ridgevale Beach

Scatteree Landing (opposite)

Chatham Fish Pier (following page)

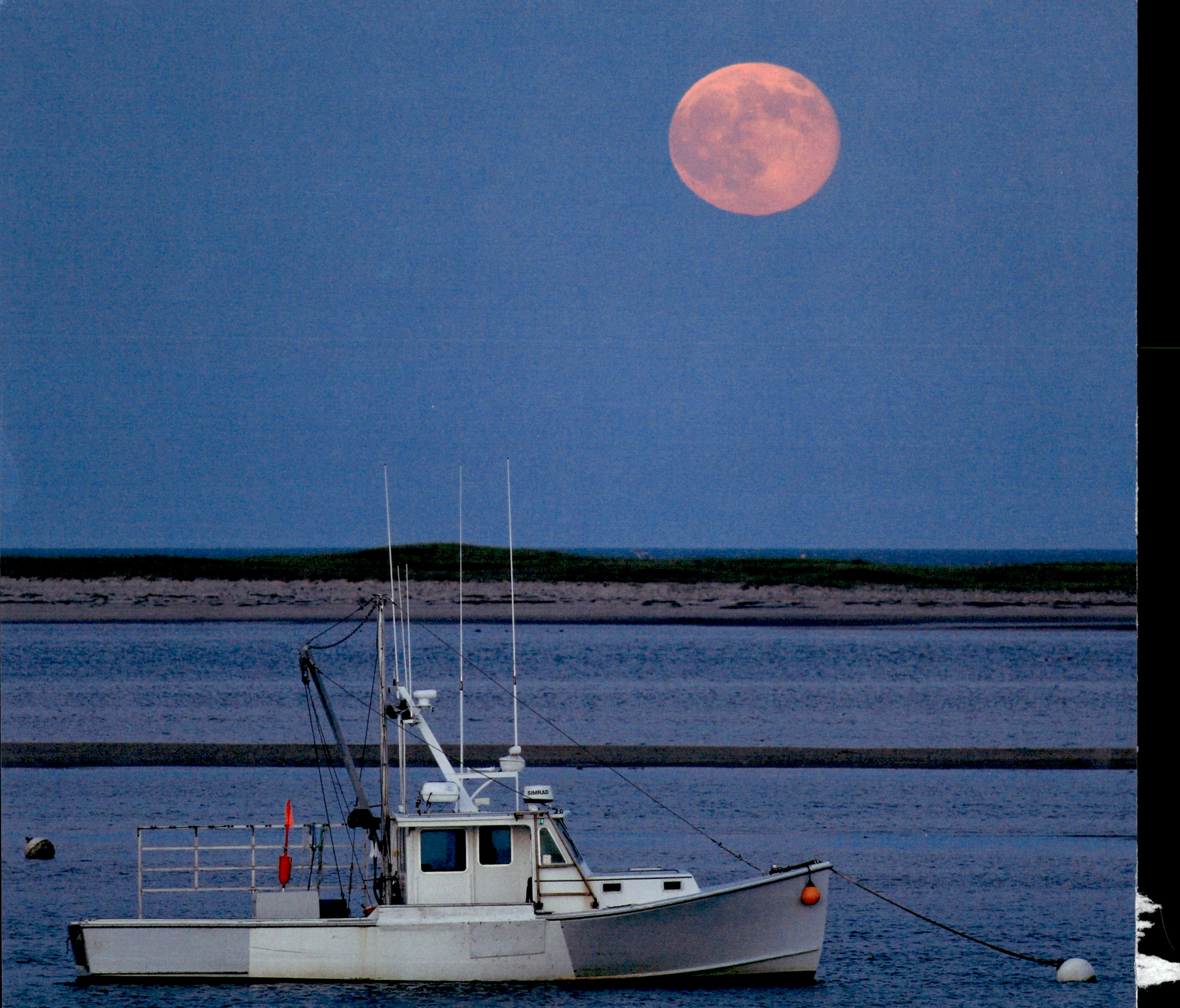
SIMRAD

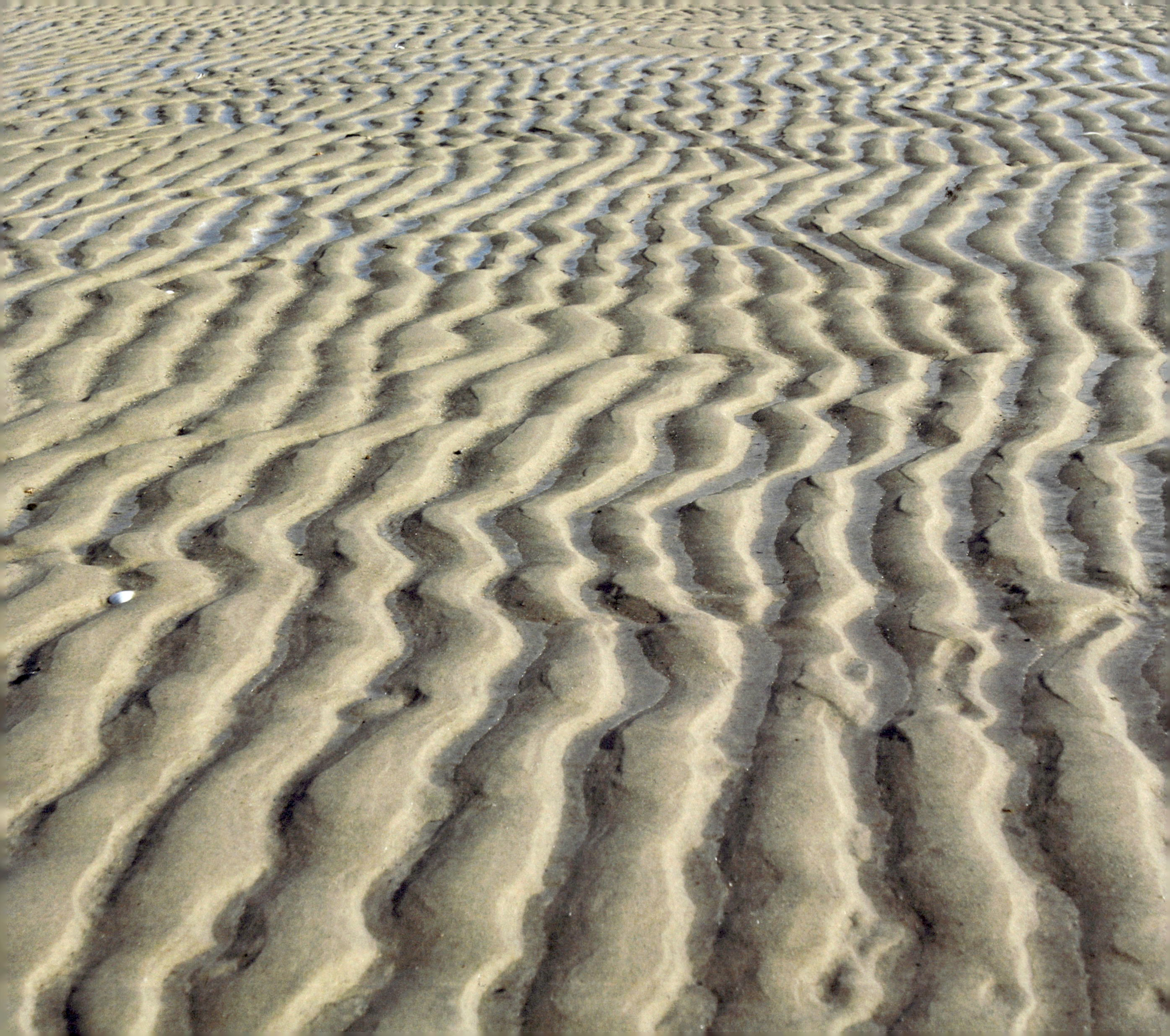